Intelligent Networks: Recent Approaches and Applications in Medical Systems

Intelligent Networks: Recent Approaches and Applications in Medical Systems

Syed V. Ahamed

Professor Emeritus,
Department of Computer Science,
City University of New York,
NY, USA

Department of Health Informatics,
University of Medicine and Dentistry,
Newark, NJ, USA

AMSTERDAM • BOSTON • HEIDELBERG • LONDON • NEW YORK • OXFORD
PARIS • SAN DIEGO • SAN FRANCISCO • SINGAPORE • SYDNEY • TOKYO

ELSEVIER

Elsevier
32 Jamestown Road, London NW1 7BY
225 Wyman Street, Waltham, MA 02451, USA

British Library Cataloguing-in-Publication Data
A catalogue record for this book is available from the British Library

Library of Congress Cataloging-in-Publication Data
A catalog record for this book is available from the Library of Congress

ISBN: 978-0-12-416630-1

For information on all Elsevier publications
visit our website at store.elsevier.com

This book has been manufactured using Print On Demand technology. Each copy is produced to order and is limited to black ink. The online version of this book will show color figures where appropriate.

Contents

Preface

Current Technological Foundation

The many dramatic impacts of the binary algebra (George Boole, 1850s), computer (von Neumann, 1940s), data networks (1950s), information (1980s), the Internet (1990s), and knowledge revolutions (2000s) are now deeply entrenched in the society. Some of the most ingrained after effects left by computers and networks are well in their sixth decade. This decade appears to that of consolidating the effects of the last 60+ years into the age of "Marxist" machines that serve the needs of all human beings rather than those of the intellectually elite, corporate tycoons, and financially secure nations. It is time for machines to turn human (at least humanist) rather than humans turning robotic. In an effort to make the tame the terabytes and gouge the gigabytes, we propose that the machines be oriented toward knowledge, concepts, and wisdom. Layers of knowledgeware, concept connectivity, and wisdom verification can envelope the teraflops supercomputers that grind out neither guidance nor axioms.

In this part, we present the impact of information age and Internet technologies. The framework to drive the raw information for the Androids, iPods, and for the information addicts is well entrenched in the backbone networks within the society. The global channels are the transoceanic fiber-optic information highways that can lead novices in a world of fantasy quite apart from the world of stark reality of science. Symptoms are here—Science Fiction Web sites, SF Ghost Hunter, SF Robotic Demons portray the trends that can put the mind into a severe tangential spin.

Science, technology, and economics at the core of human thought and social values, human dignity and total integrity at the periphery are the message of this book. This chapter is a pathway into the modern communication facilities. Here, we present the optical fiber and the deep inroads it has cut into making up most of the information revolution. Cheap transport of binary bits, longevity of service, and diversity of distances that are provided by optical fibers have altered the ways in which humans think, let alone the ways in which robots function. During the last two decades, processing, communicating, and system design are realized by strings of interwoven inventions spanning chip architecture, fiber/electronic technologies, and optical switching devices.

A robot is a vaguely humanist machine. It is artificially intelligent rather than being naturally contemplative. At a more detailed level, humanist machines though not contemplative will seek out, process, and substantiate the rationality within its processes. A robot may attempt human functions to the same extent as computer may try to compose music or play chess. In contrast, a humanist machine is more human than a machine and wiser than humans with a median level of contemplation as much as computer-generated music can be better than that from a novice composer or the programmed moves of a computer can be better similar moves of a beginner.

Humanist machines operate at the knowledge and concept levels, and robots operate at a force and displacement levels. The robotic outputs are more physical and program driven. A human controlling a robot together does not constitute a humanist machine. A contemplative human controlling the knowledge and concepts controls the force and physical levels of a robot. However, together, they do not constitute a humanist machine. The ultimate capacity of a human far exceeds that of any machine. A machine remains to be machine, but when endued with artificial intelligence, it is faster, more accurate, less emotional, and less controversial than human beings. Given that the ultimate capacity of humans is reached only by a few, the average humanist machine can outperform most of the populous, just as a computer can play better chess than most college graduates. The humanist machine is firmly knowledge and concept oriented rather than being logic and gate oriented, even though it needs all the logic and gates to work at this higher level.

The humanist machine is inclusive of all the robotics in robots and their sensory controls and response mechanisms. Knowledge, rationality, and processes are the main issues that form the core of the humanist machines. This book deals with pristine knowledge, impeccable software, and flawless processes. It also deals with space and time as they both influence human beings and machines. In a sense, the book attempts to map the perceptual, intellectual, and scientific spaces of a human mind with core, processor, and software spaces of the machine. The topics discussed in the book are as practical as the logical gates in a CPU that process binary bits. The book outlines the methodology to channel knowledge centric objects and their functionalities that affect human beings to accomplish more human than most humans, though not the best of humans. This aspect makes humanist machines distinct from traditional computers.

Historically, most civilizations have pondered about social, ethical, and fairness issues that still bewilder us even now living in a mature knowledge society. The uniqueness of this age is that knowledge is ready to be cast into silicon chips for the computers to access and process. Actions that follow are implemented by drones and robots. Processes in the knowledge domains are executed by modified logic gates. The current scenario is distinctly different. The triad of knowledge, actions, and processes has now become a high rise of modern life reaching from concepts behind knowledge that activate robotic activity in far corners of the globe and then the universe. Three outer layers of pristine purity atop knowledge, immaculate deeds atop actions, and social values checking and correcting codes atop processes can restore the integrity and identity of the original triad to withstand the onslaught of the decades to come to the knowledge society that lies ahead of us.

There are four major reasons for the explosion in the intellectual activity in the general populous: the availability of inexpensive computers, the unprecedented growth of global and backbone networks, the local area network interfacing and communication devices, and finally, the firm human drives that gravitate toward gratifying the inner most needs. Such drives bring about the best in the inspired looking for selfless love human beings. On the other hand, such instinctual drives are not always constructive. Devastation brought about by human greed, hate, and arrogance has wiped out nature and civilizations alike. This dark side of human nature can bring out violent oscillations in a streamline of progress for individuals, societies, cultures, and for almost all social entities.

In most instances, the idealistic outer attire of purity, deeds, and social values is transparent whereas modern life is getting progressively murky. In reality, human nature harbors comfort, rewards, easy living, and minimal effort. This is the basis of microeconomics. In most cases, values and ethics are readily compromised, except by a few. Factors contributing to this murkiness are the hazy perception of knowledge and the sophisticated actions necessary for retaining the purity and clarity in the ensuing processes. The fuzzy union space of knowledge (K), actions (A), and processes (P) is further shrouded by hype knowledge, willfully wrong actions, and questionable social values. In an unadulterated world, the trilogy of KAP plays out the symphony of thought in the intellectual space of the knowledge worker.

Disasters have occurred in the financial institutions, corporate settings, and international relations. Recessions leave a dark trail of hardship on citizens. Financial misconduct of executives has led to the bankruptcy of corporations. Enron and Arthur Anderson are two glaring examples from the last two decades. To add insult to injury, the malice of political leaders has brought unjust wars in the world. Humanist machines based on social justice, a well-articulated constitution, can indeed outperform humans in a well balanced social way, when humans get malicious, greedy, or emotional. Conversely, humanist machines primed with malice, greed, and hate can outperform most Godfathers from the Mafia in an evil destructive way, even when other humans' become unjust, outlaws, and malicious. An unexpected scenario can arise when these two oppositely primed super machines create a knowledge-based star-wars conflict in a very worldly setting.

Perfect rationality is not the forte of humans but total programmability is a dictate of humanist machines. Machine may not have mind, but they can be programmed to abstain from greed and hate, practice restrain, and be unbiased about the social implication of sound knowledge (K), judicious actions (A), and flawlessness of the process (P), thus titling the balance toward sanity rather than calamity.

KAP trilogy trace the future of sciences in society and the survival of society for decades. An adequate philosophy and meticulous adherence to the code of conduct and social ethics will facilitate carving the scriptures of value in information age, as did the smelting of the ferrous ore in the Iron Age. Modern machine can indeed implement such a code by validating the authenticity of knowledge, the course of actions, and the validity of processes. In a sense, what are lacking are the

KAP software, firmware, and netware to monitor the long-term drifts in the society against its own extinction.

With science, computing, and technology facilitating a seamless bondage between K, A, and P, there should be no suspicious knowledge, haphazard deeds, and erroneous processes for a long time to come. Navigation in the non-Euclidian extended space of knowledge, actions, and processes should make life an adventure, choice, and delight rather than a trap in the future or a chance of extinction.

About the Author

The author holds his PhD and DSc (EE) degrees from the University of Manchester and his MBA (Econ.) from the New York University. He taught at the University of Colorado for 2 years before joining Bell Laboratories. After 15 years of research, he returned to teaching as a professor of computer science at the City University of New York. The author has been a telecommunications consultant to Bell Communications Research, AT&T Bell Laboratories and Lucent Technologies for the last 25 years. He received numerous prizes for his papers from IEEE. He was elected a fellow of the IEEE for his seminal contribution to the simulation and design studies of the high-speed digital subscriber lines. He has authored and coauthored several books in two broad areas of intelligent AI-based broadband multimedia networks and computational framework for knowledge. His doctoral students have continued to contribute to knowledge-processing systems and wisdom machines proposed by him during 1999–2007. In 2004, he wrote the book on Scientific Innovation, for new doctoral students based on his teaching and mentoring the best of his 20 PhD students at the Graduate Center of City University of New York. He holds over 20 American and European patents ranging from slip-meters for induction motors to medical networks for hospitals. He was a visiting professor of computer science at the University of Hawaii at the Hilo Campus for the year 2009–2010 where he worked with Professors Sevki S. Erdogan and Showan M. Rahman to contribute to the art of micro-medical processing systems. The author is obliged to Professors Victor B. Lawrence, George S. Moschytz, Bishnu S. Atal, Nikil Jayant, Stanley Habib, Michael Kress, Alfred Levine, and the many unknown faculty members for reviewing the technical books written by the author.

About the Book

The overt web technology has brought about as a profound revolution in the lives of Internet users, researchers, and medical service providers (MSPs). Information and knowledge that constitute the foundations of most human activities are being constantly altered, updated, and manipulated. Both affect the applications of most disciplines and the practice of most professions. Knowledge coupled with automation and seamless connectivity with standardized procedures makes any discipline and profession amenable to computer-aided practice and perhaps to automation. When the desirable feature of total integrity in practice of professions is overlooked, the use of information technologies can be abused and the information becomes a pursuit of wealth and vanities.

Medical science and profession are exceptions because every doctor is an individual with committed oath to deploy the profession to its best use. In the same vein, every patient is an individual committed to safeguard health and welfare, just as every doctor is unique. An uneasy bilateral symmetry or a balance of power exists. The doctor being (generally) the more knowledgeable has endowed powers of prescription for drugs and services. Conversely, the patient having the capacity to choose the medical services provider holds the grip of moneys (at least in the United States) payable.

In the same vein, this uneasily balanced relationship offers a vast amount of flexibility in the interpretation of medical knowledge and the treatment of patients. On the one hand, the practice of medicine is a science, and every cure is a series of well-planned and sophisticated steps on the part of the medical staff. The procedures, subprocedures, and medical objects (drugs, instruments, equipment, etc.) have a history of innovations and enhancements, and the medical knowledge is classified by the specialty and discipline. However, patients and their reactions are distinctly individualistic. The uncertainty in the chain of a scientific process leading to the cure brings in evaluation and discretion on the part of the medical staff. Uncertain the steps toward cure may be they are logical, inductive, and rational. Discretionary steps of the doctors are always liable to be queried by teams of specialists and medical boards, and unethical practice leaves them open to law suits.

On the other hand, the patients' role of being cooperative and willing subservient during the treatment makes the position weak, especially during prolonged periods of sickness and treatment. In a sense, Internet and Web knowledge bases have diluted the power of doctors and their position in the exercise of the medical knowledge and information. In a complimentary sense, the distribution of information (via the Internet) and wealth (via the capitalistic society) has made the patients more selective from a larger and more sophisticated pool of MSPs. The delicate dyadic and symbiotic balance between patients and MSPs has shifted from country to country, place to place, and from time to time. The guidelines for reestablishing this delicate balance are currently based on wisdom and ethics rather than on power and monopoly. However, the choice and adherence to the guidelines can vary significantly.

Well conceived and documented scientific procedures directed toward treating patients as unique human beings bring a clear sequence of well-planned steps without too many discretionary choices for the individual doctors and medical staff members. In a sense, the entire global practice of medicine is well founded in science and its ensuing disciplines. Even though there is room for limited discretionary variation in the treatment of patients, the practice of healing patients needs a decisive scientific foundation. It is the object of this book to introduce machines to perform the standardized functions of being logical, inductive, and rational, consistent with web-enabled Internet knowledge bases and resources. It enables the doctors and medical staff be rigorous in their interpretation, diagnosis, and their discretionary choices. The medical machines in this book have their foundations in the procedures within the medical professions as deeply rooted as computers have in the practice of the engineering profession.

There are 3 parts and 12 chapters in this book. Part I provides the technological basis for intelligent networks and for the basis to build intelligent medical processors, machines and their networks. A platform of recent advances and new applications for medical systems is established in this part. Chapter 1 presents a brief introduction to the breakthroughs necessary in IC technologies that make medical processing feasible and in fiber-optic technologies that make communication of medical data, expertise, procedures, and knowledge possible at high enough data rates to make remote surgeries and medical robotics possible in distant locations.

Chapter 2 deals with the processors revolution over the last two decades to comprehend the complex processing of complex medical procedures, subprocedures, and microprocedures on medical super objects, objects, subordinate objects, and microobjects. Such procedures bring about major changes in the objects, such as removing a malignant tissue, curing a patient, and performing surgeries, to very minor changes such as authorizing a prescription and recording the temperature or blood pressure.

Chapter 3 deals with the explosive field of new services that the networks perform without human intervention. Machines that perform switching and network services are introduced and explored for newer medical services. Occasionally, medical services become new extensions of current and feasible network services. When complex medical services are called for, the medical machines partition strings of current/feasible services and "assemble" the instructions for these machines. Traditional computer system assemblers routinely assemble numeric and logical operations to perform a complex numeric or algebraic function such as an inverse tan function or a summation of a series. The precedence already exists. Chapter 3 further introduces the readers to switching functions in communication networks by examining the logical and number translation functions in traditional communication systems. Database technologies and devices perform much of the legwork, and communication paths for circuit-switched and data-switched networks are performed with high dependability and accuracy.

Part II has five chapters to bridge the gap between two major points in human knowledge: (a) scientific and computational aspects of technology and (b) very human and personal art of medicine. The knowledge banks at the two anchor points of the bridge are derived from knowledge banks in sciences and medicine, respectively. All the switching and routing methodologies of computer and communication systems are invoked to the pathway.

In Chapter 4, the metallic transmission media is reviewed to establish the constraint of transmission technology on the speed and extent of (medical) data through the medium. In some environments, this is the only means of communication, and the extent of possible services is easily envisioned. Signal degradation and possible errors are also explored.

Chapter 5 presents the fiber-optic media and its capabilities. Fiber-optic technology has become a default standard for most data transmission network facilities. The chapter offers a scientific basis for the very high rates and very high quality of data through such networks. For medical applications, the reasons for the choice of fiber optics barring the initial cost are established in this chapter.

Chapter 6 introduces and presents fundamental issues in microwave technology and systems. As an alternative technology, it competes favorably with fiber optics under special circumstances. Microwave mode of communication can be effectively used in remote and isolated regions. The limits and possible means of communication of medical data are presented here. Existing mobile networks are covered to indicate the bandwidth and their limitations.

Chapter 7 introduces the next-generation mobile networks (NGMN) and third-generation partition project (3GPP) around the world to integrate the medical machines and networks. The purpose is to lay the foundations and prepare the medical facilities to operate on local and a global level. Geographical and physical constraints are eliminated in the design of the NGMNs and the location of the antennas. Handover protocol and its implementation issues are being standardized by the system architecture and long-term evolution of the NGMN. In the global implementation of mobile networks, satellite communication becomes an integral part of the universal mobile telecommunications systems (UMTS) and the UMTS Terrestrial Radio Access Network (UTRAN).

Chapter 8 covers the evolution and status of worldwide intelligent networks entirely. These networks serve as a basis of the intelligent medical networks proposed in the book. All aspects of artificial intelligence (AI) (i.e., expert systems, pattern recognition, computer graphics, computer vision, and intelligent agents) and their deployment in communication networks are covered. The path-routing algorithms in communication systems and traditional AI in computer science are blended to construct the framework for intelligent medical information machines and systems.

Part III has four chapters totally dedicated to medical machines and networks. The four chapters in Part III deal with medical machines based on the design philosophy of medical processors, medical networks, AI in the science of medicine, and the deployment of nationally and internationally distributed medical knowledge bases.

Chapter 9 contains the methodology that the computer scientists have very diligently pursued in developing the architecture and composition of computers from its very inception during the late 1940s to the newer multiprocessor, multithreaded infused chip-based machines, as many as 64-bit processor VLSI chips are on the horizon. Functionality, role, and architectures of processors, bus structures, and the other three functions of three remaining components, i.e., memories, I/Os, and global Internet switches, that are now performed external to the processor chip are covered in Chapters 12 and 13 to lead up the medical machines.

Chapter 10 evolves and covers the functionality, role, and architectures of processors, bus structures of medical machines. The medical processor chip(s) plays the most crucial part. In conjunction with memories, I/O systems and global Internet switches, the medical machines will play the role of networked computers in global computing environments. Medical machines can be built in many ways as computers are built. Unfortunately, there are no centralized or standard committees to suggest global medical protocols or interfaces. Hospitals and medical centers follow their own style of conducting the medical practice as they fit. The local software designers will write medicalware macros and utilities as they see fit, and the IT engineers and network designer will simply adhere to the local directions rather than following the global medical standards.

Chapter 11 tackles the issues in the design of medical processors. These processors can only be in a genesis of computer processors and extensions of object processors. Medical processors deal with a rich array of medical subfunctions, utilities, and procedures. In addition, they contend with a rich variety of medical objects (drugs, nurses, doctors, staff, patients, accountants, etc.) that are unique and distinctive. If the medical functions are treated as "verb functions" and objects are treated as "noun objects," then the syntactic and semantic rules become complicated but not insurmountable for compiler designers to handle. The rules and grammar of "medical language" will thus be handled with a extended rules and grammar of the medical compiler.

Chapter 12 revisits the medical machines from the perspective of practical procedures in hospitals, medical centers, nursing homes, etc. If the procedures have a distinct medical code, then this code drives the machine in an error proof, sophisticated, efficient, and an optimal fashion. The subprocedures become the microcode that is assembled in view of the human and resource limitations of the hospital or the medical center where the machine is located. The composition of the subprocedure is by itself a layer of the medicalware and the compiler design.

From the hindsight of the processor technology of the last decade, the modern processors can indeed serve as medical processes. It is a debt that computer scientists owe to the medical community to provide a methodology for the programming of the medical procedures and subprocedures that can then be encoded as threads and elementary microprograms. Such micro programmable steps when aggregated as macro procedures become steps in the global process of curing ailments, treating specific medical conditions or even inventing new cures for patients. These medical microprograms reside in the caches of the new processors, and the operating systems of the medical computers guide the threads through the processes that the modern processors are built to execute.

Processor development over the last decade integrates numerous processors. These new processors integrate numerous interdependently interwoven threads because the many subfunctions in processes (graphics, visualization, MRI, surgery, etc.) were first established in the various disciplines and then presented to the computer scientists to unify these procedures as strings and threads for execution.

The four chapters in Part III break down the steps of medical processing into finite and discrete subprocedures that can be indeed executed on modern processors. Even though we present the architecture of medical processors as being the blueprints based on primitive VLSI techniques, the real purpose is to establish a neural pathway for human thought to bridge the gap between the prerequisite medical subprocedures and the programmable strings and threads in the modern processors.

The book covers the current phases of rapidly evolving computer, network, and medical fields. The emphasis has been to combine the AI aspects from computer science and the intelligent Internet aspects from networks and to import them into the medical field. Out of the enormous options available to the system scientists, only the germane and potent combinations are presented. It is possible to recombine the three disciplines and write a document with slightly different but parallel methodologies.

Part 1

Current Technological Foundation

The evolution of technology during the last few years has been unprecedented. The nature of growth in numerous areas (VLSI, processors, supercomputers, networks, and global reach) have brought about profound impacts on every phase of human life in direction's incomprehensible a few decades back. In this part of the book, the three (processing, networking, and electronic network servicing) directions that affect the medical field are presented. The focus is on medical enhancements that are feasible with the current technologies and is emerging in the economic and social arena. The pathways toward medical machines that will facilitate the practice of medicine as much as computer-aided design has facilitated the VLSI or automobile industry. The role of human beings and the medical staff is not underrated nor replaced, instead it is interwoven in the fabric of artificially and naturally intelligent environments. The AI features are embedded in AI software and intelligent agents who scan and modify the system response. The natural intelligence (and wisdom) is enforced by the medical staff that governs and monitors intelligent medical machines. In a sense, the wisdom of human beings tames the knowledge power of the machines processing at superhuman speeds.

Part 1 provides the technological basis for both the intelligent networks and for the basis for build intelligent medical processors, machines, and their networks. A platform of recent advances and new applications for medical systems is established in this part.

Part I

Current Technological Foundation

1 Information and Knowledge Revolution

1.1 Introduction

This chapter integrates networks and processors. Each plays out its own individual and dominant role in the lives of every individual. Being well founded in sciences, logic, and mathematics, processors and networks each influences the ways of our lives and degree of confidence in the outcome of results. Silicon in processors and erbium in glass each has its own influence. These aspects are introduced for processors (Section 1.2) in modern computers and for networks and their architecture in the Internet age (Section 1.3).

Processors are an integral part of networks. Networks (as in architecture and bus structures within the IC chip) are an integral part of the overall design of chip for processors. From a device and systems perspective, processing into chips is as essential as communications in networks. Processors and networks are two elements in society that have propelled human progress through the last six decades. These two elements are as inseparable as communication processors in networks or as switching networks within the processors.

From a current device and systems perspective at a microscopic level, the processing power embedded in the binary operation codes of any processor chip is as fundamental as the switching of individual communication channels in networks based on the channel address of each cell, packet, or a channel. These two underpinning concepts become evident, if Section 1.2 is read in light of Section 1.3 and vice versa. Even though Sections 1.2 and 1.3 are artificially segregated to convey their own technical significance and scientific integrity, together they convey the synergy between them. For this reason, we suggest that students read these two sections twice and the two following chapters, even though the conceptual linkage may be evident to the expert. The two following chapters have a brief evolutional history but quickly get into the recent developments of either processors in (Chapter 2) or of networks in (Chapter 3).

The numerous impacts of technologies have brought about the Internet age. During the last few decades, the life of almost every individual and social entity has picked up their influence and a great momentum. This synergy and momentum are possibly irreversible. Computers since the days of von Neumann (1945),

Intelligent Networks: Recent Approaches and Applications in Medical Systems.
DOI: http://dx.doi.org/10.1016/B978-0-12-416630-1.00001-7

networks in days of Grosvenor and Wesson (1997), then the symbiotic influence of silicon technology (about 1958) into the current silicon chip architectures, and then the doping of erbium (about 1985) into fibers are presented in this chapter. The introductory background reading material is well published in several books and kept concise in this chapter and this part of the book.

1.2   Silicon and Pentium in Processors

Silicon wafers is the material for planer transistors (Wolf January, 2002) that has been used in the IC industry since its evolution during 1950s. Pentium is the trade label (of Intel) for their $\times$ 86-compatible microprocessor architectures, designs, and features. While silicon provides the material foundations of chips, Pentium designs provide the architectural layouts and designs to realize the processor chips.

Pentium chips (Wolf, 2002) followed a long series of microprocessor chips from 8086 to 80486 from the mid-1970s to early 1990s trademarked by INTEL Corporation. During this time, the design, dependence, and low prices of the IC chip vendors have transformed industrial processes from producing gadgets to refining and optimizing the processes that are inherent in the industrial age. The industrial age assumed the size and shape of information age during the 1980s and 1990s. The momentum continues now as the information age is assuming the size and shape of the knowledge age. The common factor in these slow, steady, and sturdy evolutionary processes is the pristine human thought that monitors and facilitates social progress. In a sense, the intelligence that prompted human evolution is doing as well but in the information and knowledge domains. The linkage between the processes of the mind and the processes in the chips is embedded in the knowledge that links their functional integrity of thought and the process integration in the chips.

In the IC environments, the specialized CPU designs are tailored to the application and hardware environments. Classified by the applications and environment, three series of processors (desktop, mobile, and embedded) are commercially available. Classified by the design and architectural constraints, P5 and P6 processors dominate. Again, the P5 processors can use $0.8-0.35$ μm technologies. The P6 processors are labeled as Pentium Pro, Pentium II, and Pentium III for desktop applications. Intel has many (many) trade names for their processor chips and applications. Since the industry is mature and Intel has been a prominent source for microprocessor chips, it is feasible to find a processor chip for almost any traditional application and environment.

It appears that the traditional designs have still a long run ahead to quench the global demand for processors, the major industry leaders have been laying low in designing chips for object, knowledge, concept, and wisdom processors. To some extent, the role of Intel is comparable to the role of AT&T during 1970s when packet switching had already appeared in the horizon with greater flexibility to serve the demands of the society.

1.3 Silica and Erbium in Networks

The insertion of the emitter in semiconductor materials changed the flavor of early semiconductor industry of 1940s. Shockley (1948) had already noted the possible use of semiconductor devices for solid-state power and frequency conversion applications. However, the transistor as a semiconductor amplifier is one of the most seminal invention of the two decades of 1940s and 1950s, in par with von Neumann's invention of the blue print (the IAS machine; von Neumann, 1945) for the stored program control (SPC) for computers. Bardeen (Bardeen, 1948; Hoddeson and Vicki, 2002) and Brattain (Hoddeson and Vicki, 2002; Shockley et al., 1956) perfected the transistor[1] device as a viable electronic circuit element with innumerable applications.

The extent of change that optical amplification has brought to earlier fiber-optic industry is comparable to the extent of change that transistor brought to earlier semiconductor industry. The commonality of the theme is the amplification, even though the mechanisms for the two amplification processes are entirely different. While[2] the semiconductor amplification occurs because of the acceptor or donor dopants, the optical amplification takes place in the trivalent ion Er^{3+} as the laser active dopant for common (silica) glass fibers. This latter group of fibers is also known as erbium-doped silica fiber amplifiers (EDSFAs) generally used in transoceanic fiber links.

Since late 1980s, optical amplification has been actively pursued for deployment in fiber-optic networks. The science is precise and distances of fiber-optic links have increased dramatically. Both spatial and frequency domain properties have been studied, and the optimization of the location and length of these amplifiers are incorporated in the transoceanic fiber described in the book. As far back as early 1990s, the EDSFAs have been an integral part of most fiber-optic link design (Ahamed et al., 1997).

1.4 Impact of Computer Systems

Since the design of IAS (Institute of Advanced Study; von Neumann, 1945) machine detailing the architecture of SPC sharing the memory with data, the impact of general purpose computers expanding at an increasing rate. A well-articulated theme of intellectual pursuit can start to absorb the shock wave and ripple effects set up by the computer revolution that started in 1940s. The momentum is felt in almost every endeavor of human activity enhancing the productivity of manual effort and offering optimality in solutions for almost every need of

---

[1] Shockley, Bardeen, and Brattain all worked at Bell Telephone Laboratories during the late 1940s, when the transistor was invented and studied as a viable semiconductor device.

[2] Both semiconductor and fiber-optic industries are mature in their own individual rights. The amplification processes in both are well documented and thoroughly characterized. It is not our intent to deviate from the subject matter of this book. We merely point to the impact of fiber-optic amplification in the global fiber-optic networks as being monumental if not drastic.

individuals and social entities. The consequences are monumental and ensuing human efforts have focused on being more intellectual, accurate, and efficient. In a sense, the knowledge worker has more leisure and more creativity. The industrial revolution that offered more leisure to the public in late 1900s through the last century now bears a new label as the computer revolution that offers more creativity since 1960s. Four decades since the 1980s, the computer revolution has incubated a new wave of knowledge revolution gaining greater momentum in the twenty-first century in providing the information and knowledge for solving human problems dealing with generic needs and their gratification to the individuals, societies, and species.

Creativity invokes a deeper pursuit, to seek and command perfection in every phase of activity. Computer and display technologies have provided numerical and visual venues into creativity. For the physical activities, the laws of physics and mechanical engineering provide ample and (near) perfect solutions. Industrial robots are indeed the manifestations. For the emotional dealings, the social and ethical bounds of the immediate society provide basic and simple-minded solutions. These solutions are not optimal solutions such as those embedded in automobiles, airplanes, and spacecraft. Putting aside greed in the gratification of emotional needs, a sense of balance becomes delicate as an economic balance between the marginal amount of effort to gratify the most remote emotional need and the marginal utility in gratifying that particular need. Stated simply it reiterates Marshall's utility theory but in a triadic balance of emotion, intellect, and knowledge. Triple partial differential equations may become necessary to accommodate the role of knowledge in the post-Internet age. The combined marginal resources of any two have to be equal to the marginal utility derived in the third.

Perfection and its pinnacle are both abstract. In this book, we provide an initial basis for the structure and measure of knowledge (documented and implied) that may lead to the quantification of the steps toward the elusive goals of perfection and its pinnacle.

1.5   Impact of Networks

The impact of networks on the communication environment is akin to the impact of computers on the data processing environment. The effect of network is double folded because the digital networks evolved after computers had already made significant inroads into the processing domain. The concepts of integration (small-scale integration (SSI) and medium-scale integration (MSI)) of functionalities within the silicon chips were established. The effects of the impact have been gradually assimilated three or four decades between the mid-1960s and the mid-2010s. Processors for modern supercomputers are presented in the next chapter. The process is ongoing and the synergies between processes in computers have reached a symbiotic climax. The process is ongoing and the synergies between processes in computers have reached a symbiotic climax. The extent of intelligence, integration, and customization is high and the quality of service appears acceptable by most customers.

As early as 1960s, Bell Laboratories' scientists had started to explore electronic and magnetic media for the storage of numbers. The major impact resulted from the "planar transistor" (Hoddeson and Vicki, 2002; Shockley et al., 1956) and early promise of integration of such planner transistors for logic circuits. SSI had started and was well on the way to MSI and large-scale integration during this era. Magnetic domain technology (Henry, 1981) and the "bubble" devices (Bonyhard et al., 1970) caused a minor diversion from the use of electronic circuits and devices in the networks arena. However, it did bring a culmination to the possible use of bubble technology of the late 1960s and 1970s. Magnetic disk storage devices were gaining precedence for very large-scale information banks. They are still in vogue and used in most communication and network applications. Even in this niche, the VLSI of memory modules imposes a threat.

Intelligent networks (Ahamed et al., 2006) brought about processing capabilities for customer services. The initiation of the basic concepts behind intelligent networks was also well founded in the Bell System since 1961. The interoperability of the central offices (COs) (Telephone Laboratories, 1982) in the evolving national networks of the 1960s and 1970s needed the signaling system for national, international, and global communication. Networks were the key hardware elements in the global computer-based communication systems. Network is a mere phraseology for such cooperative, symbiotic, interoperative, interdependent, and synchronized communication systems that treat digitized data in a homogeneous and consistent fashion.

Packet switching (Ahamed and Lawrence, 1997) brought about a new wave of innovation distinct from the circuit switching deployed by Bell Systems since the days of Alexander Graham Bell (Telephone Laboratories, 1982). Cheap addressing and communication (Ahamed and Lawrence, 1997) of "packets" of information (data bits) packaged as data structures became as cheap as the processing of data in computer systems. Frame relay networks using SONET (Synchronous Optical NETwork) and then the cell relay networks using asynchronous transfer mode (ATM) have become the communication industry standard (Aprille et al., 1990) over the last two decades. The cost of transmission on shared networks was as cheap and convenient as the use of shared computers for number crunching. Both gained popularity through the 1980s and 1990s. Together the network revolution has been in full swing ever since.

1.5.1 Fiber Optics in Networks

Optical transmission was proposed during the early 1960s after the invention of the laser in 1960. The multilayered glass structure was suggested during the mid-1960s and corning glass produced a rough specimen of fiber with about 20 dB/km loss in 1970. Optical systems have been functioning with increasing capacity and sophistication. The high-quality single-mode fibers offer about 0.16 dB/km loss at 1.55 μM wavelength and about 0.25 dB/km loss at 1.30 μm wavelength. The chromatic dispersion (Ahamed, 2006) is approximately 15 ps/km-nm in the low loss window of 1.5 μm (with zero dispersion at 1.3 μm). Both features are equally attractive. Both these attributes make fiber-optic systems essential components of most modern networks.

Two major driving forces behind most broadband digital networks are the availability of high-grade fiber for transmission and the profusion of inexpensive ATM switches. The transmission issue was successfully resolved during the 1970s and early 1980s. Presently, the data rates and ranges are well beyond the projected needs of even the most digit-intensive society. Where fiber is easily available, new national and global trunk data communication are mostly based on fiber optics. Fiber is firmly ingrained in most of the trunk and shared transmission facilities within the United States, Canada, Europe, Japan, and Australia (Senior, 2008).

The deployment of dark fiber (as opposed to the "lit fiber," already in use) has opened another opportunity to bring broadband services to the globe, to a nation, and to a region. These fiber pathways are already laid out (underground or overhead) but are not in service. Such pathways can be bought, leased, or secured and be deployed for the cheapest fiber haul of data. These fibers can carry terabits per second of data with DWDM (Ahamed et al., 1997) mode with almost no dispersion effects. The individual DWDM channels each carry data at 2.5 Gb/s and there can be 160 channels multiplexed on a single fiber. Other encoding algorithms allow each channel to carry 100 Gb/s. These dark fibers offer good financial incentive for the communication industry in the developed countries where the telecom and dotcom boom and bust of the 1990s have left a wealth of underutilized national and international fiber capacity.

1.5.2 Transmission in Optical Network

Through the 1990s, high-speed optical switching was being incorporated within the optical fiber systems to offer true optical networks. Fibers can carry data at multigigabits/second rates quite dependably. Local public domain networks (such as the telephone networks) are likely to continue to deploy semiconductor switching under SPC and to deploy fiber for high-capacity, long-haul transmission. When fiber-optic backbone networks are tied into wireless networks, the hurdle for all-optical communication is the wireless link. When fiber-optic backbone networks are tied into the Internet, the only hurdle for the broadband link is the subscriber line capacity. However, FTTH and FTTC (Ahamed and Lawrence, 1997) seem to be the two distinct paths around the subscriber-loop (Ahamed et al., 1982) constraints.

Super high-speed switching for optical computing is still not practical enough for optical computers to be proven economically feasible. Networks and their switches will have to wait before they can assimilate the super high-speed switching capacity of optical systems. Currently, compound semiconductor materials cannot offer clean sharp edges for gating photons in optical signals. This scenario is similar to the delayed impact of semiconductor digital computers of the mid-1950s on switching systems of the mid-1960s. Having its inception in 1948 (Telephone Laboratories, 1982), the computer industry was already well into its prime before the first electronic switching system (1ESS) was introduced in 1965 in the communications arena.

Fiber-optic communication is deployed in most national and international communications networks. On the national scene, fiber has been introduced routinely for interoffice high data capacity channels in the United States, Canada, Europe, and Japan (Ahamed and Lawrence, 1997, 1998). Optical rates[3] OC-12 (at 622.080 Mb/s) and OC-48 (at 2488.32 Mb/s) have been achieved by commercial systems. Most information services, deploying data links at these rates, handle voice, video, and data communication needs of large and small customers. The data rates with the DWDM techniques are much higher. These services use fiber-to-the-house (FTTH) and fiber-to-the-curb (FTTC) architectures. The ATM-based bandwidth on-demand capability becomes readily feasible with all-fiber backbone and distribution architectures. In the current network environment, ATM is the implicit standard for local and global data communication. The operating cost of such services is in the maintenance of the transceivers rather than the maintenance of the fiber transmission media.

On the international scene, the first undersea transatlantic telephone cable (TAT-8) was commissioned (Telephone Laboratories, 1982; Ahamed and Lawrence, 1997) in the late 1988. The capacity is limited to 40,000 voice calls, which is double the capacity of all other copper transatlantic cables and satellites. The next fiber cable system (TAT-9) commissioned in the early 1990s handles twice this capacity at 80,000 voice calls.

More recently, any country aspiring to participate in the digital revolution has a stake in the worldwide broadband backbone. Interconnections are almost as varied as the telephone channel connects in a small region. Fiber has diminished the size of the globe for data traffic to less than 1 s (including buffer and server times) at broadband Internet speeds. The router and bridge delays are usually longer than the transmission delays. The global networks now have a flexibility to interconnect national digital exchanges to universities and hospitals alike. Knowledge banks are interconnected routinely to exchange bidirectional data, information, and knowledge. In information-rich society, the data and information banks can communicate almost instantly. Knowledge (after knowledge processing (Chapter 8) is in place), concepts, and wisdom (after concept and wisdom machine (Chapters 10 and 11) are in place) can also be communicated at Internet speeds.

There are dozens[4] (and even hundreds, locally) of fiber-optic undersea cables around the world. Network service providers around the globe are as common as

---

[3] OC rates were standardized after the optical fiber was established as a superior carrier of digital optic signals around the block or around the world. The basic OC-1 rate is 51.840 Mb/s. See Figure 1.4 for the numerical basis of this rate.

Multiplexing numerous optical channels by wave division multiplexing (WDM) and further by dense wave division multiplexing (DWDM) has led to multi-gigabit/second rates in a single strand of high-quality optical fibers.

[4] Trans Atlantic Cables: CANTAT-3 at 2.5 Gb/s; TAT-12,TAT 13 at 5 Gb/s; Atlantis-2 (12,000 km) at 10 Gb/s; Gemini at 30 Gb/s; Columbus III (11,000 km); Atlantic Crossing AC-1 (14,000 km); and Trans Pacific Cables: TPC-5 at 5 Gb/s (25000 km), Japan–USA; TPC-6 at 100 Gb/s with Soliton Technology; APCN (12,000 km) at 5 Gb/s; US/China Fiber Cable (27,000 km) at 80 Gb/s; SEA-ME-WE-3 (38000 km), in 1999, at 2.5 Gb/s initially but expanded later. FLAG or Fiber Link Around the Globe (27000 km), the United Kingdom, Spain, Sicily, Alexandria, Jeddah, Dubai, Bombay, Thailand, Hong Kong, Korea, Japan.

Internet services providers in a community. For this reason, we provide a global overview of two typical global fiber-optic networks currently serving different cultures and societies.

The TAT-8 high-capacity fiber-optic transmission system transmits 296 Mb/s data over 3646 miles. This system is equipped with 109 repeaters spaced approximately 70 km (230,000 ft) apart using coherent laser sources at 1.3 μm wavelength. Six single-mode fibers constitute the cable. The combined capacity of TAT-8 and TAT-9 has served the transatlantic telecommunication needs since mid-1990s. Transpacific (fiber-optic cable) systems link Japan, Guam, Hawaii, and the Pacific Rim states.

In order to provide the high-capacity cable linking Europe to the Asia-Pacific region, the SEA-ME-WE 2 (Southeast Asia Middle East Western Europe 2) was initiated in 1993. Singapore Telecom and France Telecom started the submarine cable project after preliminary studies during the late 1980s. Because of the success of the SEA-ME-WE 2 project, a successor project, SEA-ME-WE 3, was initiated (Ahamed and Lawrence, 1997). The later system includes 39 landing points in 33 countries and 4 continents from Western Europe (including Germany, England, and France) to the Far East (including China, Japan, and Singapore) and to Australia. SEA-ME-WE 3 (Figure 1.1) is the longest system in the world with a total length of 15,058 miles or about 39,000 km. The use of wavelength division multiplexing (WDM and DWDM; Ahamed and Lawrence, 1997) greatly increases the capacity of the networks allowing the high-quality transmission over distances as great as from Germany to Australia. The system capacity, as on August 2003,

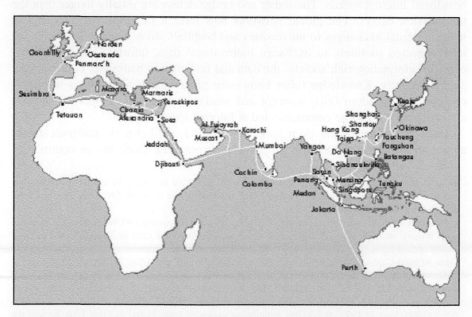

Figure 1.1 One of the recent fiber-optic (SEA-ME-WE 3 and 4) networks added to the community of high-speed backbones of the world.

has been upgraded twice. It consists of two fiber pairs, each carrying 8 wavelengths of light. Some wavelengths operate at 10 Gb/s while others operate at 2.5 Gb/s. The bandwidth in sections of the SEA ME-WE 3 network is 20 Gbit/s (as of the end of 2005) and up to 40 Gbit/s for very-short reaches.

A recent 17,400 miles (27,850 km), global long-haul network is the SAT-3/WASC/SAFE submarine cable system that provides connectivity to and from 17 countries: (1) Portugal, (2) Spain, (3) Senegal, (4) Cote d'Ivoire, (5) Ghana, (6) Benin, (7) Nigeria, (8) Cameroon, (9) Gabon, (10) Angola, (11) South Africa (Access Point)-1, (12) South Africa (Access Point)-2, (13) Reunion, (14) Mauritius, (15) India, (16) Singapore and (17) Malaysia are connected in a duplex mode. Countries (4 through 13) are on the west coast of Africa and benefit greatly from the established global economies of the West and from the growing economies of countries like India and Malaysia. The acronyms stand for third South Atlantic Telephone Cable (SAT-3), West African Submarine Cable (WASC), and South Africa–Far East (SAFE). It has been operational since April 2002 and is expected to provide a digital capacity of 120 Gb/s. In order to provide high-speed connections around the globe, the first phase was called SEA-ME-WE-3 (from the Western countries to Singapore) and ready for service since 1999, the second phase encompasses the WAT-3-WASC (countries 4–12) and the SAFE (countries 14–17) submarine cables which have been in service since 2002. In the final phase of deployment, EASSy (East African countries) ties in both SEA-ME-WE-3 and the SAT-3/WASC/SAFE long-haul fiber-optic cable networks from six locations.

Toward the end of 2005, SEA-ME-WE-4, the underwater cable connecting Southeast Asia, the Middle East, and Western Europe came into service with a capacity that is 32 times its originally designed (in 1998) capacity. It has a full capacity of 1.28 Tb/s (10 Gb/s for each of the 64 WDM channels on each of the two fiber pairs). The span is about 20,000 km. A map of the fiber backbone covering the fiber-optic net embedded in SEA-ME-WE 3 and 4 networks are shown in Figure 1.1. A more comprehensive map of the transoceanic fiber-optic pathways is shown in Figure 1.2.

These fiber-optic transmission systems facilitate the communication of high-speed data. Knowledge processing or the intelligent network functions are not an integral part of these fiber-optic systems. However, in conjunction with intelligent nodes and intelligent database systems (strategically located within the network), the fiber-optic transmission systems offer high-performance digital access for computers, knowledge bases, multimedia, video, educational, medical imaging, facsimile, and even plain old telephone services throughout the world.

Currently, the global fiber networks are underutilized. The lack of demand from the commercial sector and hence the lack of economic incentive are strong deterrents to additional growth of very high-capacity optical networks.

The recent trend in optical networks is to provide broadband and Internet service at competitive rates and make these networks scaleable for the expanding needs of the corporate community. For ease of installation and maintenance, the choice is toward passive optical networks (PONs). This approach makes PONs as affordable as the traditional copper-based technologies.

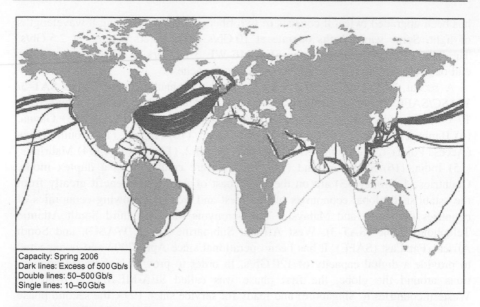

Figure 1.2 Fiber-optic pathways depicting the transoceanic data capacity of the networks since early 2006. See Figure 1.3 depicting the landing sites around the SE coast of Africa.

Over the decades, even the very early copper-based technologies adopted (T1) repeaters, line extenders, and subscriber-loop carrier systems. These technologies are discussed in some detail in Telephone Laboratories (1982). Copper-based technologies and the associated devices are likely to be short lived because of the innovations in fiber-optic line termination devices.

The transoceanic fiber-optic pathways around the spring of 2006 are shown in Figure 1.2. At present, the capacity of the intercontinental and international data traffic is immense for the needs of the world community. This is likely to be exploited during the current decade to make applications feasible and make knowledge processing and sharing economic and versatile (Figure 1.3).

Numerous digital subscriber line (Ahamed et al., 1982) or DSL and the asymmetric digital subscriber line (ADSL) technologies have staged a comeback and remain vital until the PON technology becomes so inexpensive that the FTTH or the FTTC Ahamed and Lawrence (1997) will replace the obsolete copper telephone lines.

There are inherent advantages associated with the PON technologies for reaching customers. Currently, PONs offer broadband and global access using both time-division multiplexing (TDM) and IP services at prices comparable to the copper (twisted wire pair and coaxial) based services.

Even though the installation is a capital investment, revenue opportunities for voice, video, interactive video, TV, and games are enormous. Robust optical network terminations (ONTs) allow the PON to reach the consumer premises with

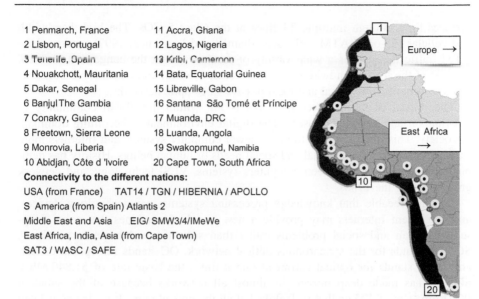

1 Penmarch, France	11 Accra, Ghana
2 Lisbon, Portugal	12 Lagos, Nigeria
3 Tenerife, Spain	13 Kribi, Cameroon
4 Nouakchott, Mauritania	14 Bata, Equatorial Guinea
5 Dakar, Senegal	15 Libreville, Gabon
6 BanjulThe Gambia	16 Santana São Tomé et Príncipe
7 Conakry, Guinea	17 Muanda, DRC
8 Freetown, Sierra Leone	18 Luanda, Angola
9 Monrovia, Liberia	19 Swakopmund, Namibia
10 Abidjan, Côte d 'Ivoire	20 Cape Town, South Africa

Connectivity to the different nations:
USA (from France)   TAT14 / TGN / HIBERNIA / APOLLO
S America (from Spain) Atlantis 2
Middle East and Asia   EIG/ SMW3/4/IMeWe
East Africa, India, Asia (from Cape Town)
SAT3 / WASC / SAFE

Figure 1.3 Recent developments in the configuration of the fiber path around SE coast of Africa and Cape Town denoting the proposed landing sites for digital connectivity to the rest of the nations.

numerous options. At the low end, the network configuration options are typically two/four POTS lines, Ethernet service, RF, and switched digital video services.

Full options of the telephony service (with all the CLASS options (Ahamed and Lawrence, 1997, 1998) and customization and all the X11 services) become feasible. Typical virtual private networking (VPN) options become available because of the large fiber bandwidth and limited programmability at the termination, which offers multiple ISP support and multiple data services, profiling for users. Multiple customer service can also be provided with an enhanced network termination for community centers, hospitals, and businesses.

CO terminations need typical data switches for CATV electronics and all the telephony interconnect options for the typical telephone services. These CO optical terminations are built to be compatible with the Class 5 switched from different vendors all around the world and offer TDM and DS1 interfaces. Simple DS0 cross-connects with carrier application make service provisioning and customization available to individual customers.

The optical networks offer a range of choices for video services and applications. The IPTV using the digital IP video format and IP network provides premium and CATV quality. Extended services, such as pay per view, VCR options, and video over TV also become options. Standard TV (SDTV) and HDTV at 20 Mb/s (or more for additional channels) are programmable options. Both Internet and CATV signals provide video content for customers. Digitized CATV and Internet video content typically flow through a high-capacity router. Other switched services flow through multiple T1 lines at the Class 5 COs. The high bandwidth and cellular (53-octet ATM cells, see Ahamed and Lawrence, 1997) nature of the ATM traffic that carries a wide variety of services solves the congestion problem in most of the lower-bandwidth video networks. Medical and educational networks stand to benefit from global and local passive fiber-optic networks.

The impact of these newer networks is felt within the global community of information and knowledge users. The digital environment is becoming dominant in society. This trend is likely to make newer computer systems and Internets more capable of serving the personal and social needs of human beings. History has demonstrated the synergy between computers systems, VLSI technology, and network growth during the 1980s.

It is foreseeable that knowledge processing systems, nanotechnology devices, and Intelligent Internets may provide a new breed of machines that solve deep-seated human and social problems rather than scientific and business problems. SONET stands for the synchronous optical network, OC stands for optical carrier, and OC-n stands for optical carrier at rate n times the basic rate of 51.840 Mb/s. SONET has made deep inroads in almost all networks because of the standard PCM time slot of 125 μs that is deployed at all the optical rates. It is also associated with the well-accepted standards for the transport of predefined frames through the network. SONET concepts are well documented in the literature (Ahamed and Lawrence, 1997).

An overview of the subject is presented in this book only to inform and assert that the network technology that is proposed for the wisdom machines and the personal behavioral networks can be implemented relatively inexpensively by SONET on fiber and ATM on SONET. The ease of multiplexing and the elegance of the hierarchy both have contributed to its global acceptance as the optical standard. The older nonsynchronous hierarchical systems such as DS1 (1.544 Mb/s), CEPT-1 (2.048 Mb/s), DS1C (3.152 Mb/s), and DS2 (6.312 Mb/s) are combined via VT (virtual tributary) streaming into a STS-1 SPE (synchronous payload envelope) signal and even DS3 (44.736 Mb/s) with path overhead into one STS-1 signal. The overall transport capability of almost all international communication carriers is thus preserved in the SONET optical networks.

SONET standards, originally proposed by BCR[5], specify the standardized formats and interfaces for optical signals. Historically, the work started as far back as 1985 to provide standard optical interfaces between major carriers (such as NYNEX, MCI, or Sprint). SONET standards address four goals. They attempt to provide a broad family of interfaces at optical rates (i.e., OC-1 through OC-192). They provide easy and simple multiplexing/de-multiplexing of the signals (such as headers and payloads) within the network components. They address the issues of the growing trend toward communication networks becoming synchronous. Finally, they provides ample overhead channels and functions (via the header blocks) to perform and support the maintenance of the network facility.

---

[5] Bell Communications Research, originally a research and development unit of Bell Operating Companies, later taken over by Telcordia Inc.

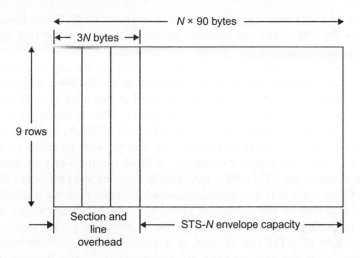

Figure 1.4 The SONET frame accepted by CEPT, ITU, and the European Telecom.

Total synchronism of all networks is unachievable and for this reason, the standard committees have accepted plesiochronous[6] interfacing signals, thus permitting the use of less than perfect timing recovery circuits in the network.

These standards, first approved by ANSI's T1 × 1 committee for standard fiber-optic transmission, were reviewed and accepted by CEPT, ITU, and the European Telecoms in the 1987—1988 time span Ahamed and Lawrence (1997) after considerable debate (the 9-row/13-row debate) about the number of rows in each of the frames. The 9-row × 90 column frame was favored by some of the European Telecoms, and the 13-row × 60 column frame was favored by the United States.

In February 1988, the Synchronous Transport Signal—Level 1, shown in Figure 1.4, was finally accepted with 9 rows × 90 columns and at a bit rate of 51.84 Mb/s. At this rate, the time duration of the frame is exactly 125 µs and this duration is necessary to get 810 bytes (or octets with 8 bits per byte or octet) at a rate of 51.840 Mb/s. Thus, one entire frame gets into the network in 125 µs (at OC-1 rate), and this is the same as the sample time of the PCM encoded speech of 1 byte (8 bits) at 8 kHz, thus maintaining the 125 µs clock duration for both the traditional voice circuits and the new SONET network.

1.6   OSI Standards and ATM Technology

Open systems interconnect (OSI) standard provides very dependable communication of data between any source and its destination. It has become the theme for

[6] The plesiochronous nature permits a small variation in the significant timing instants of the nominally synchronous signals; that is, the recovered signals may have small, but controlled, variations in their instantaneous rates or their instantaneous frequencies.

most, if not all data communication systems throughout world. Seven functions are identified in the OSI model and executed within the context of the OSI model and the network access protocol.

Stated briefly, the functions for data communication are framing and transparency, sequencing, error control, flow control, connection setup/shutdown, addressing/naming. The OSI data link layer functions are regrouped as functions of the ATM adaptation layer or the AAL (with two layers (convergence sublayer and segmentation and reassembly sublayer) and an ATM layer) for ATM. The OSI physical layer functions are handled by two (transmission convergence and physical medium) sublayers in ATM environment. A complete explanation of these functions and encoding of the five header octets of the ATM cells is presented in Ahamed and Lawrence (1997).

ATM of data transfer is a worldwide standard. It stems from the availability of a high-speed backbone in the national or global environment. It has started an era of cell relay technologies and falls under a wide umbrella of packet switching. The technological fit of ATM can be seen as a progression of X.25 technologies to frame technologies and then into the cell technologies. It also depends upon the SONET standard for the transport of data. ATM is a standard for most networks to communicate with each other provided the SONET and ATM protocol and header block information are consistently followed. ATM cells are routed and relayed by virtual circuits. Such circuits may be fabricated depending upon the traffic demands and switched and scaled by the ATM switches. These virtual networks may also be switched in the hardware at the ATM switches and/or nodes.

ATM also offers high-speed data transport capabilities. Since the ATM cells "ride" within the SONET frame, they carry all the advantages offered by transport systems embedded within SONET. The speed of transport is derived from optical rates (and thus low buffering delays), optical speeds, and low switching times (because of the simplicity/elegance in the SONET header information).

ATM is based upon packet-switched technology. The ATM packets or cells are relayed and routed throughout the network and thus are communicated between the source and the appropriate destination. Since the protocols and functions are unique to ATM, the technology for these ATM-based networks is called the "cell relay" technology as opposed to the "frame relay" technology.

ATM functionality has been embedded within a fixed size link layer (i.e., the OSI layer six, data link layer) entity. This link layer entity is the "cell" and the size of this fixed length entity is 53 octets (bytes). There are around 48 octets for the play load (or the data to be transported). Similar to the header of most packet networks, ATM cell header carries information unique to the nature of data, its functionality, disassemble and reassemble of cells and their play loads. The information contained in the header is encoded to conform to the functions within the ATM sublayers.

1.7   Conclusions

In the scientific domain, a slow and unrelenting chain of revolutions has preceded the rapid changes in the life styles of the knowledge workers in the modern society.

Pentium revolution in the semiconductor industry (1970s-present) and ATM revolution in the data transport industry (1980s-present) have implanted the information and knowledge revolutions (1990 now). The timings of these preceding revolutions have brought the human potential in scientific domain to wake up after a long slumber from the industrial revolution started in the 1800s. The two major scientific and technological implications of VLSI and fiber have been close enough to make the impact significant and sustained. Their confluence spills over most human activities. Information age appears as if it is here to stay until the human mind can conceive the macroeconomic relations between the stability of the environment and the exploitive growth of societies fueled by electronic gadgets and wireless media. Global wisdom appears too illusive in the modern scientific age for the human mind to be evolved by humans alone trapped in a traditional mode computational processing.

In this chapter, we have confined the discussion to the fields of computers and communications, and this book deals with finding a knowledge and experience-based machine to support the more exhaustive role of human action and contemplation for next few decades.

The symbiosis between humans and nature is fragile, and humans can break the balance in nature as much as nature can break the balance of human ordeals. Two glaring examples from the recent past of the dangers inflicted by humans are the global warming after prolonged CO_2 emissions and ecological damage after the Exxon Valdez oil spill. Equally disastrous counter examples are the Japanese nuclear disaster after the earthquake of April 2011 and the millions of acres of pristine forest turned into ashes after Mount St. Helens eruption of May 1980. Humanist knowledge processing and contemplative minds offer the promise of a balanced society with (accurately) calculated risks in the future in intellectual and human dimensions. The harmony between human misdeeds and nature's forgiveness will most likely be resumed, if human intellect is not subdued by greed and self-glory.

References

1. von Neumann J: *First draft of a report on the EDVAC, contract No., W-670-ORD 4926, between United States Army Ordnance Department and University of Pennsylvania,* Philadelphia, Pennsylvania, 1945, Moore School of Electrical Engineering.
2. Grosvenor ES, Wesson M: *Alexander graham bell,* New York, 1997, Harry N. Abrams, Inc.
3. Wolf W: *Modern VLSI design:* system-on-chip design, ed 3, Englewood Cliffs, New Jersey, 2002, Prentice Hall.
4. Shockley W.: US Patent Application Serial No. 35,423 filed. Private communication (during 1970s) at Bell Telephone Laboratories, Murray Hill, New Jersey. The N- and P-type materials are also presented in the application, June 26, 1948.
5. Bardeen and WH: Brattain US Patent Application Serial No. 33,466 filed. Private communication (during 1970s) at Bell Telephone Laboratories, Murray Hill, New Jersey, June 17, 1948.

6. Hoddeson L, Vicki D: *True genius: the life and science of John Bardeen*, 2002, Joseph Henry Press, and American Physical Society Homepage: *This month in physics history —November17—December 23, 1947: invention of the first transistor* (APS Website). Available from <http://www.pbs.org/transistor>.

7. Nobelprize.org: *The Nobel Prize in physics 1956, William B. Shockley, John Bardeen, Walter H. Brattain*. 1956. Available from <http://www.nobelprize.org/nobel_prizes/physics/laureates/1956/bardeen-bio.html>.

8. Ahamed SV, Lawrence VB: *Design and engineering of intelligent communication systems*, Boston, MA, 1997, Kluwer Academic Publishers. Artiglia M, Vita P, Potenza M: Optical fiber amplifiers: physical model and design issues, *Opt Quant Electron* 26 (6):585−608, 1997.

9. O'Dell TH: ASIN: 0470270845 *Ferromagnetodynamics:* the dynamics of magnetic bubbles, domains, and domain walls, NewYork, 1981, Halsted Press.

10. Bonyhard P, Danylchuk I, Kish D, Smith J: Applications of bubble devices, *IEEE Trans Magn* 6(3):447−451, 1981.

11. Ahamed SV: *Intelligent internet knowledge networks: processing of concepts and wisdom, Wiley-Interscience*, 2006; See also Ahamed SV, Lawrence VB: *Intelligent broadband multimedia networks*, Boston, MA, 2006, Kluwer Academic Publishers.

12. Telephone Laboratories Bell: *Transmission systems for communications*, Winston-Salem, NC, 1982, Western Electric Co.

13. in Chapters 16 and 17 Ahamed SV, Lawrence VB: *Design and engineering of intelligent communication systems*, Boston, MA, 1997, Kluwer Academic Publishers.

14. in Chapter 2 Ahamed SV, Lawrence VB: *Intelligent broadband multimedia networks*, Boston, MA, 1997, Kluwer Academic Publishers.

15. Aprille TJ: Introducing SONET into the local exchange carrier network, *IEEE Commun Mag, Aug*: 34−38, 1997. See also, For SONET Digital HierarchyChow M-C: *Understanding SONET/SDH: standards and applications*, Holmdel, NJ, 1990, Andan Publishers.Additional References for SONET are in (a) Bellcore, Synchronous Optical Network (SONET) Transport Systems: Common Generic Criteria, TR-TSY-000253, 1989. (b) Bellcore, SONET Add/Drop Multiplex Equipment Administration Using the TIRKS Provisioning System, Globecom, Conference Record, vol. 3, pp. 1511−1515, 1989. (c) See also Bellcore SONET Add-Drop Multiplex Equipment (SONET ADM) Generic Criteria, TR-TSY-000496, Issue 2, 1989. (d) Bellcore SONET Add-Drop Multiplex Equipment (SONET ADM) Generic Criteria for a Self-Healing Ring Implementation, TA-TSY-000496, Issue 2, 1989.

16. Ahamed SV: *Intelligent internet knowledge networks: processing of concepts and wisdom*, Hoboken, New Jersey, 2006, Wiley-Interscience, Chapter 2, also presented in Alcatel Web site at www.alcatel.com/submarine/refs/cables/iaa/semewe.htm, SEA-ME-WE-3.

17. Senior JM: *Optical fiber communications: principles and practice*, ed 3, Englewood Cliffs, New Jersey, 2008, Prentice Hall.

18. Ahamed SV: Simulation and design studies of the digital subscriber lines, *Bell Syst Tech J* 61(July−August):1003−1077, 2008. See also Ahamed SV, Bohn PP, Gottfried NL: A tutorial on two-wire digital transmission in the loop plant, *IEEE Special Issue Comm.* vol. COM 29:1554−1564, 2008.

19. Chapters 6 and 15, CLASS: Custom local area signaling services, see S.V. Ahamed and V.B. Lawrence: *Design and engineering of intelligent communication systems,* Boston, MA, 1997 and 1998, Kluwer Academic Publishers.

20. in Chapter 17 Ahamed SV, Lawrence VB: *Intelligent broadband multimedia networks*, Boston, MA, 1997, Kluwer Academic Publishers.

2 Processor Revolution(s)

2.1 Introduction

In conjunction with Chapter 1, the role of processors is placed in perspective for the social and service of modern machines for a greater array of services. The teraflops machines and supercomputers have only benefited a handful of scientists and researchers. Social machines and networks offer a greater benefit in serving public by far reaching global services such as averting disaster, sensing eminent dangers, and stopping thugs and Mafia to gain control of the social and national security of nations. In this chapter, the use of new machines is directed toward fulfilling human needs by processing knowledge to provide "satisficing" and rewarding psychological and emotional decisions. Such decisions from computer will reflect the individual human decisions from the past or the corporate decisions that reflect sound business policy. The main emphasis is on searching for optimal operations within groups of (verb) functions and optimal groups of subobjects or morphemes within (noun) objects.

Groups of actions focused on groups of objects lead to the rewards and social benefits rather than opcodes (or opcs) upon operands (as in conventional computing) lead to social computing. Networks that combine "social processors" within social networks will be the building blocks of intelligent social networks. Directed toward performing desirable and intelligent social functions, such networks will compete well with the traditional intelligent networks of the 1980s directed toward performing intelligent communication function.

We start this chapter from the inception of data and numerical processing that was introduced by von Neumann. We extend this concept to object, knowledge, medical, and wisdom processing. Technology and machines have provided the foundations, and the instinctual perhaps intellectual curiosity has provided the motivation. Incredible breakthroughs, inventions, and innovations of the last three generations have paved the way to the way we live and the comforts we enjoy. When the effort of scientists is directed toward the betterment of the society, the rewards are the prosperity as much as the adversity that results from the ill-directed the effort of thugs, Mafia, and corrupt individuals. For this reason, we reiterate the neutral mode for the pursuit of wisdom based on science, economics, and technology (SET). Such processes can be molded and enhanced for the evolution and enhancement of Internet society. The writings of Plato and Aristotle point to such an approach. However, in the converse mode, the SET processes in wisdom can be abused toward the degeneration and destruction of society, also based on the writings of Plato and Aristotle as far back as three and half centuries before Christ!

Intelligent Networks: Recent Approaches and Applications in Medical Systems.
DOI: http://dx.doi.org/10.1016/B978-0-12-416630-1.00002-9

In the more recent past, the processor revolution in the computer industry is comparable to the automobile revolution in the transportation industry. Both have influenced modern living. The later revolution during the last six decades in data and information processing is at a much faster pace, and the influence is in the human perceptual domain. The context to humans is at the emotional and psychological levels. Information, knowledge, and concepts provide garments of personality to the raw human mind. In a sense, other higher level needs reali-zation needs (Maslow, 1943), search, and unification (Ahamed, 2005) provide the motivation to seek such garments for the human mind. To this extent, the informa-tion, knowledge, and concepts processing in the next-generation processors will influence the emotional, psychological, and mental health of the generations to come, much as the evolving medical processing is influencing the physiological health of the current generation. Processing in the modern context is essential at any level of human needs (Maslow, 1943; Ahamed, 2005) much as hunting and gathering processes were at the survival level of the prior generations.

Complex processes in humans and computers are amenable to the science of morphology.[1] In the present context of processors, identification, analysis, and description of any process are feasible at two levels: (i) at the operation code level and (ii) at the operand level. The conventional opcodes (*opcs*) are a group of finely further subdivided opcodes that constitute a (verb) function directed at one or a set of operands that will experience the opcode in the processor unit of any given processor. At the operand level, operands can be numbers, logical entities, plain objects, (noun) objects, data structures, sentences, paragraphs, books, and so on. Computer scientists have classified single instruction (SI) and multiple instruction (MI) systems much as they have classified single operand (SO) and multiple oper-and (MO) systems, thus leading to the architectures of the four best-known central processor unit (CPU) designs (Stone, 1980).

In the humanist domain, processing becomes more complex due to the assistive, passive, or resistive nature of the human operands to the nature of operations. Such operations can be cooperative, neutral, or coercive. Hence, the classifications become more cumbersome and exhaustive to determine the effect of one human, robot, or machine "operator" operating upon another human, and robot or machine "operand". An in-depth classification of such operations (or verb functions (VFs)) on human and semihuman operands (or noun objects (NOs)) is presented by Ahamed (2009). Processors presented in Sections 2.9 and 2.10 transform current objects and convert them into new objects to suit different applications and scenarios in the real world.

---

[1] Morphology is the systematic breakdown, structural identification, and analysis and description of morphemes and other units in any discipline such as linguistics and biology. Words in languages, organisms in biology, shapes and forms in images, and even ideas and concepts in the human mind can be broken down, identified, and described. We extend this chain and go on to reconstitute the operation code and the operands in computer science and thus breakdown, decompose, reassemble, and reconsti-tute objects to generate new objects, images, and even new ideas and inventions, and to evolve new concepts. This is the goal of most machines presented in this book.

2.2   Earlier Processor Designs

Processor functionality is based on gating of bits and the manipulation of data structures. A typical architecture depicted in Figure 2.1 accomplishes such rudimentary functions. In 1978, the 16-bit, 8088 chip with 29,000 transistors and operated at clocking speeds of 5, 8, and 10 MHz. In 1985, the 386 chip with 275,000 transistors was already capable of multitasking. By early 1999, the Pentium processor with 9.5 million transistors was launched. By May 2005, the Intel Dual-Core Itanium with 1.72 billion transistors with 90 nm technology had been introduced. In sharp contrast, current transistor designs offer impressive reduction in size and equally impressive

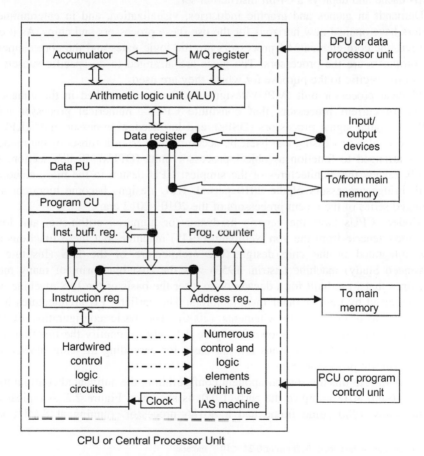

CPU or Central Processor Unit

Figure 2.1 An architecture of the first-generation processor of the von Neumann (IAS) machine (Stone, 1980) and its configuration of the PCU, DPU, bus structure, and the seven registers (accumulator (A), multiplier/quotient (M/Q), data register (DR), instruction buffer register (IBR), instruction register (IR), address register (AR), and program counter (PC)).

switching speeds. Current sizes range about 45 nm^2 and are capable of switching at the rate of about 2.3 ns^3 even as far back as 2007. Size and speed offer future designers the possibilities of performing gross macro functions that can be perceived at a conceptual level.

The technological barriers have been elegantly crossed in chip designs rather than in imagination. Such architectures are based on the 2010–2012 processors and their derivatives of the Intel Core microarchitecture. The 2 Duo, Intel Core 2 Quad multicore processors have more than 580 million transistors and are used in numerous devices, computers, and advanced systems. The second-generation Intel Core i7 mobile processor uses 32 nm technology and 4 cores and 8 threads with 8 MB cache and deploys a 64-bit instruction set.

Demands in games and graphic industries, visualization, and in entertainment centers have opened new horizons for the use these processors and chips. As it can be seen, the core elements of processors are the logic gates and the core elements of computers are the processors. The gates are arranged to do specific subsets of functions specific to the purpose for which they are used.

Medical processor unit (MPU) designs are firmly entrenched in the enhanced design of current processors that constitute CPUs^4, numerical processor units (NPUs), digital signal processors (DSPs), and knowledge processor units (KPUs). The knowledge processing can itself be accomplished from a subset of the modern CPUs arranged to function as object processor units (OPUs). In this section, we briefly review the architectures of the simplest CPU design to the more elaborate north bridge processors of the 2010 period. KPU designs become hierarchically arranged series of the recent processors of the 2010–2012 era.

Modern CPUs have the generic hardware for numeric, arithmetic, and logic functions generic from the von Neumann (1945) machine, but these functions are now integrated in the chip design. The architecture of the IAS (Institute of Advanced Study) machine (Estrin, 1953) was the first blue print of many more machines that were built for a decade or so after the basis of the IAS machine was well received by the computer manufacturers. The earlier CPU architectures have been described in detail by Clements (2006). The basic configuration of this vintage (1945) processor is shown in Figure 2.1 only to identify the functions and functional blocks. The functions are the basis for cascading the chip blocks into more powerful processor chips

In contrast to this discrete component configuration, the antiquated configuration of the 16-bit, 80186 chip of the early 1980s is shown in Figure 2.2. A typical PC in the early 1980s time frame had a 80186 processor, running at 8 MHz and

---

^{2} A silicon atom is just about 0.24 nm or 0.24×10^{-9} meters.

^{3} A light beam would have traversed only about a tenth of an inch in the time it takes for this gate to switch one bit.

^{4} In the modern days, the number of processors has increased dramatically. It is possible to build a processor for almost any function or task, ranging from arithmetic functions (calculators) to automated drones and robots deployed in battle fields. In this section we present the trail of only a few pertinent processors only because they form a basis for the evolution of the knowledge and medical processor units.

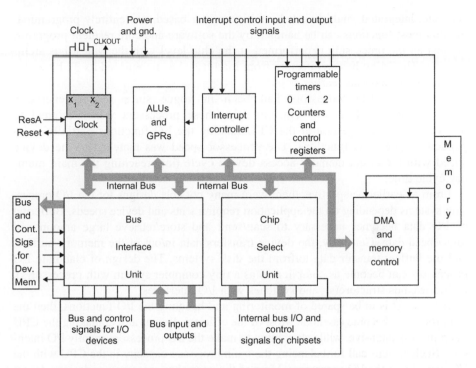

Figure 2.2 Microarchitecture of the dated chip 80186/80188 Intel Chip.

constituted the backbone of the turbo PC during the mid-1980s. It also needed a supporting 8088 processor chip for data transfers between the PC and disk or printers and at least 128K of RAM. The basic input/output (I/O) system facilitated the data transfer from the external devices.

2.3 Input/Output Processors

Conventional I/O processors have been almost nudged out of existence by the new processors[5] and their functional architecture. Greater bandwidth of up to 16 GBps (gigabytes per second), performance, and scalability simplify the board design. These newer low-cost silicon component design architectures find applicability in high-end graphics and in high-performance computing. Interconnect capacity and efficiency are both enhanced. Other processors have become so cheap, fast,

---

[5] During the era of 8086 and 8088 (1970s), Intel had evolved the 8089 coprocessor for the I/O operations during late 1970s. It shared the common system bus. With an independent clock and a set of (PROM and RAM) combination, the 8089 offered data capability to and from an external I/O peripheral.

accurate, integrated, multithreaded, multiprocessor based, and entirely programmable that most functions can be handled by the software and core resident programs. Almost all the processing is performed at the chip level with the widest bus architectures. The 64-bit bus architecture from Intel has already replaced its 32-bit architecture almost a decade earlier.

Independent I/O processors had been in vogue since second-generation machines of the IBM-7094 era. Initially, these processors were designed to relieve the data congestion at the CPU making the I/O functions partially independent of the CPU functions. The processor speed was matched to the device speed with the direct memory access device cycle time reaching the main memory cycle time.

From an earlier perspective, there were many possible designs for the I/O processing systems depending on the application requirements and device speeds. Buffering of I/O data becomes necessary to scan/send and store/retrieve large amounts of high-speed data. Generally, the device transfers data in/out of the memory buffers, and the buffers transfer data to/from the disk systems. The design of elaborate I/O processors can become as complicated as a tiny computer system with processor(s), memories, bus structure(s), and switches with I/O interfaces.

If the CPU is to be spared of monitoring and handling the I/O functions, then the I/O processors become essential. Most of the efficient designs aim at making the CPU main process intensive, while attempting to make the I/O processors equally I/O intensive. Such designs call for balancing the main processor capacity in the CPU with the I/O capacity in the I/O processors. Most of the normal microcomputer designs do not usually demand such stringent design requirements.

Sequentially and/or interrupt-driven I/O devices and direct memory access (DMA) (Stone, 1980) devices are generally available for numerous applications. The I/O interfaces can also be highly variable. The application requirements (e.g., for audio, video, graphics, and medical) usually set the primary constraints and limits on the design and integration of the overall system. Speed, buffer capacity, and bus structures with the I/O processors are the intermediate design variables.

For the sensing and monitoring applications, where large blocks of data (e.g., high-definition visual scenes, transient astronomical observations) need bulk transfers, dedicated I/O processors may become essential. Single and multiple buffering techniques facilitate the smooth transfers from external devices to computer memories. When the data scans are performed at regular intervals, the buffer control can be driven by the clock and counters if the clock speed is much faster than the sampling clock. Limited extent of real-time processing of the sampled data is also feasible in the I/O processors. For example, extremely accurate and high-speed sampling multiprocessors may be deployed. In a sense, the I/O interfacing can be as demanding as the design of a very low-level computer with serial, parallel, interrupt, and DMA capabilities.

In some of the specialized commercial I/O processors in the 2010 time frame, as many as 25 simultaneous, DMA channels and up to 12 serial ports may be active in order to scan and collect environmental data. The hardware and software methodologies of the graphics processor units (GPUs) can be imported into the I/O processing because of a graphical display in a very specialized output device. The I/O processors are generally used for high-speed data inputs. If A to D and/or D to A conversion is one of the considerations in the reception of external data, the conversion time also plays a significant role in the continuous operation of the system. The situation is resolved by specialized I/O processors, just the specialized graphics processors to resolve particular application needs.

2.4 Display/Graphics Processor Units

The rudimentary features of graphics processors are sometimes integrated and built into the modern core CPUs. It can incorporate high definition (HD) coupled with media processing and high performance. Some of the CPUs and GPUs are integrated into a single chip as shown in Figure 2.3. The Intel HD graphics 3000 and 2000 chips use the more recent 32 nm technology throughout, thus reducing the

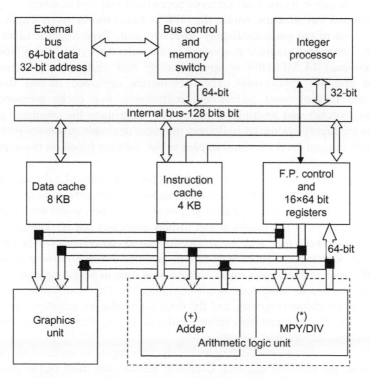

Figure 2.3 A typical CPU configuration that could be used as a GPU unit from the late 1980 era.

power consumption and size. Faster 3D and more-realistic renderings of complex gaming and real objects are thus feasible.

The earlier versions of display devices, their display processor units (DPUs), the cathode ray tube (CRT) technology are obsolete now. Cursor input in the CRTs is very antiquated for the last two decades. Their software was primitive, and the display functions and colors needed dramatic enhancements and are not discussed here. The flat panel technology and the availability of very fine granularity and color options have rendered new venues for machines to carry the visual impact deep in the minds and thoughts of scientists and researchers alike. The impact in every scientific and social direction of progress is monumental.

Only for the sake of completeness, we very briefly cover the pathway that has led to modern display technology. During their introduction, the GPUs served as the intermediate processors between the CPU and the graphic devices. The GPUs were initially built to relieve the CPU from the display functions and continue with the application-based processing. Earlier designs (e.g., Intel 82786 graphics coprocessor) adapted a separate configuration but the later CPU architectures absorbed the basic GPU configurations within the larger Very Large Scale Integrated (VLSI) chips that were offering larger capacity, dependability, and yield. Typical configuration of a CPU from the 1980s that could also be deployed as a GPU is shown in Figure 2.3. The GPUs for movie industry are far more specialized and sophisticated.

The internal bus structure within the GPU is based on the word length and the instruction set of the graphics/display processor unit. Typically, the older (1980s and early 1990s era) graphics processors and accelerators (the Intel 80860, i860, 1989) delivered 13 MFLOPS or approximately half million vector transformations for graphics applications. The architecture deployed 10 bus structures, integer and floating-point adders and multipliers, two cache memories, and numerous switches and multiplexer units. The algorithms for computer graphics functions are highly optimized to deliver the most desirable processor power consistent with desired level of visual impact to the viewers based on the application requirements.

The graphics processors were as powerful as the CPUs almost a decade earlier. In fact, the VLSI technology is the same and some GPUs outperform traditional CPUs for specific applications. Processors for graphical inputs and outputs have specialized requirements. Most of the graphical and display processes are accomplished in real time and need to keep pace with the application-based computations. When the entire systems are designed for special applications (such as distance learning, remote surgery, MRI, stock market, and games), the response time of both (application oriented and graphics oriented) subsystems needs consideration. The communication capacity is influenced on channel capacity, and the three (computation, graphics, and communication) basic design parameters influence the accuracy, clarity, and quality of the output displays, movies, and pictures.

Graphical user interfaces (GUIs) provide the user inputs to applications programs that generate the resulting displays. Graphical devices are main output devices for computer to communicate with the users. In certain applications such as computer games and movie making, the perception time of the users and viewers becomes crucial. When the computer systems are dedicated to movies, the graphics processing systems can become as elaborate and intricate as mainframe/supercomputers.

The balance between the processing power and graphics display capability becomes an option for most of the designers of standard desktop and laptop computers. In the customized systems, the processing powers are based on the choice of the CPU and graphics processor chips that are compatible with the CPU. For intensive graphics applications, independent graphics processors are deployed. Some of the modern low-cost computing systems have integrated GPUs built in the overall architecture.

GPU computing has become a specialty in its own right. It is seen as a viable alternative to the traditional microprocessor-based computing in high-performance computing environments. When used in conjunction with selected CPUs, an order of magnitude gain in performance can be expected in game physics and in computational biophysics applications. The parallel architecture of the GPU is generally used to accelerate the computational performance. These GPUs handle a broad range of process-intensive complex problems with a visual insight into the nature of changes that occur as the computation progresses.

Integrated graphic products (chips and chipsets) generally found in notebook computers offer the compromise of having reasonably high-level graphic display capability while cutting power consumption and cost. However, they share the bus and main memory (MM) of the computer reducing the overall performance level. Such products are unsuitable for any high-end graphics applications.

Intel's Graphics Media Accelerator (GMA) chips and chipsets are dedicated to higher quality and faster operations. The GMA 500 has been in production since early 2000. Operating core speed is 200 MHz and it uses four unified pipelines. The technology is 130 nm, and it shares 128 MB memory with the main computer. As a sharp contrast, the GMA 4700MHD series chip set has a core speed of 640 MHz and deploys 10 unified pipelines with 65 nm technology sharing as much as 384 MB of main memory. Other GMA series (600, 900, 950, X3000 (in 2006), X3100, 4500M, and 4500MHD) integrated products are also available. Compatibility issues with the OS and the main CPU unit are critical in performance, speed, and display quality.

High-quality memory cards with their dedicated memory can deliver superior performance and speeds for the highest quality graphic and video applications. Numerous low priced graphic cards such as Matrox Millennium G550 (32 MB), ATI Radeon 9800 Pro (256 MB), ATI (X1950, X1800, etc.) to the higher priced (Nvidia's Geforce 7600 GT, 9700 GT, PNY Nvidia Quadro NVS 420 graphics adaptor with two GPUs and 512 MB and a maximum resolution of 2560×1600, etc.) are available. These newer processors have distinctive features[6] (e.g., smoothness of transitions, three-dimentional (3D) renderings, and true colors).

---

[6] These devices and their identification are for illustration only but they provide a snapshot of the graphics chips and adaptors during the Summer-2011 time slot.

2.5   NPUs and Array Processors

Much as GPUs were aligned to the visual (gaming, movie applications); the NPUs were geared to the numerical manipulation. Such requirements are commonly encountered in research, scientific, and are needed for accuracy in the user applications. Accordingly, single and double precision devices were available for simple and matrix operations. The Intel coprocessors (8087, 80287, 80387, and even 80487 for a very short time) provided numeric support for their (8086 (1978−1990), 80286 (1982−1990), 80386 (1985/6−2007), and 80486 (1989−1991), respectively) CPU chips. In the early versions, the NPUs were used as an appendage to the CPU to overall performance of the computer by forcing the NPU to perform numeric functions. A series of NPU architectures were developed during the 1970s and 1989. In most cases, the NPU has been integrated within the main CPU architecture for almost two decades.

The more recent CPU designs incorporate the essential numeric and graphic functions entirely. A variety of multimedia (audio, video, media creation, and multithreaded gaming applications) functions can be accomplished in the Intel®, Pentium®, 900 sequence (extreme edition) processor. This particular processor has dual-core processing, with hyperthreading and virtualization technologies. It accommodates two of 2-MB level 2 caches, and front side bus at 1066 MHz for maximum bandwidth. Execute disable bit provides additional hardware security, and the processor permits streaming for single instruction multiple data (SIMD) extensions to accelerate the performance of most applications including multimedia, video, audio code/decode functionality. 3D graphics and image processing functions can be performed in this processor environment.

Array processors (also known as vector processors) provide an example where a large number of SIMD architectures are deployed in conjunction with numerous NPUs. Generally used for matrix and array operations, array processors perform large matrix operations (such as multiplications and inversions) at high speeds due to massive parallelism. Bus configurations and switches are designed accordingly to assure that most of the identical numeric functions (such as additions, multiplications, and divisions) can occur simultaneously to be able to reduce the overall execution time for matrix and vector functions.

Array processing has found applications in the solution of numerous engineering and scientific research and problem solving. When the problems become specific and complex boundary conditions apply, their numerical solutions become the logical (if not the only) recourse. Array processing becomes invaluable in most cases. Large matrices can be multiplied and inverted in a few milliseconds.

In graphics and image processing, array processing techniques facilitate the recognition of objects, the embedded patterns, and any differential properties in arrays of pixel frames. In image modification and enhancements, differential or correlated pixel image (or their arrays) maps detected after pixel array processing yield new characteristics in the original image(s). Results from applications of vector processing in genome, evolution, and cancer researches offer new insights into the microscopic methodologies of nature. At the other extreme, time-lapse photos of galactic snapshots of individual terrestrial objects in space, pictured from space probes and microwave radio telescopes, offer new insights into the macroscopic forces that shape the planets, galaxies, and the universe.

In social setting, objects such as human beings, communities, societies, and nations can be processed by object-processing techniques (see Section 2.8) well founded in image processing. Rather than pixels captured in snapshots, the attributes of superobjects, objects and subordinate objects, their subattributes, and their structural relationships are tracked. The conditions for stability of the structure of objects need to be processed and deduced by "social array processors." After such "social object array processors" enhance the time lapse "object images" of such social objects, the forces that alter the social dynamics can be as easily recognized as the core of malignancy in a cancerous tissue. It can be treated by surgical removal (police force) or by ("socialized radiation" techniques, or commando forces). Such social malignancies can also be cured by social medicine such as rehab of mentally disoriented terrorists, drug abusers, sex offenders, and children abusers.

2.6 Digital Signal Processors

Some of the elaborate digital processors can be as complex as wafer scale integrated microcomputers. Typically, these simplistic processor chips are not too expensive, and again, the processing is not as extensive but application dependent. Hence, there is proliferation of the types and architectures in the design of DSPs. For example, in the DSPs, the voice communication industry would focus on the high density packet voice signal processing and depend on the complexity of the coder/decoder (codec) as opposed to DSPs used in the digital subscriber lines. The interfacing, pin configuration, and power requirements would also vary accordingly. Specialized communication processors in the numerous types of (e.g., plain old telephone services (POTS), cellular to the ATM-based fiber optic) networks generally have special racks dedicated to digital signal processing via their "channel units" Ahamed and Lawrence (1997a). In a sense, the communication industry of the 1960s has provided a firm platform for the DSPs for any application, for any place, anywhere ranging from outer space data collection systems to EKG monitoring system for stabilizing the heart beat of patients.

Initially, DSPs were built as especially programmable processor units that convert external signals (mostly analog) to digital formats and then to process the signals to generate new sets of accurate and programmable output parameters. These external parameters can in turn be used to control the environment and feed into other sensing and monitoring systems to control the stability or the optimality of the overall systems.

The DSP units are in use for numerous industrial, production, and robotic applications. For the production-oriented and robotic lines, the place for DSPs is firmly entrenched. The specific design of the units is tailored to the particular industrial, production, or control environment. The nature of applications dictates the choice of finite number of operations and *opcs* that are embedded in DSP chipsets. The life-long task of many digital designers is to optimize the performance and the optimality of a particular DSP to a particular task.

The need to tailor DSP design for any specific application brings about wide varieties of the DSP architectures. From a conceptual perspective, it is possible to transform the simpler CPU design methodologies into DSP designs. The VLSI chip design engineers incorporate the details to implement the DSP with a minimum number of gates and at clock rate to offer a response fast enough for the applications. At the current state of technology, the computer-aided VLSI design software offers ample freedom of architectures and for the chip manufactures to offer a marketable product in less than a month. Being highly specific to the application and less versatile, the DSP chips are generally less expensive than CPUs, if there is sufficient demand. For customized designs, the costs can be relatively high, and the solution sometimes lies in using the less expensive DSP with necessary peripheral I/O devices.

For the applications of moderate complexity, modern DSPs provide serial, synchronous, and asynchronous interfaces, 64K−256K, 16-bit words with multiprocessing capability in each programming and I/O space. Pins for external interrupt signals and interrupt service routines are also provided. The PC is generally pushed into a hardware stack, thus providing the built-in return capability after the interrupt servicing is complete. Eight level nesting is common even in the low-level modern DSPs. Scanning the system for periodic or infrequent inputs is also a programmable option. Scanning, conversion, and direct memory transfer features are generally available.

Modern applications can range from DSPs for digital subscriber loop (DSL) transceivers to stream processors capable of delivering up to 512 GOPs Mandl and Bordiloi (2011). The program code driving the recent DSPs also plays a vital role in realizing the highest overall performance. The modern processors are flexible enough to be used for a variety of applications needing signal, image, and video processing. Massive parallelism is deployed in recent (2007−2008) DSP architectures. Most of the emerging process-intensive embedded applications (such as high definition encoding, video processing, image processing, search operations, encryption, and wireless communications) stand to benefit from the new breed of DSP chips with highly specific code to drive them and realize the data parallelism through the processors. The direct memory access capability is usually built in the high-end processor chips.

2.7 Recent Processors

The changes in the design and the architecture of the processor are evident, but the functional blocks and functions performed are essentially the same, even though the components are interconnected differently and the speeds are incredibly faster.

As in all competing environments, the numerical functions of the processors, the memories, the switches, the bus structures, and the I/O processors remain firmly embedded in the silicon and Pentium technology. Conceptually, it is feasible to retune each component to have the integrated functionality of the functionalities of any/all other four components and build microcomputer chip (chipsets) for each of the components. In fact, it is evident that the complexity of the modern processor chips of the last two decades to be as complex as (if not more complex than) the computer(s) of the prior decade. The comparison of complexity is valid in the memory chips as well. The breakthroughs in the organization of functions and their hierarchy and the lithographic processes to make the chips and keep such costs low and affordable make up for the triple exponential growth of processing power. An equally good parallel of these symbiotic developments (fiber optic, wireless, and cellular technologies) in the domain of data transmission exists. These well-synchronized breakthroughs have made the unprecedented growth of Internet a reality. Faster, precise, and diligent we have become, but emotionally poorer and disconnected we have emerged!

Data, information, and visuals are everywhere, but knowledge, concepts, and wisdom are scarce. We suspect that knowledge, concepts, and wisdom being the by-products of human intellect, creativity, and contemplation ride atop silly processes in dumb processors. Enhancements of human intelligence, comprehension, and values have failed to keep abreast of artificial intelligence, technology, and photolithography. We do not have a solution this impasse. It is perhaps due to the fact that processes as powerful and fast is too much of a challenge for ill-educated population of the world. Use of devices is not intelligence-based in the civilized societies and is not an intelligence but an excuse not to be able to differentiate the desirable, the neutral, and the undesirable objects (Nose) and events (Vs.) integrated over a lifetime. Perhaps Aristotle was right in indicating that the values behind truth, virtue, and beauty are eternal, infinitely (in a manner of speaking) slower than the pet flops the processors can provide.

The microarchitecture of a typical 2007−2008 period processor by Intel is depicted functionally in Figure 2.4. The infusion of CPU and the GPU is shown at a microarchitectural level in the processor designs that followed. The 2011 technology and designs are greatly enhanced from this figure. Sixty-four processor chips are being built for special applications, and the prediction are for 1024 processors much before the end of this decade. Multithreading is also conceived to enhance performance and to make the chips oriented for complex functions. There is a good chance that the 22-nm technology will permit the infusion of more functions CPU, GPU, I/O processors, and all the necessary bus switching functions with their own controllers.

The reduction in size and the enhancements of gating speed of transistors both foster greater processing power. The sophistication of the resource allocation and control in the operating systems for the new processor-based machines is indicative of the possibilities that machines can indeed be made more complex and even humanlike, if the computer scientists are challenged intellectually and financially,

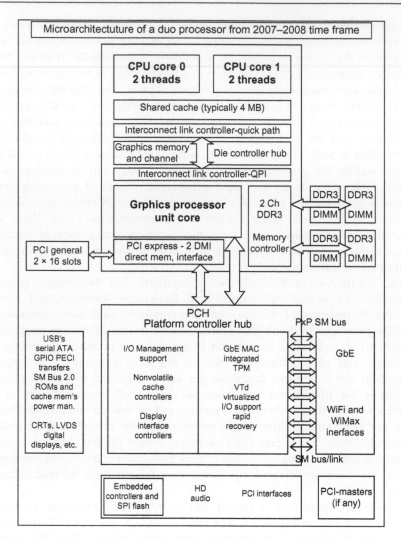

Figure 2.4 Microarchitecture of a duo processor from the 2007−2008 period.

by the multinational corporations. The direction for true commitment to the welfare of the society is in building machines for the public (as Karl Marx would say) or building automobiles for every household (as Henry Ford did in 1920s). The gaming systems for building more 3D display graphics software may serve the fancies of a few, and even that to paralyze the intellect of youngsters as they while away their lives.

Building knowledge processors for knowledge machines with their own operating systems will be a landmark achievement in making machines more

Table 2.1 Snapshot of Intel's Penryn Duo and Pentium Family of
Processors 2007–2009 Time Frame

	Manufacturing Process	Transistor Count	Die Size
Intel Core Duo (Penyrn)	45 nm	410M	107 mm^2
Intel Core 2 Duo	65 nm	291M	143 mm^2
Intel Pentium 4	0.18 μm	42M	217 mm^2
Intel Pentium Pro (P6)	0.50	5.5M	306 mm^2
Intel Pentium (P5)	0.80	3.1M	294 mm^2

Note: Intel logic technology development process names P1264 P1266 P1268 P1270 P1272 with lithography of 65, 45, 32, 22, and 16 nm, respectively. The first production of these processors was in 2005, 2007, 2009, 2011, 2013. The processing and lithography are developed in two or more distinct departments.

subservient to humans rather than making humans the robotic extensions of mindless machines.

Pentium processors of the 2004–2006 periods had transistor counts ranging from 3.1M (P5) to 42M (Pentium 4). The manufacturing process was reduced from 8.80 μm to 0.18 μm. The die size ranged between 294 and 217 mm^2 respectively. For the duo-core processors, in the 2006–2008 (Penyrn and Nelalem) processors that followed the Pentium series, the transistor count increased dramatically reaching up to 410M and die size shrank to 107 mm^2 using 45 nm manufacturing process. For the 2009–2010 (Westmere and Sandy Bridge) processors, the 32-nm technology is becoming more and more popular.

The next logical extension of the knowledge machine is the medical machine with its medical processor (adopted from the new infused processors of this decade) with multithreaded human and medical tasks. Some of the processors designed during the years 2005 and 2007 are characterized in Table 2.1.

For most processors, the system bus still plays a vital role in the transfer of data, programs, instructions, and external elements that constitute the entire computer. However, the discrete components, such the floating-point processor units (FPUs), the arithmetic logic units (ALUs), and the decoders, become integrated within the CPU chip. The block diagram of the Duo Conroe chip (late 2006–2007 period) is shown in Figure 2.5.

As shown in Figure 2.5, the instruction fetch via the system bus, initial decoding, queuing, microcode decoding, buffering, scheduling, floating-point processing, arithmetic logic, and functions in this duo-core processor are done at the chip level together with caching and flow-control functions performed in hardware.

The progress toward more powerful processors has been gradual, but a variety of designs architectures and capabilities have accrued over the last few years. The major strides in the application software and filmware have not kept pace with the availability of the processors and their ever-growing capabilities. Significant developments in operating systems and application packages have failed to keep pace. Human aspects in social and humanist computing are the most neglected areas.

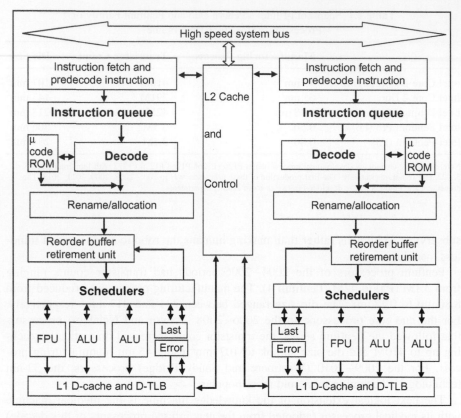

Figure 2.5 Block diagram of the functions in the Conroe chip of the 2006−2008 time frame. Not all the designs from chip manufactures gain popularity, nor are they extensively used. Some chips, their designs, and processes are discontinued simply because of lack of demand for them, or newer powerful chips takeover the functions. The chips, chipsets, and their supporting environments are usually optimized for the application.

If the functions are mostly hardware based, the chip flexibility becomes constrained, thus limiting their use and lifespan. The converse is also true. Thus, the survival of the fittest chip lies in its programmability of more and more generic (sub) functions that are most desirable in most applications. At this fine level of choice, the decisions become business and profit oriented. However, the conceptually well-founded designs linger on. The goal toward the reduced power consumption (with the rapidly diminishing die sizes) has been ear marked to be pursued through the middle of the decade past 2010.

The Intel Quad Core Nehalem Processor (Xeon X5550) introduced in 2012 offers programmable functions and adaptive performance. It offers dual caches (L2−4 × 256 KB, L3−8 MB) and the layout is shown in Figure 2.6.

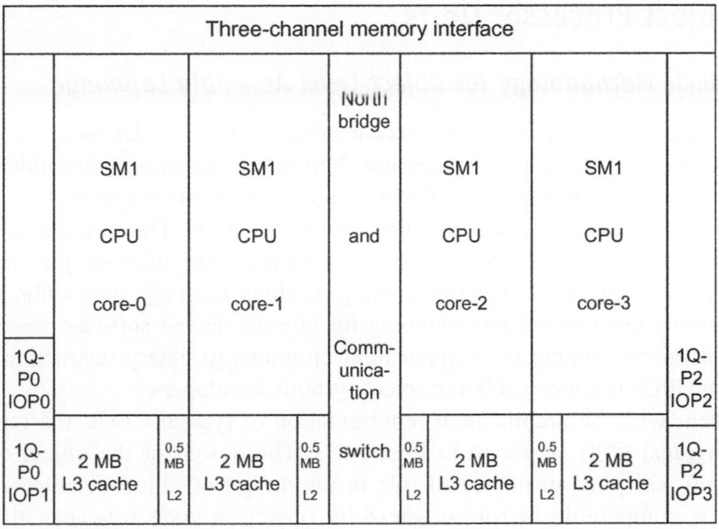

Three-channel memory interface									
				North bridge					
	SM1	SM1				SM1	SM1		
	CPU	CPU		and		CPU	CPU		
	core-0	core-1				core-2	core-3		
1Q-P0 IOP0					Comm-unica-tion				1Q-P2 IOP2
1Q-P0 IOP1	2 MB L3 cache	0.5 MB L2	2 MB L3 cache	0.5 MB L2	switch	0.5 MB L2	2 MB L3 cache	0.5 MB L2	2 MB L3 cache	1Q-P2 IOP3

Figure 2.6 Chip layouts of the Intel Quad Core Nehalem Processor with 731 million transistors, 8 MB (4 × 2 MB) L-3 cache and 4 of 0.5 MB L2 units. Each core size is 29.6 mm² placed on a 19. × 13.5 mm die-sized chip.

2.8   Digital Object-Processing Environments

Sampled data object processing has been in vogue since the introduction of the object-oriented programming and the early days of computer graphics. However, the more powerful object-processing functions occur with object-oriented sophisticated programming language commands. Data structures that represent objects are processed in a mathematical sense as the objects undergo realistic/physical changes (e.g., when a ball bounces, when a bell is struck, when a wave rolls, when a flower blooms). Complex groups and collection of object entities may thus be processed quickly and accurately. The processed objects and their attributes represent the newly computed properties of the objects or object groups. Complex chain of processes may thus be processed sequentially or in parallel. Pipeline and parallel object processor can thus be readily built using primitive VLSI technology.

The advent of more recent processors simply uses the inexpensive chip functions and documented binary code to execute such digital object processing. The net effect is these DSPs offer cheaper, faster, and accurate chips that can be used in robotics, computer games, and in real-time drone planes. Unfortunately, the technology can also be used in wars and destructive machines.

2.9   Object Processor Units

2.9.1   Basic Methodology for Object Level Assembly Language

The modern processor chips of this decade offer a firm foundation and reason for adapting these chips for object processing. Multiple processors, independent cache, DMA features, independent chip selection features for microprograms all contribute to the adaptation of these chips as object processor chips. The basic principle that every macro object processing can be degenerated into microscopic instruction that can be reassembled as object-processing machine language instruction will lead to the assembly-level object programming for object-oriented software systems. The software hierarchy ranging from application programs to binary instruction code of the modern CPUs is conceivable for object systems developers.

Consistent with the architectural representation of typical CPUs, the representation of a typical OPU is shown in Figure 2.7. The design of the object operation code (*Oopc*) will play an important role in the design of object-oriented machine. This role is comparable to role of the 8-bit operation code (*opcs*) in the design of IAS machine during the 1944–1945 periods. For this (IAS) machine, the *opc* length was 8 bits in the 20-bit instructions, and the memory of 4096 word, 40-bit memory, corresponds to the address space of 12 binary bits. The design experience of the game processors and the modern graphical processor units will serve as a platform for the design of the OPUs and hardware-based object machines.

The evolution of instruction set from the earlier machines (such as IBM 360-series) provides a rich array of guidelines to derive the instruction sets for the OPUs. If a set of object registers or an object cache can be envisioned in the OPU, then the instructions corresponding to register instructions, (R-series), register-storage (RS-series), storage (SS), immediate operand (I-series), and I/O series instructions for OPU can be initially designed.

Specialized instruction set will need a thorough expansion to suit the object and medical applications. It is logical to foresee the need of control object memories to replace the control memories of the microprogrammable computers. The instruction set of the OPU is derived from the most frequent object functions such as (i) single-object instructions, (ii) multiobject instructions, (iii) object to object memory instructions, (iv) internal object–external object instructions, and (v) object relationship instructions.

The separation of logical, numeric, seminumeric, alphanumeric, and convolutions functions (see Chapter 3) between objects will also be necessary. Hardware, firmware, or brute-force software (compiler power) can accomplish these functions. The need for the next-generation object and knowledge machines should provide an economic incentive to develop these architectural improvements beyond the basic OPU configuration shown in Figure 2.7.

2.9.2   Design Variation of OPUs

The designs of OPU can be as diversified as the designs of a CPU. The CPUs, I/O device interfaces, different memory units, and direct memory access hardware

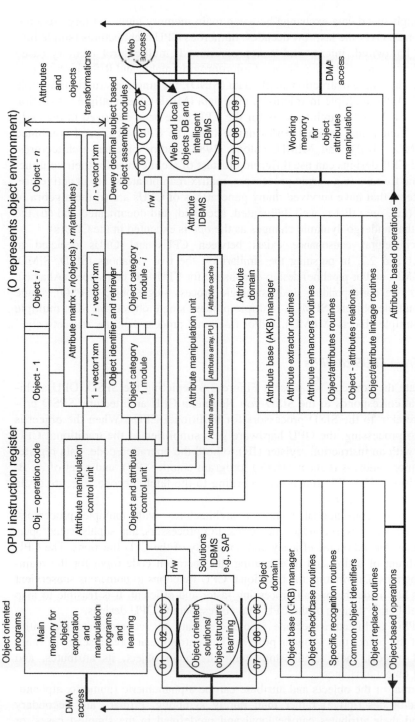

Figure 2.7 Schematic of a hardwired object processor unit (OPU). Processing n objects with m (maximum) attributes generates an $n \times m$ matrix. The common, interactive, and overlapping attributes are thus reconfigured to establish primary and secondary relationships between objects. DMA, direct memory access; IDBMS, Intelligent, data, object, and attribute base(s) management system(s); KB, knowledge base(s). Many variations can be derived.

units for high-speed data exchange between main memory units and large secondary memories. Over the last few decades, numerous CPU architectures (single bus, multibus, hardwired, micro- and nanoprogrammed, multicontrol memory-based systems) have come and gone. Some of microprogrammable and RISC architecture still exist. The single instruction single data (SISD), the single instruction multiple data (SIMD), the multiple instruction single data (MISD), the multiple instruction multiple data (MIMD), architectures for the CPU have been deployed in the early designs. Efficient and optimal performance from the CPUs also need combined SISD, SIMD, MISD, and MIMD, (Stone, 1980) and/or pipeline architectures. Combined CPU designs can use different clusters of architecture for their subfunctions. Some formats (e.g., array processors, matrix manipulators) are in active use. Two concepts that have survived many generations of CPUs are (i) the algebra of functions (i.e., *opc*) that is well delineated, accepted, and documented and (ii) the operands that undergo dynamic changes as the *opc* is executed in the CPU(s).

An architectural consonance exists between CPUs and OPUs depicted in Figures 2.1 and 2.7. In pursuing the similarities, the five variations (SISD, SIMD, MISD, MIMD, and/or pipeline) design established for CPUs can be mapped (Ahamed, 2009) into five corresponding designs; single process single object (SPSO), single process multiple objects (SPMO), multiple process single object (MPSO), multiple process multiple objects (MPMO), and/or fractional process pipeline, respectively.

2.9.3   From CPUS to OPUs

To illustrate the concept, we present Figure 2.8 depicting the SPSO, OPU architecture that corresponds to the SISD von Neumann CPU architecture. SPSO processors are akin to the SISD processors for traditional CPUs. When the object is immune to processing, the OPU hardware gets simplified to the traditional CPU hardware with an instruction register (IR) to hold the operation code, data register (DR), memory address register (MAR), program counter (PC), and a set of A, B, and C registers. The CPU functions according to the fetch, decode, execute cycle (FDE) in the simplest case.

The ensuing conventional computer architectures with multiple processors, multiple memory units, secondary memories, I/O processors, and sophisticated operating systems depend on the efficacy and optimality of the CPU functions. The CPU bears the brunt of action and of executing the operation code (*opc*) for the mainstream programs. Distributing the traditional CPU functions to numerous subservient processors has made the overall processing faster and efficient. It is feasible to map the more elaborate designs of the CPU into corresponding OPU designs.

The SPSO architecture becomes more elaborate to accommodate the entire entropy of the object that is under process. The entropy can have a series of other dependent objects, their relationships with the main object, its attributes, and dependent object attributes.

The format of the objects and attribute can be alphanumeric (numeric, alphanumeric, and/or descriptive) rather than purely symbolic. Primary and secondary objects and their attributes can be local and predefined in the simplest cases, or

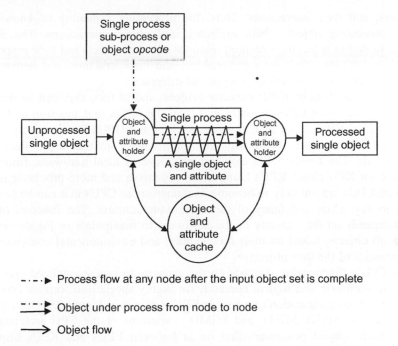

Figure 2.8 Simplified representation of a SPSO processor that operates on a single object and its attributes. When it replaces the FPU and ALU in the layout for Figure 2.1, the system can be forced to work as a simple von Neumann object computer.

they can be Internet based and fetched from the world wide web or the WWW knowledge banks. The execution of a single knowledge operation code (*kopc)* can influence the entropy of the single object via the secondary objects and attributes. In essence, numerous caches are necessary to track the full effect of the single *kopc* process on the entire entropy of the single object in the SPSO processor.

It can be seen that the machine configurations for other types of architectures, i.e., SPMO, MPSO, MPMO, and pipeline object processors Ahamed (2009) can be derived by variations similar to those for the SPSO systems. In the following sections, we present the change for a MPMO type of object processor and object machine.

2.10   Knowledge Processor Units

Object and knowledge processing have a significant functional and thus architectural commonality. Both OPUs and KPUs process objects, their attributes, their interrelationships, and their structure. Both interpret, recognize, and alter the properties of objects per se. Knowledge is indeed derived from objects, their nature, attributes, and their interactions. Thus, the processing capability of knowledge entails processing objects, their attributes, and object interactions. The KPUs process further to detect the structural relations between objects and their properties (i.e., their attributes, their interrelationships, and their structure) and derive new properties, concepts, and perhaps insight and inference.

Numerous designs of KPUs become evident, and in fact, they can be derived from the varieties of CPUs initially and then the CPUs that function as GPUs, and finally the CPUs that can also serve as CPUs and GPUs The creativity of the individual KPU designer lies in matching the hardware architecture to the application needs. The newest CPU architectures serve as ideal hardware, filmware, and MW for KPU chips. KPUs being more expensive and more processor intensive than CPUs are unlikely to become as numerous as CPUs that can be personalized to any whim and fancy of the chip manufacturers. The function of the KPUs depends on the capacity of the hardware to manipulate or juggle (global and local) objects, based on their own syntax, and environmental constraints in the semantics of the user objective.

The CPU's functionality depends on the capacity to execute stylized operation codes on arithmetic and logical operands (in highly specialized formats and date structures). The configuration of a simple KPU is shown in Figure 2.9. Other variations based on SIMD, MISD, and MIMD[7] variations of the CPU architectures can be built. Object processors that lie in between CPUs and KPUs bring in another degree of freedom because KPUs can deploy OPUs, much like CPUs can deploy ALUs and NPUs. Sequential, pipeline, and parallel execution of operations on objects in KPUs gives rise to at least eight possibilities: SKI-SO processors, SKI-MO processors, MKI-SO processors, and MKI-MO processors. Now if SO and MO processors have SOI-SO, SOI-MO, and MOI-SO (pipeline structure) processors, and MOI-MO (pipeline and/or multiprocessor structure) processors have variation embedded within themselves, then at least eight design variations become evident. The SKI-SOI-SO is the simplest to build while the MKI-MOI-MO is the most cumbersome to build. From the first estimate, the hardware for the simplest KPUs should be an order of magnitude more complex than the IBM 360 CPUs (even though these CPUs deployed the microcode technology).

---

[7] A brief explanation of acronyms for this section is presented. CPU, central processor unit; KPU, knowledge processor unit; ALU, arithmetic logic unit; NPU, numeric processor unit; SIMD, single instruction multiple data; MISD, multiple instruction single data; MIMD, multiple instruction multiple data; OPU, object processor unit; SKI-SO, single knowledge instruction-single object; SKI-MO, single knowledge instruction-multiple object; MKI-SO, multiple knowledge instruction-single object; MKI-MO, multiple knowledge instruction-multiple object; SO processor, single object processor; MO processors, multiple object processors; SOI-SO, single object instruction-single object; SOI-MO, single object instruction-multiple objects; MOI-SO, multiple object instruction-single object; MOI-MO, multiple object instruction-multiple object; SKI-SOI-SO, single knowledge instruction-single object instruction-single object; MKI-MOI-MO, multiple knowledge instruction-multiple object instruction-multiple objects.

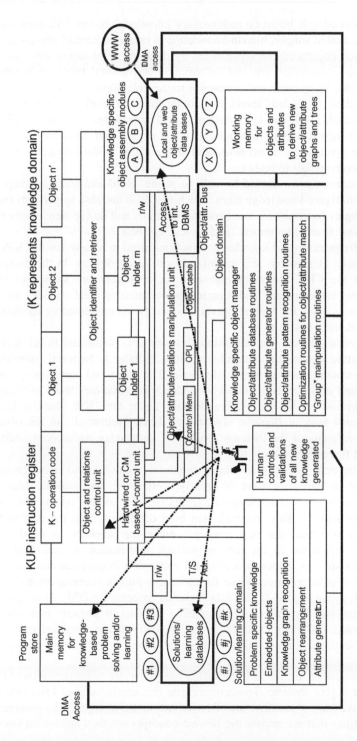

Figure 2.9 Switch S-1, open for execution mode for knowledge domain problem solving; closed for learning mode. The learning programs "process" the existing solutions and are able to extract objects, groups, relationships, opcodes, group operators, modules, strategies, and optimization methodologies from existing solutions and store them in object and corresponding databases. The architecture permits the KPU to catalog a new object in relation to existing objects and generate/modify existing pointers to and from new objects.

Knowledge processing is based on rudimentary knowledge theory (Ahamed and Lawrence 1997b). Stated simply, human knowledge is clustered around objects and object groups. Such objects can be represented by data and information structures. Data has numerous representations, and information has several forms of graphs and relationships that bring order and coherence to the collection of objects. Such a superstructure of data (at the leaf level), objects (at the twig level), and the object clusters (at the branch level) can constitute a tree of knowledge. Specific graphs, moreover, relationships that bind information into a cogent and coherent body of knowledge, bring (precedent, antecedent, and descendant) nodal hierarchy in a visual sense that corresponds to reality.

Knowledge processor units should be able to prune, build and shape, reshape, and optimally reconfigure knowledge trees, much as CPUs are able to perform the arithmetic (and logic) functions on numbers and symbols and derive new numbers (and logical entities) from old numbers (and logical symbols).

All the most frequently used knowledge functions need a review for the KPU to perform the basic, elementary, and modular functions on objects. In the design considerations of the CPU, the more elaborate AU functions are known to be decomposable into basic integer and floating-point numeric (add, divide, etc.) operations. Similarly, complex logical operations can be reconstituted as modular (AND, OR, EXOR, etc.) functions.

Knowledge-bearing objects can be arbitrarily complex. Numerous lower level objects can constitute a more elaborate object entity. Similar to bacterial colonies, knowledge superstructure have dynamic life cycle. The order and methodology in the construction and destruction of such knowledge superstructures leads to "laws of knowledge physics" in the knowledge domain under the DDS classification 530−539 Traditional laws of Boolean algebra and binary arithmetic do not offer the tools for the calculus of the dynamic bodies of knowledge undergoing social and technological forces in society.

However, if the new laws for the flow, dynamics, velocity, and acceleration of knowledge can be based on a set of orderly, systematic, and realistic *kopcs*, then these laws can be written as machine executable routines that operate on the knowledge bearing objects. This approach is a bold digression from the approach in classical sciences where the new concepts enter the sciences as symbolic and mathematical equations. In the present society, information is exploding as multimedia WWW streams, rather than graceful expansion in coherent and cogent concepts embedded in information. Time for extensive human contemplations is a rare luxury. Much as we needed digital data scanning systems for DSPs in the past, we need a machine-based common sense, sensing systems to separate junk level information (Ahamed, 2009) from knowledge-bearing information. Knowledge filtering, discussed in Section 2.4, accomplishes this initial, robust, sensible, and necessary humanist tasks.

The current scenario of science and innovation has given rise to the deployment of technology before it gets obsolete. To accommodate this acceleration of knowledge, we propose that we have a standard set of basic and modular *kopcs*. The complex knowledge operations that encompass the newest concepts are then assembled from the basic set of internationally accepted standard of *kopcs*. The proposed representation for the dynamics of knowledge paves the way between concepts that create new knowledge and the technology that uses such knowledge.

2.11 The Microknowledge Processor Unit

Microknowledge processors are the functional equivalents of control memory controlled CPUs. The assembly level instruction on typical CPUs is taken over to the particular address in the control memory and the mircoinstructions are executed upon the operand to complete the original assembler level instruction.

In the knowledge environment, the process gets cumbersome because the knowledge objects are data structures with other objects related to the main knowledge centric object (KCO) and each of the objects can have attributes and customized relationships. Hence, the micro-KPU needs to perform all the hardware and closely associated software functions such as performing the syntactic and semantic checks and making sure that the micro-*kopcs* are fed into the microknowledge processor at the execution time.

Most registers in the traditional CPUs need the structure of cache memories or stacks. These enhanced structures substructures to hold other related objects caches or their addresses. The affected attributes of objects also need address and data space to store the effect of *kopc* in any knowledge assembly level instruction.

The basic concept behind the micro-KPU is shown in Figures 2.10−2.12. These diagrams are based on three laws dealing with the following: (i) the concept

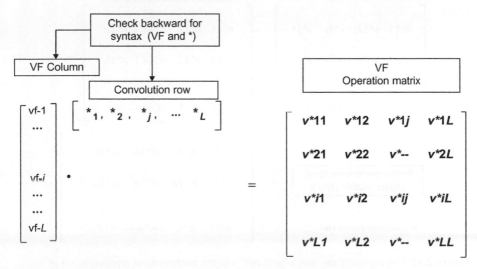

Figure 2.10 Generation of VF operation matrix from verb function (VF) and its corresponding convolution*.

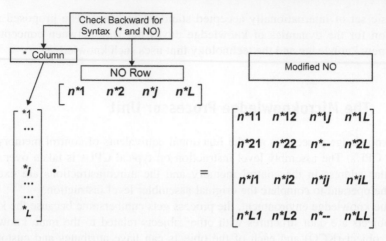

Figure 2.11 Convolution ⊗ operation on the original row of noun objects (NOs) and the resulting matrix of modified NOs.

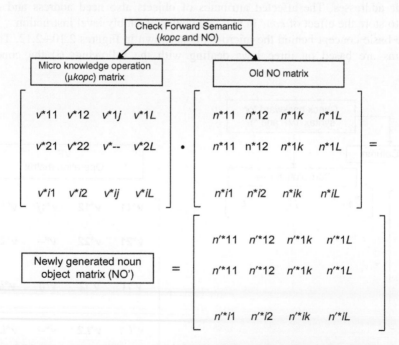

Figure 2.12 Generation of the new object NO′ and the mathematical representation of a microknowledge operation code ($\mu kopc$) as it is executed on an old noun object NO to evolve a new noun object NO′.

of segmentation of (verb) functions Figure 2.10, (ii) only selected actions can be implemented on corresponding NOs Figure 2.11, and (iii) behavior is founded on convolution (*s) of VFs upon NOs. The computational framework to convert these ideas is presented in Section 2.11.1.

> *Fragmentation:* Larger actions are based on decomposable smaller actions.
> *Grouping:* Actions and objects are grouped, and they abide by the syntactic and semantic laws of behavioral grammar.
> *Convolutions:* Human behavior that results from (VF ⊛ NO) abides by Marshals law in maximizing derived utility of the resources expended.

2.11.1 Effect of Fragmentation of VFs

Human behavior is a set of associated and smaller subsets of well-sequenced actions. Any action can be broken down into smaller action. Each smaller action can be written as

$$VF = \sum vf_i, \text{ where } i \text{ ranges from 1 to } L \text{ steps}$$

Stated alternatively,

$$VF = A \text{ column}^8 \text{ of } vf_i\text{'s}; i \text{ ranging from 1 to } L \text{ smaller vf's.}$$

Actions involve at least two components: an active object ("doer") and a passive object ("done upon"). The "doer" can be a human being whose behavior is being considered, and "done upon" is the old noun object NO. When the *kopc* is completed, the new noun object NO′ is generated in the micro-KPU. There are at least two matrix functions involved to generate the new noun object NO′. The new object NO′ is evolved after the microknowledge operation code (μ*kopc*) knowledge operator matrix is multiplied by the old noun object matrix, NO (see Figures 2.10–2.12).

In general, knowledge application programs (KAPs) accomplish major functions in the knowledge domain. When a KAP is compiled and assembled, a series of steps in the smaller knowledge assembly language program (KALP) is generated after syntactic check and semantic check for all the knowledge objects in the KAP. These steps in the KALP follow a series of well-defined FDE cycles as the program is executed. Any knowledge level program/subprogram/miniprogram, and microprogram can be written as a series of fine steps of the nature VF⊛NO.

2.11.2 Effect of Grouping of NOs

NOs generally consist of other NOs, and they are represented as trees or as matrices. When an action occurs on an object NO, the other NOs in the group also get affected. To represent this effect, a matrix multiplication is suggested where the VF operation $(L \times L)$ matrix is multiplied by $(L \times L)$.

---

[8] It is proposed that any verb function can be performed in its own context and syntax thus leading to a $(L \times L)$ matrix in Figure 2.10. It appears impossible to perform any function on any noun in an unknown context and in an unknown syntax.

$$VF * NO \equiv \sum_{i=1}^{i=L}(vf_i) \bullet \prod_{j=1}^{j=M} (*_j) \bullet \sum_{l=1}^{l=N} (no_k)$$

$$[VF \equiv \sum_{i=1}^{i=L}(vf_i)], \quad [* \equiv \prod_{j=1}^{j=M} (*_j)] \text{ and } NO \equiv \sum_{l=1}^{l=N} (no_k)$$

Figure 2.13 Algebraic representations of any knowledge process ranging from a major knowledge program to a microknowledge operation ($\mu kopc$). It implies that any verb function (VF) can be decomposed into a series of smaller (verb) functions, any process ($\circledast$) consists of a series of microprocesses, and the effect of the process on noun object (NO) is the combined effect of the microprocesses on each of the elements (no's) that constitute the main noun object NO.

The law of fragmentation permits the breakdown of VF, $\circledast$, and NO. The algebraic representation of KAP is shown in Figure 2.13. It becomes essential to perform a syntactic and semantic check before any KAP can be executed in a computational environment. The syntactic check ascertains that the process requested can be performed in the hardware and software constraints of the computer and the semantic check ascertains that the process requested is indeed valid and legal in context to the noun object upon which the process is being executed.

2.11.3 Architecture of a Convolver

Knowledge processing is more complex than data or text processing and the implication of each step of knowledge processing needs scientific and/or economic justification. In addition, if a KAP calls for an optimization, then the utility of each of the steps of the KAP needs to be evaluated and tallied against the resources required for that particular step or procedure.

When only one VF, or vf_i, is convolved with one noun object NO or no_k then a simple "convolver" (Figure 2.14) will suffice[9] to bring about a (VF$\circledast$NO) or ($vf_i\circledast_j no_k$). Other architectural variations, such as one vf, multiple no's (equivalent of SIMD, MISD, or MIMD) configuration can be derived.

In a wider sense, the utility of the process (VF$\circledast$NO) needs to justified. The derived utility is determined solely by the natures of (VF, $\circledast$, and NO) or by the natures of (vf_i, $\circledast_j$, and no_k). In reality, however, a series of no_k's are involved

---

[9] The term "convolver" is designated as hardware that enforces a verb function on a noun object. It is akin to an adder or multiplier. In the knowledge domain, at least one verb and one noun is implied in every statement that modifies an object. The implication is that an active verb modifies a noun or alters its state. The action of the verb varies dramatically depending on the verb and the noun and become a convolution rather than a simple add, subtract, multiplier, divide, etc., or any logical, vector, matrix, etc., function. Hence the symbol is chosen as a * and written between *VF* and *NO*. The convolver in its simplest form would be an ALU, vector, graphic, signal, etc., processor depending on the syntax and semantics of its usage. In more complex form it could be a digital amplifier, a sensor or a synthesizer.

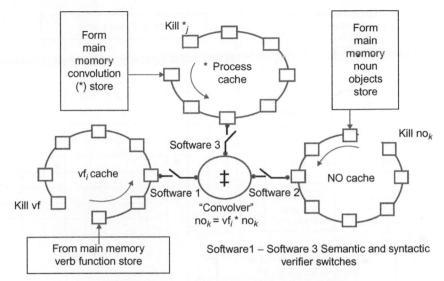

Layout fo a microprocessor to implement a micro KPU
for the convolution (vf$_i$ * no$_K$) to generate a new noun object no$_K$

Figure 2.14 Location of a "convolver" in a μKPU. The "convolver" forces the completion
of a microknowledge operation (μ*kopc*) on one or a series of possible no's. Typically,
a series of no$_k$'s are involved since the process yields different utility for each no$_k$. Similarly,
the utility is different for each possible variation of vf$_i$ and for ⊛$_j$. When these options are
available, the utility of each combination is evaluated to find which combination or solution
yields the best utility or results.

since the process yields different utility for each no$_k$. Similarly, the utility is
different for each possible variation of vf$_i$, ⊛$_j$, and no$_k$. When these options are
available, the utility of each combination is evaluated to find which combination or
solution yields the best utility or results. Three different caches for vf$_i$, ⊛$_j$, and no$_k$
are necessary and are shown in Figure 2.15. Other architectural variations (such as
one vf, multiple no's, multiple vf's, multiple no's) of the microknowledge processor will require multiplicity of stacks for VFs, ⊛s, and NOs.

The computation or the estimation of the expected utility of any μ*kopc* or
microknowledge function becomes necessary if the process involves optimization
or the selection of the best utility that will result from one or more combinations of
vf$_i$, ⊛$_j$, and no$_k$. A series of vf$_i$, ⊛$_j$, and no$_k$ are stored in their respective caches
and the process then selects the best combination of vf$_i$, ⊛$_j$, and no$_k$. The resulting
utilities are illustrated in Figure 2.16.

If the knowledge program KAP calls for combining the three elements (VF, ⊛,
and NO) from local knowledge bases (KBs) with the corresponding elements
from the WWW KBs to find the best solution for the KAP, then the coordinates
of each of the elements in the local and the WWW KBs need accurate tracking.

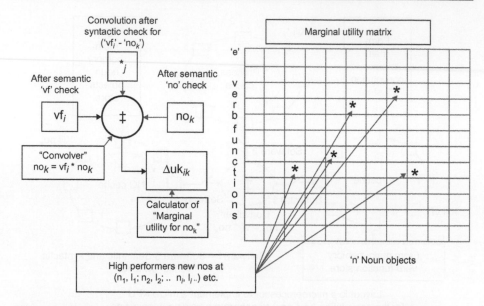

Figure 2.15 The plot identifies the combination of $vf_i, \circledast_j$, and no_k yielded the highest utility from convolving various VFs, $\circledast$s, and NOs available from the local knowledge and expertise. These combinations are analyzed for the utility of the highest performers in a pushdown stack that stores the top choices of new objects NOs. When the choices are limited, an exhaustive search may be performed. When the search is expanded to WWW knowledge bases, as shown in Figure 2.17, the search algorithms are made intelligent and self-learning to reach the best solution(s).

The utilities also need to be computed and tracked. The effort can be time and resource consuming. Hence, the tacking of the local sets of (vf_i, $\circledast_j$, and no_k) modified by the corresponding and documented WWW sets of (vf_i, $\circledast_j$, and no_k) are stored in a 3D matrix of the coordinates of the three elements of knowledge for the final human evaluation of the derived utilities. One of the possible configurations of this type of microknowledge processor is shown in Figure 2.17. Fine-tuning of the final solution is thus postponed to human judgment in view of committee of joint decision.

One of the by-products of this type of micromanagement of the composition of knowledge is the enhanced creativity in the optimal combinations of the two sets of local and WWW (vf_i, $\circledast_j$, and no_k). New VFs, $\circledast$s, and NOs will be evolved to maximize the utility in one or more directions. When the criterion for selection is social benevolence, the machine yields the best social innovations. When the criterion for selection is best molecular structure for drugs (allergies), the machine yields possible sets of drugs innovations (for allergies).

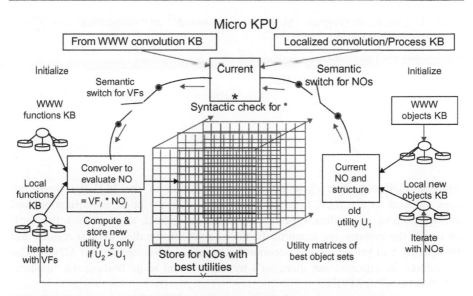

Figure 2.16 Verb functions and noun objects are drawn from both local knowledge expertise and KBs, and verified against the Internet KB to ascertain the utilities derived from the newly synthesized noun objects. The marginal enhancement of utility is tallied against the marginal cost to make the most valid economic choice for the newly generated object NO′. The derived knowledge centric object (KCO) is likely to be a flawless and perfected KCO based on the constraints imposed on the choices of VFs, ⊗s, and NOs.

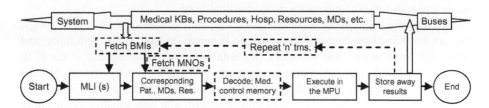

Figure 2.17 Flowchart of the simplest medical computer.

2.12 Micromedical Processing

Micromedical processors are discussed in detail in Chapter 11 and only the concept is introduced here. In the medical domain, if a medical assembly language program (MALP) that is generated after compiling, assembling, loading, and linking the medical application program (MAP) is represented[10] as "summation" (or $\sum$) of basic medical instructions (BMI),

$$MALP = \sum_{1}^{nm} BMIs, =$$

or

$$\text{any } MAP = \sum_{1}^{nm} \{MVF \text{ corresponding MNOs}\}$$

then the FDE repetitive cycle during the execution of the MALP follows the steps outlined for the KLP. In addition, the detailed description, identification, and authorization of all medical objects, the particular patient, the doctor(s), the staff, the drugs, the therapy, the instruments, the equipment, the diet, the test results, and the security and privacy issues become the "medical noun objects" or MNOs. The procedures, instrumentation, therapist's treatments, and so on become the "medical verb functions" or MVFs.

The coordinated execution of the instruction (MPF⊛MNO) corresponds to the nano- or a micromedical step in the curing or healing of the patient (pat.). Largely, the doctors (MDs) and medical staff being intelligent and trained perform these long strings of micromedical functions quite adeptly. However, the medical machine can be and needs to be programmed to perform these procedures efficiently, dependently, and securely subject to the available resources (Res.). Accordingly, the flow chart for simplest medical computers, depicted in Figure 2.17, needs to be enhanced to reflect the additional constraints (added security, privacy, preferences, special needs and features, etc.) necessary in the medical field.

The training of the medical staff is based on medical science, device technology, and accurate implementation. The rigorous training infused with intelligence and great skill leads to one side of aspect, dependability, and predictability of the FDE cycle in the MPU. The entire process becomes a small part of the overall process of treating the patients. The individual traits of the doctor and the doctor–patient relationship add different variations of care, concern, and individuality to the entire process of treating patients.

The architecture of the CPU of any moderate speed computer with enhanced memory capabilities can be forced to process the medical procedures for patients at a (very) rudimentary level. Enhanced memories will hold executable programs for the microprocedures assembled onto the standard procedure for the patient in the

---

[10] In a conceptual framework, the following equations simply state the any major medical treatment or procedure for any patient is an organized collection of minor processes or procedures. The sequential or parallel nature of these minor functions is embedded in the symbol $\sum$ that forces the medical machine to complete the major medical treatment or procedure in view of the limitation of the resources of the medical facility, staff, and the knowledge bases of the specialists, doctors, and staff. The medical machine expands these series of minor medical processes into executable program code that can be executed in the medical facility by the staff and medical resources.

special hospital, medical center, or even the country in which the procedure is going to be performed. These subprocedures will be intelligently assembled based on knowledge bases that use artificial intelligence (AI). For this reason, we expect a high-level language software (the compiler-assembler-loader-linker software chain (Detmer, 2001)) of the IMS to be significantly different from that of traditional computer systems. We also foresee that adapting the set of assembly level procedural instructions will be tailored to the specific medical facility, thus calling for facilities dependent assemblers. This type of adaptation is routinely made for computer systems at installation time, depending on the hardware in that particular system.

Dual processors and elaborate error checking offer dependability and security of data. The error checks not only verify the processing but also the validity of the results based on the AI-based expected outcome. Any unexpected findings are referred to the physician team on duty. Results of procedures will be entered into a patient database. Opinions and subjective comments will be entered onto a voice-activated message retrieval system. Pictures, X-ray, and CAT scans will be entered onto a visual database of the computer system, making the IMS a truly multimedia system.

2.13 Conclusions

Processor revolution is an ongoing and continuous process. The explosion in the types and capacity of the newer and specialized processors is testimony to the need for gaming, medical, movie, and other object-oriented applications. In this chapter, we have presented two new concepts the designs for hardware-based object-oriented processing and for knowledge processing. The designs are extensions of the architecture of hardware rather than an additional layer of software, objectware, or knowledgeware to support the humanist aspects in computing. In reality, such hardware-based system will perform faster than layered software systems. The concept of the processor power should be measured as KNOPS (knowledge operations per second) rather than FLOPS (floating-point operations per second). It is our contention that GFLOPS and TFLOPS machines and supercomputers should be tamed to operate as MKNOPS humanist machines that serve society and public.

In this chapter, we have also introduced the concept of microprogramming knowledge based operations into fragmented VFs and introduced the conceptual framework for the basis and design of micromedical processors. The philosophy is borrowed from the design of RISC computers and microprogrammable CPUs. Such machines will bring the design and programming of knowledge machines in the domain of software engineering and the design of medical machines in the domain of medicalware. Fragmentation of NOs is performed by Internet search of the morphemes objects that surround the main noun object. Fragmentation of medical NOs is equally feasible by searching for the basic fragments of biology and physiology that constitute any medical object. When microprocedures are convolved with micromedical NOs, a micromedical process is invoked. Multiplicities of such processes are indeed any medical events/function (e.g., falling sick, healing, surgery, recovery).

References

1. Maslow AH: A theory of human motivation, *Psychol Rev* 50:370–396, 1943, See also Maslow AH: *Motivation and personality*, New York, NY, 1970, Harper & Row.Maslow AH: *Farther reaches of human nature*, New York, NY, 1971, Viking Press.
2. Ahamed SV: An enhanced need pyramid for the information age human being. In *Proceedings of the Fifth Hawaii International Conference, Fifth International Conference on Business, Hawaii, May 26–29, 2005.* See also, An enhanced need pyramid of the information age human being. Paper presented at the International Society of Political Psychology, (ISSP) 2005 Scientific Meeting, Toronto, July 3–6, 2005.
3. Stone HS, Introduction to computer architecture, computer science series, New York, NY, 1980, Science Research Associates. See also Hayes JP: *Computer architecture and organization*, ed 2, New York, NY, 1980, McGraw Hill.
4. Ahamed SV: Chapter 2. In *Computational framework for knowledge: integrated behavior of machines*, Hoboken, NJ, 2009, John Wiley & Sons.
5. von Neumann, J.: First draft of a report on the EDVAC. Contract No. W-670-ORD 4926. Between the United States Army Ordnance Department and University of Pennsylvania, Moore School of Electrical Engineering, June 30, 1945. See also, Burks AW, Goldstine HH, von Neumann J: U.S. Army Report Ordnance Department, 1946.
6. Estrin G: *The electronic computer at the institute of advanced studies, mathematical tables and other aids to computation*, vol. 7, Princeton, NJ, 1953, IAS.
7. Clements A: *The principles of computer hardware*, USA, Oxford, England, 2006, Oxford University Press.
8. Ahamed SV, Lawrence VB: *Design and engineering of intelligent communication systems*, Boston, MA, 1997, Kluwer Academic Publishers.
9. Mandl P, Bordiloi U: General-purpose Graphics processing Units Deliver New Capabilities to the Embedded Market, www.amd.com/US/_layout/ reference 2011. See also, Vendor specification of DSP chips such as Texas instruments, AMD, NVIDIA, etc. Powerful general purpose GPUs from these venders can be used as DSPs.
10. Ahamed SV, Lawrence VB: *Intelligent broadband multimedia networks*, Boston, MA, 1997, Kluwer Academic Publishers. See also Ahamed SV: *Intelligent internet knowledge networks*, Hoboken, NJ, 1997, Wiley-Interscience.
11. Detmer RC: *Introduction to 80 × 86 assembly level language and computer architecture*, 2001, Jones & Bartlett Publishers. See also Rudd WG: *Assembly level programming and the IBM 360 and 370 computers*, 2001, Prentice Hall.

3 Services Networks Explosion

3.1 Introduction

Network service is an age-old offering. Telephone service has been in vogue since the era of A.G. Bell and his early telephone starting in 1874. These earlier networks provided bidirectional telegraphic connectivity and rudimentary voice communication over metallic transmission lines. When the monopoly of the Bell System was finally broken by the consent decree imposed by Judge Greene (in the early 1980s) resulting in numerous independent Regional Bell Operating Companies (RBOCs), the expansion of network services became a common practice to make these RBOCs more profitable and competitive. Providing basic telephone services was rendered the obligation of a regulated entity.

Many momentous changes have taken place in making new services feasible as easily as executing well-designed and documented service programs. The most significant trend evolved when intelligent networks (INs) were introduced after the divestiture of the Bell Systems in *circa* 1986. Stemming largely from the switching and communication capabilities of networks, the explosive growth has ignited the Internet services and broadband communications. The network switches have enjoyed the tremendous growth and dependability of the Very Large Scale Integration (VLSI) industry and the network links have all the rewards of the fiber optics industry. The rewards are compounded to the extent cost of transmission of user data channels over network is almost nonexistent, and the cost of switching of these channels is vanishingly small. This opportunity envisioned by entrepreneurs during the 1980s and 1990s has benefitted the user greatly. Intelligence has been embedded gradually to make such services attractive and affordable. The impact has been gradual in most industrial and manufacturing environments. However, one of the last groups to benefit from such a dramatic technological breakthrough appears to be the medical and humanist service providers. It is the object of this and the following chapters to open the doors of technology from computer-based networks and industries into the active arena of medical and social-based service providers.

In particular, we start from the impact of INs. In a sequence, the INs in the United States evolved as IN/1, IN/1+, IN/2, and Advanced Intelligent Network (AIN). These INs (especially, IN/1+, IN/2, and AIN in the United States and equivalent European INs, especially the Telecommunication Management Network (TMN) and Intelligent Network both combined as TINA) made the programming and offering of new network services economical for the network users and very easy to deploy for the network managers. In the short run, these innovative features offered by the INs an

Intelligent Networks: Recent Approaches and Applications in Medical Systems.
DOI: http://dx.doi.org/10.1016/B978-0-12-416630-1.00003-0

attractive source of revenue stream as the IN/1 services. The growth of these services was dramatic, though not comparable to the growth of small scale integration (SSI)- and medium scale integration (MSI)-integrated circuits.

Initially, the public service offered by the more advanced INs (such as IN/2 and AIN) did not provide the economic incentives for the network administrators to develop and evolve specialized network languages. The basic concepts and innovations have brought about significant changes in the traditional telephone services networks.

Four most dominant developments are:

> the growth of switching systems (from the traditional electronic switching systems in traditional telephone networks through the add—drop multiplexors (ADMs) in the asynchronous transfer mode (ATM)/synchronous optical network (SONET) environment to the gateway switches in the Universal Mobile Telecommunication System (UMTS) terrestrial radio access network (UTRAN)) and their control,
> the transmission media (from unshielded open wire pairs to the single mode fiber in transoceanic fiber networks) and its optimal performance,
> the signaling systems (from voice commands of operators to evolved signaling system 7 (SS7)) and their global standardization, and
> the associated protocols (from substandard interoffice protocols in the Bell System to the TCP/IP five-layer Internet protocol stack) that direct the underlying networks to execute the necessary functions in an optimal and consistent fashion.
> From the current perspective, all networks behave as programmable computerized systems that perform as smaller programmable elements performing functions just as well as computers that execute application or scientific programs.

Networks have evolved into massive groups of computer controlled switching and services facilities for customers and other participating network nodes. The support of other service nodes (medical centers, universities, emergency centers, or other commercial service vendors, etc.) may be acquired, solicited, and even required. Being distributed in nature, network nodes (and their own localized computer-controlled facilities) act in conjunction and cooperation with one another. In the older switching systems, the signaling in its protocol format was delivered by especially secure and most dependable signaling networks (Bell Telephone Laboratories, 1982). Every node had connectivity and access to the signaling network. However, with the advent of packet, frame and cell switching the use of signaling network has fallen precipitously, the worldwide acceptance of frame relay systems with embedded ATM cell structures, and the TCP/IP protocol, the need for the older, expensive, signaling systems in the conventional formats as it was used in the earlier plain old telephone systems (POTS) is no longer essential. Signaling has become easy and elegant as assembling the appropriate VLSI chips that execute the signaling functions in the appropriate protocol format in the programmed fashion for the service(s) requested by the customers or from a corresponding network node.

3.2 Switching Systems in Services Networks

Switching systems play a crucial role in the programmed services that networks can offer. Identification of service requests, its validation, authorization, collection of billing information, duration of service, etc. are performed and tracked by the switching systems. The information so gathered can be localized or centralized at commercial centers. The information is based on the caller ID and the service logic programs (SLPs). The protocol for the service is then initiated at the switching centers and dispatched to other nodes in the specialized nodes (such as knowledge banks, medical centers, 911 and polices, etc.) or to other switching centers for call, packet, or channel connectivity.

Operator switching was the earliest form of a telephone switch in networks even though computer switches were automated from the inception based on machine instructions. Numerous short-lived early versions of switches (rotary switches, relay switches, step-by-step, etc.) were introduced in the telephone environment (Ahamed and Lawrence, 1997). These switches were phased out as the transistorized switches became popular through the 1950s and 1960s.

3.2.1 Local Switching Environments

In 1965, the first software-driven (stored program controlled, SPC) Central Office was commercially introduced as the No.1 ESS™ switch in Succasunna, New Jersey. The hardware in this Central Office was not totally software controlled. Numerous subsystems (such as, line scanner, signal distributor, and central pulse distributor) are combined into a basic hardware unit to interface with the line and trunk circuits and perform local functions. They are monitored by their own program control. The switching network interconnects different segments of the communication path depending on the need and availability. This switch was primarily electromechanical in nature. Because of the software considerations, the No.1 ESS switch-based Central Office (*circa* mid-1960s) was still designed specifically to handle the communication functions in real time with the dependability in (about 2 h downtime) and life span of (40 years) typical Central Offices. The usual switching element was the ferreed switch to make or break a single connection at a time under high-speed centralized control. The centralized control for the first No.1 ESS is driven by one group of programs (about 90 different ones) with about 100,000 words. With the growth and number of specific services demanded from the No.1 ESS, the program size increased rapidly to 250,000 words of code. The program word for the No.1 ESS is 44 bits (37 data bits and 7 bits for single error correcting hamming code and parity). The program store size is 131,000 words and each generic Central Office could have as many as 12 program stores for handling as many as 65,000 lines in parallel. The cycle time is 5.5 μs.

Other major developments that rapidly followed the introduction of the No.1 ESS architecture to the switching systems were the No.1A ESS switch. Integrated circuits and faster clock rates offered greater call-handling capacity. This development is similar to what happened when the second-generation computer systems were introduced in the late 1950s and early 1960s. Translation of operational code and software code with the No.1 ESS permits growth and expansion in the telecommunications industry that is typical of the late 1960s and 1970s. The No.1A ESS is capable of serving up to 128,000 lines and 32,000 trunks with a total capacity of 10,000 erlangs. This number translates to 36 million (3600 × 10,000) call seconds per hour, since each erlang is equivalent to 3600 call seconds per hour (ccs, or "centi calls per second"). On the average, one erlang (36 ccs) is sufficient traffic load to keep one trunk busy for 1 h because there are only 3600 s in the hour.

In a sense, the No.1 ESS initiated the impact of computerized control onto local switching—something that computers had initiated in the data processing field, but 21 years earlier. Numerous other Central Offices (No. 2 ESS, No. 2B ESS, and No. 3 ESS switches) were also introduced during the late 1960s and early 1970s, but the impact of the switches was not as dramatic since the systems addressed the growth and speed aspects of switching systems. The microprogrammed control of the processor (a feature of third-generation computer systems) was introduced to the switching system in the No. 3A ESS switch with faster logic and automatic code conversion for the No. 2 ESS switch. Most of these switches provided sound economic justification for rapid expansion, and they provided a foundation for the eventual development of networked systems.

3.2.2   Switching in Toll Environments

The electronic translator, consisting of the SPC processor No.1, was introduced within the 4A Crossbar Toll System in Grand Rapids, Michigan, in 1969. This toll system was the first system to include some of the same functions and features of computerized systems. For example, the system could have the Centralized Message Accounting System, generally known as CAMA for local and toll billing. This system also included the peripheral bus computer to interface to the 4A/electronic translator system (ETS) that monitored the system performance in service. However, the major enhancement to the system included the ability to accommodate the Common Channel Interoffice Signaling (CCIS) between processor-equipped switching systems. With the introduction of the full-fledged 4A/ETS, the telephone system was transforming itself into a computerized network for telephone systems with limited network capabilities but with a great potential to grow.

3.2.3   Number 4ESS

The next major step in toll switching is the 4ESS toll switching system. This machine is a logical (and managerial) extension of the No.1 ESS switching system to reduce the fixed costs and the running expense, and to provide flexibility with the changing socioeconomic climate of the early 1970s.

The processing capabilities for toll, the more sophisticated toll network resource and channel allocation, and the pulse code modulation (PCM) transmission and switching capabilities were also included in the 4ESS switch. The first 4ESS switch was capable of handling about half a million calls per hour with a trunk capacity of over 100,000 calls per hour. This switch provided a benchmark for the capacity and reliability of trunk switching systems.

To a degree, the 4ESS switch initiated the impact of computerized control onto toll switching—what computers had initiated in the data processing field 29 years earlier. The trend in the communication industry brought all the rewards to the digital processing and handling of telephonic information in the early stages. More recently, this same trend has evolved into networks that make any relevant information accessible to anyone authorized to receive it, at any time, and at any place with any degree of accuracy and resolution within the framework of security and the legality of exchange of information.

As a telecommunications switching facility, the recent 4ESS switch completed as many as 800,000 calls per hour as the call attempts reach about 1,200,000 during peak calling periods. More recently, similar strides have been made in retaining the compatibility between the 4ESS switch and the more modern communication systems and networks. Typically, the existing 4ESS switch is capable of interfacing with the SS7 via its common network interface and the digital services implementation with CCITT (International Telegrarph and Telephone Consultative Committee, now International Telecommunications Union (ITU-T)) Q.931 standards. The switching platform functions with a spatially separated time-multiplex switch capable of interconnecting numerous time slot interchange units. The "B" (that is, the DS0 at 64 kbps) channel integrity is retained in this switch. Total synchronization between the switching clock and the network clock is retained throughout the 4ESS switch. In its current design, the 4ESS switch can also interface with DS-3 carrier systems initially and then with the SONET-based transmission facilities.

The introduction of the new processor (1B) to replace the original processor (1A) in the 4ESS switch has contributed to the increased call-handling capacity of the switch. The expanded volume that the switches handle is expected to increase at an approximate rate of 5% every year. The demand for the 800 number, cellular, fax, and video messaging is likely to remain high. Rather than replacing the switch with the newer 5ESS switch, a more economical and feasible alternative is to replace the processor. For this reason, the new processor is designed to function at a call-handling capacity 2.4 times greater than that of the original processor. The speed and memory access is more than doubled. The reliability is enhanced, and operations and maintenance are streamlined. The overall switch (the 4ESS) capacity with the new processor is expected to be over one million calls an hour—a super Pentium chip for a massive PC.

3.2.4 Number 5ESS

The introduction of the first single-module 5ESS switch in 1982 (in Seneca, Illinois), and then the introduction of the multimodule 5ESS switch in 1983 (in Sugar Grove, Illinois), started another major trend in Central Office capabilities. In essence, the integrated architecture and time division digital switching that is inherent in this machine provides for most of the distributed processing and multifunction capabilities for the expanding telecommunication market. The configuration of 5ESS (*circa* late 1990s) is shown in Figure 3.1.

During the era of electronic switching system, the impact of the 5ESS was considered monumental until it was overshadowed by the optical switches for the SONET frame relay systems and ATM cell relay systems. However, these optical switches perform broadband switching, while the electronic switches perform

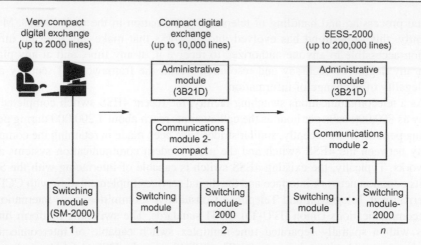

Figure 3.1 Configurations of a 5ESS switch. All the three configurations can serve newer digital local and business service needs. The smaller configurations may also be interfaced into remote-switching modules, PBX line groups, and remote integrated service line groups. The modern 5ESS supports wireless, and toll services and IN functions and gateway switching in all network architectures (Alcatel−Lucent, 2013).

channel switching and time slot allocations. Both these very powerful switching schemes and their capabilities are discussed further in the book.

During its inception, the 5ESS switching machine offered several distinct features:

It is a single system that served all the applications: operator, local, toll, and international. It provides for digital switching between numerous subscriber loop carrier systems and interexchange carrier circuits (the T family or the E family popular during 1980s and 1990s), making the transition to newer digital services easy and elegant. It also interfaced with the analog interexchange systems.

It has a modular approach in the hardware and software design, which permits adding newer devices as technology evolves and which allows itself to interface with the older generation switching systems (e.g., the 4ESS switch or the older 5ESS systems).

Its hardware modularity permits gradual growth as the network and service demands increase. This permits a cost-effective deployment of Central Office resources. Being mostly digital in devices and its control, it has a reliability comparable to, if not better than, most computer systems. Extra error correction stages and parallel functionality of the CPUs permit quick and dependable retractability of any call-processing step(s).

The computer orientation of the switch design permits local and centralized maintenance by running diagnostics in any module, combined modules, extended subsystems, or global systems. The operations, engineering, and maintenance functions become much simpler.

The 5ESS operating system, being modular and encoded in a higher-level language (the C language), permits Central Office capabilities to be added easily. The system is portable and modular to be customized to the particular Central Office need. New digital services and new IN services within the Service Switching Points (SSPs) can be accommodated by altering the flow control within the call-processing environment; such network services can include the detection of the trigger condition, database lookup in a network information database or invoking an intelligent peripheral (IP), or exercising an SLP.

The 5ESS-2000 switch in the American environments contended with both the broadband services and IN functionality of the 1990s. In addition, this newer 5ESS platform permits enhanced processing capabilities, as they exist in the IN environments, and servicing capabilities with simpler operations, administration, maintenance, and provisioning (OAM&P) as discussed in Bell Telephone Laboratories (1982) and Ahamed and Lawrence (1997). Servicing capabilities include handling as many as 200,000 lines, newer remote-switching modules with line capacities of 20,000 lines, wireless services, etc. The provisioning aspect is unique to most of the recently designed ESS platforms for the United States and Europe. The reliability of the 5ESS platform was better than that of most computer facilities and recorded (as of December 1994) to be at zero failure in the first 7 months of its installation in eight countries.

Numerous other digital switches also exist. In Europe, for example, Siemens' EWSD® and Ericsson's AXE® systems perform comparable functions. Equivalent systems in Japan have also been built and function with similar precision and dependability.

The switching module (SM-2000) of this machine permits its interfacing with the fiber-optic nets using the synchronous digital hierarchy (SDH), with optical carrier-1 (OC-1) (as far back as 1994) through OC-12 carrier capabilities. Numerous other vendors are integrating the optical rate switching (OC-1 through OC-48) with conventional broadband switching. In addition, hybrid fiber coaxial (HFC) cable service providers have digital access into the conventional switches and thus are able to provide better (i.e., 64 kbps PCM toll-quality telephony services) to their customers. This is seen as an added attraction to sell the Cable Television or CATV service and the video-on-demand services to appear in the future. The HFC services and facilities link with the broadband networks and are now available in most developed countries. Data rates of up to 1.3 Gb/s have been reported in Austria.

The recent versions of the 5ESS® switch has a full range of capabilities that can be expected for modern local and trunk facilities. Network intelligence is a dominant feature of the 5ESS of this decade and the expanded wireless network services. The interfaces are adaptable and can link with the networks and carriers of the last decade including the landlines and wire lines of the past two decades.

3.2.5 Switching in ATM and Sonet Environments

Traditional electronic switching systems have been on a steady decline since optical switches at major gateways around the world and wireless channel switching at mobile telephone stations at local population centers in most major cities have both gained worldwide acceptance as being more economical, dependable, and programmable.

Bulk optical switches facilitate global and massive national switching, whereas channel and cell relaying can be accomplished at cellular base station of wireless networks. At the intermediate level, wideband digital cross-connect switches (WDCSs) and ADMs provide OC (OC-1 through OC-n) switching. Some of the configurations of the recent switches are depicted in Figure 3.2.

Networking has been a discipline in its own right through the 1980s. Electronic switching systems provided the hubs for the older carrier systems such as DS-1 through DS-3 or DS-4 systems discussed in Ahamed and Lawrence (1997) and AT&T (1985). The global acceptance of the synchronous transport standard (STS) and the (9×90) STS-1 frame with 3-byte section and line overhead for 87 byte in a STS-1 envelope has made global and transoceanic switching as easy as connecting the USB devices to a PC or a USB hub. The basis for this flexibility and connectivity is the concept of the 125-μs time slot for the frame. The OC rate, n can vary from 1 to 192 depending on the optical rate of the fiber medium carrying the SONET frames (Aprille, 1990).

Frame- and cell-relay systems with their own distinctive overheads ($3n$ bytes for an OC-n frame) and 5-byte ATM header (for the 53-byte cell) has replaced the expensive and intricately programmed ESS's in most instances. The transition is still complete as the networks are already established in many urban areas.

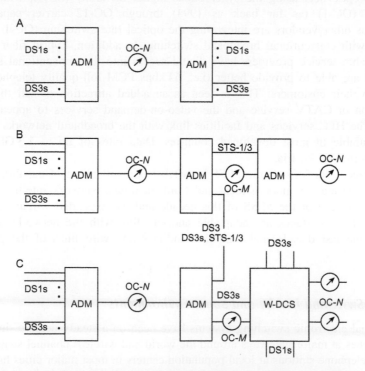

Figure 3.2 Configurations of wideband networks. (A) Point-to-point using ADMs, (B) network extensions using ADMs, and (C) combination of ADMs and WDCSs.

3.3 The Role of Signaling Systems

Signaling systems play a crucial role of dispatching appropriate commands in their own prerequisite protocol format to other elements of the network such that the service request(s) can be completed. In the earlier networks, both the signaling and its protocol were simple. However, with an explosion in the types and nature of specialized and programmable services provided by the modern networks, signaling its associated protocol has grown elaborate and cumbersome. Signaling has also undergone an evolution in its right. Now it has become standardized by the efforts of ANSI, CCITT, and ITU during 1980s and 1990s. The advanced SS7 provides ample flexibility to command the network to perform local and global network and customized routine and special services.

3.3.1 Signaling in the Communication Environment

Automated signaling systems brought numerous features and expanded the range of services and applications. In summary, most of the earlier signaling provides two basic functions: supervision and addressing. Supervisory functions monitor the network functions and, hence, the network control. They also provide the information for billing and accounting. This signaling must also be appropriately sequenced to ascertain the typical functions within the circuit-switched networks (e.g., call setup, monitor, connect, hold, charge, and release). At a detailed level, the most rudimentary circuit-switched call needs nine specific functions between the Central Office and the calling/called parties:

Initiate a call request (detect off-hook status, calling party).
Indicate that dialing may commence (provide dial tone).
Transmit called station identification (number collection and number transmit).
Alert the called party (send out ring current).
Alert the calling party (send out ringing tone, incomplete call, or busy tone).
Indicate that the call is received (off-hook status, called party).
Stop alerting signals to both parties (stop ring current; stop ring signal).
Monitor the call progress (off-hook status of both parties and send billing information on the calling number).
Release the Central Office path for both parties.

Each of these functions has a certain signal(s) associated with it. These signals are executed in the right sequence under stored program or logical control from the hardware, much like the control signals from the CPU within a computer.

Such numerous signaling sequences, appropriately matched to the specific operations, exist for all the necessary network functions. In the early days, each telephone environment proceeded haphazardly in accomplishing these necessary functions with its own localized standards. As a result, the differences and incompatibilities between the major telephone environments around the world have prevailed until ANSI and CCITT (now ITU) standardized the signaling systems, CCIS (for interoffice signaling, first installed in 1976), and SS7 (for customer and

Central Office signaling). However, numerous other types of signaling systems have existed and will continue to exist around the globe. In concept, these networks with their peculiar signaling can be compared to mainframe systems that functioned with their own sets of unique logic instead of standard binary logic (AND, OR, EX-OR (exclusive-or), etc.) found in computer systems. If this were the case, it would lead to chaos, if not a collapse in the computer industry!

3.3.2 Applications of Signaling

In the conventional telephone environments, there are three areas of applications where signaling is crucial. The first area is the exchange of control information between the station (customer) and the Central Office. The second area of application is between Central Offices dealing with trunks and the channel allocation and its control. The third area of application deals with special services and the functions and controls associated with such special services (like Private Branch Exchange (PBX) trunks and PBX tie trunks). Each of these applications is discussed next.

In the first area of application, there are three basic types of signals dealing with the station (customer) loop. Loop signaling deals with the special treatment of long loops where range extension signaling becomes necessary. Basic station signaling deals with the control or change of DC currents (on-hook, off-hook), the signals originating at the station. For example, dialing, touch-tone signals, clicking, and operator alerting), and finally the ringing from the Central Office are performed by this signaling. Of these signals, the dominant and well-accepted ones are the touch-tone signals, which uniquely combine a frequency from a low-frequency group with a frequency from a high-frequency group to identify a decimal digit (0–9) or the * or # symbol. The frequencies in both groups are carefully chosen to be uncommonly rare in the spoken language. Coin station signaling needs the usual station signaling plus the coin collection signals to and from the Central Office (announcements and tones with each coin drop).

In the second area of application, there are two types of signaling: loop-reverse-battery and E&M lead signaling.[1] The former type is used for one-way call origination (for one-way trunks) and is applicable to metallic facilities only where the current and the polarity are both sensed. Sometimes this type of signaling can also be used with carrier facilities. The E&M lead signaling is appropriate for two-way call origination and requires a facilities-signaling system for all applications. In the metallic facility, the appropriate signaling is the Bell System DX system (to detect the changes in the DC resistance, voltage, or current conditions during DC signaling). In an analog trunk facility, the appropriate signaling is the single frequency (SF) in-band signaling system. In the digital trunk facility, selected bits in

---

[1] E&M leads exist between the terminating sets and the signaling equipment in the Central Office. These leads control the currents in the trunks and in the relays in the switching systems. The M-lead conveys the per-channel signaling input status (special services, DC signaling, in-band signaling, or out-of-band signaling); then, the appropriate signaling is applied to the circuit via the E-lead.

the information stream provide the signaling information for the control of the communication channel.

In the third application, that is, the special services application, both the first and the second types of signaling are necessary. In addition, if there are any coin services or tie trunks associated with the PBX subscribers, then additional signaling protocol and interfaces become essential. The loop type and E&M signaling systems are both modified for these special services.

3.3.3   End-To-End Signaling

Facilities-signaling systems are necessary to carry signaling information from its source to a destination. Compatibility of the signaling transmission techniques with the type of facilities is essential. Generally, there are five major types of facilities-signaling techniques: DC, in-band, out-of-band, digital, and the CCIS signaling. These signals can themselves be continuous, spurt, or of a compelled variety. The continuous signals indeed monitor the channel during its transmission procedure (e.g., call progress state). The spurt signal is generally associated with short duration address information and supervisory functions. These are generally used with the CCIS backbone network signaling. The compelled mode of signaling is used for highly reliable communication systems (e.g., international calling, secure network, and so forth). Here, every change of state is acknowledged, and each step is precisely monitored throughout the network.

3.3.3.1   DC Signaling

The dated mode of signaling deals with the detection of balanced and unbalanced line currents, the reversal of polarity and changes of resistance that may occur as the station sets are being used. For example, the on-hook/off-hook condition causes a flow of line current in the loop. This change is picked up by the line scanner, which enhances the scan rate to detect the dialing pulses. Each dial pulse (DP) is a quick on/off click at the Central Office. Such pulses are counted and collected (by electronic Central Offices) or are actually used in the "step-by-step" Central Offices to make the connections to the called party.

In-band signaling can be SF, multifrequency (MF), or the touch-tone signaling. SF provides for on-hook and off-hook signaling with the presence or absence of a 2600 Hz signal. A typical duration of 50 ms is usually adopted to prevent false triggering of voice frequency. MF allows for different combinations of two of the four audio frequencies (350, 440, 480, and 620 Hz) to accomplish the signaling states (such as, ringing, busy, and so on).

Out-of-band signaling employs the unused part of the 4 kHz voice frequency channels allocated to the user. Typically, the N1 carrier system in the United States uses signals at 3700 Hz in a continuous format similar to SF signaling. E&M lead interfaces are used for this mode.

3.3.3.2   Digital Signaling

This type of signaling over the digital carrier facilities is a form of out-of-band signaling. Per-channel signaling is usual with one or two bits allocated for signaling within the digital bit stream. A typical example of this type of signaling is carried by the 193rd (or $24 \times 8 + 1$) signaling bit in the T1 carrier systems at 1544 kbps. The sampling rate of this bit is about 1000 bits per second because the T1 frame repeats 8000 times a second and every channel is accommodated in 8 bits or one byte. The signaling systems vary depending upon the D1, D2, or D3 channel banks, which are discussed further in the companion volume "Design and Engineering of Intelligent Communication Networks."

3.3.3.3   CCIS Signaling

This modern mode of signaling is a truly facilities-independent and standardized signaling system accepted throughout the world. Greatly expanded as SS7, it handles most of the signaling for newer digital services and IN functions. Most of the currently manufactured switching systems stringently adhere to this standard. With the SPC switches, this interoffice signaling system eliminates the need for a per-trunk signaling interface. Instead, a single data link containing multiplexed signaling information is used. This data link passes through a signal transfer point (STP) and serves multiple trunk groups from the office. This signaling system removes the need for the older loop-reverse-battery, the E&M signals, and DP or MF addressing.

3.4   Protocol and Interfaces

A protocol becomes necessary for the orderly exchange of information between computing and communicating environments. It can be visualized as a logical abstraction of a process and the steps that must occur to permit two or more machines to exchange information. In networks, the protocol performs three basic functions: (a) establishment of necessary conventions, (b) establishment of an accepted or standard communication path, and (c) establishment of a standard data element with which the data will be exchanged.

These three basic protocol functions need monitoring and vigilance prior to the actual flow of information. Any foreseeable errors need detection and appropriate remedy. Real or virtual data-path requirements need to be mutually accepted, recognized, and established. Failure to connect should be appropriately handled. Finally, the start and end of data blocks need accurate identification such that a block of data (or numerous blocks of a sequence) may be transmitted and received, or swapped. The term "handshaking" is sometimes used when two units of information engage in a controlled two-way transfer of data. A series of interlocking steps via appropriate signals (such as, ready-to-send-to; ready-to-receive-from; data-flow-to; receipt-acknowledge-from; send-complete-to; completion-acknowledge-from) ensures the flow of data between the two units (to and from) the sender and the receiver. When the interfaces concerning which data is exchanged become standardized, numerous devices and device types may be used freely.

For example, an RS-232 interface may be readily used for printers from numerous vendors, or even printers and plotters. When information is exchanged in a complex environment (such as, multiple users through an intermediate network), the role of protocols and interfaces becomes elaborate. When two users have user processes (segments of their programs) running on two different machines (logical or physical), and the users exchange information, then a sequence of steps (depending upon the protocol used) facilitates the exchange process.

This protocol has enough order and structure embedded in it to permit the process to communicate with the host computer. This computer in turn reuses the information provided and employs its own protocol structure to cross the interface between the computer and the packet switch. The forward path for the transmit information continues and, in the process, provides enough information for the receiving process to respond back to the sending process via its own host computer. Standard interfaces exist for the logical pathways to be established throughout the network. The interface at Layer 1 is the physical interface defined as the RS-232 electrical interface and X.21 standard.

At the second level, the link control procedure becomes essential. One of the commonly used controls is the high-level data link control (HDLC), even though the synchronous data link control (SDLC) introduced by IBM and the advanced data communications control procedure introduced by ANSI also prevail. At the third level, the network control protocol for packet networks is the internationally accepted X.25 protocol. For the ISDN environment popular during 1990s, the protocol established is called Q.921 and Q.931 for Layer 2 and Layer 3, respectively.

3.4.1 IN Environments

In the IN environment, there is an innermost functional layer with three sections that facilitate the network functionality. These IN functions (AT&T, 1985) do not correspond, nor overlay, the Open Systems Interconnect (OSI) functions in its seven layers. However, these functions are addressed to invoke a new OSI-based exchange of IN signals to follow the universal OSI model that will be inclusive of the generic IN functions.

The innermost layer of the IN is an interface consisting of three major software modules: (a) operation support system (OSS) for the switching to occur, (b) signaling, engineering, and administration system (SEAS) for transmission of data through the network, and (c) service management system (SMS) for network services to be adapted according to technological and social changes.

The first section permits the local and global switching within the network for the flow of information. The second section permits the transmission of data throughout the network, thus ascertaining the accurate flow of information throughout the network. The third section permits the introduction, management, and monitoring of network services as they start to become available and as users become accustomed to the new intelligent services available.

At the outer layer, the human IN interface may be necessary sometimes. Examples of such interfaces exist at operator interfaces that made the telephone systems work or consoles that make computer systems run. Thus, the type and number of interfaces for the network start to become clear. For example, the network operator interface discussed in AT&T (1985) with OSS, SEAS, and SMS, or service vendors at switching systems and the transmission systems interface, with the network hardware for the switching and transmission functions. Because the network devices are computer based, they also need an appropriate software interface with OSS and SEAS. The subscribers and the network users interface with the network hardware, software, or both, depending upon the nature and extent of their usage. The interface standards and their corresponding protocols are well accepted in the internal control of INs. Vendors of IN services thus have some flexibility in organizing the interaction and cross-communication within their individual services.

However, great uniformity and consistency exist for the communication between the major IN components. The most significant step taken in the control of the overall networks and the cross-communication between major building blocks of INs is the use of X.25 protocol between SCPs, SSPs, and STPs. Furthermore, for the interfacing of the ISDN and broadband services and communication pathways, Q.931 and Q.921 are accepted standards. It is interesting to note that all the ITU-T (formerly CCITT) recommendations are rigorously being followed in the general communication paths between the major IN components. For example, the various INs presently implemented in the United States and Europe use the X.25 packet communication through the SS7 network linking the SSPs, SCPs, and STPs. When ATM becomes the international standard for "cell relaying," and when a fiber "backbone" signaling network is established, then the current X.25 switching will be upgraded in the IN arena for the signaling of IN control information. This gradual evolution to all fiber and all ATM will be a major chapter in the genesis of the telecommunications industry.

Another major contender for the transport of data is the HFC system. The current thinking is to allocate enough capacity for a wide variety of services ranging from POTS to video-on-demand and video conferencing. The newer HFC systems will tie into the telephone carrier-system hierarchy to permit traditional telephone type service at comparable cost but better quality and in addition carry the CATV type of services. A set-top box will permit the separation of services. In addition, the upstream capability becomes essential for video service requests and for POTS. Fiber to the curb (FTTC) makes ATM services feasible to the desktop. However, new FTTC installation is not economically justifiable in all circumstances, especially in established metropolitan areas where the economic activity is also likely to be very high.

When the HFC integration in the CATV industry is complete and economically proven, the excess capacity of the system is likely to be deployed for novel video services on a sound business footing. When these services become available, the architecture of the IN networks for CATV and HFC environments are likely to follow its own evolutionary path.

The generic intelligent medical network (IMN) concepts based on evolution and developments of modern INs (see Chapter 8) will emerge by the end of the decade. Such intelligent broadband networks have already found implementation during the last decade and provide valuable linkage to most of the knowledge bases around the globe.

3.4.2   Protocol Objectives and Implementation

The three main objectives of most protocol system are as follows:

First, the separation of control and data (or "data transparency") is achieved.
Second, the synchronization of two or more ends of a protocol in close correlation is maintained.
Third, the resources are managed and shared efficiently.

Communication protocols tend not to be comprehensive in accomplishing these objectives but do function efficiently within the network. Very detailed and comprehensive protocol can become too elaborate to be implemented and be wasteful. These protocols tend to have a layered structure, and the different layers have supporting objectives since the entire layered structure must have common objectives. One typical example of a specific supporting objective is flow control, which is indeed a part of the common protocol objectives.

Layering generally implies a vertical structure with levels (such as, application level, user level, host level, and packet-switch level via a Data Circuit Terminating Equipment—DataTerminal Equipment (DCE—DTE) interface) and predefined functions within these levels. Sometimes these levels may assume a side-by-side structure with independence between them.

Within the HDLC procedure, data transparency is achieved by bit stuffing and a special frame character. At the X.21 level, the physical separation of the leads causes the separation of signal and data. Other techniques may also be employed in different types of protocol. Sequencing the flow-control mechanisms keeps the frames synchronized. Buffering and multiplexing is related to management and sharing of resources in most network environments.

3.4.3   ATM-Based Signaling

The optical rates currently available (up to 4—8 Gbps) for the transport of data are much too high to be directly integrated in the existing telecommunication networks. The SONET frame, lasting for 125 µs, can carry a large amount of information as the payload (2349 bytes) even at the OC-3 rate. While this size may appear perfectly reasonable in the local area network/metropolitan area network/wide area network (LAN/MAN/WAN) data environment, it can be perceived as being too large for other (like switched virtual service, SVC, or permanent virtual service, PVC) types of application in business and industry. In the trunk environment, numerous low rate data channels are multiplexed onto the fiber trunk with its own particular protocol, framing and bit designations for rates ranging from T0 to T3 or

E0 to E3. However, recent applications are not always circuit switched, but are becoming more packet and message switched. Hence, the idea of having the SONET was to carry smaller packet sizes (frames) in the packet-switched mode.

Due to their compact size and ability to ride within SONET frames, packets or "cells" becomes more appealing. In a sense, ATM is an extension of the signal transport concept that SONET itself relies upon. Cells provide user level interfacing packets and SONET frames become the photonic network transport packets. ATM standards outline the efficient (and perhaps the elegant) techniques to bridge the gap between multiplicity of users and vast variety of light-wave devices that will make up the network. However, until such networks are a reality, ATM can be used to supplement DS-2 and DS-3 networks.

The ATM cell format has an optimized structure (Figure 3.3) to be transferred efficiently and effortlessly over virtual channel, virtual and transmission paths. With a standardized 5-octet (byte) header and 48-octet payload, the cell can deliver user data (payload) through most user and network interfaces by decoding the 5-octet header data. These details are explained further in Figure 3.5.

ATM of data transfer is a worldwide standard. It stems from the availability of a high-speed backbone in the national or global environment. It has started an era of cell relay technologies and falls under a wide umbrella of packet switching. The technological fit of ATM can be seen as a progression of X.25 technologies to frame technologies and then into the cell technologies, as depicted in Figure 3.3. It depends upon the SONET standard for the transport of data. ATM is a standard for

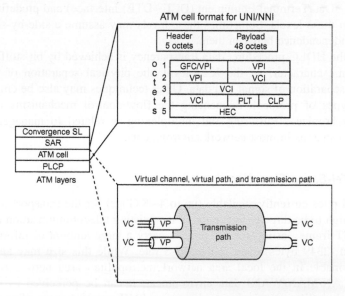

Figure 3.3 ATM cell format: structure and its transport on the virtual channel, virtual path, and transmission path. NNI, network—network interface; PCLP, physical layer convergence protocol; SAR, segmentation and reassembly; SL, sublayer; and UNI, user—network interface.

most networks to communicate directly with each other, provided the SONET and ATM protocols and header block information are consistently followed.

ATM is based upon packet-/cell-switched technology. The ATM packets or cells are relayed and routed throughout the network and thus are communicated between the source to the appropriate destination. Since the protocols and functions are unique to ATM, the technology for these ATM-based networks is called the "cell relay" technology as opposed to the "frame relay" technology. Frame relay technology is used to carry data in the last generation data networks such as circuit-switched digital capability or CSDC at 56 kbps, fractional T1 rates via T1 carrier, and even DS-1 and DS-3 networks.

ATM functionality has been embedded within a fixed size link-layer (i.e., the OSI layer six, data link-layer (DLL)) entity. This link-layer entity is the "cell" and the size of this fixed length entity is 53 octets (bytes). There are 5 octets for the header block and 48 octets for the payload (or the data to be transported). Similar to the header of most packet networks, ATM cell header carries information unique to the nature of data, its functionality, disassembling and reassembling of cells and their payloads. The typical ATM cell format for the user—network interface (UNI) and network—network interface (NNI) are shown in Figure 3.4. The information contained in the header is encoded to conform to the functions within the ATM sublayers.

ATM cells are routed and relayed by virtual circuits. Such circuits may be fabricated depending upon the traffic demands and switched and scaled by the ATM switches. These virtual networks may also be switched in the hardware at the ATM switches and/or nodes.

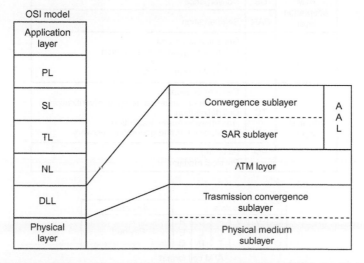

Figure 3.4 Encapsulation of the ATM layers within the data link and the physical layers of the OSI reference model.

ATM also offers high-speed data transport capabilities. Since the ATM cells "ride" within the SONET frame, they carry all the advantages offered by transport systems embedded within SONET. The speed of transport is derived from optical rates (and thus low buffering delays), optical speeds and low switching times (because of the simplicity/elegance in the SONET header information).

ATM standards are applicable within LAN/MAN/WANs. ATM standards are applicable to private LANs, campus networks, or any other data network, and thus these networks can be connected to public, regional, or national ATM networks. They can also serve the needs of broadband service by functioning via connection-oriented ATM switches.

3.5 OSI and ATM

The ATM signaling protocol meets with all the OSI standards and satisfies all the layer requirements of the OSI model. ATM functions occur at the sixth DLL and seventh (physical) layer of the OSI model. The top five OSI layers remain intact, and after the fifth layer, the ATM adaptation layer (AAL) begins. The organization and conversion to the ATM environment is shown in Figure 3.5.

In OSI standards, seven functions are identified for the network access protocol. These functions are framing, transparency, sequencing, error control, flow control, connection setup/shutdown, and addressing/naming. These functions (regrouped as

Layer		Function
ATM adaptation layer	CS	Convergence
	SAR	Segmentation
ATM layer		Generic flow control Cell header generation/extraction Cell VPI/VCI translation Cell multiplex and demultiplex
Physical layer	TC	Cell rate decoupling HEC header sequence generation/verification Cell delineation Transmission frame adaptation Transmission frame generation/recovery
	PM	Bit timing Physical medium

5 octets						48 octets
G F C	V P I	V C I	P L T	C L P	H E C	Payload

ATM cell format

Figure 3.5 ATM layer functions and ATM cell format.

	Class A	Class B	Class C	Class D
Timing relation between source and destination	Required		Not required	
Bit rate	Constant		Variable	
Connection mode	Connection oriented			Connection less

Examples of service classes

Class A Circuit emulation; constant bit rate
Class B Variable bit rate, video, and audio
Class C Circuit connection-oriented data transfer (FR)
Class D Connectionless data transfer (SMDS)

AAL-Mapping

Class A	Class B	Class C	Class D
AAL1	AAL2	AAL3/4, 5	AAL3/4

Figure 3.6 Six functions of the AAL to the OSI-RM higher layers for the different (A−D) classes of services.

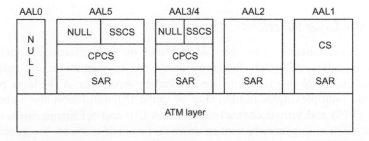

Figure 3.7 AAL structure between ATM layer and network layer of the OSI-RM. CPCS, common part convergence sublayer; SSCS, service-specific convergence sublayer; SAR, segmentation and reassembly; and SL, sublayer.

six functions as shown in Figure 3.6) are handled by the two sublayers: AAL and ATM layer as shown in Figure 3.7.

The traditional DLL now has two distinct layers: the AAL and the ATM layer. The ATM network starts from the ATM layer down and this layer may interface with the traditional DS-1, DS-3, and SONET networks. This is where the existing trunk and high-speed networks (DS-1 and DS-3) and evolving SONET get integrated via the ATM layer. ATM node-to-node connection may be established at the ATM layer.

3.5.1 AAL Functions

The AAL is also subdivided into two sublayers: convergence sublayer (CS) and segmentation and reassemble (SAR) sublayer. For the upper layers, AAL handles the transmission errors through the network: single errors are corrected and multiple errors are detected, leading to cell rejection. The effects of segmentation of data (into discrete payloads) among cells are also handled by this sublayer. The flow and time-control functions are also enforced within this sublayer. Lost or error-ridden cells are also resurrected from the network (by requesting retransmission).

In addition, the necessary DLL functions of the OSI, the AAL also performs a distinctive ATM function to the extent that it provides four (A through D) classes of service. The A and B class services requiring timing relation between source and destination are connection oriented. Only class A service is at a constant bit rate. Classes C and D do not require timing relation between source and destination and are both variable data rates. Class C is connection oriented, whereas class D is connectionless.

Class A is exemplified by circuit emulation mode with constant bit rate service, for example, 56 kbps CSDC lines. Class B is exemplified by variable bit rate video and audio services. Class C is exemplified by connection-oriented variable rate data transfer, such as frame relay applications, PVC/SVC, ranging from 56 kbps to 64 kbps to 1.544 Mbps, etc. Finally, class D service is exemplified by switched multimegabit data service (SMDS). To provide these four classes of services, AAL assumes four formats, as shown in Figures 3.6 and 3.7.

3.5.2 ATM Layer Functions

The ATM layer functions with the AAL to make the OSI reference model's DLL functions complete. Although, the convergence and segmentation, and reassemble part of the OSI level two functions are handled by AAL. The ATM layer provides for: (a) the multiplexing/demultiplexing of cells; (b) translation the virtual path identifier (VPI) and virtual channel identifier (VCI); and (c) management of UNI. The third function is generally broken down as two subfunctions: the generic flow control (GFC) and the generation/extraction of the cell header. In a sense, it completes the functions that AAL did not finish, but allows for the node-to-node connection in ATM networks.

3.5.3 ATM Physical Layer

The ATM physical layer is also divided into two distinct sublayers: the transmission convergence sublayer (TCS) and the physical medium sublayer. Together they perform all OSI reference model physical layer (layer one) functions or level one functions.

3.6 TCS Functions

There are five functions at the TCS sublevel: cell rate decoupling, header error check (parity) header sequence generation/verification, cell delineation, transmission frame adaptation, and transmission frame generation/recovery. Each of these functions is tailored to fit the cell structure (5-octet header plus 48-octet payload) and the "frame" that carries these cells. Though tailored to map efficiently into the SONET/SDH frames, these cells may also be mapped into DS-3 or even DS-1 frames.

3.6.1   Physical Medium Sublayer

This last sublayer performs two basic functions: it permits the bits to communicate between any given points in the network by maintaining the bit timing function and it facilitates such bits to traverse the physical medium.

3.6.2   ATM Header and ATM Functions

The interface becomes important in the format of the header block. At the UNI and at the NNI, the five header octets convey the information to the ATM layer to service the AAL (see Figure 3.6). This five-octet header block of ATM cell permits the ATM switch to perform the GFC, VPI (virtual path identification), VCI (virtual channel identification), playload type (PLT) identification, the cell loss parity (CLP), and the header error check. The arrangement of the bits and octets at UNI/NNI are shown in Figures 3.3 and 3.5.

It is to be appreciated that the AAL function becomes crucial, since the four classes of services (A through D, discussed earlier) have their own specific requirements. For this reason, the AAL has a flexible functional structure (format) depending on the class of service. Six such structures (AAL0 through AAL5) are identified and shown in Figure 3.7.

AAL0 is transparent and has a null structure. It does not perform any function and is specifically not used (at present) for any of the service classes. AAL1 structure performs the CS and SAR functions. It is suitable for class A, constant bit rate, and connection-oriented services needing a timing relation between the source and destination. AAL2 structure performs only SAR functions. It is suitable for class B, variable bit rate, connection-oriented services not requiring timing relation, and video/audio services. AAL3, AAL4, and AAL5 structures greatly overlap. All of these perform the SAR function. However, the CS is subdivided into yet another two sublayers: the service-specific convergence sublayer (SSCS) and common part convergence sublayer (CPCS). All three AAL structures handle class C, variable rate, connection-oriented, and frame relay type of services. For class D, it is a connectionless variable rate and SMDS that is handled by AAL3 or AAL4 structures.

3.7   ATM as a Global Standard

ATM is a generalized standard that can encompass a large number of existing networks (such as the general T1/E1, T3/E3; optical, OC-1 to OC-48, computer, campus, LANs, MANs, and WANs) with appropriate bridges and routers. Networks have their own idiosyncrasies based on the economic forces that make them viable. For example, the T1/E1 networks are geared toward twisted wire pairs and used in the trunk/subscriber environments and CATV networks have been geared toward carrying analog TV information in the homes, etc., but mostly, networks carry information through complex hierarchy of media switches by responding to the network commands via the signaling systems. The photonic network carries pockets

(rather than packets of data) of photons through the optically sealed fiber environment. However, at the transceivers (transmitters/receivers), the bits of data get
encoded/decoded as pockets of photons and bits of data are recompiled as bytes of
information.

The ATM standards particularly facilitate an easy and elegant integration of the
existing digital carriers and the 53-byte ATM cells onto to the SONET frames
transported by these networks. The integration into the broadband ISDN is equally
simple and elegant. Most general networks may be integrated with the ATM environment by appropriate protocol converters and bridges/routers.

3.7.1 ATM Building Blocks and DS-N Rates

Typically, there are *six* building blocks: the hub, bridge, router, brouter, the LAN/
MAN/WAN switch, and the transport media. Numerous varieties of terminal equipment are connected to the ATM network access node, which interconnects to the
ATM hub and other nodes. The configuration and the interconnection depend upon
the type of application (LAN/MAN/WAN) for which the ATM is being deployed.

The interface issue is generally handled by ATM interface/adapter cards.
Currently, there are *four* interfaces: the high-performance parallel interface, the standard ATM, the standard SONET, and DS-3. The ATM bridge handles the connection
between typically Ethernet and ATM networks, thus facilitating their coexistence in
the same campus or LAN. The ATM router interfaces between two ATM networks.

3.7.2 ATM Switch and DS-N Rates

The ATM switch is significantly different from the traditional switch (e.g., ESS)
and functions by multiplexing (based upon the VCI/VPI) and path availability, not
on time division multiplexing. The cell size is fixed at 53 octets. This does not
have variable length frames, nor is it fixed at lengthy time slots. The capacity is
determined by the peak-rate cell allocation and is not a fixed rate allocation of
frames or time slots. Finally, the cell multiplexing is statistical rather than deter-
ministic. Essentially, the ATM switch provides the switching fabric (i.e., interconnection between any input to output ports), the cell buffering, and the contention
resolution.

The ATM switch (broadly characterized as campus, LAN/MAN/WAN, and hub)
has also been operational at numerous (eight; 1993 data) locations providing ATM,
frame relay, SMDS, Ethernet, Fiber Distributed Data Interface (FDDI), broadband
ISDN, and T3 to OC-3 (to other ATM switches) switching. Such switches are commercially available (from at least seven vendors; 1993 data). As many as 32 ATM
ports (1993 data) can be supported. The ATM switch throughput is as high as
12.8 Gb/s (1993 data) and is likely to increase by many orders of magnitude over
the next decade. The ATM interface is as high as OC-12, even though typical rates
range from DS-3 to OC-3 rates (1993 data). Most of the ATM interface is for fiber,
even though some ATM switch vendors provide an ATM interface at 155 Mbps
over class 5 unshielded and shielded twisted wire pairs for campus and premises

wiring. The LAN interfacing for most of the ATM switches is Ethernet, token ring, and FDDI (supervision, gateway, and even node-to-node communication).

ATM hubs are also being manufactured by numerous vendors throughout the world with AAL5 structure and for the older PVC and SVC switching. Typical (1993 data) interfaces are at 45, 100, and at 155 Mbps. Bridge, router, and brouter devices are available to build complete ATM networks.

3.7.3 ATM Media

Three viable media exist. Fiber offers very high bandwidth at a modest cost, some amount of implementation difficulty, and high skill maintenance (Lightwave Staff, 2012). Coaxial cable offers relatively high bandwidth (up to 400 MHz; the digital capacity depends on coding algorithms) with a high cost and a medium amount of difficulty in implementation and maintenance. The unshielded twisted wire pairs have the lowest capacity (about 100–155 Mbps at about 30 m), but cost, implementation, and maintenance are quite low.

3.7.4 ATM Network Configurations

For LAN applications, the architecture usually incorporates ATM switches, hub(s), and interfaces. In MAN applications, the architecture typically includes the ATM router, ATM switch, and ATM mux/demux (in addition, to the ATM–LAN building blocks). For wide area public networks, the architecture includes ATM frame relay switch, ATM–SMDS, ATM access node, and ATM multiplexing facility. For the wide area private network access, the ATM building blocks that are necessary may be as few as the switch, concentrator, and gateway.

3.7.5 ATM and Earlier Data Networks

ATM (or a major section of the standard) has been adapted by numerous private networks. Data system vendors provide for frame relaying at data rates ranging from 56 kbps to the DS-3 rates with all five (AAL1–AAL5) types of AAL structures. The vendors also provide for DS-3 and isochronous T1 data with AAL1, 3, or 4, and 5 structures. Numerous vendors offer frame relay systems for X.25, HDLC, Systems Network Architecture (SNA)/SDLC at 56 kbps to E3 rates with the AAL5 structure. T1/E1, T3/E3, and OC-3 rates with the AAL5 structure are also offered. For example, General Datacom offers frame relay Ethernet, T1/E1 by circuit emulation, also with its own AAL. Other vendors offer SMDS and selected rates between fractional T1 and DS-3 rates with AAL1, 3/4, and 5 structures. Alcatel Data Networks offers frame relay, HDLC, SDLC, 64 kbps to E1 rates, and SMDS rates ranging from 2 to 16 Mbps.

Fiber-optic technology, its efficacy, and its global reach are well documented and accepted throughout the world. In a very concrete fashion, the SONET/ATM standards have been proposed and well received in most nations and appear to be the most popular for raw data communication. The TCP/IP protocols are standards that are generally used in the Internet environments.

3.8 Conclusions

Data communication standards are well established for most applications, and the OSI hierarchy provides a means for the data to be communicated between applications running on widely dispersed computer systems. Internet communications are generally handled by using the five-layer TCP/IP reference model presented in Section 7.4. In a sense, the status of data and Internet communication is based on two well-designed and established reference models.

Even though the protocols and interfaces for the older networks and carrier systems were satisfactory and dependable, the digital networks of the present generation enjoy the precision and accuracy of modern computer systems. To this extent, the digital revolution has affected the networks arena though not the medical networks arena. INs have the potential of providing the communication aspects of medical functions and subfunctions; they do not have the interfaces and protocol for medical networks. It is the responsibility and the requirements of the developers of medical-ware (MW) to evolve MW a step beyond knowledge-ware (KW) and two steps beyond software (SW) and firmware (FW).

References

1. Bell Telephone Laboratories: *Engineering and operations in the bell system*, Indiana, 1982, Western Electric Co, or see Ahamed SV: *Intelligent networks*, *Encyclopedia of telecommunications*, 1982, Academic Press, Chapter 9, pp 159−174.
2. Ahamed SV, Lawrence VB: *Intelligent broadband multimedia networks*, Boston, MA, 1997, Kluwer Academic Publishers.
3. Alcatel−Lucent: *Alcatel−Lucent 5ESS® switch* (website). https://support.alcatel-lucent.com/portal/productContent.do?productId=5ESS, 2013. Accessed March 2013.
4. AT&T: *Telecommunications transmission engineering*, vol. vols 1−3, Indianapolis, IN, 1985, AT&T.
5. Aprille TJ: Introducing SONET into the local exchange carrier network, *IEEE Commun Mag* vol. August:34−38, 1985. See also, for SONET Digital HierarchyChow M-C: Understanding SONET/SDH: standards and applications, Holmdel, NJ, 1990, Andan Publishers.Additional References for SONET are in (a) Bellcore, Synchronous optical network (SONET) transport systems: common generic criteria, TR-TSY-000253, 1989. (b) Bellcore, SONET add−drop multiplex equipment administration using the TIRKS provisioning system, Globecom, Conference Record, vol 3, pp 1511−1515, 1989. (c) See also Bellcore SONET add−drop multiplex equipment (SONET ADM) generic criteria, TR-TSY-000496, 2, 1989. (d) Bellcore SONET add−drop multiplex equipment (SONET ADM) generic criteria for a self-healing ring implementation, TA-TSY-000496, 2, 1989.
6. Lightwave Staff: PON, VDSL, cable equipment sales continue growth in 3Q12, *Lightwave Mag* vol. December 4:1990.

Part 2

Intelligent Network Environments

Intelligent networks (INs) have evolved from a long and rich heritage of communication networks. The sophistication in the design of INs stems from the seminal and patented works of Bell, Marconi, Tesla, Zworykin, Schawlow, Townes, and numerous other communication scientists. Being at the top of an evolutionary ladder, the current INs have benefitted greatly from the breakthrough invention of Shockley, Bardeen, Brattain, as the three-electrode element (Transistor). Then the innovations in the VLSI and processor industry to develop cheap IC circuits have also enhanced the feasibility of INs. Further, the advent of packet switching based on Aloha networks has made the implementation of INs practical, cheap, and dependable. Finally, the discovery of Maurer, Schultz, Keck that silica-glass fiber-optic material can make fiber a viable media for signal transmission, has made the digital revolution cheap, dependable, and very accurate.

The five chapters in this part of the book are (a) Transmission Media in Networks, (b) Optical Fiber in Modern Networks, (c) Wireless Networks, (d) NGMNs, 3G and 4G Networks, and (e) Evolution and Developments of Modern Intelligent Networks. These chapters offer the platform to gracefully conceive and build the medical machines and networks. The obstacles appear in the design of generic building blocks of medical processor units (MPUs) and the intelligent medical network (IMN) modules. To circumvent the two hurdles, we present the seminal designs of object processor units (OPUs), the architectures and methodologies for parallel processing, etc. in Part 1 and extended in this part. The generic building block of all INs the SSPs, SCPs, SMSs, the CCISS6 and SS7, and finally the IPs are also presented in Part 1 and extended in context to the transmission media deployed in the evolving next generations of 3G and 4G networks and finally the impact of evolution and developments of modern INs.

These components and their evolution presented in this part, derive an guideline toward building the future medical machines and IMNs. Evolutionary aspects are also included in these components and their design to circumvent possible pitfalls in the development of MPUs and IMNs. Such shortcomings and pitfall are now evident (in hindsight, of course) during the evolution of INs.

Modern NGMNs the 3G and 4G networks do not compete directly with landline optical networks for medical applications due to the statistical nature of atmospheric media. The conditions that favor these 3G and 4G mobile networks for the last link with the patients and medical service providers are delineated in Chapter 7. The NGMN organization and component vendors are aiming toward making mobile data communication as dependable and secure as the modern fiber-optic networks.

The evolution and developments of modern INs presented in Chapter 8 provide a methodology for the designing secure medical knowledge bases and their interoperability to provide medical knowledge and expertise with complete precision and total accuracy. Global medical knowledge bases and access poses a special challenge to the medical knowledge base designers and their addressing for the Internet TCP/IP protocol. Waraporon[1] has demonstrated that intelligent interstate (cities in NJ–NC–TX–NY) query-response times for Internet-based medical application to range between 2 and 16 s (average time ~6–8 s) under high-traffic conditions during 2005–2006 timeframe. The corresponding intelligent international (US–Germany–Thailand–Tokyo–Bangkok) query-response times for Internet-based medical application to range between 10 and 60 s (average time ~10–20 s) under high-traffic conditions during 2005–2006 timeframe. The major cause for the delay was tracked down to the local lines in the distant countries (except Germany and Japan) with a 56-kbps modem access.

[1] Waraporon N: *Intelligent medical databases for global access*, Ph.D. Dissertation at the Graduate Center of the City University of New York, 2006. Also see Waraporn N, Ahamed SV: Intelligent medical search engine by knowledge machine. *Proc. 3rd, Int. Conf. on Inf. Tech.: New Generations*, IEEE Computer Society, Los Alamitos, CA. 2006 and Waraporn N: Results of real time simulation of medical knowledge technology (MKT) system for medical diagnosis on distributed knowledge nodes. *ITNG*, 2007, pp. 265–270.

4 Transmission Media in Networks

4.1 Introduction

Recently, fiber and wireless have taken over most of the media space of copper, cables, and electrical conductors in the world of communications, especially in the United States. The choice of media for high-speed services differs from country to country. When it is necessary to deploy the plain old telephone service (POTS) lines to provide Internet type of services (twisted wire-pair, TWP), copper media can still be a reasonable choice. In this chapter, we present a very short glimpse at this phenomenal migration in the choice for media from copper to fiber and from copper to wireless.

In this chapter, the traditional copper media is reviewed briefly to indicate that the network explosion is a result of the advance in the older technologies and the final impact of the semiconductor industry onto the transmission technology that enhanced the network capabilities by many orders of magnitude. For example, the open two-wire copper media was meant to carry voice signals in the range of 400–2400 Hz. The present-day digital subscriber loop capacity carries 2.048 megabits per second (Mbps) for the high-speed digital subscriber line (HDSL) to (16 or even 24 Mbps (in exceptional environments for downstream data)) Mb/s for the asymmetrical digital subscriber line (ADSL) +2 lines. Downstream rates of 16 Mbps are offered in Germany and France where most of the subscriber loops are free of discontinuities and bridged taps (Ahamed and Lawrence, 1996, 1997). HDSL and ADSL architectures are presented in detail in Ahamed and Lawrence (1997) for the United States subscriber loop environments.

This chapter presents the most significant developments in the copper media to contend with the digital age of the current century. Even though many had predicted a slow but sure death of the copper media in digital networks, the transmission and terminal technologies of the past two or three decades puts copper media for the "last mile" (Ahamed and Lawrence, 1997) to the customer as a possible contender for Internet services.

4.2 Traditional Copper Media

Over the evolutionary phase of most voice networks, a large amount of copper in the form of wires has been used to carry electrically encoded information bearing signals. Copper is a very good conductor (resistivity 1.712×10^{-8} Ohms/m, 25°C)

Intelligent Networks: Recent Approaches and Applications in Medical Systems.
DOI: http://dx.doi.org/10.1016/B978-0-12-416630-1.00004-2

of electrical signals, being next to silver (resistivity 1.617×10^{-8} Ohms/m, 25°C). It is cheap, readily available, durable, and ductile. It is used for overhead wires, TWPs, coaxial cables, Cable TV (CATV) distribution systems, and for TV broadcast cable (twin-cable). For the communication networks, copper medium has played a significant role, and it retains a sizable (but diminishing) foothold in most established networks. Two well-established networks that depend heavily upon copper for distribution of information are the traditional telephone networks and the CATV networks.

The unshielded twisted wire-pair (UTP) group of conductors has five categories: Category 1 is deployed for ordinary telephone lines and Categories 2 through 5 are generally used for data. The bandwidth can be as high as 4, 10, 20, and 100 Mbps. The signal is influenced by electromagnetic induction (EMI) and crosstalk. The high signal attenuation and signal contamination general limits the range to about 100 m, even though TWPs of up to 3.41 miles (about 5.5 km) in the subscriber loop environment (Ahamed and Lawrence, 1996). With electronic range extension and possible load coils (Ahamed and Lawrence, 1997), the voice frequency signals have been conveyed up to 4.5 miles (7.3 km) in the remote rural sections of the United States for telephone voice communication.

The shielded twisted wire-pair (STP) group of conductors offers protection against signal contamination adequately over limited distances. Five types (1, 2, 6, 7, and 9) of STPs are generally offered. The first two types, 1 and 2 use #22 American wire gauge (AWG) wire with two or four telephone wire-pairs, respectively. Types 6, 7, and 9 use #26 AWG wire and types 6 and 7 have two and four pairs, respectively. The STPs tend to become more expensive than the coaxial cables. The types 1 and 2 STPs were used for T1 carrier systems (Ahamed and Lawrence, 1996, 1997) with embedded repeaters, in the United States.

More recently, the impact of fiber has been dominant and resounding. Fiber as a viable alternate both for long haul and for local distribution of information is firmly established. The impending hybrid-fiber/coax technology (including the fiber-to-the-curb (FTTC) and fiber-to-the-home (FTTH) systems) and cellular wireless "last mile" both pose as serious contenders for the continued role of copper as an electrical signal carrier. However, the continued tendency of the data services providers to use the copper already in networks as digital subscriber lines (DSL) (ITU G.992.5 for ADSL +2 applications up to 2 miles) has prolonged the use of copper media in the digital networks. Passive optical networks and numerous types of DSL services now offered in conjunction with hybrid fiber coax (HFC) networks deploy the existing copper lines already in place between customer premises and central offices.

The limited bandwidth of the copper media, especially the TWPs, has been a topic of serious contention, but the transmission engineers have been able to push the limit further and further by improvement of the terminal devices that "couple" with the media. In the era of sophisticated signal processing, the characterization (attenuation and dispersion) of the transmission medium is not the challenge. Instead, the contamination (crosstalk and stray electromagnetic coupling) within the medium and from extraneous sources of signal contamination that makes the copper medium unacceptable for dependable data communication. Hence, the scientists attempt to isolate the effects of contaminants that cannot be accurately characterized. There is a statistical estimation of the damage they cause but not a scientific methodology to eliminate them. The scientific breakthrough will result when and if it becomes possible to force the copper medium innately to "couple" the electromagnetic fields for the signal and "uncouple" them for the noise. New transmission materials that perform signal processing at the atomic/molecular levels may result. Such fabricated compound semiconductor materials for optical devices have been successfully deployed.

For these reasons, a true parallel between the two (copper systems versus fiber optic) systems mode of operation cannot be drawn. Optical systems offer a clear edge over the copper-based systems for deployment. In the same vein, the redeployment of (spatial) cells and micro cells in wireless and cell phone by using multiple base stations delivers the final blow to the copper-based systems. Over the last two decades, both fiber-optic and wireless technologies have made monumental strides. Barring any long-range ill effects of microwave radiation, the slow demise of copper as a viable contender of data communication is a long drawn conclusion, except in some remote and specialized application. ADSL (for up to 12 Mbps downstream) and ADSL +2 (for up to 24 Mbps downstream) still prevail where the copper media needs to be deployed and fiber-optic lines are not installed.

The current integrated optical technologies for transmission and broadband switching can leave behind some of the older communication technology in a state of premature obsolescence. The utilization of copper already in place as a medium to carry voice and data in the subscriber loop environments appears to offer economic incentive for a few network owners around the world. Some of the older communication networks are heavily invested with established metallic connections to almost every household. Deploying copper (by itself) for new communication is an undesirable alternative in most cases.

In most of the older telephone networks, the subscriber loops are used in star topology to connect individual subscribers to the nodal Central Office or to a remote terminal (RT). These RTs are in turn served by a higher capacity carrier system from a Central Office. Recently, these carrier systems are integrated with the optical systems and carry data at Synchrohous Optical Network or the SONET [OC-3 (at 155.520 Mbps) or at OC-12 (at 622.080 Mbps)] rates over optical fiber. These Central Offices themselves have trunks or other high capacity lines (OC-12 or OC-24) for interconnections to other Central Offices in widely dispersed geographic areas. In some rural areas, the subscriber loop remains as the last link for distributing information to the end user and becomes the first link to receive the information from the user. This dual requirement from the loop to serve as both the first and the last link of a conventional telephone network is due to duplex nature of voice communication systems.

4.2.1 Wire-Pairs

Wire-pair environments differ significantly from country to country and from one region to another. A large number of factors influence the nature of the telephone loop-plant environment where wire-pairs are used extensively. Two (open and twisted) types of wire-pairs are used in the loop plant.

4.2.2 Open Wire-Pairs

Open wires strung on top of poles (Bell Telephone Laboratories, 1982) still exist in some areas even though they are no longer actively installed in most countries. The existing open wire-pairs still used in the United States for metallic connection to the Central Office, usually consists of bare copper wire of 0.080, 0.104, 0.128, or 0.165 in. The wire-pairs are generally mounted on poles spaced at about 130 ft. Frequent transposing and close spacing between the pairs tends to provide immunity to noise and power frequency EMI. It also helps reduce crosstalk from other wire-pairs. Some older carrier systems ranging from 15 to 150 miles (O-type for 16 single-sideband two-way voice grade channels on open-wire) were implemented. However, these carrier systems were also quickly adapted to TWPs, coaxial cables, and even microwave radio systems in order to deal with problems of terrain, population density, pole-line congestion, and environmental conditions including rain, ice, sleet, frost, and high wind.

4.2.3 Twisted Wire-Pairs

TWPs (AT&T Telecommunications Transmission Engineering, 1985) to carry voice and data generally exist in most national networks. Composition of a 12–50 bundle pairs of a composite 600 TWP cable in the United States is shown in Figure 4.1. The TWP connections to the customer premises were originally provided for voice traffic with a limited bandwidth of 200–3200 Hz. Since the inception of POTS, the terminating devices have become more and more adaptive and IC oriented. In 1950s, the cost of these components has plummeted rapidly. More recently, this scenario has initiated the investigation of complex circuitry at the subscriber line termination to enhance the data rate.

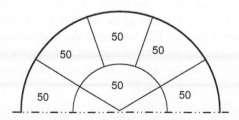

Figure 4.1 Half-section of a 600 TWP cable section. Other size cables are also manufactured for use in the subscriber loop environments.

4.2.4   Unshielded Twisted Wire-Pairs

Much of the metallic signal carrying color coded, bound in bundles, and enclosed in sheaths. Typically, media consists of the twisted metallic wire-pair. TWPs are typically waterproof coating, corrugated aluminum and steel shields, and/or polyethylene jackets are used outside the core insulation of the TWPs. The choice of the outside material depends upon the type of application and the environmental protection most desirable. Immunity against electrical interference and physical protection are offered by metal clad cables, whereas resistance to corrosion is provided with polyethylene cladding.

Being cheap and relatively indestructible, UTP (AT&T Telecommunications Transmission Engineering, 1985) is used within Central Offices, sometimes between Central Offices, mostly within the loop plant to reach the subscribers, and usually within the customer premises. Mostly the wire-pairs have a random twist along its length. They have been manufactured to range between six wire-pair units and several thousand wire-pair units. Physically, individual wire-pairs are bundled to occupy the innermost bundle or one of the outer bundles within the physical cable.

4.2.5   Shielded Twisted Pairs

Shielded wire-pairs have the same type of makeup as the new untwisted wire-pairs. In addition, there is a metallic shield between cable pairs. This metallic shield modifies the field distribution substantially to the extent that the propagation properties of the cable are themselves altered or even degraded. Due to eddy currents, any loss in the shield shows up as additional copper loss. To prevent any build up of voltage in the shield, a single drain wire is connected between the shield (and foil in most cases) and the outside sheath. Such cables are sometimes referred to as screened cables. Shielding itself takes two forms: braided shield and foil shield, each offering different electrical properties. Sometimes the braided shield find use in applications below 100 MHz and foils shields find use in applications above 100 MHz. The grounding connections of the sheath at either end of the cable, also influence the net reduction of the electromagnetic pickup in shielded wire-pairs, in addition to the connectors and cross connects.

The shielded wire-pairs can become slightly more bulky and less flexible, thus crowding the conduits in which the cables are buried. These shielded wire-pairs are also heavier, which makes the installation more labor intensive. The process of including the STP in the networks becomes difficult and expensive. Even though these wire-pairs are used in some premises distribution systems (PDS), they are not as widely used as the UTP.

4.2.6   Wire-Pairs for High-Speed Data Services

From the very modest rate of 32 kbps in the late 1970s (Ahamed and Lawrence, 1997), the DSL rates in the subscriber loop environments have climbed to E1 rates at 2.048 Mbps in the early 1990s. In the United States,[1] H0 (5B+D; 384 kbps), H1 (11B+D; 768 kbps), and T1 (23B+D; 1.544 Mbps) rates are being actively considered. In other countries, 1.024 Mbps or 15B+D and 2.048 Mbps or 30B+D are being considered. These rates also play a part in mode of operation. In the full-duplex mode, full-rate bidirectional data is transmitted over one wire-pair. In the half-rate duplex, bidirectional half-rate is transmitted over two wire-pairs. In the simplex modes, twice the wire-pairs are used, but the directionality is isolated. Hence, the frequency at which loops should be characterized depends upon the HDSL rate and mode of operation. A series of scatter plots for all the loops in the 1983 loop survey database at discrete frequencies of 40, 60, 80, 120, 160, and 200 kHz is presented in (Ahamed and Lawrence, 1997).

The potential use of TWPs as high-speed digital lines reaching every subscriber at medium rates is high. If this digital capability may be economically realized, then wire-pairs become one of the most viable carriers of digital data to the homes of millions of subscribers. The limits of such wire-pairs as carriers of very high-speed data over very short distances may also considered. Accordingly, the discussion had been focused in two major areas for data distribution to the subscribers. First, in the general subscriber loop environment rates to the T1 and E1 are currently being considered. Second, for very short loops in the tight local area environment that may include PDS rates, up to 155 Mbps is feasible over very short distances (typically about 300 ft) with extremely high-quality wire-pairs (such as category 5 UTP) where the twist and insulation quality are both tightly monitored. This application of the UTP in the PDS environment is presented further in (Ahamed and Lawrence, 1997). The quality of echo cancellers and near-end cross-talk noise eventually govern the implementation and the realization of the multi-megabit and possibly fractional gigabit per second TWP data carrier systems.

4.3 TV-Cable Media

4.3.1 CATV Network Topology

Most CATV networks generally use a standard topology for the distribution of the TV channels. The *five* elements of most, older CATV networks are depicted in Figure 4.2. *First*, the head end, consisting of a transmitter and multiplexer, combines signals from satellites, special long distance antennas, local signals, local studios for community access, video machines, etc., and other signal sources. *Second*, the trunk cables and the broadband trunk amplifiers are 2 kft, going to different population centers to service various communities. *Third*, the distribution cable reaching the customer homes with bridged amplifiers boosts the signal for multiple or cluster homes with line extenders. The *fourth* element is the cable drop

---

[1] During late 1980s, the B and D rates were standardized at 64 kb/s; except for the (2B+D) rate of 144 kb/s when D is at 16 kb/s.

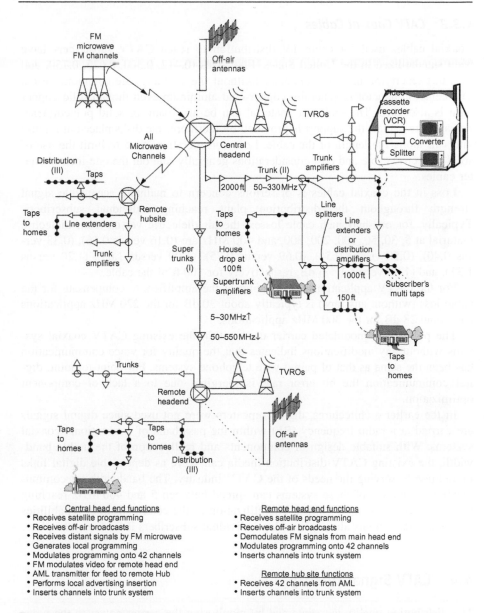

Figure 4.2 Typical CATV architecture for distribution of TV signals. Note that the fiber connections are not included.

permitting TV signals to reach the customer premises. For the *fifth*, the internal in-home wiring goes to the converter/descramblers and TV sets. The distribution system and the flexible drop account for about 90% of the actual TV-cable footage. A fiber optic supplemented architecture is discussed in Section 4.6.

4.3.2   CATV Coaxial Cables

Coaxial cables used for cable TV distribution to reach CATV subscribers have been standardized in the United States. Five sizes (0.412, 0.500, 0.625, 0.750, and 1.00 in.) specifying the outer diameter (without the cladding) are commonly used. The center conductor is generally copper-clad aluminum even though solid copper wire is also used. The dielectric material can be air, foam, or solid polyethylene. For air-core cables, the support is provided by thermoplastic disks placed at regular intervals along the length of the cable. Loss considerations tend to limit the use of solid dielectric cable and cost considerations generally rule out the one-inch diameter cables.

Loss in the coaxial cables is of serious concern to maintain acceptable signal strength throughout the distribution plant reaching individual subscribers. Typically, for one-half inch cable losses, the air dielectric versus foam dielectric material at 5, 30, 50, 100, 200, 300, and 400 MHz are (0.16 versus 0.16), (0.38 versus 0.40), (0.50 versus 0.54), (0.69 versus 0.75), (1.00 versus 1.08), (1.20 versus 1.31), and (1.39 versus 1.53) dB, respectively for 100 ft of the cable.

For the CATV applications, the spacing of the amplifiers to compensate for the cable loss (without any taps) is typically about 30 dB for the 220 MHz applications and about 28 dB for the 300 MHz applications.

The pulse code modulated carrier used within the existing CATV coaxial systems without any modifications indicates that the quality for voice communication has been the same as that of paired wire telephone systems. For point-to-point, digital communication the bit error rate is marginal due to a lack of component optimization.

In the earlier architectures, digital repeaters were not used since digital signals are carried at a radio frequency (RF) within the pass-band of conventional coaxial systems. With suitable design of components and reallocation of the usable bandwidth, the existing CATV distribution media can serve as dependable digital links in addition to serving the needs of the CATV industry. The bandwidth for communication over most of these systems can spread between 5 and 400 MHz reaching over distances of about 20 miles. The utilization of the communication capabilities of the coaxial systems already reaching individual subscribers is far from complete.

4.4   CATV Signal Quality

The distribution quality is maintained by monitoring the carrier power to the noise of the system. Most cable systems aim to maintain the carrier to noise power ratio in the order of 46 dB and maintain the two composite (second order and triple beat) signals at about or below −53 dB. The signal level at TV is on the average of about 0 dBmV or 1 mV.

Sometimes it is necessary to boost the signal quality. Occasionally, the digital video is transported over the cable. Adding fiber interconnects in the CATV network also enhances the signal quality. Analog-video fiber technology carrying

6—12 video channels is used, even though the ongoing research is for 30—40 NTSC channels over one fiber for distances in the range of 20—25 km. Currently, this technology is used for studio quality transportation of TV signals from remote earth stations, studio-to-head end video transport, etc. It is expected that when this technology matures, fibers running between nodes located at approximately the sixth trunk amplifier can directly insert broadband signals (combining 30—40 channels) into the coaxial network. Each node is thus capable of serving an area with about 1.5-mile radius. In essence, this is an inexpensive fiber backbone of the CATV network.

4.5 Digital Capabilities of CATV Systems

The cable can carry digital traffic and special services based upon the data exchanges and two-way digital communication such as video, text, electronic publishing, home security, and digital audio programming. However, to date, the public response to such data service offering is very low. Some CATV companies that had offered such services have retracted them because of the lack of demand. Thus, the CATV network is focusing most of the attention on efficiently and economically carrying video programs. For the present, it appears that the CATV networks are likely to remain entertainment oriented rather than becoming competitive in data transport and communication type of services.

4.6 Hybrid Fiber Coax Systems

Fiber capacity and its economic advantage to long-haul multiple gigabits of information are well documented in the telecommunications field. Fiber and its impact in the trunk and carrier systems are well suited, even in the older and more established POTS network. However, the capacity for the newer multimedia services (needing megabits per second data capacity) still remains to be completely exploited. The proposed HFC systems take advantage of providing a "fiber-backbone" network with ultra-high capacity and quality. This carries data from video information providers, and broadband switches for entertainment, broadcast CATV, distance learning, etc., to "fiber nodes" and then span the "last couple of miles" via coaxial cables to reach the residences and business.

Coaxial cables for CATV reached over 50 million households in the United States in 1990, thus enabling 55% of households to access cable television. Immediately 87% of the households could have been connected to the existing cable services. The rate of growth is sustained at 1% per year thus offering a high potential for services (such as CATV, ATV, HDTV, video, picture, multimedia teleconferencing, interactive and participative video games, etc.) to grow in the residential markets. Providing access via cable and distribution via fiber combines the superb capabilities of both media for integrated broadband networks.

All the HFC networks are not likely to make a quantum leap toward becoming entirely digital and all at once. Most of the 1990s HFC systems used analog-video techniques through the end of the decade. The evolution of the analog CATV laser (typically known as distributed feedback laser) permits the direct modulation of amplitude modulated multiplexed signals. In 1994, these lasers permitted 80−110 channel capacity, improved end of life sensitivity, analog/digital capability, higher splitting ratios, and optical redundancy. Laser technology for CATV applications is still being customized to the fibers of the HFC systems. In a laboratory environment at room temperature, quadrature phase-shift keying techniques, as far back as mid 1990s have been used to demonstrate up to 60 channels through 24 km of fiber.

The deployment of fiber at the head end of a CATV distribution facility (see Figure 4.2) as fiber optic super-trunks (instead of coaxial super-trunks) brings a range of about 12 miles of passive transmission to the fiber-optic hub. Typically, the maximum number of trunk cascades reduces from 32 to about 12. If a fiber is developed to provide a fiber backbone in the CATV environment, it is foreseen that the maximum number of trunk cascades reduces still further to 4. In the fiber to the feeder architecture, about 500 residences would be served by one optical hub receiving optical signals from the head end. The overall number of traditional super-trunk, trunk, and feeder amplifiers would be dramatically reduced, thus

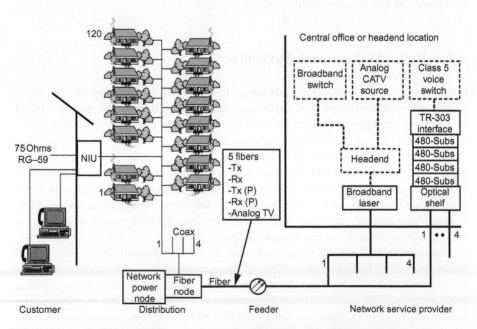

Figure 4.3 HFC system architecture. P, phone; NIU, network interface unit; Tx, transmit fiber; Rx, receive fiber; CATV, cable television; TR-303, transmit/receive interface in Class 5 switch; RGn, cable type.

improving the video quality, the power requirement, and also the maintenance of the CATV plant. The replacement of trunks and super-trunks with fiber has been an ongoing process in the United States since 1988–1989. A typical architecture of a HFC is shown in Figure 4.3. Here, the fiber node uses an optical transceiver, and a linear bidirectional split band RF amplifier for the coaxial segment to handle the upstream/downstream signals.

As can be seen, there is ample bandwidth for further application in the fiber part of the HFC network. A bottleneck exists in the cable part of the HFC network because the coaxial bus between the fiber node and the 120 homes has to accommodate an entire bandwidth from 5 to 750 MHz, since 5–50 MHz can be used by conventional upstream and telephone signals. The overall broadband access architecture proposed (Ahamed and Lawrence, 1997) to/from the network service providers (with head end, broadband data, and telephone services) from/to the individual home within the HFC network is depicted in Figure 4.3.

Appropriate switching and software control in the newer network will permit symmetric and asymmetric flow of network information. Digital and programmed control (via stored program control in the switching systems) will permit high reliability and high quality of a mixture of customized telecommunication and entertainment services. It is the object of the fiber-coax network to bring in the impact of digital technology and to carry a broad spectrum of multimedia services to the household rather than CATV or ATV services that plain old cable TV brings to the public.

In a sense, this network is likely to become the successor of the POTS network, making the existing cables serve as access and/or distribution systems and making room at the top for fiber to carry much higher capacity data. However, the analogy stops here since CATV systems are not generally bidirectional to the same extent as POTS networks. Some of the services (such as distance learning, video-on-demand, enhanced pay-per-view, broadcast CATV, video-catalog rather than bidirectional interactive TV, video-conferencing, and video-telephony) become more compatible with the new network. Converting the existing CATV plant for complete bidirectionality is expensive if not impossible. For services needing complete bidirectionality, other networks architectures incorporating microwave, all fiber networks with FTTH or FTTC become more appealing for high bandwidth. For the very low bandwidth voice/facsimile application, the cellular radio network comes in as a strong contender.

The major drawbacks of the existing POTS and CATV networks are eliminated in the newer fiber-coax network. *Five* major factors that make the older telephone network unsuitable for multimedia services are: (a) the narrow bandwidth, (b) labor-intensive nature for changes or new services, (c) relative inflexibility in the type of video/interactive services, (d) high initial and operating cost, and (e) limited switching and interconnect capability. Further, the three major factors that make the CATV networks unsuitable for multimedia services are: (i) it had been mostly analog and carrier modulated and (ii) unidirectional. Earlier CATV systems were less reliable than the POTS or computer networks but are becoming competitive with other network.

4.7   Networks of the Future

The evolution of next generation networks is an economic proposition rather than a technological process. From the current perspective, the network and processor speeds are sufficient to conduct most of the data and information-based services satisfactorily. New demand for services from the medical, educational, and security from the social sector need the professional touch that the computer and network scientists have demonstrated in the past. Many revered laws of economics exist for the corporate entities to invest in the development of the medical ware, education modules, and security software. Typically, the expected rate of return on the capital invested needs to be justified to the politicians, senate members, and the economists.

4.7.1   Political and Socioeconomic Forces

Truly, the economic climate of different countries varies drastically and the temperament of decision makers can be volatile. In many circumstances, dramatic strides in modern network installations have been made because of the political leaders and their attitude toward computer and network technologies. In small countries, wireless networks and ADSL technologies appear as the most viable contender (e.g., Bosnia and Herzegovina). In other countries where railroad systems are extensive (e.g., Malaysia), planting the fiber along the tracks offers an edge. Fiber and wireless technologies in combination can offer the advantages of rapid installation and cost in medium-sized countries.

In most cases, the development of network in a country is a well-planned and evolutionary process. In the stable countries, the networks of the future bear an entrepreneurial flavor. The role of government can become subsidiary. In the haphazardly developed countries, the evolution of intelligent network services can only be retarded.

In the overly driven profit-seeking countries, the abuse of network flourishes as the spread spam, false advertisements, and deception increases. Truly optimum development of a network to serve the needs of any society or community is a delicate balance between attitude of citizens and a good legal framework.

4.7.2   Abuse of Intelligent Networks and Medical Machines

Intelligent networks can be abused more effectively and in a more devious fashion. The programs can also be tailored to suit the client. After all, Nixon tried to cover up Watergate and Bush tried to hide the nonexistent weapons of mass destruction in Iraq by trying to sneak deception in news networks.

Medical networks seem to follow a similar track but on much smaller scale. In a society where moderation is the norm, medical networks can bring the best of medical services, drugs, and therapy to the community. The parallelism exists for other countries where excessive profiteering from the medical services can lead to confusion, though not chaos. All the laws of microeconomics govern the installation of medical machines and networks.

Intelligent medical networks can also be programmed to propose expensive alternatives, to suggest unnecessary surgeries, and to prescribe only proprietary and expensive drugs. When such practices are camouflaged in the execution of medical application programs, the malpractice of the medical informatics profession can become convincing to the less literate patient community. The role of legal policies becomes evident, and traditionally these corrective mechanisms are much slower and tedious to be operational.

4.8   Conclusions

The needs of the cable TV subscribers had been substantially different from the needs of the subscriber for information and intelligent network services. Some of the newer services (such as shop-at-home and video-on-demand) have features that overlap video and intelligent network services; they have not established a firm-hold in the communication industry. It is a fond hope of the intelligent network service providers that such services can be met by intelligent wide-band networks (such as broadband ISDN and ATM). The possible entry of the fiber-coaxial networks as viable carriers in the multimedia services to the home, makes the status quo of traditional analog CATV networks less and less likely to be able to provide a rich variety of intelligent network services.

The impact of digital encoding of video information and the HDTV technology are likely to have a strong impact on the TV broadcast and TV production industry. This effect is likely to persist throughout the decade and well into the twenty-first century. The slow and insidious trend in the TV environment is to go digital like most of the other communication systems. The rewards of digital TV environment are already documented and the HDTV picture quality rates dramatically superior to the analog TV quality. When this technology reaches a viable commercial status, the emerging high capacity all-digital networks are well equipped to bear the digital video signals both for transport (typically the fiber-optic backbone and ATM technology) and for distribution (typically fiber to home facility, fiber-coax facility, or perhaps a new digitized CATV network environment).

Intelligent network services over most of the commercial media have been flourishing over the last two decades. The role of all metallic media (of the past) is less promising than the role of mixed network technologies (e.g., fiber and wireless, fiber and coaxial, and satellite and coaxial). Providing medical and intelligent medical service over metallic media appears less than desirable (except in a few remote locations and small countries where ADSL + technologies are deployed) in view of the dependability and security expected in the medical field. In essence, some form of broadband service is more desirable than the POTS.

References

1. Ahamed SV, Lawrence VB: *Intelligent broadband multimedia networks*, Boston, MA, 1996, Kluwer Academic Press.

2. Ahamed SV, Lawrence VB: *Design and engineering of intelligent communication systems*, Boston, MA, 1997, Kluwer Academic Publishers.
3. ITU G.992.5 (01/09/2009), an ITU standard. A survey of recent Internet articles for most countries ranging from Austria to UAE at http://en.wikipedia.org/wiki/G.992.5, about 64 countries have the ADSL +2 services offered over "bonded ports" (to reduce cross talk effects). Further information on the ADSL +2, see http://www.itu.int/rec/T-REC-G.992.5/e. About 6 countries have the ADSL +2 services offered over "bonded ports" (to reduce cross talk effects). For technical discussion of ADSL see Chapter 6, Reference 4.2.
4. Bell Telephone Laboratories: *Transmission systems for communications*, Winston-Salem, NC, 1982, Western Electric Co. also see Bell Telephone Laboratories: *Engineering and operations in the bell system*, IN, 1982, Western Electric Co.
5. AT&T Telecommunications Transmission Engineering, Volume 2 Facilities, New York, NY, 1985. Also seeBell Laboratories: *Engineering and operations in the bell system*, 1977, Western Electric Co., Chapter 9.

5 Optical Fiber in Modern Networks

5.1 Introduction

The impact of fiber on the communication industry is as profound as the impact of silicon on the electronics industry. The later innovations for refining the purity of glass and for the capacity to be pulled in dual cylindrical fibers of different refractive indices offered the breakthrough for its deployment as global data carrier. This chapter presents the use of optical fiber for carrying all types of data, including medical data, images, information, and knowledge.

More recently, plastic fiber is a viable contender for very short distances and for instrumentation. Use of plastic fiber may offer special advantage in the medical field, and we propose special half-pulse width data encoding to get a better signal to noise performance.

The possibility of using lightwave for communication was proposed as far back as 1880 by Alexander Graham Bell; after 26 years John Tyndall (Reville) performed the light transmission experiments over a dielectric conductor before the Royal Society in England in 1854. Optical transmission was seriously considered during the early 1960s after the invention of lasers at Bell Laboratories, in 1960. The multilayered glass structure was suggested during the mid-1960s, and a rough specimen of fiber with about 20 dB/km loss was produced by Corning Glass in 1970. Optical systems (Senior, 2008) have been functioning with increasing capacity and sophistication. Large capacity, immunity from stray electromagnetic interference, low weight, and cost are the chief attractions of the optical fiber waveguide (simply stated, optical fiber) medium. The highest quality single-mode fiber drawn during the late 1980s offers 0.16 dB/km loss at 1.55 μm wavelength and less than 0.35 dB/km at 1.30 μm wavelength. These lower loss limits are due to intrinsic scattering in the silica glass rather than manufacturing tolerances in drawing the fiberglass. The chromatic dispersion is also equally attractive at approximately 15 ps/km-nm for the explanation of the units of measurements for chromatic dispersion in the low loss window of 1.5 μm (with zero dispersion at 1.3 μm). Specially designed fibers further reduce the overall dispersion to about 17 ps/km-nm at 1.5 μm band and prove satisfactory for laser sources without chirp or drifting wavelength of the photonic energy emitted. These two effects, light loss (or attenuation) and chromatic smearing (or delay distortion effects), eventually limit the product of bit rate and distance through the fiber carrying information. Since there is only a single mode in the single-mode fibers, the light through these

Intelligent Networks: Recent Approaches and Applications in Medical Systems.
DOI: http://dx.doi.org/10.1016/B978-0-12-416630-1.00005-4

fibers does not suffer modal dispersion effects but is susceptible to chromatic dispersion effects.

Fibers are dielectric waveguides. A subset of the classic Maxwell's equations (Stratton, 1941) lead to the fields that coexist in the fiber. Since the material is (largely) linear and isotropic without free circulating currents and devoid of free charges, the basic equations for the signal propagation are derived from the basic Maxwell's equations that relate E, B, H, D, and the traditional relations between D and E, B and H. The two scalar wave equations governing the distribution of the electric and magnetic intensity are as follows:

$$\nabla^2 E = \mu\varepsilon \frac{\partial^2 E}{\partial t^2} \quad \text{and} \quad \nabla^2 H = \mu\varepsilon \frac{\partial^2 H}{\partial t^2}$$

From the applications point of view, the complexity of the detailed analysis (Reville) for such field distributions in general environment is unwarranted since the fiber structure is cylindrical. Considerable simplification can be gained by the approximate, but adequate, model known as geometrical optics, due to the cylindrical structures of the core and the cladding. To explain the concept, consider a fiber with distinctly different optical densities for the core and cladding. At the interface, there are two effects: refraction and reflection. Both affect the propagation of light. When the optical density is graded as a function of its diameter, a combination of the refraction and reflection along the radius effect the recapture and the propagation of light through the fiber core.

Three crucial layers of the fiber are the core or the inner most layer and the cladding and the outer protective jacket (Marcuse, 1972; Barnoski, 1989). The core and cladding together provide the optical environment for the lightwave(s) through the fiber. The cladding is tailored to be an integral part of the fiber geometry to contain and propagate the light. The core has a slightly higher optical density (index of refraction) than that of the cladding. The optical density of the core material or silica glass is higher (1.46−1.5) than that of the air from where the light is incident. This affects the propagation in two ways: first, the velocity in the denser medium is reduced; second, the direction is changed by the conventional rules of refraction. The net effect of the two is a realignment of the rays of light toward the axis of reference or the axis of the fiber.

At the core−cladding boundary, *two* types of rays exist. *First*, consider a ray of light at the core−cladding boundary that is refracted in the cladding and is bent toward the axis of reference. This ray travels some distance in the cladding until it approaches the cladding−jacket boundary where the absorption loss is high, due to the lossy portion of the outermost cladding, and due to the scattering of the ray at the rough cladding−jacket interface. This ray, which enters the cladding and moves toward the jacket, is lost and will not appear to any measurable extent at the end of the fiber.

However, the *second* type of ray of light, which is incident at the core−cladding boundary at a low angle of incidence (i.e., with respect to the axis of the fiber), does not enter the cladding at all, but is reflected internally and guided toward the axis of the fiber. Hence, the extent of capture of the light in the core depends upon the angle of incidence at the core–cladding boundary. The laws of reflection dominate the propagation in the recapture of the light within the core, and this is the carrier of information to the far end of the fiber. The limiting angle for the cutoff for reflection to prevail over refraction depends upon the relative difference between the optical densities of the core and cladding.

The problem can also be completely stated by considering three propagating electromagnetic waves: incident wave at the core–cladding boundary; refracted wave propagating away from the boundary; and reflected wave that reenters the core. The boundary conditions from both sides of the interface may be enforced, and simply enough, such an algebraic exercise leads to Snell's law, which asserts that the ratio of the optical densities equals the ratios of the cosines of the angle of incident ray and the angle of trajectory ray. Stated simply with respect to Figure 5.1, the relation becomes

$$n_{core} \cdot \cos(\theta_{core}) = n_{cladding} \cdot \cos(\theta_{cladding})$$

or the reciprocal relation

$$n_2/n_1 = \text{cosine } \theta_1 / \text{cosine } \theta_2$$

subscript 1 refers to the core and subscript 2 refers to the cladding. The critical angle is simply inverse cosine (n_2/n_1) these ratios (n_2/n_1) can be made very close to

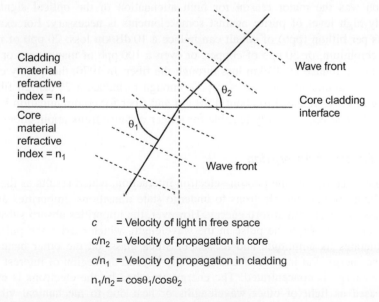

c = Velocity of light in free space

c/n_2 = Velocity of propagation in core

c/n_1 = Velocity of propagation in cladding

$n_1/n_2 = \cos\theta_1/\cos\theta_2$

Figure 5.1 Refraction at the interface of core and cladding.

unity (typically the value is 0.99), thus most of the light gets trapped or internally reflected totally in the core, and is received at the far end of the fiber. The critical angle in this case is as follows:

$$\theta_c = 8.109°, \text{ at the core} - \text{cladding boundary}$$

and it signifies that rays of light incident from the core with an angle $<8.109°$ (with the longitudinal axis of the fiber) will be totally internally reflected. Extending this computation of the critical angle, the rays that can possibly subtend an angle of $<8.109°$ at the core−cladding boundary can enter the core (from the air) only if they subtend an angle $<(n_{core} \, 8.109°)$. Stated alternatively, the critical angle, θ_c, in this case is approximated as follows:

$$\theta_c = 11.84° \text{ to } 12.16°, \text{ at the air-core boundary}$$

with the longitudinal axis of the fiber for typical fiber waveguides, since the typical values of n_{core}, lie between 1.46 and 1.5.

5.2   Properties of Silica Glass Fiber Material

5.2.1   Attenuation

The loss of optical energy that a light pulse experiences as it travels down the fiber is called attenuation. Two causes for the loss of energy are absorption and scattering. In the early fabrication of fibers (mid-1960s to early 1970s), impurities by absorption was the major reason for high attenuation of the optical signal. An extremely high level of purity against some elements is necessary. For example, two parts per billion (ppb) of cobalt can induce a 10 dB/km loss; 20 ppb of nickel, iron, or chromium, or 50 ppb of copper, or even a 100 ppb of manganese or vanadium can each induce 10 dB/km loss through the fiber. In 1970, the quality control of the fiber manufacture process was poor enough to induce a 20 dB/km fiber. In 1972, the loss was reduced to about 4 dB/km and fiber for communication became scientifically and economically feasible for longer distance trunk applications.

5.2.2   Effects of Absorption

Absorption is caused by the photon−electron interaction, which results as the propagating light prompts the electrons to undergo state transitions. Impurities and the silica glass material both absorb energy. However, the impurities absorb substantial amounts of energy from the pulse in the wavelength, which carries the pulse, and thus obliterates its amplitude and its shape. Silica glass, on the other hand, does absorb the energy, but in a waveband generally beyond the region of interest where the pulse energy is concentrated. The energy absorbed by the electrons is eventually released as light of other wavelengths or heat due to mechanical vibration within the material.

5.2.3 Effects of Scattering

Scattering, as the term implies, is caused by the energy in the rays that leaves the fiber due to the imperfection of the geometry of the fiber. The measure of the imperfection is its relation to the wavelength of the light through the fiber. Thus, at the imperfection, a certain amount of light leaves the fiber at the same wavelength as it reaches the imperfection.

Silicon dioxide (SiO_2 or silica glass) is a noncrystalline material. The atoms are arranged in a somewhat random fashion where any incremental volume of the material does not hold the same number of atoms. The light through the glass does interact with the electrons in the material however small the interaction may be. Rayleigh scattering caused by the weak interaction (absorption and reradiation at the same wavelength, but delayed in phase) of the light with the electrons in the glass structure represents a theoretical lower limit on the attenuation of the particular type of glass for a given wavelength. A typical loss curve at various wavelengths is depicted in Figure 5.2. The Rayleigh scattering limit for 0.85 μm wavelength (from GaAlAs light sources) is about 1.6 dB/km and varies inversely with the fourth power of the wavelength. However, the lower limit of the loss is about 0.5 dB/km at 1.3 μm and less than 0.2 dB/km at 1.55 μm. The newer sources of light and matching optical detectors have been investigated and successfully fabricated and deployed for high-quality fibers fabricated with 0.16 dB/km loss at 1.55 μm light.

The presence of the OH radical (water) offers strong absorbing resonance at about 1.4 μm wavelength. This "water peak" effect is due to the lingering presence of some of the OH radical in the fiber core material. Total eradication of this peak

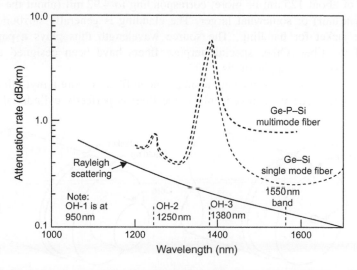

Figure 5.2 Typical loss curves for silica glass fibers. The lowest theoretical loss (about 0.16 dB/km) occurs at about 1550 nm where the scattering loss and the absorptive loss are about the same.

has not been successful, and the fiber system designers avoid the 1.4 μm wavelength for this reason for silica glass fiber core material. At wavelengths greater than 1.6 μm, the absorption loss in silica glass in and by itself starts to increase rapidly, and viability of optical systems using this material does not exist.

This does not mean that the other materials have the same restrictions (OH and Rayleigh limits) and that they cannot be used for other types of fibers. Some materials offer a theoretical loss limit of 0.01 dB/km, but the practical use within a scientific and economic system has yet to be demonstrated.

5.3 Single-Mode Fiber

5.3.1 Physical Features

The fiber core made of silica glass has a diameter of about 5 μm. This diameter corresponds to 0.19685 mil (1 mil = thousandths of an inch) for single-mode fibers (Figure 5.3A), which sustain a single mode of propagation through it. The wavelength of the light through the fiber is generally chosen to be a fraction of the core diameter. For the fine core diameter or single-mode fibers, the diameter is generally a small multiple of the wavelength of the light through it.

The cladding has a refractive index or optical density slightly lower than that of the core. The difference of the optical densities can range between a fraction of a percent and a few percentage points. However, the discussion to follow asserts the need for proper proportioning of the optical densities in relation to the ratio of the fiber diameter to the wavelength of the light through it. The cladding diameter is of the order of about 125 μm or more, corresponding to 4.92 mil (about the diameter of a human hair) or somewhat larger. The cladding is generally surrounded by a protective jacket for handling. The source wavelength thus plays a part in the choice of the fiber. Other special purpose fibers have been designed and constructed for particular applications.

The perfect single mode through a single-mode fiber is more a myth than a reality. The single mode is achieved only if the fiber is perfectly cylindrical, and the

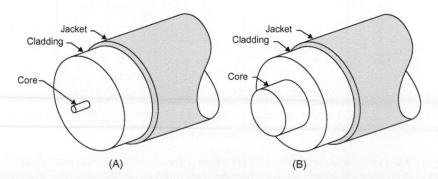

(A)   (B)

Figure 5.3 Physical configurations of the single (A) and multimode (B) fibers.

manufacturing tolerances (however small) force the tiniest modal degradation or polarization. Both modes traverse the length of the fiber at very slightly different velocities, and this effect, though very small, does linger on as the polarization-mode dispersion effect.

5.4   Multimode Fiber

5.4.1   Physical Features

The core diameter of the multimode fiber is much large ranging from 10 times the wavelength to a 100 times the diameter of the wavelength of the light through it. This has a profound effect upon the attenuation and dispersion of light through it because rays of light trapped in different modes travel different distances through the fiber, and thus the extent of attenuation and dispersion will not be the same. The cladding is thinner and has about the same external diameter; and it is enclosed in a protective jacket like the single-mode fiber.

5.4.2   Physical Makeup

Typically, numerous optical fibers are bundled to make up the inner core of an installation cable. Circular (Figure 5.3B) and ribbon structures are used.

For the circular cables, the strength members are at the center, with the fibers around the periphery, with a sheath to hold the entire structure. For the ribbon structure, encapsulation is used to fill the space between a bundle of fibers and the outermost jacket, which also holds the strength members.

As many as 12 ribbons with 12 fibers in each have been fabricated and enclosed in circular copper-clad steel sheath helical wiring for strength members with an outer diameter of 1.2 cm. This ribbon structure permits easy gang splicing of the different ribbons.

5.5   Effect of Larger Core Diameter

Now consider a different geometry with a much larger core diameter, typically 50 μm, $n_2/n_1 = 0.99$, and the same source of light with a typical wavelength of 0.66 μm in the core. The value of D/λ is 1/75 radian or $0.8°$. The value of θ_{max} (for a fiber with cosine $\theta_{max} = n_2/n_1 = 0.99$) is about 8.1°, and there are 10 rays (i.e., 8.1/0.8 since there are no fractional modes) that can coexist in each direction away from the axis, thus leading to 20 rays in two dimensions. For the three-dimensional fiber, the total number becomes about 20×20 or 400. With this relation between the parameters for the fiber, many hundreds of modes can exist, giving rise to multi-modality in the fiber; and every one of these modes has some finite extent of propagation delay through the fiber.

5.5.1 *Effects of Optical Energy Distribution in a Waveband*

The second major reason for the pulse spreading is due to the presence of optical energy at numerous wavelengths in the light emitted from LEDs and perhaps a chirp in the laser source. Different optical wavelengths travel at different speeds. The range of light from LEDs and other noncoherent light sources may become quite broad (over 5% of its nominal value). The optical density or the index of refraction of silica glass is sensitive to the wavelength and is evident as the prism effect upon white light. This effect shows up because the propagation speed will vary with wavelength if the second derivative of the index of refraction with respect to wavelength is not zero. This effect, known as material dispersion, is measured in ns/(km-nm) and is characterized by the variation in delay (measured as ns/km of fiber length) with respect to the change in wavelength (nm). In Figure 5.4, the typical material dispersion effect is plotted for silica glass over a range of wavelengths. It is easy to see that the material dispersion effect can be sizable (in fact exceeding the modal delay spreading in graded index fibers) under certain conditions. At 0.85 μm wavelength, the dispersion is about 0.1 ns/km-nm. If the optical band spread from an incoherent LED is 50 nm, then the pulse spread between the two extremes of the wavelength is 5 ns/km. When the pulse width is only 20 ns at 50 Mbps, then pulse spread due to material dispersion becomes significant.

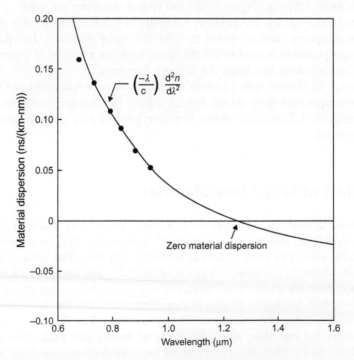

Figure 5.4 Typical material dispersion features for silica glass fibers.

The spectral spread of coherent light sources (laser) is small, and the effects of material dispersion can be low. However, silica glass offers one other attractive feature; at 1.3 μm, the material dispersion crosses zero value and the optical attenuation is low (0.5 dB/km; a low enough value, though not the least). For this reason, many lightwave systems are built with components around a nominal wavelength of 1.3 μm.

It is possible to design single-mode fibers in which the waveguide propagation effects can counter the material dispersion effects. The net effect is that the frequency of net zero dispersion is shifted. Also, single-mode fibers with uniformly low dispersion effects over a significant band of wavelengths can be fabricated. This type of fiber design permits the concept of multiplexing numerous channels over preassigned optical wavelengths through the same fiber, thus leading to wavelength division multiplexing (WDM) of the wavelength parameter through the fiber with low dispersion of the pulses in the many wavelength bands.

The spectral spread of coherent light sources (laser) is small, and the effects of material dispersion can be low. However, silica glass offers one other attractive feature; at 1.3 μm, the material dispersion crosses zero value and the optical attenuation is low (0.5 dB/km; a low enough value, though not the least). For this reason, many of the earlier lightwave systems were built with components around a nominal wavelength of 1.3 μm.

It is possible to design single-mode fibers in which the waveguide propagation effects can counter the material dispersion effects. The net effect is that the frequency of net zero dispersion is shifted. Also, single-mode fibers with uniformly low dispersion effects over a significant band of wavelengths can be fabricated. This type of fiber design permits the concept of multiplexing numerous channels over preassigned optical wavelengths through the same fiber, thus leading to WDM of the wavelength parameter through the fiber with low dispersion of the pulses in the many wavelength bands.

As the transmission capabilities are pushed higher and higher, the optical properties other than transmission loss become increasingly important for the fiber. Representative of these properties are the dispersion (chromatic and polarization) effects and scattering (stimulated Raman, stimulated Brillouin, cross-phase modulation, and four-photon mixing). These limitations affect the various optical systems differently and each system needs to be simulated, studied, and experimentally verified.

Bit rates, distance, transmitted power, and the number of channels through the fiber influence the ultimate capacity of an optical system. Once again, the optical system is much more than the fiber and the system components (the sources, the multiplexers, the detectors, the de-multiplexers, etc.); each exerts its own influence in an individual and in a combinatorial fashion, on the performance of the system. Good quality fibers offer attenuation loss of about $0.16-0.2$ dB/km at $\lambda = 1.55$ μm and $0.32-0.35$ dB/km at $\lambda = 1.3$ μm. For this reason, the fabrication of complex lightwave system is an elaborate computer-assisted iterative process that minimizes the bit error rate (BER, typically $<10^{-9}-2 \times 10^{-10}$) of up to 20 Gbps over $80-100$ km. The eye closure penalty is a good measure for these optical data transmission systems. Computer simulation (Elrefaie and Romeiser, 1986; Ahamed and Lawrence, 1989) systems yield accurate time domain results and waveshape generated after transmission through elaborate optical systems.

Although it is possible to limit the effects of dispersion (Elrefaie et al., 1988; Wagner and Elrefaie, 1988; Ahamed, 1988), modal delay lingers on. This effect cannot be canceled by the two (i.e., waveguide and material) dispersion effects. The total delay distortion (when both modal delay and dispersion are present) is the square root of the sum of the squares (of the individual spreads in nanoseconds per kilometer).

The transmission capacity of appropriately designed fiber far exceeds the capacity of other media. Even if the fiber is used to a capacity that is four orders of magnitude less than its ultimate capacity, it surpasses other media for high-volume communication systems. Existing communication systems that have been deployed by national and international communications networks have other restrictions, such as switching and intelligence, to channel the fiber capacity. On the national scene, fibers have been routinely introduced for interoffice high data capacity channels in the United States, Canada, Europe, and Japan. Optical rates of 565 Mbps and OC-12 rates of 622.080 Mbps have been achieved by commercial systems.

Optical amplification adds another dimension of gain and cost reduction in the deployment of fibers in long haul transoceanic networks. Some of these gains are currently realized (see Sections 1.5.1 and 1.5.2) in the transoceanic FO cables now being deployed throughout the global networks around the world.

5.6 From Glass to Plastic

Plastic fiber optics media is viable for small networks. The current applications include data distribution in aircraft and automobiles. Plastic fiber systems being an order of magnitude less expensive than silica fiber-optic systems and being more robust have applications in other traditional data communication systems. Possible applications are in high-rise office buildings and premises distribution architectures. The signal to noise ratio (SNR) for optical rates up to 2.5 Gb/s and for link lengths up to 5 km is feasible, even though the signal level becomes too low for the PIN diodes. The quality of components affects the performance dramatically and their impact should be simulated in detail.

The two categories (poly(methyl methacrylate), PMMA and perflorinated, PF) of commercial plastic fibers are readily available. The simulations for the PMMA plastic fiber are generally available (Kahande and Ahamed, 2008) to offer a window and envision other applications for this new breed of optical fibers.

Acrylics such as PMMA is a thermoplastic material that is transparent, mostly unaffected by moisture and offers favorable strength-to-weight ratio. Plexiglas®, Lucite®, and Acrylite® are generally classified as acrylics and offer high light transmission with a refractive index of about 1.49. It can be easily heat molded without loss of clarity. Prolonged exposure to moisture, or even total immersion in water, does not drastically affect the mechanical or optical properties of acrylics. Most commercial acrylics have been UV stabilized to withstand weather and to resist prolonged exposure to sunlight. The signal attenuation in the older PMMA plastic optical fibers (POFs) can be ranged between 90 and 100 dB/km in the 550 nm range. The attenuation can be as high as 450–500 times that for glass fibers (0.16–0.2 dB at 1550 m) and for this reason, the viable fiber length is correspondingly shorter. For the older PF POF, the attenuation can be ranged from about 25 to 75 dB in the 1000 nm range, and about 140–370 times that of glass fiber. When the PMMA fiber length is short (<100 m), the performance is satisfactory (SNR in the range of 44–26 dB), though not comparable with the performance of silica glass fibers.

Table 5.1 provides the simulated results (Kahande and Ahamed, 2008) for various optical data rates and fiber lengths with full-width pulse encoding and the cheaper LED optical source. A typical eye diagram for this type of plastic fiber-optic transmission system is shown in Figure 5.5. Table 5.2 provides the simulated results for various optical data rates and fiber lengths with half-width pulse encoding and laser optical source. A typical eye diagram for this type of plastic fiber-optic transmission system is shown in Figure 5.6. The variation in the design of these inexpensive POF systems can provide a significant change in the SNR (and the dependability and the BER of the system) at the detector.

With longer lengths of PMMA fibers, the clarity does not suffer but the signal strength becomes too low for any recovery of the transmitted signal after 1 km of fiber length. At 5 km and at 10 Gb/s, the system becomes entirely unacceptable for any serious consideration. The noise due to the PMMA fiber *per se* depends on the bit rate and fiber length and drops precipitously from 5 Gb/s to 10 Gb/s at the 5 Km.

The WDM alternative for POF systems has not been studied even though the simulation platform is capable of providing all the necessary results. It is not evident if the WDM techniques are viable and/or desirable for POFs.

Table 5.1 Binary Code, Full-Width Pulses, High-Quality LED, and PMMA Fiber

Fiber Length (m)	Rate (Gb/s)	SNR in dB						
		Encoder (Gr 1)	Source LEDs (Gr 1)	Filter (Gr 1)	Fiber PMMA	PIN (Gr 1)	Detector (Gr 1)	Comments: Gr 1 Is the Best Grade in Current Databases
50	1.75	394	43.5	36	35.3	30.3	28.7	Marginal
50	2.0	394	37.3	31	30.7	27.3	26.0	Acceptable?
100	1.75	394	43.5	36	36.0	30.3	28.7	Marginal
100	2.0	394	37.3	31	30.8	27.2	26.0	Acceptable?

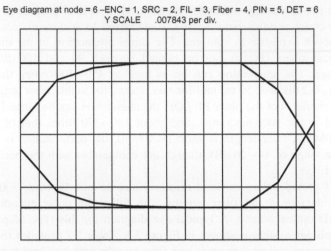

Eye diagram at node = 6 –ENC = 1, SRC = 2, FIL = 3, Fiber = 4, PIN = 5, DET = 6
Y SCALE   .007843 per div.

Figure 5.5 Typical eye diagram with full-width pulse encoding for plastic fiber-optic transmission system.

Table 5.2 Binary Code, Half-Width Pulses, Laser Source, and PMMA Fiber

Fiber Length (m)	Rate (Gb/s)	SNR in dB						Comments: Gr 1 Is the Best Grade in Current Databases
		Encoder (Gr 1)	Source (Laser)	Filter (Gr 1)	Fiber Type PMMA	PIN (Gr 1)	Detector (Gr 1)	
50	1.0	394	394	135	129.8	40.17	40.12	Good
50	1.25	394	394	135	132.0	40.17	40.12	Good
50	2.0	394	394	135	131.6	40.17	40.17	Good
100	1.0	394	394	135	129.9	40.38	40.23	Acceptable
100	2.0	394	394	135	129.9	40.38	40.23	Acceptable
100	2.5	394	394	135	128.1	40.38	40.23	Acceptable

5.7 Conclusions

High-quality silica glass fiber-optic systems provide dependable and accurate error-free transportation of medical (or any) bulk data. The bandwidth of optical systems can be tailored to the need of the medical application. In most commercial networks, the quality of service (i.e., latency time and BER) is negotiable. Dedicated fiber-optic networks linking medical facilities over local or metropolitan areas

Eye diagram at node = 6 –ENC = 1, SRC = 2, FIL = 3, Fiber = 4, PIN = 5, DET = 6
Y SCALE   .0031763 Per div.

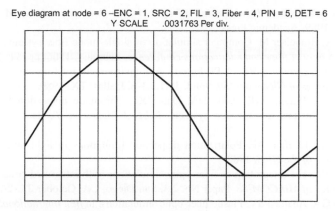

Figure 5.6 Typical eye diagram with half-width pulse encoding for plastic fiber-optic transmission system.

provide the best service, and network links and services offered by commercial network operators provide adequate service for most applications.

Plastic fibers do not degrade the signal over short distances and are suitable for transmitting medical data. The signal attenuation can pose a problem when the medical facilities are widely distributed. When the cost of the system is not a serious factor, existing local area links (if any) may be deployed. When bandwidth requirement is a serious factor, inexpensive plastic fiber systems provide a possible solution. The design optimization strategy for POFs needs to be evolved much like the design strategy for the silica optical fibers or the digital subscriber lines. Theoretical studies coupled to an intelligent and automated computer-aided design (Kahande and Ahamed, 2008) platform provide the basis for standardization of the possible architectures and the ideal characteristics for the components. A study of possible applications, architectures, and components characteristics will provide the POF industry to mature as a viable contender in a targeted segment of data communications market.

References

1. Reville W: *Life and work of John Tyndall*, Cork, University College. Available from < http://understandingscience.ucc.ie/pages/sci_johntyndall.htm > . Accessed february 2013.
2. Senior JM: *Optical fiber communications: principles and practice*, ed 3, Englewood Cliffs, NJ, 2008, Prentice Hall.
3. Stratton JA: *Electromagnetic theory*, New York, 1941, McGraw Hill Book Company.
4. Marcuse D: *Light transmission optics*, New York, 1972, Van Nostrand Reinhold Company.

5. Barnoski MK, editor: *Fundamentals of optical fiber communications*, ed 2, London, England, 1989, Academic Press.
6. Elrefaie A, Romeiser M: Computer simulation of single-mode fiber systems, conference record. In *optical fiber communications conference*, February, 1986, pp. 54–56.
7. Ahamed SV, Lawrence VB: A PC based CAD environment for fiber-optic simulations. In *Proceedings of Globecom '89*, vol 2, 19.1.5.1-6, Dallas, TX, 1989.
8. Elrefaie AF, Wagner RE, Atlas DA, Daut DG: Chromatic dispersion limitations in coherent lightwave transmission systems, *IEEE J Lightwave Technol* 6(5):704–709, 1989.
9. Wagner RE, Elrefaie AF: Polarization dispersion limitations in lightwave systems. In *Proceedings of the OFC*, 1988.
10. Ahamed SV: The integration of fiber-optic simulations with integrated circuit design. In *Proceedings of MILCOM'88*, Paper No. 2.3, San Diego, CA, October 23–26, 1988.
11. Kahande GA, Ahamed SV: Plastic fiber-optic simulations. In *fifth international conference on information technology new generations*, ITNG 2008. See also Kahande GA: *Simulation, design and engineering of plastic fiber-optic systems*, 2007, PhD Dissertation, City University of New York.

6 Wireless Networks

6.1 Introduction

Much like the landline technologies, wireless technologies have also evolved from analog to digital framework. The older networks evolved to be analog and suffered from all the usual drawbacks, and are less favored. As the digital wireless architectures, devices, standards, and VLSI chips have become, and are currently becoming, available, the emphasis has shifted to all-digital wireless networks. Circuit- and packet-switched networks can both interface with the wireless core networks being currently introduced under the watchful direction, and coordination of the third-generation participation project presented in Chapter 7. The thrust is toward the establishment of the packet switched core for the next generation mobile networks (NGMN) that can interface with the current circuit switched core networks. Suitable interface requirements, standards, and protocol are necessary and being developed.

Wireless communications encompass mobile/portable radio systems. In contrast to landline communications, wireless systems offer special advantages when voice/ data systems require field automation, close communication with mobile employees/robots, and disaster recovery. Field automation permits widely scattered production units to work in close synchronicity and collaboration, and under tight control. Typical examples of this work dynamic include petrochemical oil refining systems, geophysical observation centers, and others. In the case of land-based centers, for example, numerous command units in a military operation need close contact with each other and also with the central command units. In addition, close control is essential when robots are deployed to work under hostile conditions. Natural disasters can also completely ruin the physical line of continuity for essential communication (e.g., a copper or fiber link). The telephone companies suffered from the San Francisco earthquake and the Central Office fires at the New York exchange and at Hinsdale, Illinois. In all of these disastrous conditions, wireless techniques have been the telephone company's bypass. This is an alarming trend for the traditional plain old telephone service (POTS) and public switched telephone network (PSTN) environments because the complete potential of these very short wireless links is not completely utilized. In this section, we present the wireless technologies and their implications for the areas of communications and intelligent networks (INs).

Most wireless systems stem from the deployment of the atmospheric/space media for radio waves. Communications facilities based on the age-old single

Intelligent Networks: Recent Approaches and Applications in Medical Systems.
DOI: http://dx.doi.org/10.1016/B978-0-12-416630-1.00006-6

sideband (SSB) amplitude modulated (AM), frequency modulated (FM), and satellite systems have evolved and been successfully deployed for decades. Frequency division multiplexing techniques are fundamental in the communication of speech and very low-rate, voice-band data during the early days. Television and wide band and special services data are also carried by the radio systems. Such systems could be used to carry modulated radio signals across the street to over 4000 miles. Wireless links and systems have been preempted by fiber-optic links and systems, except in special terrains and in satellite and space applications. Being insensitive to the amplitude of the signal, FM modulation techniques offer distinct advantages over the AM procedures.

Short-haul radio systems (up to 250 miles) were deployed for localized interstate and feeder services. Long-haul radio terrestrial (up to and beyond 4000 miles) and satellite systems were generally used for distance and backbone application. FM techniques depended on linear microwave amplifiers with sufficient gain in the communication of radio signals. Linearity, bandwidth, and power handling capacity had been the constraints in these microwave communication systems. Band edge (non)linearity and intermodulation noise restricts the capacity of these systems.

Repeaters and their spacing offer some relief for enhancing the range and the dependability of signal transmission through the atmosphere. Historically, 2-, 4-, 6-, 11-, and 18 gigahertz (GHz) band have been deployed in the United States. But the systems can be customized to suit the terrain and weather conditions of different regions of the world. Water vapor and rain offer serious limitations at 11 GHz and higher frequency bands.

Multiple signal paths, and abnormal and variable signal refraction effects cause serious concerns in maintaining signal quality through the wireless media. Change in humidity temperature and pressure waves (due to weather conditions) all contribute to the deployment of the wireless media for high-quality signal transmission.

External noises, multiple signal paths, abnormal refraction of radio signals, and signal fading offer new barriers in the use and deployment of radio systems for medical applications. In a sense, the extensive use of radio systems for medical applications is less desirable than other refined fiber-optic or coaxial systems. Signal attenuation, nonlinearities, intermodulation(s), and noise phenomenon are generic to most communication systems. However, these signal contaminants are most manageable in fiber and then in the coaxial systems.

In this chapter, the focus is on speech and voice communication for medical applications. Medical data, information, and knowledge also suffer serious degradation in the wireless systems.

6.2   Wireless Technology from Older Networks

Typically, the advanced cordless phone and modified cellular techniques become necessary for the more recent and full-fledged applications of personal, wireless communication systems. Voice and data communication are both implied. Each of these systems and techniques has implicit features and limitations. The wireless networks and as service providers, the architecture is geared toward serving *five* potential types of customers: (1) portable in-premises users, (2) mobile on-the-street users, (3) fixed location indoor/outdoor users, (4) commuters (train and plane), and (5) globe trotters.

The devices, interfaces, protocols, and characteristics of networks are optimized to suit the particular application. The partially unregulated environment (airtime tariff structure) offers enormous opportunities and challenges to network builders. The technology, though in its formative stages, is sufficiently mature and is not a financial barrier. The procurement of lease to certain services, channels on the air-waves, security, and legal clearances appear to be the major obstacles.

6.3   Modes of Operation in Older Technologies

There were *three* variations in the operation of earlier mobile radio systems. *First*, in mobile radio systems with two-way radiophones (e.g., citizens band radio), the system offers no privacy to listeners. In the typical citizens band radio systems, 40 channels are allocated, and the system uses any channel that happens to be free. *Second*, in the unichannel dispatching systems (e.g., open channel taxi dispatch) only one channel is allocated. All the users share this common channel. On the allocated channel a group of users (e.g., drivers) may talk only to the operator and not to each other. There is no privacy among the different users. *Third*, in individu-alized radio paging systems, the operator signals or beeps a particular receiver. The receiver may then go to a nearby telephone to get the message from the operator.

More recently, in later packet radio systems, the receiver has multiple access control. Numerous scattered devices transmit to the same receiver without interfer-ing with each other's transmissions. Mobile or portable terminals are feasible, and wireless receive-and-transmit capability is necessary. The data to be transmitted is formed into a packet by the transmitting control unit and has the address of the receiving unit and the transmitting terminal. Only the addressed receiver responds with an acknowledgment if the packet appears to be free of errors. The transmitter awaits this acknowledgment for a certain period and retransmits the packet if the acknowledgment is not received.

Traditional telephony over the wireless medium dates back to 1978 when Telepoint service was introduced in the United Kingdom as an alternative to con-ventional pay phones. In a sense, Telepoint acts as the "wireless last mile" between the pay phone subscriber and the Central Office. The concept materialized as the second-generation cordless telephone (CT2) where subscribers, in general, could access the CT2 telephone network systems, but by using a different band of fre-quencies. The third-generation (CT3) systems and the small wireless private branch exchanges (PBXs) followed immediately.

From the network perspective, the wireless PBXs, cell sites, cell bases, and wireless switching offices also exist (Figure 6.1). They may be integrated with most circuit-, packet- or message-switched networks to perform POTS, data,

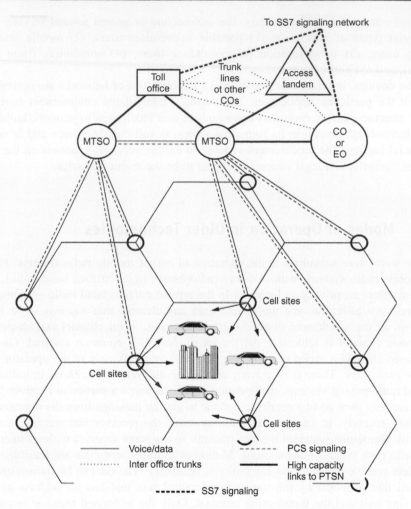

Figure 6.1 Network perspective of wireless communication. (a) Communications between
the mobile units and cell sites by using inward-directed antennas at alternate cell sites to suit
the topography of the area, providing access in the presence of obstructions in the
communication area. (b) Access to and from the public-switched telephone network (PSTN)
to the PCS. CO, Central Office; EO, end office; MTSO, mobile telephone switching office;
PCS, personal communication services; PSTN, public-switched telephone network.

packet, message, broadband services, or even IN services. Private communication
systems, personal communication networks, or even multicampus educational networks are examples of being able to administer, interconnect, switch, signal, monitor, and communicate with almost anyone, anywhere, and at any time.

The rapid growth of wireless technologies during the last decade has drastically
altered the nature and scope of radiotelephony. The remaining sections of this chapter
discuss these developments in more detail, as well as the growth of cordless

telephones, cellular radio, and personal communication networks. The changing architectures of these systems are indicative of the growing need for such communication systems, and of the potential of the technologies as they are currently being deployed.

6.4 American Perspective (Older Technologies)

Historically, radiotelephones encompass *four* types of services: (1) mobile telephone service (MTS), (2) improved mobile telephone service (IMTS), (3) Metroliner telephone service, and (4) advanced mobile phone service (AMPS).

As far back as 1938, under the Federal Communications Commission (FCC) ruling for regular service, the MTS deployed 40 kHz channel spacing with the base transmit in the range of 35.26−35.66 MHz and the mobile transmit in the range of 43.26−43.66 MHz. Only 10 channels are feasible under ideal conditions with the channels so widely spaced (40 kHz). The FCC's original authorization further limited the channels to four. For the IMTS, duplex mode, in 1964, the FCC allocated two frequency bands: the 152.51−152.81 MHz band for base transmit and the 157.77−158.07 MHz band for mobile transmit. Eleven channels are feasible with 30 kHz spacing. In 1970, the FCC allocated the higher 454.375−454.65 MHz band for base transmit and the 459.375−459.65 MHz for mobile transmit. Twelve channels are feasible with 25 kHz spacing. These two later systems make up the IMTS service. The two systems were identified as the "MJ" in the 150 MHz band and the "MK" in the 450 MHz band, each with a range of about 50 miles. Provided by AT&T, these systems were greatly oversubscribed from the mid-1970s when they were initially introduced. The demand for the MJ and MK channel services was intense, already creating a demand for the wireless telephone service.

The Metroliner telephone service (New York to Washington) operates in the 400 MHz range. Nine zones along the 225-mile stretch of railroad with fixed radio transceivers automatically hand over any call in progress from one zone to the next without any interruption of calls in progress. This service system is considerably simpler than the other mobile radio services because the transmitters and the receivers are along a well-defined path in clear terrain.

In 1974, the FCC also permitted the deployment of 870−890 MHz for base transmit and 825−845 MHz for mobile transmit. With a bandwidth of 20 MHz for each direction, 666 channels are feasible at 30 kHz spacing. This has been the basis for rapid growth of the high-capacity AMPS, which offers a very wide range of voice/data services (and perhaps some IN services). This type of service is planned to work within the constraints of a cellular planned network. The allocated bandwidth is used repeatedly in the cellular structures that overlay the serving areas. Thus, the capacity increases greatly, especially if the cells are also designed as micro- and picocells (Figure 6.2). For the current systems, research and design is centered around making the most use of the band for new advanced services and telecommunications of data/voice fax, paging, and other services. Most of the second-generation cordless systems (CT2), telepoint, and other similar phone systems operate in this band throughout the world.

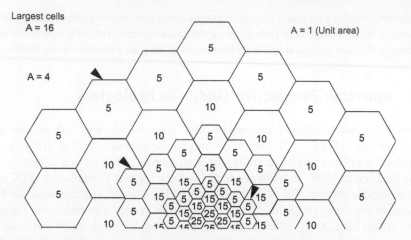

Figure 6.2 Reduction of cell sizes to serve increasingly congested areas. In this case, a maximum of 25 channels are deployed in the center with the smallest cell area. The number of channels is reduced, and the cell size is increased to accommodate the traffic patterns accordingly. In this case, only five channels are allocated for an area 16 times the size of the smallest cell. Other variations are also feasible.

Once again in 1992, the World Administrative Radio Conference (WARC) allocated a total of 230 MHz (in two radio frequency (RF) bands, 1885−2025 MHz and 2110−2200 MHz) for the development of the CT3 systems. Out of this frequency allocation, two 30 MHz bands are for mobile satellite applications (1980−2010 MHz uplink and 2170−2200 downlink). In this higher band, entire networks (such as personal communication networks) with advanced network services need to be explored, developed, tested, and deployed. The economic viability and social acceptance is yet another issue. Such networks can be implemented with a cellular "backbone" for pocket transceivers.

Most mobile phones (including the CT2 category) and their limited services operate within the 30 MHz to 1 GHz band. Over 1 GHz (the bandwidth allocated for the CT3 category), moisture and climate start to influence the communication and can make the frequency space unusable for mobile telephony for the present. The problem areas in these applications include bringing down the size and weight of the devices, the power budgeting in adjoining cells, complete privacy, signal interference and degradation, and possible radiation hazard from too many devices concentrated in small areas. In the United States, by common usage, personal communication networks and personal communication services operate in the 1800−2000 MHz band via a well-designed microcell architecture using code division multiple access (CDMA). Some of the cellular radio services in the 800−900 MHz range also satisfy the service categories expected from the personal communication networks. Intelligent services are expected to become available in both the cellular radio and the personal communication environments.

6.5   European Perspective (Older Technologies)

The Universal Mobile Telecommunication System (UMTS) played a significant role in the development of the newer third-generation products and standards for future public land mobile telecommunications. Four dominant types of mobile systems have existed (especially in Europe) and include:

1. Cellular systems, which are based upon the global system for mobile communication (GSM) adapted from the Pan-European, second-generation digital mobile system.
2. Cordless systems, which are based upon digital European cordless telecommunication, also referred to as "CT2" for "cordless telephone second generation" and "CT3" for "cordless telephone third generation."
3. Paging systems, which are based upon the European radio messaging facilities.
4. Private mobile radio systems in the United Kingdom.

The European community organized its third-generation wireless communication effort under the auspices of Research and development for Advanced Communication in Europe (RACE). The effort for the RACE-1 project in Europe is concentrated in eight broad areas:

1. fixed network and its functional specifications,
2. mobile systems and services,
3. equalization,
4. modulation and coding,
5. channel management and cellular coverage,
6. signal processing in mobile communications,
7. broadband mobile systems,
8. other related technology, such as antenna design in relation to the CT3 band.

As a follow up, RACE-2 project was started. This project directs its efforts toward realizing the third-generation systems and organizing its work in a functionally oriented, top–down fashion, which ensures that the systems specification meets requirements and that technical support is available for CT3 mobile communication systems and products.

UMTS has provisioning for the bearer services as they are defined in the GSM and ISDN context. These "bearer" services may be in the circuit- or packet-switched mode. Supplementary ISDN services are likely to be supported by the UMTS. As mobile telephony starts to gain popularity, the 8, 16, and 32 kbps and the unrestricted B2 channel services are likely to become part of the UMTS consideration. The applications for the new wireless services can be quite diverse, such as low-rate video, image document retrieval, audiovisual services (though not multimedia), video telephony, and so forth.

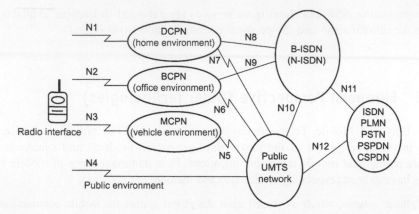

Figure 6.3 Architecture and interfaces for the generic universal mobile telephone systems (GUMTS) network. DCPN, domestic customer premises network; BCPN, business customer premises network; MCPN, mobile customer premises network; BISDN, broadband ISDN; N-ISDN, narrow-band ISDN; UMTS, universal mobile telephone system; ISDN, integrated services digital network; PLMN, public land mobile network; PSTN, public-switched telephone network; PSPDN, packet-switched public data network; CSPDN, circuit-switched public data network.

In concept, most of these systems have a radio interface with each other as they span the "last few wireless miles" to serve the mobile user. From this network access point with the radio interface, access into the other existing networks, DCPN, BCPN, MCPN, or public UMTS networks (Figure 6.3), could be over any of the communication media, such as fiber, coaxial cable, microwave, or even the twisted wire pairs in the ADSL/HDSL[1] mode (ITU G.992.5, 2009).

However, since these networks and their architectures are evolving, designers prefer to make the network/network access via fiber links, terrain permitting, or via very small aperture terminal links to span remote inaccessible areas. In many instances, a microwave radio link is also provided to handle localized and overflow traffic from cell sites to the public UMTS network.

Both the public UMTS and ISDN networks provide access to fixed networks, such as the PSTN, packet-switched public data network (PSPDN), and circuit-switched public data network (CSPDN). The typical architecture and interfaces are also shown in Figure 6.4. There are 12 interfaces (N1−N12) shown in this figure, and the first four are reserved for the user terminal or the radio access port to the UMTS. The remaining eight interfaces provide network-to-network access. The architecture of the UMTS provides for much more than the interfacing for radiotelephony. In a generic sense, this architecture can be tailored to suit most wireless environments. Then, these networks had been integrated into the established

[1] ADSL/HDSL—asymmetric digital subscriber line/high-speed digital subscriber line discussed in detail in reference ITU G.992.5 (1997).

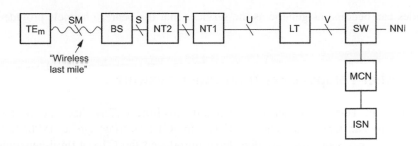

Figure 6.4 Access provisioning for the wireless to the wired and/or optical environments. TE$_m$, terminal equipment—microwave; SM, "S" interface for the mobile roamer; BS, base station; NT1, NT2, network terminations; S, T, U, and V, ISDN standardized interfaces; LT, line termination; SW, switch for the mobile telephone/wireless environment; MCN, mobile control node; ISN, information storage node; NNI, network-to-network interface.

networks, such as the landline networks such as PSTN, PSPDN, CSPDN, ISDN, and broadband ISDN (BISDN).

The mobile units access the network by way of a microwave channel using their specific terminal equipment (TE) links into a base station (BS). Consistent with ISDN interfaces (*circa* mid-1980s), there are four (that is, R, S, T, and U) interfaces with NT2 and NT1 network terminations and one "LT" or line termination (Ahamed and Lawrence, 1996). The switch (SW, typically circa 4ESS (Anderson et al., 1994) in the United States and the series of Alcatel-Lucent Central Office electronic switches (Alcatel-Lucent, 2013), EWSD (Chapuis and Joel, 2003) switches) has access to the mobile control node (MCN) and information storage node (ISN). In addition, the switch also provides the access to the rest of the customer networks. These two nodes, MCN and ISN, are essential for the mobile roamer environment and are an integral part of the switch resident within the MTSO as shown in Figure 3.14.

The network-to-network interface (NNI) provides for the signaling and protocol conversions to and from the wireless communication environment with the "wired" and/or the "optical" communication environment.

The implementation of the UMTS is based upon layering of the generic and implicit functions. Three logically distinct groups of functions emerge in the graceful integration of future UMTS networks and the more evolved public networks. The first group of functions deals with the mobile telephony aspects, the second group with call control aspects, and the third group with the bearer-channel control. The first layer, called the mobility call-control layer, has paging entity, paging control, customer mobile access control, database, and universal personal telecommunication routing point control. The second layer, called the call-control layer, has mobile user agent control, and customer access and call control. The third layer has the bearer control. These layers span and deal with the mobility issues at the first layers, with its five sublayers, and also the control of the bearer-channel generic within the ISDN environment. It is interesting to note that the services that UMTS provides can become as generic as the services that the bearer channels provide in ISDN.

6.6 Other Perspectives from Older Networks

The European Telecommunications Standards Institute (ETSI) had endorsed the interim European technical standard (IETS) for CT2 as long ago as 1990. Some vendors (e.g., Ericsson from Sweden) have introduced the CT3, a third-generation digital cordless telephone system, namely the DCT900 series to be coupled into the PBX markets. Other countries (such as, Australia, Austria, Canada, Finland, France, Hong Kong, Italy, the Netherlands, New Zealand, Spain, Switzerland, and West Germany) have all endorsed (some reluctantly) the CT2 and/or the CT3 cordless digital telephone systems. The allocation of the carrier frequencies and the acceptance of CCITT wireless standards and protocol are strongly indicative of the direction and the magnitude of the impact of wireless communication.

In the Japanese digital cellular (JDC) standard, there have been three bands. At the low end of the carrier spectrum, the uplink lies between 940 and 956 MHz and the downlink lies between 810 and 826 MHz. For the high bands, the JDC has 1429−1441 MHz and 1453−1465 MHz for the uplink, and 1477−1489 MHz and 1501−1513 MHz for the downlink. The carrier spacing is 25 kHz, with quadrature phase-shift keying (QPSK) modulation. By comparison, the North American Digital Cellular (NADC) standard deployed 30 kHz spacing with the same QPSK modulation. The carrier bit rate proposed for JDC is 42 kbps (i.e., VSELP[2] is 11.2 kbps), as opposed to NADC 48.6 kbps (i.e., VSELP is 13 kbps). Like the other standard digital cellular systems (GSM and NADC), JDC also permits eventual integration with the ISDN network via standard ISDN protocol.

6.7 Technological Perspective

Numerous technologies converge into the wireless telecommunication arena. The effective utilization of bandwidth (by using the same spectral band in nonneighboring cells) allows for mass production of devices. The sophisticated customer sharing of a limited group of channels, which is microwave-operated and microprocessor-based, allows for an acceptable number of tries for each call completion. Initially (*circa* 1985), this concept originated in trunked telephone systems. Some of these earlier systems operate under the analog modulation techniques, but the modern trend is to bring the digital revolution into wireless. The techniques of frequency division, time division, and code division are becoming more and more interesting. The net effect is accurate communication, higher capacity, cheaper price, and more mobility.

---

[2] VSELP—vector sum excited linear prediction. For a complete list of acronyms, see Appendix A.

6.7.1   Transmission Considerations

Signal loss along the propagation path is an uncertain phenomenon at best. The effects of terrain on the scattering of the radio waves along the desired path are the greatest uncertainty. Propagation is influenced by *three* major physical processes: (1) specular reflection, (2) diffuse reflection, and (3) diffraction.

First, specular reflection occurs when the signal permeates two dissimilar media. The linear dimensions of the surfaces are large in comparison with the wavelength of the signal. This type of reflection is not unlike the imaging properties of mirrors governed by Snell's Law predicting the equality of angles of incidence and of reflection. However, when the terrain is rough and the ground is not horizontal, then the reflected signals and paths can be numerous, causing delay in differing amounts by adding time to the net received signal on the "direct path." Typically, the received signal is distorted, dispersed, and delayed in varying degrees as the mobile unit travels, especially through built-up areas, or as the media or terrain characteristics change.

Second, scattering also causes multipath fading or diffuse reflection. The many reflections from obstructions may reinforce or block the main signal, thus demanding consistent receiver performance over a very wide, dynamic range. Doppler shifts, generated by the movement of the mobile unit, give rise to two sideband frequencies (signal frequency $+f_d$ and signal frequency $-f_d$). Standing wave patterns also exist, which are due to severe reflections from obstructions ahead of the mobile unit.

Finally, diffraction of radio signals results when the line of sight between the transmitter and the receiver is obstructed by rough terrain. The diffraction patterns can differ considerably, depending upon the extent of protrusion along the line of sight.

Interference due to thermal and environmental noises causes effects very similar to the fading effects of multipath signals. The phase and envelope of the narrowband noise output after filtering are quite similar to those of the radio signal carrier that has passed through a multipath fading medium. The *five* typical sources of environmental noise for the mobile radio environment are:

1. atmospheric noise varies from place to place and season to season, especially in the very low end of the signal band to about 20 MHz,
2. urban, suburban, and man-made (fabricated) noises,
3. galactic noise,
4. solar noise,
5. internal receiver noise.

Primarily, man-made atmospheric noise results from vehicular ignition, power line noise and corona discharges, industrial equipment, and even fluorescent lights. From nature, lightning, sunspot activities, starbursts, meteor trails, and the aurora borealis also contribute to some noise, however insignificant it might be.

The mean and standard deviation of automotive noise in four types of areas (business, residential, rural, and remote areas) have been published by the National Bureau of Standards. Typically, the mean noise figure falls at an approximate rate of about 28 dB per decade with its value being the highest in the business areas at about 80 dB relative to kT_0B, where k is the Boltzmann constant, T_0 the reference temperature (290 K), and B the effective receiver bandwidth. The residential and the rural noise levels are about 6 and 12 dB below the business noise levels. The standard deviation exhibits wide fluctuation. For the business areas, the standard deviation σ- increases with frequency in the 10−100 MHz band, whereas it shows a steady fall from about 2 MHz for the residential and rural areas.

Delay spread is another significant factor in mobile radio communication. When the transmitter transmits an impulse function to the receiver, the multiple paths through the medium cause a much wider signal at the receiver. The peakiness of the received signal indicates the multiplicity of the paths. Under idealized conditions, a single, slightly spread-out pulse may be received due to media dispersion. In general, numerous peaky pulses are received and each peak is suggestive of a dominant path. If a large number of obstructions (and, thus, a large number of reflections) are present, then the received signal is a smear of such reflections that are received. These reflected signals are delayed in time because of the varying lengths of their path. The signals that travel farther along longer paths lose signal strength, and the trails become vanishingly small. However, their interference must be signal processed (or canceled) from the next time slot or the duration when the information-bearing signal arrives.

Typically, the best and the worst estimation of path loss over flat and hilly terrains are essential in the cell design and cell-site locations. Signal loss due to foliage can vary by about 10 dB between summer and winter. Signal loss through tunnels is also highly dependent on frequency. From the measurement at about 1000 ft inside the Lincoln tunnel (an underwater roadway between New York City and New Jersey), the loss is about 40 dB at 150 MHz, 14 dB at 300 MHz, and 4 dB at 1 GHz. Street orientation also becomes significant in some cases due to the "channeling effects." The street width, building spacing, and the signal wavelength (frequency) all play a part in modulating the signal. Typically, the detailed computational approach provides the most dependable estimate for the effects of urban geography on mobile radio systems and their cell-site locations. A considerable number of analytical models are available for estimating signal loss and degradation. Detailed computational models are also available for predicting the signal degradation for mobile wireless applications within most metropolitan areas.

In most applications, it is essential to realize that the media is highly variable and only statistical techniques have any bearing in the real world. Most of the statistical communication techniques are applicable in this environment, leading to a very good probability that the designed systems and devices, in combination, will work in any given application, location, environment, or terrain.

6.8   Wireless Technologies in Other Networks

The concept of "the wireless local loop" had been already familiar in the United States and Canada. Some of the technologies that are relatively immune to wireless appear to be fiber and fiber/coaxial technologies geared toward the multimedia and entertainment industries. In the former case, the rate, the range, and the cost favor the initial investment of fiber. In the second case, where the possible demand for data in businesses and industry is very high, the fiber backbone may be desirable for very high-speed data tied into high-rate cable capacity. The broadband fiber and loop access switching and transport technology, coupled with the residential access of cable television, makes the fiber/cable combination a serious competitor to all wireless technology. The established foothold of cable in video and TV service offers an added attraction. Finally, the expectation of the public favors the quality of high-definition television video/entertainment service over the fiber and/or cable service, rather than over wireless.

6.8.1   Traditional Landline Applications

The wireless technologies have exerted a steady influence in traditional landline local area networks (LANs), metropolitan area networks (MANs), and wide area networks (WANs). For example, in LAN applications, spread spectrum, infrared, CT2, CT3, personal communication networks, RF identification systems, and narrow-band radio can all carry voice/data to some extent or another. The spread spectrum technologies for LANs have been delivered up to 300 kbps in hilly terrain. For time division multiple access (TDMA), burst rates up to 8 Mbps may also be sustained in indoor settings over 60−100 ft. The bit rate for most LANs is at 4, 10, or 16 Mbps, or much higher rates for optical networks. For MAN applications, a variety of networks exists at very low rates compared to fiber rates, including cellular phones, conventional radio, trunked radio, FM sideband, TV vertical blanking interval, microwave, and paging networks. For WANs, two-way mobile satellite, very small aperture terminal (VSAT), pocket radio, and meteor-burst techniques exist. Various technologies have existed for use in voice and data communications. The following sections give an overview of each of them.

6.8.2   Trunked Radio Communications

Trunked radio communications are valuable for 30- to 50-mile voice/data communication. Being privately owned, these systems are shared and can be cost-effective if the use of channels is maximized. Trunked radio service can be fixed or mobile. Channel allocation is done by scanning for a free channel, or requesting a master station to assign, confirm, or deny a request. Signaling is done by way of a reserved channel, and the user is unaware of the channel-allocation process. The capacity of IMTS far exceeds that of existing trunked radio for trunked radio to be a serious contender (for the present) in the LAN-to-LAN or LAN-to-WAN interconnect.

6.8.3   Spread Spectrum Transmission

Spread spectrum transmission (SST) techniques permit frequency hopping from one frequency to another in a pseudorandom fashion. Transmitters and receivers both follow the same pseudorandom sequences and remain in synchronization, thus staying in continuous contact. This concept is desirable when secrecy and security are essential for communication (i.e., in military or control communications). In direct sequence modulated systems, a carrier is modulated with a digital sequence much higher than the bandwidth of the information signal. In the frequency-hopping systems, the carrier frequency is shifted at discrete increments by a distinct pattern determined by the code sequence, which in turn determines the order of the frequency usage. In time-hopping systems, the timing of transmission (typically a short duration of time slices) is influenced by the code sequence. In the time-/frequency-hopping systems, both the transmitted frequency and transmission bit rate are determined by the code sequence. In the "chirp" or pulse FM systems, the carrier frequency is swept over a wide band during the interval of the pulse. These techniques offer distinct privacy of information, even though they waste bandwidth.

6.8.4 Code Division Multiple Access

In the CDMA, frequency spreading is used rather than frequency hopping. Thus, information is camouflaged rather than chopped. Wireless LANs, mobile satellite communication, and cellular digital telephone are possible beneficiaries of CDMA. Privacy of communication is a key constituent in CDMA wireless techniques. It is also robust against impulse noise and other electromagnetic interference. It is relatively immune to fading because the adjoining (or "hopped") frequencies do not all fade during the same time.

6.8.5 Cellular Radio

Cellular radio systems use the microwave frequency optimally by limiting the transmit power and then using the same spectral band many times over in a small area. Diversity of calling times permits a few hundred channels to serve as many as a hundred thousand customers, thus reducing the overhead. Radio modems still play a minor role in digital communications. As opposed to voice message dispatch systems, computer dispatched message systems can have the error correction at both ends of the wireless links. These modems can send low-speed data.

6.8.6 Mobile Satellite

Mobile satellite systems using geosynchronous satellites permit very wide area of messaging and paging services. Mobile receivers with directional antennas permit low- to medium-speed data communications feasible at almost any location (weather and terrain permitting) by way of VSAT networks. Peer-to-peer networking is feasible because the remote unit has some degree of flexible control (channel selection, switching, and hand over) over the base stations. Short, bursty traffic patterns (as they exist in IN functions and services) are well suited to wireless networks.

6.8.7   Infrared

Infrared communications using line-of-sight laser sources provide good links for T1, E1 rates, 4 Mbps (token ring), 10 Mbps (Ethernet), and 16 Mbps (token-ring bridge) applications. For short, indoor, point-to-point, and point-to-multipoint applications, the inexpensive light-emitting diode devices are applicable. These devices may use antennas along roofs, floors, or walls for communicating, and reflectors for directing infrared signals up to 10 Mbps over short distances. Incorporated as nodes on LANs, they provide computer-aided control in the production process and to robots. Careful installation and maintenance is mandatory for such wireless systems.

6.8.8   Meteor Burst

Meteor-burst communication takes advantage of reflections from trails left by tiny particles that sporadically enter the earth's atmosphere. As they traverse, these particles leave behind trails about a meter wide and as long as 25 km. Consisting of ionized gases, these trails occur about 100 km high and can last as short as a few milliseconds or as long as a few seconds. Radio signals targeted toward such meteor trails are bounced back to earth up to distances of 2000 km and can be received for the short duration of the life of the trail. However, the occurrence of the trail can be extrapolated from early observation, and on an average, these meteors fly past the earth every 6–8 min. Hence, in effect, they provide a free, but very short-lived satellite without launching it, and being galactic, they are tamper-proof by humans. If a packetized data stream is to be communicated, then the free transport is provided if the transmitter and the receiver priorly know that data will be exchanged. Typically, these systems operate in the 30- to 50-MHz range.

6.8.9   Very Small Aperture Terminal

VSAT supports a data rate of up to 56 kbps, or sometimes higher. These terminals work with antennas pointed to the geosynchronous satellites orbiting at 22,300 miles in the sky (Ahamed and Lawrence, 1996). Commercial satellite-service vendors lease a telephone/data line to the subscribers from an uplink facility and, thus, provide access to most remote places equipped with these large antennas to receive and transmit data. Remote and rural areas are the chief beneficiaries of the VSAT wireless technology.

6.8.10   Radio Frequency

RF identification systems are able to scan a small microelectronic tag fastened on a moving object. Three types of tags are feasible: passive, active, and locally powered. The passive, reflective devices reflect an incoming RF beam, thus encoding its unique identification upon the signal. The active stages of these devices contain a battery source and have memory for buffering and user programmability as an option. They are still reflective and only modify the transmitted signal. The locally powered tag actively communicates a considerable amount of information to the receiver and vice versa. Another closely related technology is the automatic locating service for vehicles that can find a vehicle(s), and compute the speed and track its movement.

6.9 Techniques and Models

Significant analytical techniques and a corresponding array of simulation models are available for the design of wireless communication systems. These techniques offer analysis of flat terrain and multipeak terrain for signals as the mobile unit traverses the cells. The effects of multiple reflection due to single- and multiple-antenna systems can be formulated under the best and worst conditions. Short-term fading models exist. Rayleigh, multipath, and selective fading simulators are also available. Thus, fading, based upon envelope and phase, can be determined. Doppler effects and standing wave patterns can also be evaluated accurately for a given set of conditions. In a sense, these effects must be considered in proper proportions and scales for each application, and this is where the statistical communication theory and computer simulation become valuable.

6.9.1 Modulation

Various modulation techniques, amplitude, phase, and frequency offer special features suited to the fading character of the environment. AM techniques are suitable to the fading effects. However, FM techniques, when deployed wisely, offer reasonable immunity against fading and some types of noise interference. Digital modulation techniques for these applications consist of five major selections:

1. coherent binary AM (also known as phase-shift keying or PSK),
2. FM with discrimination,
3. coherent frequency shift keying (FSK),
4. noncoherent FSK,
5. differential PSK.

Typically, voice is converted to data via any of the speech encoders and decoders (codecs), ranging in rates from 64 to 32 kbps pulse code modulation (PCM), adaptive-delta pulse code modulation, and delta modulation meeting the CCITT specification on speech quality. Wide ranges of codecs are feasible from linear predictive coding and adaptive predictive coding, requiring as few as 2.4−32 kbps adaptive-delta modulation codecs with 30 dB signal-to-noise (SNR) ratio and 45 dB dynamic range.

In the nonfading channels, the coherent binary AM (PSK) provides best overall performance even though the phase correlation is necessary for coherent detection. The noncoherent FSK, though the simplest to implement, has the least desirable performance. When channel fading is a concern, the PSK system outperforms the coherent FSK by about 3 dB for the digital voice signals. Although they are quite inefficient in using bandwidth, spread spectrum systems, can also be used when secrecy and security are essential. A certain tolerance to fading is also a feature of the spread spectrum systems. In spread spectrum systems, there are five types of modulation techniques:

1. direct sequence modulated systems,
2. frequency-hopping systems,
3. time-hopping systems,
4. time-/frequency-hopping systems,
5. "chirp" or pulse FM modulation systems.

The main contender for mobile radio application is the time-/frequency-hopping system. Although complicated to implement, this system is being actively developed. It is also referred to as continuous phase discrete frequency modulation, or as the frequency-hopped differential phase-shift keying modulation. These systems offer good immunity to interfering signals.

The modified SSB systems also hold considerable promise. The prime objective is to enhance the signal-carrying capacity of existing mobile RF bands. In a 1978 FCC report, a new SSB system is proposed that uses companding[3] to reduce bandwidth and uses amplitude companding to increase the SNR ratio. This particular system, called the SSB frequency/amplitude system, needs considerably less channel separation (typically this is of the order of 2.0–2.5 kHz, whereas the traditional FM systems need about 15 kHz). Only amplitude companding needs about 3.0–3.5 kHz. These techniques are suited for speech wireless applications, rather than all data systems for wireless communications.

In European settings, the following techniques are being considered: constant envelope modulation—typically, Gaussian minimum shift keying (GMSK) and Gaussian timed frequency modulation (GTFM)—and bandwidth-efficient linear modulation—that is, quadrature amplitude modulation (QAM) and band-limited QPSK. Amplifier linearity over the dynamic signal range becomes essential. Variable rate trellis-coded modulation is also a viable contender, although the disposition is for GMSK.

6.9.2 Interference

The interference problem in mobile radio systems is unique because the media is open and the frequencies are reused many times over. Co-channel interference arises from another signal in the same band, but from a different user. An approximate measure for this type of interference is the "near-end to far-end ratio." The ratio of path losses at distance d and d' is evaluated. Expressed as decibels, the loss

---

[3] "Companding" is changing the step size to accommodate a wider dynamic range. See Appendix A for a complete list of acronyms.

follows a 40 dB-per-decade slope, and the ratio in decibels can be approximated as 40 times log (distance ratio). This interference is not significant deep inside the individual cells, but it can become significant as the mobile unit approaches the cell boundaries. Many mobile radio systems have a frequency allocation plan that monitors the use of the frequency band in adjoining cells. The adjacent channel interference (rather than co-channel) can also become significant in mobile radio systems. Two other interferences are also significant: (1) intermodulation interference in multichannel, frequency division multiplexed systems and (2) intersymbol interference in digital systems. In the digital systems, the eye closure in the Y direction has two significant components: the Gaussian noise and the Rayleigh fading. The timing jitter is also influenced by clock instability in the receiver, the static misalignment of timing signals, and the time-delay dispersion effect of the medium. In the QAM systems, the computations need to be extended in the real and imaginary dimensions of the signal space.

6.10   Integrated Technologies and Intelligent Platforms

The trend over the last two decades is integration of the most cost-effective technologies and the optimal (proven, dependable, and error free) platforms. Fiber-optic technology has cut deep inroad and most older platforms, established by AT&T (now at&t), Bellcore, EWSD, NTT etc., are converting their interfaces to suit the demand for intelligent social and network services.

Built on age-old technological foundations presented in this chapter, the services and their platforms have been enhanced substantially. Interfaces and software are continually updated to meet service requirements. Even though these services are data (numerical) and information (text) oriented, they are not knowledge or wisdom oriented. Only generic object-oriented processing, processing of personal–social object relationships, can bring about intelligence in the personal (Ahamed and Lawrence, 1996) and medical domains presented in this book.

At the top layer of control, numerous new entries to the integrated technology markets offer intelligent optical services, such as optical layer management, remote provisioning, real-time monitoring, and reconfiguration of optical pathways through the world. Reduced operating expenses and high reliability are achieved by using these interactive and (self) monitoring capabilities.

Intelligent peripheral equipment also makes the optical capabilities more versatile and manageable. For example, optical amplification, signal splitting, and no loss distribution of optical data and information in high-density traffic nodes make the optical integration of services (though not truly intelligent) flexible and economical. Typically, the high-bandwidth customer traffic is not disrupted and the makes the high-end control of optical network services and customization easily incorporated in existing optical networks.

6.11 Conclusions

In this chapter, the physical and technological basis of wireless network is presented. The wireless technologies are mature and wireless networks from any application (medical, emergency warning, educational, etc.) can be interfaced with traditional network using standard interfaces and protocols and extensively used in remote area, monitoring systems, aviation industry, etc.

Wireless technologies had been suggested as early as 1890s, since the days of Marconi (1897) and Tesla (1901) but evolved slowly compared to the metallic line-based telephone systems suggested by Bell (1876) and actively deployed through 1990s. In the Bell System environment, wireless communication had been studied in detail. The signal degradation due to noise in all aspects of communications had been analyzed. In the landline applications, the signal recovery was targeted before being completely buried in noise. However, with the advent and deployment of satellite communications systems, wireless technologies received particular interest in developing new coding algorithms and noise control in wireless communication systems. The era of NGMN (discussed in the next chapter) had started to accommodate dependable mobile network architecture and their configurations.

References

1. ITU G.992.5: *Asymmetric digital subscriber line 2 transceivers (ADSL2)—Extended bandwidth ADSL2 (ADSL2plus). A survey of recent Internet articles for most countries ranging from Austria to UAE*, 2009 (website). Available from < http://www.itu.int/rec/T-REC-G.992.5/e >. About 64 countries have the ADSL + 2 services offered over "bonded ports" (to reduce cross talk effects). For technical discussion of ADSL, see Ahamed SV, Lawrence VB: *Design and engineering of intelligent communication systems*, Boston, MA, 1997, Kluwer Academic Publishers.
2. Ahamed SV, Lawrence VB: *Intelligent broadband multimedia networks*, Boston, MA, 1996, Kluwer Academic Press.
3. Anderson TW, Carestia PD, Foster JH, Meyers MN: The evolution of the 4ESSTM switch, *AT&T Tech J*. November/December:93−100, 1996.
4. Alcatel-Lucent: *Alcatel-Lucent 5ESS® switch*, 2013 (website). Available from < https://support.alcatel-lucent.com/portal/productContent.do?productId=5ESS >. Accessed April, 2013.
5. Chapuis RJ, Joel AE Jr.: *100 years of telephone switching*, Amsterdam, 2003, IOS Press.

7 NGMNs, 3G, and 4G Networks

7.1 Introduction

The mobile telephone industry has offered vast economic incentives for the network service providers. Coupled with intelligent network (IN) and limited personal services, the mobile services provided to the customers are limited by the intelligence embedded in the mobile service base stations. The role of the base stations in the earlier configurations of the 1970s and 1980s was to provide telephone service connectivity and handover functions necessary to maintain base station contact as the users moved from cell to cell.

Currently, vendors are attempting to offer partially converged services, network function virtualization and Switched Digital Network (SDN) architectures with additional and enhanced quality of services. More recently, the possibilities of providing multiple bands operating in a multimode to the users are envisioned. Cost effectiveness and economy of scale are yet to be realized or at least during the second half of the decade of 2010.

From *a fun*ctional perspective, global roaming, security issues, machine-to-machine communication/services, and operator-deployed open access small cells are some of the concerns that resolution before next generation mobile networks (NGMNs) can be classified as a fully converged mainstream global network. The operations, administration, and maintenance requirements become necessary for the end-to-end connectivity in mobile networks. These issues have been successfully resolved in the traditional networks over a time. Mobile communication brings its own set of issues due to nature of transmission through the medium. Uncertainties about signal path and noise characteristics due to the natural and man-made interference cause the wireless media make less dependable than the fiber optic, cable, Hybrid Fiber Coaxial (HFC), and so on media for communication. However, in remote areas, for band limited and for handling emergencies, the wireless technology becomes necessary and desirable.

Wireless network had been expanding dramatically during the last decade. It is estimated that the subscriptions for mobile broadband subscribers (for every 100 people) have increased from about 5 in 1998 to about 67 in 2009. The cellular telephone subscribers have increased from <0.1% to about 9.5%, whereas the plain old telephone subscribers have changed from about 13% to about 17.8% reaching a peak of about 19% in 2005.

Mobile communication facilities have contributed most radically to the growth of wireless systems. It is estimated that there are approximately 120 million subscribers in the western hemisphere for the third-generation partnership project (3GPP) by the

Intelligent Networks: Recent Approaches and Applications in Medical Systems.
DOI: http://dx.doi.org/10.1016/B978-0-12-416630-1.00007-8

end of 2010. The growth includes the High Speed Packet Access (HSPA) predictions in Latin America and Caribbean that integrates 64 networks in 27 countries from Panama to Chile in South America.

Unguided flow of multimedia information from (almost) any location to (almost) any other location is being realized through the wireless media. The routing and channeling are processed by intelligent mobile networks and the base stations. As far back as late 1940s, researchers at Bell Laboratories (an R&D unit of AT&T before the divestiture of the Bell System) had envisioned the possible deployment of radio communications. Tesla and Marconi already demonstrated the viability of wireless radio equipment during the late 1890s.

Mobile networks can encompass the (very) wide variety of systems ranging from every type of metallic media (wires, cables, bundles, buses, printed circuits, etc.) to every type of atmospheric media (air, free space, ether space, outer space, etc.). The even aquatic mediums (for marine communication systems) can become a viable contender in the (near) future. Almost any technique of communication is a candidate for mobile networks to deploy. Ranging from dial-up, telephone, digital subscriber lines, integrated services digital network (ISDN), ethernet, packet switching, including code division multiple access (CDMA) and cellular digital packet data (CDPD), frame relay, cell relay, asynchronous transfer mode (ATM), broadband, and Bluetooth to general packet radio service (GRPS), global system for mobile communication (GSM), cellular radio, and any formal mode of communication all fall within the wider realm of mobile networks.

Intelligence in mobile networks is derived by implanting intelligent peripherals. Processing, service routing, and provisioning are accomplished in the intelligent peripherals (IPs). Similar to IPs in conventional INs (see Chapter 8), these add-on devices provide the customer with a wide variety of data, voice and/or video services. In the WiMAX and IP multimedia subsystem (IMS) environment, the IP interfaces with IMS client applications and the IP sublayer provides for the quality of service. The details are presented further in this chapter.

IPs can be distributed or centralized, and the service provided can be restrictive or extensive depending on the type of NGMN. IP functionality can range from low-speed voice/data or broadband multimedia services. The connectivity to the IPs itself can be metal-based/fiber or wireless. The design of NGMN has enormous flexibility, and the architectures can vary significantly. In a sense, the NGMN and fourth-generation (4G) networks are a supernetwork atop of all other networks much like a supercomputer is a network of smaller modular computers.

Satellite networks, wireless wide area networks (WANs), metropolitan area networks (MANs), local area networks (LANs), and private access networks (PANs) together form the composite (and heterogeneous) network for multiple hops through the 3G (third-generation) and 4G networks to provide customer access around the globe. Sensor networks that get activated to provide on-demand services (see Tsunami networks, section 8.5.2) can also be served via the NGMN supernetwork. In these networks, generally the last link is wireless from the base stations, and the stations are (generally) linked by landlines (metallic/fiber).

IMS integrates the Internet services (easy to use, affordable, multiple usage, multiple user devices, broadband, multimedia services over IP, and global roaming) and deploys the participation of Wi-Fi, 2G, 3G, wireline, WiMAX (service band 2.5 GHz, and 2.3 GHz, WiMAX) operators that have globally distributed greatest concentrations in Western Europe.

The first-generation (1G) systems communicate only voice signals (advanced mobile phone service (AMPS), European and Japanese formats for voice signals), the second-generation (2G) devices carry voice, data, and low-rate signals (IS-95, GSM, packet data control protocol (PDC) signals). The 3G devices can carry data at higher rates and support voice, data, and multimedia (video) streams (typically wideband-CDMA (W-CDMA), TD-SCDMA, HSPA, CDMA2000, EV-DO/DV type of signals up to 2 Mbps). While Wi-Fi offers a distributed customer-centric approach at data rates from 2−100 Mbps up to 1 Gbps for the UWB systems. The 3G and the long-term evolution (LTE) (normal and advanced) systems offer a vertically integrated service-provider approach in the wireless access.

The International Telecommunication Union (specifically, the Radiocommunication (ITU-R) standardization sector) has initiated to bring broadband services in the mobile communications arena. Efforts toward the next generation of International Mobile Telecommunications-Advanced (IMT-A) systems have been ongoing since 2000.

7.2   Objectives

The NGMNs aim at providing mobile broadband services for the users. Strategies and standards aimed toward LTE and evolved packet core (EPC) development become necessary to realize fully converged network services. Reduced antenna space requirements Multi Antenna Technology Antenna Co-Site Solutions, multiple antenna technologies Multi-Antenna Technology Compact Antenna Solutions, NGMN whitepaper small cell backhaul requirements NGMN Whitepaper Small Cell Backhaul Requirements (2012), and security in LTE backhauling NGMN Whitepaper Security in LTE backhauling (2012) are being investigated during the first half of this decade (2010).

The main objective of the NGMN architecture is to accommodate the circuit switched and packet switched user traffic in an integrated, coherent, and dependable fashion. An overview of the integrated NGNM is presented in Figure 7.1.

Network and customer services are well established in the landline environment. Landline networks provide connectivity to the knowledge bases widely distributed throughout the globe. In the current NGMN configurations, Internet connectivity provides connectivity to the knowledge bases and to a few intelligent services via the policy and charging rules function (PCRF) (explained in Figure 7.4). These newer NGMNs use the landline resources extensively and depend on the circuit and packet core backbone networks.

The PCRF is imposed at the serving gateway (SGW), packet data network gateway (PDNGW), and PDN interfaces. In comparison with the evolved IN environment in the landline environment, the functionality of the PCRF is still rudimentary. The intelligent NGMN evolution has the history of IN evolution in the public telephone and services networks in the United States, Europe, and Japan Ahamed and Lawrence (1996).

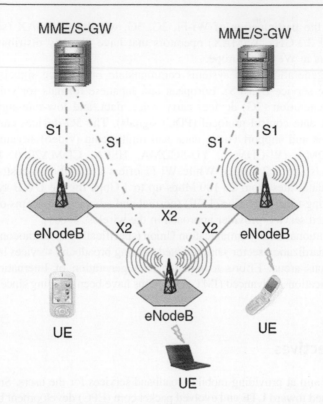

Figure 7.1 Schematic of a NGMN. *Note*: All NGMNs do not fit this representation. UE, user equipment; MME, mobility management entity; GW, gateway. The eNodeB evolved after NodeB was installed in the prior architectures of mobile networks. The functionality and interfacing of the eNodeB have been enhanced dramatically in the evolved networks such as E-UTRAN; eNodeB and links X2, S1, etc. are presented further in Figures 7.3 and 7.4.

7.3   Configurations

Numerous nodes (NodeBs that communicate with users) and radio network controllers (RNCs) make up the universal mobile telecommunication system (UMTS) terrestrial radio access network (UTRAN). UTRAN is a key element that makes up the 3G core UMTS network and provides access between RNCs, user equipment (UE), and the core network (CN) via the logical interface (luB). Figure 7.2 illustrates the connectivity between elements UE, NodeB, RNC, and the CN through three logical interfaces Uu, luB, and (luCS and luPS) between the four elements. An RNC may also communicate with another RNC via the fourth interface luR.

In the evolved packet systems (EPSs), the cells (Figure 7.3) connect to eNodeB, and eNodeBs connect to the mobility management entity (MME) via S-MME interface. The MME can communicate with each other via the S10 interface, while the eNodes communicate with each other via the X2 interface. The details of the traffic flow pattern in next generation evolved systems are depicted in Figure 7.4.

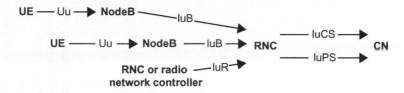

Figure 7.2 Traffic flow from users at UE to the core network (CN).

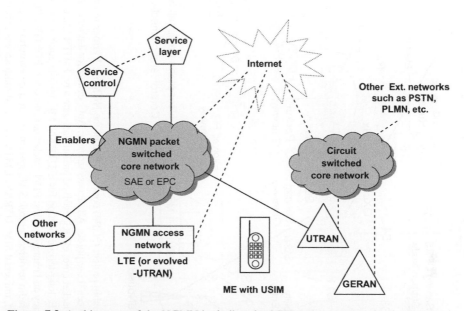

Figure 7.3 Architecture of the NGMN including the 3GPP enhancements for the proposed future networks for the broadband IP-based cellular networks of the future with bit rates up to any beyond 1 Gbps (see Table 7.1). GERAN, GSM EDGE radio access network; LTE, long-term evolution for evolved-UTRAN; ME, mobile equipment with authorized SIM; NGMN, next generation mobile network; PLMN, public land mobile network; PSTN, public switched telephone network; SIM, subscriber identity module; UMTS, universal mobile telephone system; USIM, universal SIM; UTRAN, UMTS terrestrial radio access network; SAE, system architecture evolution for evolved packet core or EPC. *Note*: For a complete list of acronyms, see Appendix 7.A.

7.4 Five-Layer TCP/IP Reference Model

The evolving 3GMN configurations should be considered in conjunction with present Internet environment where the TCP/IP is extensively deployed. It is briefly presented here for the sake of completeness. The TCP/IP (in comparison to the traditional seven-layer OSI model and its own protocol) has five levels for Internet and deploys the TCP/IP five-layer reference model shown in Figure 7.5. This reduced level model

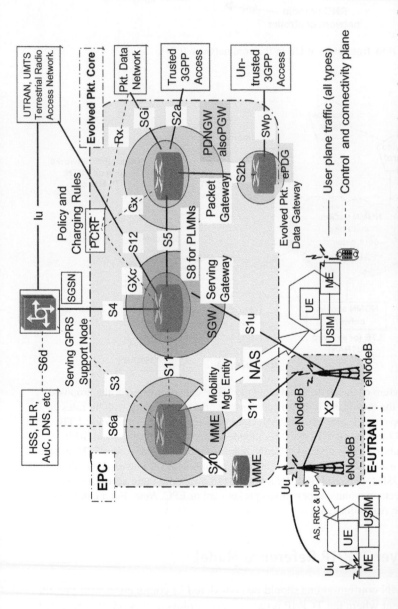

Figure 7.4 Brief topology of the third-generation partnership project (3GPP) configuration of the NGMNs. Various reference points S-x, X-x, etc. also exist to facilitate the protocols to be transferred between these points. AS, access stratum; AuC, center for authentication; DNS, domain name system; EIR, equipment identity register; EPC, evolved packet core; ePDG, evolved packet data gateway; E-UTRAN, evolved UTRAN; HLR, home location register; HSS, home subscriber server; LTE, long-term evolution for E-UTRAN; ME, mobile equipment; MME, mobility management entity; NAS, nonaccess stratum; PCRF, policy and charging rules; PDN, packet data network; PDNGW, PDN gateway; PLMN, public land mobile network; RAN, radio access network; RRC, radio resource control; SAE, system architecture evolution; SGSN, serving GPRS support node; SGW, serving gateway; UE, user equipment; USIM, universal SIM; UTRAN, UMTS terrestrial radio access network; UP, user plane.

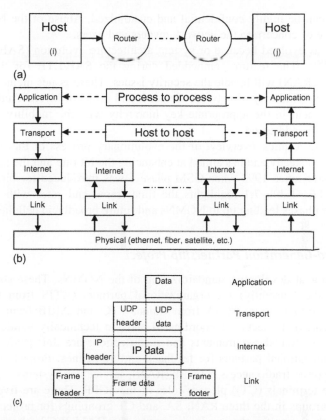

Figure 7.5 Depiction of the five-layer TCP/IP reference model or the TCP/IP suite, or just the Internet model: (a) network topology, (b) data flow, (c) encapsulation of data through the three lower TCP/IP layers.

jumps from the application layer to the transport layer with network, data link, and the physical or hardware layers below. Some of the earlier models (such as the Cisco Academy and RFC 1122, Internet STD3) had suggested three and four layers. It is evident that the transport, Internet, and link layers play a crucial role in providing the connectivity between application (at the application level) layer to the physical layer.

7.5 Evolving NGMN Capacity and Configurations

The NGMNs will make all the sophisticated network services available to the wireless and mobile users now common in the circuit switched IN (Stratton, 1941) environments. Under the careful scrutiny of the 3GPP, specialized and customized network services, which were the privy of more established landline service providers, will become efficient, popular, and foolproof for the local, national, and global wireless users. Security is of prime importance as the networks are wireless and services can be highly confidential and customized. Abuse of the NGMN and its services are of concern to the network owners and users.

The EPS has evolved because of system architecture evolution (SAE) and LTE of the NGMNs. The features embedded during the SAE/LTE for the evolved UTRAN (E-UTRAN) will handle the security issues. These issues include the security requirements, security of network elements and protocol layers. Authentication and key agreement in the appropriate key hierarchy with the mobility of network users will also be addressed.

In evaluating a quick overview of the evolutionary process of the NGMN, the growth has been steady and has aimed at enhancing the bit rate and the access to the mobile networks since 1993 when GSM phase 1 was introduced for bit rates from 9.6 to 14.4 kb/s. Table 7.1 highlights the time frame and rates with the advent of each major phases leading up to NGMNs and future broadband cellular networks.

7.5.1   Third-Generation Partnership Project

The 3GPP aims at developing standardization of the NGMNs. These standards are prepared by the (currently) six organizational partners (ATIS from the United States, ETSI from Europe, CCSA from China, TTC and ARIB from Japan, and TTA from Korea). Projects are coordinated and are technically validated for the specification. Technical requirements and specifications are thus passed on to the ITU and organizational partners for feedback and guidelines. Project coordination is directed to three (radio access network (RAN), service and systems aspects (SA), CN, and core terminals (CT)) plenary roles of the 3GPP. There are five, five, and six working groups in the three RAN, SA, and CT groupings for project coordination each with a specific charter. For example, the RAM WG3 takes care of the RAN to wired transitions; the SA WG2 group studies the architectural aspects.

Typical architectures of the NGMN are shown in Figures 7.1, 7.3, and 7.4. Network evolution is presented next, and architectural enhancement is shown in

Table 7.1 Evolutionary Timeframe from 1993 into Future BB IP-Based Cellular Networks

Time Frame and Specification	Project	Digital Rate (Range)
1993 Phase 1	GSM	9.6−14.4 kbps
1996 Rel. 96	HSCSD	14.4−56.6 kbps
1997 Rel. 97	GRPS	14−171 kbps
1988 Rel. 98	EDGE+	384 kbps−1.3 Mbps
2000 Rel. 3	UMTS	144 kbps−2 Mbps
2002 Rel. 5	HSDPA	1−21 Mbps
2004 Rel. 6	HSJPA	1−12 Mbps
2007 Rel. 7	HSPA + NGMN	11−42 Mbps
2009 Rel. 8 (and WiMAX)	LTE BB IP based	50−100 Mbps
Future (and WiMAX)	LTE-A cellular networks	100 Mbps−1 Gbps

BB, broadband; IP, intelligent peripheral; Mbps, megabits per second.

these figures. Access is controlled via two stratums (access stratum (AS) and non-access stratum (NAS)) that permit mobile equipment (ME) to communicate data to the E-UTRAN and MME, respectively. The evolved NodeB (eNodeB) in the E-UTRAN environment will take over the radio resource control (RRC) functions and all the necessary functions of NodeB from the UTMS environment. It also serves as the end point for AS with RRC and user plane functionality.

The MME provides for the mobility within the EPC. It serves as the end point for the NAS and selects the appropriate gateway for the UE. The UTRAN is to have access to the serving GRPS support node (SGSN) and to the SGW nodes in the EPC.

Trusted and untrusted network access to the PDNGW of the EPC is treated differently. This permits the trusted PDN access such as IP multimedia systems and other operator handled IP services to gain immediate access to the gateway. Policy and charging rules are enforced via the PCRF reference point that monitors the flow of data at the corresponding reference point at the serving gateway SGW, PDNGW, and trusted PDN reference points shown in Figure 7.4.

In perspective, the user equipment communicates with the eNodeB via the Uu interface. The eNodeB communicates with other eNodeB, MME, and SGW via the X2, S11, S1u and interfaces. The X2 interface is to minimize the loss of packets due to user mobility. It also stores the unsent and unacknowledged packets and forwards them to the user(s). There are S interfaces for the user and control planes to communicate between MME, SGW, PDNGW nodes. The extraneous nodes and network nodes also signal via the S3, S4, S12, SGi, S2a, and SWp interfaces and are further presented in Figure 7.4. Appropriate protocols are necessary and available for the NGMN and the 3GPP configurations to function in a dependable and a coherent fashion. Security of user data, privacy, and network issues are of prime importance to assure error and attack proof performance from the evolving NGMNs. The functionality is assured by strict adherence to the interface and protocol structure and requirements now available in the public domain.

7.5.2 The Role of the eNodeB

The eNodeB functionality offers more integrated functions than the original NodeB in the prior configurations of the 2G and 3G networks. Being simpler and more streamlined, there should be fewer variations in the architecture of the eNodeB. Modulation and demodulation and channel coding and decoding for the radio interface are handled at this node. In addition, the RRC (allocation and deallocation of radio channels), handover processing and decisions, and OSI Layer 2 protocol for the radio interface are also handled by the newer and eNodeB nodes.

7.5.3 Evolved Packet Core

This CN has at least five components: the MME, the home subscriber server (HSS), the SGW, the PDNGW, and the PCRF gateway.

The MME handles the security procedures (user authentication, ciphering, and integrity protection), the terminal/network sessions including identification and collection of idle channels. The user subscriber (ID and addressing) information and the user profile information in HSS are invoked via the S6 interface. Any radio path ciphering and integrity information specific to the user is also stored in the HSS. The SGW links the packet data to the E-UTRAN. It serves as an anchor node for data transfer point until the next handover. The PDNGW links the packet data to the PDN. Packet filtering and virus-infected packets are removed from the network at this gateway. Finally, the policy decision function (PDF), charging rules function (CRF) are housed in the PCRF server. Additional constraints may also be temporarily interjected by this server.

7.6 The Ongoing Evolution

The evolution of the wireless NGMN is an ongoing phenomenon. The network in the packet switched arena and also the continued deployment of the sophisticated protocol for user and service provisioning are likely to continue till all the intelligent services can be instilled in the NGMN and that the subscriber—user demands exist. The economic justification for these newer networks is firmly entrenched in the business needs and user demands. The social processes and the human elements in using the sophisticated service provisioning the 3G UMTS and their services need to be reexamined based on future social and business requirements.

The continued survival and growth of wireless networks are a harsh economic reality. The enhanced marginal utility provided by these newer networks should justify the tariff on such services; conversely, the enhanced costs of implementing the networks should be compensated by the revenue stream thus created. Any likely effects of economic recession and business can only cause delay in the implementation of the possible services offered by the 3G UMTS networks.

Numerous technical, implementation, and standards issues remain to be resolved before the 3G and 4G mobile networks can deliver all the services such as true Internet quality, on-demand bandwidth, global roaming, remote connectivity, and global access. The issues that have retarded the expansion of the 2G and current 3G mobile networks can linger into the NGMN era. Affordability lingers as a serious issue deep down the exponential growth predicted.

7.7 Conclusions

The communication and multimedia networks have brought about an intense change in society. Fiber-optic backbones and wireless access networks are the primary catalysts. The social implications and intellectual strides have been profound, especially in the lives of students and future knowledge workers. The integrated effects have a long lasting impact. Processors and networks together can only double, if not more, the impact. Society has its inertia and resistance to such changes, even though the students and elite may absorb the impact and change gracefully.

In a sociological sense, such a change can widen the generation gap more dramatically in the future and cause rifts in the young and old generations that constitute the society. If knowledge is power, it is likely to be centered with the younger generations, making the younger generation more powerful than ever before. This power drift is evident in most of the western nations and has started to surface in Japan, China, and India. In this chapter, we have presented technological foundations for processing, manipulation, distribution, and communication of knowledge that bring in the sociological changes. From a knowledge perspective, there is no balancing force to restrain the trend except that the capital investment markets are generally controlled by the mature and elite in the populous. Knowledge may provide reason and power but the direction of the power is money. In retrospect, reason, power, and money do not always synergize coherently or conformably.

Wireless and mobile networks have enhanced these sociological changes further. When the intellectual inertia is low, the shockwave of change travels further thus accelerating the change. Their impact on the personal life is comparable to the impact of computer systems and networks in business life. The social and behavioral shifts are likely to continue in the immediate future. The uncertainty lies in the personal and social demands that the global wireless networks will offer to the society. Economic validation of such services remains to be realized for the business vendors. Saturation of consumer demands for such bandwidth could be as much of a reality as the demand for terabits per second capacity of the transoceanic fiber networks.

Social and humanist aspects that accompany these networks have a serious impact on the society and more so on the educationally elite but emotionally naïve segments. Since human psychology is not likely to change drastically in a decade or two, the adjustments between the two generations (computer literate, network proficient and unskilled, illiterate) can be painful if not combative and conflictive. In some instances, the social shock waves have been more painfull (French Revolution) than in other instances (British Imperialism in Africa and India).

Appendix 7.A List of Acronyms

7.A.1 General Acronyms in Wireless

ADPCM adaptive delta pulse code modulation
ADSL asymmetric digital subscriber line
AM amplitude modulation
AMPS advanced mobile phone service
BC bearer control
BCPN business customer premises network
BISDN broadband ISDN
BS base station
CATV cable television
CCITT consultative committee of ITT, now ITU-T
CMAC customer mobile access control
CPDFM continuous phase discrete frequency modulation
CSPDN circuit switched public data network
CT2 cordless telephone second-generation
CT3 cordless telephone third generation
DCPN domestic customer premises network

EO end office
ERMES European radio messaging facilities
FCC Federal Communications Commission
FDM frequency division multiplex
FH-DPSK frequency hopped differential phase-shift keying
FM frequency modulation
FPLMTS future public land mobile telecommunications
FSK coherent frequency shift keying
GMSK Gaussian minimum shift keying
GSM global system for mobile communication
GTFM Gaussian timed frequency Modulation
HDSL high-speed digital subscriber line
HDTV high definition TV
IM intermodulation
IMTS improved mobile telephone service
IN intelligent network
ISDN integrated services digital network
ISI intersymbol interference
ISN information storage node
ISO international standards organization
JDC Japanese digital cellular
LAN local area network
LED light-emitting diode
LPC linear predictive coding
LT line termination
MAN metropolitan area network
MCN mobile control node
MCPN mobile customer premises network
MJ early wireless system introduced by AT&T in the 450 MHz band, circa1970s
MK early wireless system introduced by AT&T in the 150 MHz band, circa1970s
MTS mobile telephone service
MTSO mobile telephone switching office
MUA mobile user agent
NADC North American digital cellular
NNI network-to-network interface
NT1, NT2 network terminations
PBXs private branch exchanges
PC paging control
PCM pulse code modulation
PCS personal communication services
PE paging entity
PLMN public land mobile network
PMR private mobile radio in the United Kingdom
POTS plain old telephone service
PSK phase-shift keying
PSTN public switched telephone network
QAM quadrature amplitude modulation
QPSK band-limited quadrature phase-shift keying
QPSK quadrature phase-shift keying modulation
RACE research and development for advanced communication in Europe

RF radio frequency
S, T, U, and V ISDN standardized interfaces
SM S interface for the mobile roamer
SSB single sideband
SSB-F/A single sideband frequency/amplitude
SST spread spectrum transmission
SW switch for the mobile telephone/wireless environment
TDMA time division multiple access
TEm terminal equipment-microwave
UMTS universal mobile telecommunication system
UPT universal personal telecommunication
VSELP vector sum excited linear prediction
WAN wide area network
WARC World Administrative Radio Conference

7.A.2 Acronyms in Modern Wireless Networks

3GPP third-generation partnership project
AS access stratum (RRC and UP)
AuC center for authentication
AV authentication vector
DNS Domain Name System
EIR Equipment Identity Register
EPC evolved packet core
ePDG evolved packet data gateway
E-UTRAN evolved UTRAN
GERAN GSM EDGE radio access network
HLR home location register
HSS Home subscriber server
IMS IP multimedia subsystem
IP Internet Protocol, Also used for intelligent peripheral
LTE long-term evolution for E-UTRAN
MAC medium access control
ME mobile equipment (and hand phones)
MME mobility management entity
NAS nonaccess stratum
NGMN next generation mobile network
PCRF policy and charging rules function
PDCP packet data control protocol
PDN packet data network
PDNGW PDN gateway
PLMN public land mobile network
PUCI protection against unsolicited communication in IMS
RAN radio access network
RAT radio access tandem
RLC radio link control
RRC radio resource control
SAE system architecture evolution
SGSN serving GRPS support node

SGW serving gateway
UE user equipment
UP user plane
USIM universal subscriber ID module
UTRAN UMTS terrestrial Radio access network

References

1. Multi-Antenna Technology Antenna Co-Site Solutions: This document provides the solutions of co-site antenna to reduce the antenna installation space and requirement for 2G/3G/4G. On the web at www.ngmn.org/under the heading Publications/ Technical_NGMN-n-p-mate-multi-antenna_technology_d1.pdf, accessed April 2013. See also, NGMN project report: multiband multimode, requirements—multiband multimode technology, evolution and global roaming, by NGMN Alliance, January 4, 2013, published by the Programme Office of NGMN Ltd., Friedrich-Ebert-Anlage 58, 60325 Frankfurt am Main, Germany.
2. Multi-Antenna Technology Compact Antenna Solutions: This document provides the solutions of compact antenna to reduce the difficulty of antenna deployment for information sharing. On the web at NGCOR_Phase_1_Final_Deliverable.pdf. See also, Multi-antenna technology, antenna co-site solutions, August 31, 2012, published by the Programme Office of NGMN Ltd., Friedrich-Ebert-Anlage 58, 60325 Frankfurt am Main, Germany.
3. NGMN Whitepaper Small Cell Backhaul Requirements: This NGMN white paper aims to help move the industry forward by clarifying consensus around the operators' requirements for small cell backhaul. On the web at NGMN_Whitepaper_Small_Cell_ Backhaul_Requirements.pdf (2012), published by the Programme Office of NGMN Ltd., Friedrich-Ebert-Anlage 58, 60325 Frankfurt am Main, Germany.
4. NGMN Whitepaper Security in LTE Backhauling: This paper is an NGMN informative contribution on the subject and aims to provide a common terminology and some high-level scenarios to introduce to Industry a few possible implementations for security in LTE backhauling. On the web at NGMN_Whitepaper_Backhaul_Security.pdf (2012), published by the Programme Office of NGMN Ltd., Friedrich-Ebert-Anlage 58, 60325 Frankfurt am Main, Germany.
5. Ahamed SV, Lawrence VB: *Intelligent broadband multimedia networks*, Boston, MA, 1996, Kluwer Academic Press.
6. Stratton JA: *Electromagnetic theory*, New York, NY, 1941, McGraw Hill Book Company.

Additional References for NGMN

Frattasi S, Fathi H, Fitzek FHP, Katz M, Prasad R: Defining 4G technology from the user perspective, *IEEE Network Mag* vol. 20(1):35—41, 2006. IEEE 802.16 Broadband Wireless Access Working Group.
Fazel K, Kaiser S: *Multi-carrier and spread spectrum systems: from OFDM and MC-CDMA to LTE and WiMAX*, ed 2, Hoboken, NJ, 2008, John Wiley & Sons.
Ergen M: *Mobile broadband including WiMAX and LTE*, New York, NY, 2009, Springer.
Kato T: Next generation mobile networks, *Fujitsu Sci Tech J* vol. 48(1):2012.

Part 3

Intelligent Medical Environments

The four chapters in Part 3 deal with medical machines based on the design philosophy of medical processors, medical networks, artificial intelligence (AI) in the science of medicine, and the deployment of nationally and internationally distributed medical knowledge bases.

Chapter 9 contains the methodology that the computer scientists have very diligently pursued in developing the architecture and composition of computers from its very inception during the late 1940s to the newer multiple processor, multi-threaded infused chip-based machines. As many as 64 processor VLSI chips are on the horizon.

Chapter 10 evolves and covers the functionality, role, and architectures of processors, bus structures of medical machines. The medical processor chip plays the most crucial part. In conjunction with memories, I/O systems and global Internet switches, the medical machines will play the role of networked computers in global computing environments. Medical machines can be built many ways as computers are built. Unfortunately, there are no centralized or standard committees to suggest global medical protocols or interfaces. Hospitals and medical centers follow their own style of conducting the medical practice as they fit. The local software designers will write medical-ware macros and utilities as they see fit and the IT engineers and network designers will simply adhere to the local directions rather than following global medical standards.

Chapter 10 also summarizes the role of network and Internet technologies in the medical field. As much as processor technology has evolved, network technology has kept pace. As much as silicon and the high-k dielectric gate[1] have contributed

---

[1] Chris Auth et al.: 45 nm High-k+ metal gate strain enhanced transistors, *Intel Technology J* 12(2):77−89, 2008. For the 45 nm technology node, high-k+ metal gate transistors have been introduced for the first time in a high-volume manufacturing process [1]. The introduction of a high-k gate dielectric enabled a 0.7x reduction in Tox while reducing gate leakage 1000x for the PMOS and 25x for the NMOS transistors. Dual-band edge work function metal gates were introduced, eliminating polysilicon gate depletion and providing compatibility with the high-k gate dielectric. In addition to the high-k+ metal gate, the 35 nm gate length CMOS transistors have been integrated with a third generation of strained silicon and have demonstrated the highest drive currents to date for both NMOS and PMOS. An SRAM cell size of 0.346 μ^2 has been achieved while using 193 nm dry lithography. High yield and reliability has been demonstrated on multiple single-, dual-, quad-, and six-core microprocessors.

to the performance of processors, so much have fiber and erbium contributed to the transport of data from one knowledge bank to another. Processing of data and information that was the forte of CPUs has become merged with switching and graphics in the newer more powerful processors of this decade. Network transmission is much understood and deployed by the optical fiber and wireless cellular industries. Massive and global network switching is gradually being shifted in the domain of optical switches and the communication processors in laptops, iPods, and androids.

Chapter 11 tackles the issues in the design of medical processors. These processors can only be in a genesis of computer processors and extensions of object processors. Medical processors deal with a rich array of medical sub-functions, utilities and procedures. In addition, they contend with a rich variety of medical objects (drugs, nurses, doctors, staff, patients, accountants, etc.) that are unique and distinctive. If the medical functions are treated as "verb functions" and objects are treated as "noun objects", then the syntactic and semantic rules become complicated but not insurmountable for compiler designers to handle. The rules and grammar of "medical language" will thus be handled with a rich rules and grammar of the medical compiler.

Chapter 12 revisits the medical machines from the perspective of practical procedures in hospitals, medical centers, nursing homes, etc. If the procedures have a distinct medical code, then this code drives the machine in an error proof, sophisticated, efficient, and optimal fashion. The sub-procedures become the micro-code that is assembled in view of the human and resource limitations of the hospital or the medical center where the machine is located. The composition of the sub-procedure is by itself a layer of the medical-ware and the compiler design.

8 Evolution and Developments of Modern Intelligent Networks

8.1 Introduction

This chapter covers a wide span of technological strides that make intelligent medical networks conceivable in the first quarter of this century. Monumental inventions and innovations have been made during the last three decades. We present such breakthrough inventions in the society that are germane to modern intelligent networks. Even though medical intelligent networks are their infancy, the trend is well established. The emergence is eminent if not inevitable. From a perspective, the society and medical community is not deriving the full benefits of the intellectual, information and Internet ages of modern day. The purpose of this chapter is to close the gap between the current technologies and the future medical needs for all digital medical age to offer the populous accurate, scientific, and well-founded science of medicine and healing and to offer the medical profession "knowledge-based" tools rather than the raw information-based searches through the Web space.

Globally, intelligent network (IN) technologies are mature and self-sustaining. The IN evolution and development was a global effort until the establishment of the intelligent network conceptual model (INCM) proposed and standardized by ITU after the telecommunication management networks and intelligent network or the TINA network proposed in 1990s. The TINA architecture is well founded and documented as the IAS documentation by von Neumann in the late 1940s. The development of INs has been a continual process since 1990s, much as the development of the computer industry since 1950s.

8.1.1 Packet-Switching Phenomenon

Generic packet/frame/cell networking principles are applicable to all the data networks such as LANs, MANs, WANs, and the Internet. They share the resources and use adaptive routing. The geographical size and expanse dictate the classification as a local area network (LAN), metropolitan area network (MAN), or wide area network (WAN). Transmission paths are not dedicated, and the traffic and network conditions dictate the actual allocation of routes linking the network nodes. This network nodes work cooperatively and cogently to move the data from one node to another node. Most of the modern networks use actual network statistics to route the traffic adaptively. Any node handles the traffic that it can pass without

Intelligent Networks: Recent Approaches and Applications in Medical Systems.
DOI: http://dx.doi.org/10.1016/B978-0-12-416630-1.00008-X

offering undue delay to the local or to the transit traffic. The algorithms in the original/revised ARPANET (Abramson et al., 1970) or other networks (Tymnet, I/II (Schultz, 1980), SNA, IBM, Manual, etc.) get the packets from node to node with minimal delay.

There are only two building blocks to any network: the nodes and the links. There are abundant varieties of nodes and links. Most nodes have switching functions embedded to guide the packets to their destinations. As the header information is decoded, the routing is then performed; thus, the packets may arrive via any route, but they are sequentially assembled before delivery at the destination node.

8.1.2   Explosive Growth

The consent decree (NYTimes, 1982) imposed by Judge Greene at the time of divestiture of the Bell System in United States, during the early 1980s, offered a host of economic opportunities to the telecommunication service providers. The typical players in this arena have the seven Regional Bell Operating Companies (RBOCs, whose combined research effort is gathered within Bellcore), General Telephone and Electronics, and the numerous smaller independent local companies which serve locally distributed customers.

Major inventions resulted in providing IN services to the willing and paying customers in the society. A shock wave and its ripple effect still prevail as intelligent Internets for many different services in education, government, medicine, etc. The absorption of the newer technologies has proceeded on a relatively slow basis. However, in the case of the Internet, growth of both its technology and its social acceptance have been phenomenal since its inception. The video and then the digital services have quickly become popular in western society. Now the Internet and Internet services appear to be integral to the functioning of educated western societies. The users have become more information-oriented during the last two or three decades, and this trend are likely to gain more momentum. Society, with its affluent users, is moving away from a product-oriented society to an information-oriented society. The economics of an information society is different from the economics of the Adam Smith society. In the modern times, society is likely to be more educated and is likely to respond more quickly.

These factors tend to make the inventions be absorbed faster, and the invention—technology—rewards cycle spins faster. Inventions thus get extinct and obsolete more quickly. The older Internet architecture and its services are examples of this phenomenon: a revelation to the inventors whom their inventions and the ensuing technology should be valuable and timely. The medical field appears to lag in absorbing the precision, efficiency, and optimality that digital age has to offer, even though the fields of education, business, government, security, etc. are already well along the way.

Most countries realize that an investment in the Internet can catalyze economic activity. For this reason, the public sector looks at the Internet the same way into the transportation industry but with a global impact and the information highways inter-netting the knowledge banks. We have every reason to expect a super-geometric growth for the Internet, and perhaps a slightly less dramatic growth for the Internet-related businesses. The financial opportunities have awaited the full utilization in many directions, such as social networking and knowledge services.

8.1.3   Revolution to Damped Steady State

The explosive growth of packet-switched networks, switching systems, fiber-optic technologies, and global networks had splintered the directions of building, utilization, optimality and deployment of networks, INs, and intelligent Internets. The inventions and their direction is more streamlined and better focused during the last few years as the investors become aware of the social needs and aspirations of an educated society.

The role of (older) ANSI and current ITU is noteworthy in making the INs become global and standardized. The convergence of the IN technologies has resulted. The US, European, (especially, French, Spanish, Italian), and Japanese networks tend to follow standards imposed by ITU especially in the global intelligent wireless and mobile networks. The stability in IN growth in these two directions is becoming more and more visible.

8.1.4   Transition to Optimal Communications

Total optimality in communication is an impractical goal, since the social needs can change dramatically from community to community, time to time, culture to culture. However, some innovations and technologies such as semiconductor, laser, satellite, CD, and fiber optics endure. IN and Internet designers can iteratively optimize network components and configurations. Some of the realistic goals are to reduce the waiting time, increase the accuracy, connect to the appropriate knowledge bases, reduce user frustrations, and provide most appropriate information most of the time. From a statistical perspective, these service requirements demand adaptive if not (very) INs, components, agents, and software. Thus, an appropriate design becomes essential and customized to the service goals. For medical applications, total accuracy and patient privacy add additional software modules and security measures (such as firewalls, encryption, and error correction) to the network components and configurations.

8.1.5   Asynchronous Transfer Mode and Methodology

The asynchronous time division-multiplexing framework provides a foundation for high-speed asynchronous transfer mode (ATM) networks (Rayan, 1994). Typically oriented toward the evolving synchronous optical networks, the ATM approach takes advantage of the ultra high speeds of fibers already in use. These networks depend upon the extremely low bit-error rates and the high switching rates of the optical channels. Fixed time slots carry information packed from different channels over the physical media. The size of the packet in each slot is fixed. Each subpacket from different channels, called a "cell," carries its own header. The cell can be identified and switched by a specific label in the header. The term asynchronous is derived from the fact that the same connection may exhibit an irregular occurrence pattern. Most of the existing techniques of the packet-transfer mode follow the aspect of filling packets on demand for service. Actual demand for data transfer monitors the filling of individual cells.

ATM has gained momentum through the 1990s, the universal ports of the advanced intelligent networks (AINs) (rather than the slightly archaic Universal Information Services (UISN)) will be able to interconnect with these networks. The standardization of the signaling protocol, the impact of fiber optics, the availability of inexpensive hardware, and the progression toward ATM make it necessary to reconsider the revitalization of the national networks of the developing economies. Network architecture for these countries has a very special character. An architectural variation of the IN can be implemented to accomplish a multiplicity of functions quite economically for the developing countries.

The traditional distinction between the circuit-switched network and the packet-switched network has all but vanished because the fast packet switching is inherently built in the ATM. Now, ATM is the replacement for nearly all networks, with fiber, wireless, fiber and wireless, or fiber and cable as the replacements for the traditional telecommunications media. With this technology comes the era of cheap and universal ATM switches trying to become the replacement of the massive electronic-switching systems (ESS). Optical switching prevails even though all photonic-switching looms on a distant horizon.

8.1.6   From SCP'S to Stand-By Servers

The service control points (SCPs) discussed further in the chapter had been essential to provide the early IN functions have been replaced gradually by servers and lookup databases. The lookup function remains; when a network service is requested, the SCP provides the supplementary data, address, or methodology (programs, utilities, etc.), to complete the request. Such supplementary information can be stored in any database and servers can take over the SCP functions, especially in small networks. The service can indeed be any type of service and the role of servers in any network is that of providing supplementary information to complete any task or function.

The seminal American Telephone and Telegraph Co. (AT&T) patent (Weber, 1980) for IN is based on the inclusion of real-time database capabilities in communication networks. Address lookup of circuit-switched connections of plain old telephone service (POTS) to dynamic path routing of SONET frames is routinely done by the fast high-volume servers in networks.

8.1.7   Backbone Networks to Network Clouds

Ownership of entire networks by corporation is still common, but the ability to share the network resources is the more common practice. For example, the mobile networks share the bandwidth allocated in certain bands with numerous users and service providers. The transoceanic fiber links share the available channels for most of media service providers, and so on. In essence, the concept of traditional backbone high-speed networks is being replaced by clouds of many networks that provide (data) transport services. The path that any packet, frame, or cell may take from its source to destination is dynamically routed by the routers embedded in the "clouds" rather than assigned physical connections or switches, except in very localized subscriber loop environments.

In network simulation programs (OPNET, 2013; Sheffield Hallam University), this scenario is handled by a statistical distribution for network delays and such parameters are dynamically updated depending on the network conditions and the channel load in different segments of the "cloud".

8.2 What Are INs?

INs carry and communicate information with distinct algorithmic adaptation. Adaptability occurs at a local or global level. Local adaptability is administered by the programs resident at the nodes within the network. Global adaptability is administered by the coherent functioning of the node to process requests from another node and thus accomplishes global and extraneous functions.

Numerous distinct networks (Ahamed and Lawrence, 1997) can and generally do coexist within the IN. These subnetworks operate coherently and cooperatively in the intelligent functioning of the overall network. In fact, the predictable and accurate response from the entire network is also a dominant requirement for its acceptance in the user community. The endpoints of the INs provide the user access. Information and data may flow in and out of the INs in any standard form (voice, digitized voice, multimedia, or encoded data bearing any type of information). Typical examples of the endpoints may range from individual user terminals or even plain old telephones, to entire exchanges or even gateway offices tying the network to other national exchanges.

In the context of hardware, intelligence resides in the design, architecture, and algorithmic performance of the integrated circuit (IC) chips. The hierarchical interconnection that permits the ICs to function as network components also contributes to the hardware intelligence. In the context of software, intelligence is coded as programs, utilities, or modules. It resides in the active memories of computers during the execution phase. In the context of firmware, intelligence is placed into the control memories of the monitoring computers through microcode.

8.2.1 Basic Building Blocks

In the specific and implemented versions of INs in the public domain, the basic building blocks of INs have been defined in a much narrower sense. As an overview, these (at least) *six* basic building blocks have been identified as SSPs, SCPs, STPs, SMSs, IPs, and signaling network(s).

8.2.1.1   Service-Switching Point

Service-switching points (SSPs) are physical or logical entities generally located at or in close proximity to the switching systems that contain call-processing software.[1] There are *two* aspects of the SSP: (a) the physical switch that performs the switching function and (b) the logical software modules that reside within the switch forcing the execution of the SSP functions. The term SSP is sometimes used to refer both the physical and the logical modules; therefore, a certain amount of caution is necessary in the interpretation of the term. The switching system, which hosts the SSP, may be an end office or a tandem switching facility. Generally, an access tandem (AT) houses the SSP and may receive Freephone calls (800 calls) from other ESS™ Central Offices, step-by-step switching systems, or even crossbar offices. The ATs housing the SSPs use common channel signaling (CCS) to facilitate interoffice signaling and allow the facilities to use interexchange carriers (ICs). The SSPs react to the specific triggers from the customers. In response, the SSPs transmit queries to a centralized SCP within the network. Generally, these database machines can be viewed as highly efficient and dependable computer systems that react to user input, such as the 800 number. In general, the user input can be a specific service request, such as an alternate billing number or a private virtual network (PVN). When the SCP responds to the query from the SSP, the SCP instructs the switching system to complete the call attempted by the user. The call-processing software of the switching system is then invoked to complete the call.

The voice facilities of the network relay the user information between the customers and the SSPs. The queries to the SCP are passed via the interoffice signaling system (SS7) and are made into information packets via the CCS7 network (or the evolved signaling network, Section 8.2.1), which consists of highly dependable packet switches. These switches are called signal transfer points (STPs, see Section 8.2.1.3), which perform context-dependent signal transfer within the signaling network.

8.2.1.2   Service Control Point

Defined as a physical or a virtual node within the IN, the SCP contains the active database of customer records. SCP is a database system that provides critical routing and switching information to the SSPs. The architecture of the SCP depends on the nature of the IN hosting the SCP. The medical-services based SCP will be substantially different from the SCP in an IN/1+ or IN/2 network. Within the architecture of the IN/1+, *three* distinct types of databases (800 number, alternate billing service (ABS), and PVN) can reside in its SCP. This database is actively queried from the SSPs within the network to seek and obtain service-completion

---

[1] Call-processing software monitors the completion of individual steps necessary to complete any call through the network. Typical steps for a circuit-switched voice call are: accept the complete sequence of digits, complete ringing connection, supply ringing signals by alerting called and calling party, detect response from called party, disconnect the ringing path, establish voice path, await hang-up at either party, disconnect the voice path, and release the connection.

information; hence, the optimal and effective management and utilization of this database is critical.

Certain sophistication in the hardware and software hierarchy is essential to make the SCP handle the high volume (several million calls per hour) and diversity in the information sought from the SCP, depending upon the types of services and subservices provided. In a sense, the design of the SCP should be considered a highly efficient parallel processor and data storage-retrieval computer system. The input and output processing need special attention. The SCP operating environment is relatively well defined, and its functional requirements are clearly delineated both by the architectures of IN/1 and by the CCSS7 requirements. Thus, the hardware design assures consistency with the operational environment (STP, SMS, and SSP), the type of processing accomplished (database functions, their updating, security, error-recovery, and duplication), and the interfaces with the other network components (SS7 network, other signaling networks, service management systems (SMSs), security systems, and so forth).

8.2.1.3 Signal Transfer Point

STPs are distributed within the CCS network (see Section 8.2.1.6). The STP nodes are high capacity, extremely reliable packet switches for the transportation of signaling information between SSPs, SCPs, and other STPs. In rare instances, the SSP and STP functions are combined as one node. The four main functions of the STP are performing: (1) error-free message routing, (2) protocol processing, (3) address translation, and (4) message routing database look up.

STPs provide terminations for numbering signaling links from 256 to approximately 1024. They process up to 5000 or more messages/packets per second. The packet delay is typically less than 0.1 s. Four of the six types of STP links terminate at the STPs, and the inter-STP traffic can become quite heavy for interarea calls. The link rates started at 2.4 kbps, enhanced to 4.8 kbps, and presently work at 56 kbps in the United States. Some of these links can also operate at 9.6 kbps. The STPs contain the translation information necessary to forward the database queries from the SSPs to the appropriate SCPs. Traditionally, the CCS network works in the packet-switched environments, and the STPs constitute highly reliable packet switches, operating as two physically separated (and duplicated) pairs within the CCS network to ensure network integrity, even in cases of fire and natural disaster.

The querying Central Offices may consist of a variety of digital and/or analog switches. The minimum configuration requirement for analog switches to communicate with the STP is a stored program controlled switch (SPCS) with a digital adjunct associated with it for CCS capability. The digital switches may be all digital or remote from the digital switches, such as a carrier serving area (CSA) serving point having CCS capability.

The STP also needs some fundamental database support for performing optimal signal transfer and selecting the appropriate SCP. With appropriate software support, the STPs in the CCS can relay the control information in the CCISS7 signaling format throughout the network and respond to SSP queries, and relay responses.

8.2.1.4 Service Management System

The SMS function is intricately tied with the functions of the SCP. In fact, the SMS is an off-line support facility used to enter customer data into the SCP's databases within the IN/1 environment. It is also used to enter the call-processing software into the SCP. The SMS communicates with the SCP through interface cards that process the BX.25 protocol used for communication between SMS and SCP. The SMSs also need a series of front-end processors to link with the dual buses, which provide data paths between the SCP's other front-end processors (discussed further in this chapter) and the SCP's bank of central processing units (CPUs). Generally, these front-end processors may be implemented by deploying microcomputer chips with appropriate interfaces.

In the IN/1 framework, new SMS modules are necessary for each new IN/1 service. To further group the software in the SMS environment, three sets of SMS software have emerged for the IN/1, the first generic IN. These sets are the SMS/ 800 for the 800 services, the database administration system (DBAS) for the ABS, and the SMS/PVN for the PVN.

Standardization and uniformity are desirable among the software modules for these three well-accepted IN/1 services. The number of SCPs in the IN/1 can start to increase as the number of individual service providers grows, since each provider can have an individual SCP for the particular type of service. However, if the SCPs of each of the service providers have to respond in a consistent manner, then the SMSs that drive the SCP must be functionally transparent. For this reason, standard forms of SMS/800, DBAS, and SMS/PVN have been created in the United States for IN/1, the RBOCs, and for the Bell client companies (BCCs).

The functionality and the architecture of IN/1+ and IN/2 through the early and mid-1990s that the SMS design philosophy has undergone considerable reorientation. This reorientation happened because of the enhanced service-independence concept that is essential to the working of IN/1+ and IN/2.

8.2.1.5 Intelligent Peripheral

IP or its functional equivalent was introduced for the additional functions (e.g., message recovery and new network service installations), deemed necessary for IN/1+ (in the American environment) customers. IPs will have their own localized switching facility to contact newer vendors of additional telecommunication services or carriers.

The intelligent peripheral (IP) for IN/1+ is a stand-alone, network-compatible element (Haas and Robrock, 1986), which can be connected to a switching system. The signaling to and from the IP is communicated via the SS7 network to STPs in the IN/1+ network. IPs also transfer voice and data to and from switching systems. In view of routing efficiency, the IP is generally connected to only one switching system, even though a switching system may have numerous IPs. Remote physical locations of IPs are acceptable in IN/1+ architecture.

The IP is a new entity that performs very specialized functions in the network. Specialized and evolving telecommunication resources may be provided in the network to be used with the introduction of newer IN/1+ services. Some of these resources include customer-specific announcements and/or service-specific announcements, voice synthesis, digit collection, and voice and data encryption. The IPs may contain resources to interact with call participants. These devices may be triggered by the customer inputs, such as the voice or the preprogrammed digits that initiate certain network responses.

Every IP has an adjunct service point (ASP) (Wojcik, 1991), which responds to the network requests to use its telecommunications resources. The ASP interacts with the service logic interpreter (SLI/1+) of the SCP/1+ within the limitations of the IN/1+. The subset of SS7 that deals with the transactions capabilities applications part (TCAP) is used in the ASP-to-SCP communication via the STP in the network. The ASP module has control links to the switching fabric of the IP and to the numerous resources within the IP. The IP communicates with the switch by way of its voice/data lines. The IP is accessed by two groups of users: the caller when an IN/1+ service is demanded by the customer, and the operating-company personnel as new services are being configured. A typical example of the first case occurs when customers may want to recover an announcement stored for them. Upon customer verification (identification code or voice analysis) by the IP resource, the stored announcements may be made available to the customer by the database from which the announcement was retrieved. In a typical example of the second case, the operating-company personnel may be attempting to provide a new service by using the functional components (FCs) of the network-resource-management facility and the associated IP. The SSP/1+, which hosts the SLI/1+, responds to the input, and the SLI/1+ makes contact with the IP by way of the intermediate STP/1+.

These functional building blocks of INs are essential for the transition of telephone networks to become intelligent. The phased introduction of INs during the 1990s needs considerable standardization and uniformity in design and functionality. The standards committees, ITU-T—International Telecommunications Union-Telecommunications Standardization Sector (formerly CCITT—International Telegraph and Telephone Consultative Committee)—and ANSI—American National Standards Institute—have identified a majority of functions, interfaces, and protocols. These standards have been published and are available in most of the major telecommunication libraries.

A certain amount of intelligence is encompassed in the conventional analog networks, such as the POTS network. The Central Offices that serve as nodes of the older POTS networks are primarily for the use of analog voice telephones.

These high-capacity networks become a part of the long-haul facilities that, in turn, carry multiplexed voice and data traffic within the country. This mode of network design and evolution is not appropriate to the projected services of the networks in modern societies. In a sense, networks can only leapfrog forward rather than evolve. The recent innovations are too many and too powerful to be ignored. Internet working, broadband information highways, and the distribution of critical

resources and intelligence are the more basic concerns rather than providing telephone access and POTS capability.

Four of the lower levels of the Central Offices are EO, Sectional, Tandem, and
Primary as they existed in real networks. Classified according to the functions, the
end offices bear no through traffic (Figure 8.1) and provide communication to and
from the customers. The intermediate, Sectional offices permit through traffic
between Central Offices and the Tandem Central Offices permit both end traffic

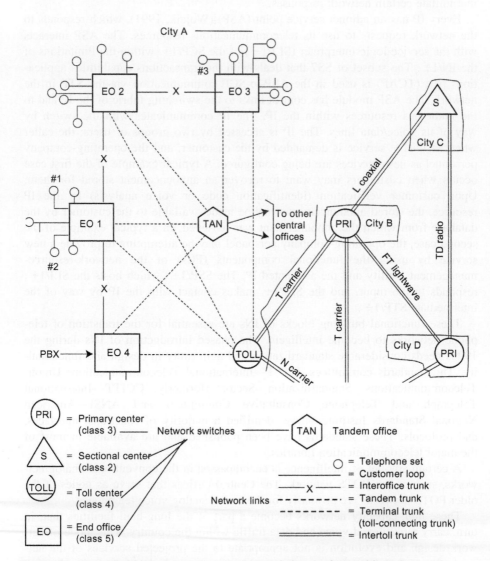

Figure 8.1 Generalized interconnections between switches (nodes) and links in an older
telephone network (ca. 1980s and 1990s). The modern mobile networks have a much more
evolved architecture.

and through traffic. The Primary offices carry intercity and toll traffic. *Two* formats of links are: (a) the high-capacity trunk lines and (b) the lower capacity local distribution or subscriber loops or lines.

8.2.1.6   Signaling Network

Signals in networks force network components to function in a prescribed and predetermined fashion to complete a task in providing a specific service. Having started as being very rudimentary (e.g., DC signaling), it has evolved to a very elaborate CCISS.

The implementation of Common Channel Interoffice Signaling (CCIS) started in the United States in 1976. Hardly a network then, CCIS was simply a link connecting two toll offices: the 4A toll crossbar office and the first deployed 4ESS™ switch toll center. After having proved its worth and potential, the link became a network over the 8 years that followed until divestiture of the Bell System. The signaling standard used was the CCITT (now ITU) approved System 6 and was crucial to proving the advantage of the digital CCS over the single-frequency and multifrequency techniques used earlier. Typical of the advantages that have been documented are the reduction of call setup time, from about 10 to 2 s, thus improving the utilization of network resources. Additional benefits included improved reliability, reduced fraud, call tracing, call-process acknowledgment, and optimal call routing.

8.3   Events Leading up to INS in the United States

8.3.1   Early American INs

There are two major directions of force on the evolution of the public domain INs in the United States. First, the carriers of major data transport facilities around the country are evolving a special type of network intelligence to monitor and implement the network performance requirement from a data-throughput point of view. Optimal utilization of network switching and transmission facilities to maximize revenues is the major design criterion. With the advent of high-speed fiber-optic systems that deploy multiple gigabit capacity in digital pipes, it is essential to be able to add, drop, and cross-connect channels appropriately from the digital superhighways spanning the country. Second, regional operations in the more densely populated areas of the United States are developing the capability to provide new IN services (IN/1, IN/1+ , and IN/2 architecture).

8.3.2   Evolutionary Aspects of American Networks

Public domain communication networks can only evolve. The size and expanse of these networks make even incremental changes in their functioning and administration expensive and time-consuming. The American telephone network is an example of this situation. A majority of this vast national network was owned by a single organizational entity (AT&T) until the divestiture of the Bell System in 1984. This majority ownership status prevails in most public national networks.

The recent public domain INs, which are built around standard interfaces and standard signaling systems, are able to control, monitor, and administer new services in the evolving networks. The introduction of integrated services digital network (ISDN) services and capabilities is based upon the deployment of the existing telephone networks (and the CCIS (Wojcik, 1991) network) in the United States and around the world to provide new digital services to a large and diversified customer base. Similarly, the introduction of the most rudimentary IN (IN/1) is also based upon the deployment of the existing telephone network (and the CCS network) in the United States and around the world to provide a layer of sophisticated, network-based, and value-added services, as well as novel information services. Sophisticated signaling capability is a prerequisite for all novel IN services.

In the context of enhancements to existing communication networks, the service-oriented networks are derived as new architectures of information processing nodes (e.g., SPCS systems, SSPs, real-time database facilities, and SCPs) through advanced signaling systems (e.g., SS7 (Ahamed and Lawrence, 1997)) to provide value-added service. At the most fundamental level, selected nodes are chosen and enhanced to perform more than the typical communication functions they perform in telephone systems. These nodes are interfaced with customers providing them with more convenient, economical, and quicker services (such as 800 number, ABS, and Green Number Service (GNS)). At a more advanced level, the functions within the INs are varied and dispersed and can be tailored to the need of individual communities. The databases can also be dispersed and tailored to provide lookup or look-forward services using quick and economical computer-based methodologies.

The major steps toward the evolution of the INs during the last three decades are presented in Figure 8.2. There are no technical barriers to overcome for implementing the IN/2 and AIN-type of INs. For this reason, the implementation will progress through the 1990s. However, when the fiber backbone is sufficiently in place, it is expected that Service Net-2000 will incorporate SONET and ATM technologies to deliver IN services based upon frame relay and cell technologies. Typically, such services will be based upon processes now used in knowledge processing for medical, educational, and financial applications, and for video telephony and multimedia in entertainment. Service Net-2000 is an AIN/2 type of INs.

8.3.3 Events Before INS in Europe and the INCM Model

8.3.3.1 Early British Telecom in Digital Derived Services Network

The *two* major business divisions in British Telecom are the national networks division, which caters to telephone and specialized services, and the local exchange networks. In addition, the British Telecom International and British Telecom Enterprises participate in the overall telecommunications environment. The digital derived services network (DDSN) was developed in conjunction with the advanced 800 network.

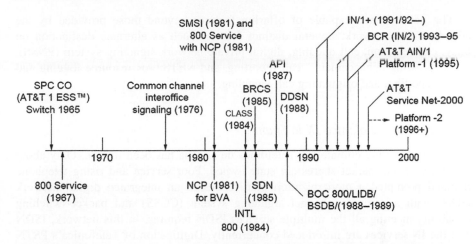

Figure 8.2 Timeline for the major technical changes that have preceded the fully evolved INs in the United States. API, attached processor interface; AIN, advanced intelligent network; BOC800, Bell Operating Company 800 Service; BRCS, business residence custom services; BVA, billing validation application; CLASS, custom local area signaling services; DDSN, digital derived services network; DSDC, direct services dialing capabilities; IN/1+, intelligent network/1+; LIDB, line information database; NCP, network control point; SDN, software-defined network; SMSI, simplified message service interface; SPC CO, stored program controller Central Office; Service NET-2000, SONET-based AIN/2.

The primary example of this network, in its limited capabilities, was the original British Telecom DDSN. The service capabilities of this network were conceived and implemented by AT&T. The DDSN was commissioned in 1986 with the Freephone, or the 800 service, capabilities. In 1989, the advanced Freephone (similar to the advanced 800) services were introduced. Similar services have been in place in Spain (late 1991) and in Italy (1992). These networks use the AIN implementation methodology and provide the services initially envisioned by IN/1+ and IN/2. These services and the architecture of the network are conceptually similar to those of the INs as envisioned by Bell Communication Research for the RBOCs. In fact, two of the Bell operating companies (Ameritech and Bell South) have plans to follow the AIN Release 0 services platform to introduce their own AINs.

The analog-derived services digital network (ADSN), implemented in two stages, had already offered the Freephone (0800) service since 1985 and the premium (0898) service since 1986. Eight participating analog switching nodes in ADSN have been replaced by digital switches, thus converting the ADSN to a DDSN and offering full IN services in the United Kingdom. The five building blocks of the network are: 5ESS® switching systems, network control point (NCP), network subscriber transaction, administration, and recording system (NETSTAR), network services complex (NSCX), and multifunction operating system (MFOS).

The network was capable of offering features beyond those provided by the advanced 800 network. Several distinct features such as alternate destination on busy, call rejection, call queuing, digital private network signaling system (PNSS), call-processing enhancements, call reporting, and NETSTAR resource logging and usage reporting, and originating call signaling.

8.3.3.2   Early Telefonica IN in Spain

The socioeconomic climate for Telefonica de Espana has been unique. Only about one third of the market shares are state owned. Poor service and rising telephone demand prompted a modernization plan to design an integrated digital network (IDN) with a common channel signaling system (CCSS) and packet-switching capability meeting all the multiple services ISDN requires. In this network, ISDN and the IN services are introduced concurrently. Digitization of Telefonica's PSTN gave rise to the very first (2B+D) service at 144 kb/s, and 30B+D services at 2.048 Mb/s in the early 1990s. The existing *four*-level hierarchy of the network with local, primary, secondary, and tertiary exchanges is not unlike the American network hierarchy of Central Offices. A tandem switch may be added between the local exchanges. The signaling, facilities and administration are considerably different from those in other national exchanges and are unique to Spain.

These proposed services of the early Spanish IN includes: malicious call trace, call diversion with immediate, no-reply, absent subscriber signaling, traffic restrictions with outgoing call barring, incoming call barring, incoming call barring for diverted calls, alarm call service with casual alarm call, and regular alarm call. Additional services includes abbreviated dialing subscriber control, hot line service with direct connect and timed hot line, call waiting, three-party service, calling card, televoting, and personal number.

8.3.3.3   Early Societa Italiana per l'Esercizo and Azienda di Stato per i Servizi Telefonici in Italy

The state controls the Italian postal and telecommunication services. *Two* major organizations constitute the Ministry of Post and Telecommunications Societa Italiana per l'Esercizo (SIP) and Azienda di Stato per i Servizi Telefonici (ASST). Some of the early services offered by the SIP segment of the Italian Network were local telephone customer relations, design and construction of local, sector, and district telephone networks, local telephone and auxiliary services and long-distance telephone services with ASST, and border international telephone service as agreed with Italian and Foreign administration.

Some of the early services offered by the ASST segment of the Italian network were design and construction of the domestic telecommunication between the compartments and international network, long-distance communication with SIP, international telephone communication with European and neighboring countries and islands, and other administrative duties with the concessionaries.

8.3.3.4 Early French IN Environments

The French IN effort has a rich and trailing history. During an explosive surge of growth for the French PSTN during the mid 1970s, an archaic version of the VPN concept was in place for industry. Four Alcatel E10N3 exchanges in the Paris area could be used in the transit mode to provide interconnect capability for large businesses via leased lines. The service called Colisée provided switching of leased lines within the framework of the exchanges. Service details, private numbering options, detailed billing, etc. were provided to the large business customers of Colisée. The service has ISDN capability with an added Alcatel (MT25) exchange and provides interconnect with other PVNs from other carriers. A precursor (Numero Vert, Freephone, or called-party billing) service to the IN/1 services was in place as early as 1983 followed by calling card (Carte Pastel) in 1989. The architecture of the early versions have the PSTN exchanges (Alcatel E12s) connect to the SSP served by the SCP with routing database, service database, and charging center. The more recent French IN provides for independence of the service provisioning form network implementation and its evolution from the PSTN. Further, the concept of offering new and innovative services from service-independent elementary functions is exploited to offer services quickly and efficiently.

The French Telecom's IN has *three* layers. *First*, the functional layer consists of the SCP, the routing database tied into the charging center, and the billing system. This complex is supported by the conventional SMS and its database management system (DBMS) with the service creation environment (SCE) and the service management access point (SMAP). The service data point (SDP) and its DBMS will support the SCP functions with the service data for the individual customers in providing the specific service.

Some of the early services for the French IN include typical IN/1 services including the Numero Vert, Carte Pastel, Call Me Card service, and the Transgroupe (the VPM service). The evolution follows the introduction of the ITU-T CS-1 features in the SSPs and provisioning of the ISDN services. The evolution of the IPs is geared toward separating the IP platforms to provide general services to most SSPs and to provide the interface.

8.3.4 INCM for Generic World Wide INS

In the INCM model, ITU-T has facilitated the gradual assimilation of communication networks into INs. It came about approximately 11 years after the initial architectures from Bellcore during early 1980s. The Bellcore AIN work entails an implementation of the functions over the physical planes of the network and these two indeed constitute the two lower planes of the INCM. The AIN Release 1 is a proposed physical architecture from Bellcore that integrates other technologies and platforms with the future INs. AIN 0.1 architectures include the SSP, the SCP and their interface; interfaces between SDPs and SCPs; and finally interfaces between operation systems, the SSPs and SCPs. AIN 0.2 adds the interface between SSPs and IPs.

In perspective, the evolution of the ITU-T's INCM model is not unlike the evolution of the more generic ITU-T's open systems interconnection (OSI) model. In the standardization of earlier (OSI) model, ITU-T has facilitated the gradual evolution of all networks into communication networks. The generic OSI model also came about after the circuit-switched network of the numerous network owners (such as AT&T, GTE, BNR, PSTN, and the TELCOs), the packet-switched networks of the computer companies, and the rudimentary signaling networks of the already existing communication networks were already in place. Layer 3 functions were already being implemented (though not as efficiently and elegantly in the older networks) in the early 1980s in a functional sense in both the circuit and the packet-switched networks; then came the OSI model that gracefully integrated the entire telecommunication networking functions in its role within one seamless communication entity.

Germane to the ITU-T standard is the *four*-plane INCM: (a) the service plane, (b) the global function plane, (c) the distributed service plane, and (d) the physical plane. These four planes facilitate introduction and implementation of new IN service shown in Figure 8.3. They encompass and address the original questions (regarding the service logic, service logic programs (SLPs), service interaction, service independence, and the original functional entities) posed by the original IN/2 Bellcore model and discussed in the following sections.

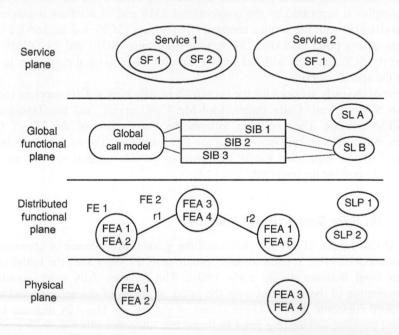

Figure 8.3 INCM proposed by ITU-T (formerly CCITT). FE, functional entity; FEA, FE action; i*N*, interface to any Node *N*; PE, physical entity; r*N*, relationship to any Node *N*; SF, service feature; SIB, service-independent building block; SL, service logic; SLP, service logic program.

In specifying the upper two levels of the INCM, ITU-T has played an elegant role of globalizing the IN architecture at a functional level and again at a physical level.

8.3.5 Major Events Encompassing INCM

The earlier developments in the ESS industry (1965–1985) in the United States, Europe, and Japan had streamlined the integration of the VLSI and computer-based processor technologies into the communication industry. The earlier software industry from the computer environments throughout the world was well integrated into the design of operation systems, utilities, logic programs, and utilities of all the switching systems around the world.

American-based 4ESS, 5ESS, the European-based Alcatel's (Earlier generic E-10 and MT25 systems, now Alcatel-Lucent 4 and 5ESS), Siemens' EWSD, Ericsson, and the Japanese-based NTT's, Nippon switches all deployed a rich admixture of VLSI-based hardware platforms and their associated layers of software.

Since the interfaces, software layers for the INCM, and the protocols were well in place by the year 2000. Major events influencing transfer and communication of multimedia content is presented in Figure 8.3. The effects of these events have been spectacular on all most all aspects of intelligent communication systems and networks (Figure 8.4).

Intelligence in networks has become highly distributed as the distributed processing in computer systems. It is feasible to build intelligent HW/SW modules and place them in most networks such as security, educational, and medical networks. Software modules and intelligent agents in any network can substantially alter its functionality, operation, and its response.

The basic computer systems and facilities (the hardware, software, and firmware) that control, monitor, process, and channel information through the network have become an integral part of INs. The flow of the information takes place over appropriate channels within the network. Information also flows within a diversity of participating networks.

Channels are assigned dynamically, switched, and reallocated to carry the information from node to node, customer to customer, or workstation to workstation. The facilities that actually switch channels may be Central Offices, switching centers, private branch exchanges (PBXs), or even satellites that relay information. The actual transport of the information is carried out over transmission facilities of the network. Such facilities may span a small laboratory or become extensive to span a nation or the whole world, or be sent into deep space to relay planetary information. The size of the network or its geographical expanse is inconsequential to its nature.

The functioning of any generic IN depends upon the *four* essential components. *First*, the interfaces (I) provide for the flow of information into and out of the network. *Second*, the monitoring computers (C) supervise and control the flow of information via the various "channels" according to software modules in the computers. *Third*, the switching systems (S) switch the channels and complete the

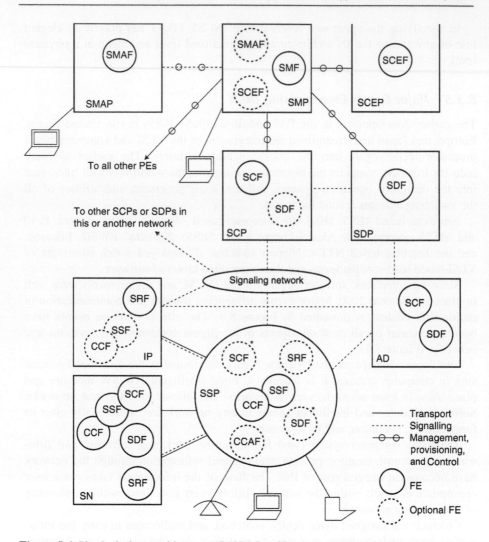

Figure 8.4 Physical-plane architecture (Q1205 Specification) proposed for the telecommunication management network or TMN and the IN or the TINA network. *An SSCP PE includes the SCF and SDF FEs as core elements. AD, adjunct; CCAF, call control access function; CCF, call-control function; FE, functional entity; IP, intelligent peripheral; PE, physical entity; SCEF, service creation environment function; SCEP, service creation environment point; SCF, service control function; SCP, service control point; SDF, service data function; SDP, service data point; SMAF, service management access function; SMAP, service management access point; SMF, service management function; SMP, service management point; SN, service node; SRF, special switching function; SSCP, service switching and control point; SSF, service switching function; SSP, service switching point.

physical (electrical, microwave, optical, satellite, etc.) or logical channels between the users interfacing with the network. Finally, the associated transmission facilities (T) carry the electrical, optical, or microwave signal in the appropriate medium to convey and communicate the information.

The increasing network topology and its geographical expanse in the United States called for nodes in the network. These nodes are called the STPs. Germane to the CCIS network, the STPs prevailed well before any emergence of an IN was implemented anywhere (not until 1981). Before the divestiture of the Bell System in mid-1980s, the CCIS network operated with 10 regional signaling sectors in the United States.

Each region contained two STPs. The locations of these individual STPs within the regions were chosen with due consideration to survival and recovery of the network after natural disasters and disastrous network conditions.

Three types of links span these STPs. Type *A* links connect the switching offices with the STPs. Type *B* links connect the STPs of neighboring (adjoining) regions. Type *C* links are specially balanced, mated pairs that interconnect STPs within regions. The user offices (i.e., the Central Offices) and the STP interconnections in the CCIS network are shown in Figure 8.5. In a sense, the links, STPs, and the switching nodes that communicate with the STPs within this network all have unique logical and geographical addressing capabilities.

8.4   The Evolved SS7

CCIS6, approved during mid-1970s, by CCITT (now ITU) and deployed in the United States, underwent yet another scrutiny starting in 1980. International standards for implementation using a layered protocol structure were the ultimate goal for voice, data, and any other multimedia communication around the world. This quest also resulted in the OSI seven-layered reference model with the higher layers geared toward applications and the lower layers geared toward network and transport of data. The layered or modular approach to specify the communication protocol is the framework of CCS7. The standard was approved by ITU in 1984 and published in mid-1980s.

In a sense, the SS7 has an evolutionary architecture of its own. The exchange of signaling information also follows the OSI model. Thus, all the features inherent in the OSI data exchange model exist in the exchange of signaling information in the SS7 network. The SS7 network architecture in the United States has undergone considerable enhancement during the 1980s. In divestiture of the Bell System, the resulting numerous local exchange carriers (LECs) have increased the number of STPs dramatically. Provisioning for the access and interconnection between the STPs needs more numerous links and more types of links. The increased numbers of INs and Internet connections being installed have required a far greater sophistication in the signaling environment. The SS7 environment addresses these needs effectively, resulting in a much more versatile architecture and protocol compared to the earlier signaling systems.

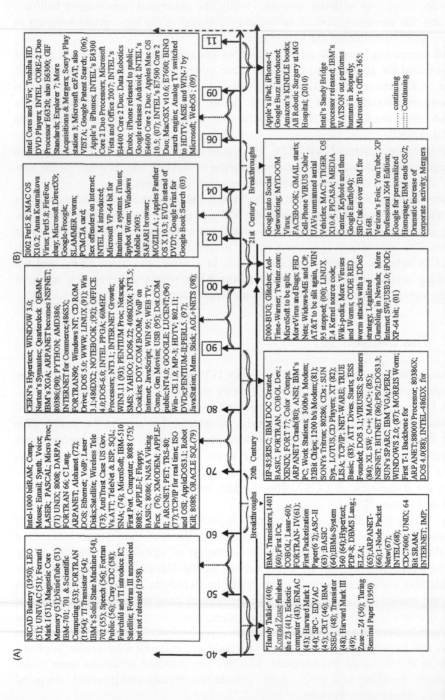

Figure 8.5 (A) Major computer, network innovations affecting network of twentieth century. Social forces are also included. (B) Major computer, network and media innovations since 1990 affecting INs. Major corporate and social forces are also shown to indicate their influence on the evolution of INs.

In the composite functions of signaling and communication, the signaling flows through the SS7 network and the user information flows through the communication network (in all circuit-switched configurations). The interdependence is as essential as the interdependence of control circuits and data paths in computers. The analogy is complete, and the composite network can be built like a cosmic computer with distributed processing and switching capabilities. There is no single switching system (or CPU) that controls all functions; instead, many localized switches (or CPUs) control cooperatively.

Six major links are identified in the CCS7 network and shown in Figure 8.6. The first *three* links, that is, *types A, B, and C*, correspond to those discussed earlier in the section "CCIS Network" that describes the CCIS6 network. *Type D* links interconnect local STPs with the regional STPs to query IN-type of information from the regional SCP. *Type E* links interconnect the other independent carrier with the AT or the SSP node of the IN. Finally, the *type F* link interconnects the non-SSP type of end office with the SSP.

The link rate for CCS7 is normally at 56 kbps, although 64 kbps is likely when data transparency in ISDN is clearly available. These links can also operate at 9.6 kbps. When ISDN is completely implemented, its bearer channels may serve as the CCS7 links. With a total transparency in the CCS7 network, most of the IN functions, such as 800 Service, CLASS™, and interoffice data transport, become realizable. Selective call rejection, caller identification, and automatic call back features can be introduced by simple programming steps within the SSPs of IN/1+ and IN/2.

In a microprogrammed environment, the flexibility depends upon the nature and number of microinstructions and programs resident in the control memory. On the

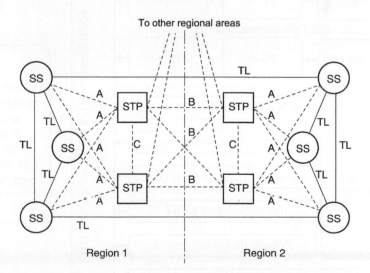

Figure 8.6 Typical interconnections of STPs in the CCIS network. SS, switching systems; TL, trunk lines. Only the "A" lines are duplicated to guard against link failure. Typically, the SSs have numerous TLs.

other hand, the adaptation of the networks depends upon the FCs, the SLI, the associated SLPs, and finally the data stored in the network information database (NID). These network information modules generally reside in the SCPs.

8.5 Global INs

8.5.1 Overview of Global INS

INs have evolved much as computer systems have evolved. During the maturity of IN architecture, numerous countries and many vendors have participated in the evolution. The globally accepted architecture is the INCM model because of the ITU efforts and the culmination of the TINA architectures. Figure 8.7 depicts the efforts of many organizations that have evolved their own interim configurations.

8.5.2 Commonality and Consistency of INS

Networks are also akin to vastly distributed computer systems. In fact, networks can be considered widely dispersed computer systems, rather than locally distributed processors. The converse, however, is not true; that is, computer systems, at their current stage of sophistication, are not widely distributed communication systems. Network intelligence is also similar to a distributed intelligence coded into

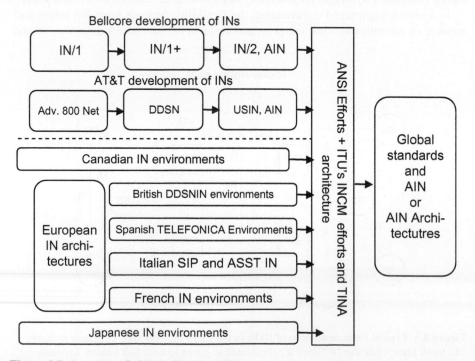

Figure 8.7 Overview of global effort for AIN.

computer software and operating systems. Both systems perform complex functions depending upon the hardware architecture, the nature of operating systems, and the application programs that drive them. Both types of systems have been significant beneficiaries of the powerful concept separating the control signal path from the data-flow paths, even though this principle has been rigorously followed in computer systems from the days of von Neumann. Both systems deploy their hardware and software resources by optimal, adaptive, and load- or traffic-dependent algorithms. The designers of both systems built in service independence into the hardware, software, and firmware. Generally, these concepts are inherent in the computer systems built and used in the computers around the world. The worldwide communication systems have not been as adaptive and programmable. For this reason, recent attention has been focused upon the standardization of the network hardware, software, interfaces, and the protocol to permit easier global communications.

The need for signaling to control the IN is established, and it closely parallels the need for operation-code-driven control signals in computer systems. The control of the IN is directly exerted by the SS7 network constantly communicating with the SSP, STP, and SCP. A typical configuration of the SS7 signaling network is shown in Figure 8.8. In this context, the SS7 consists of two basic parts: message

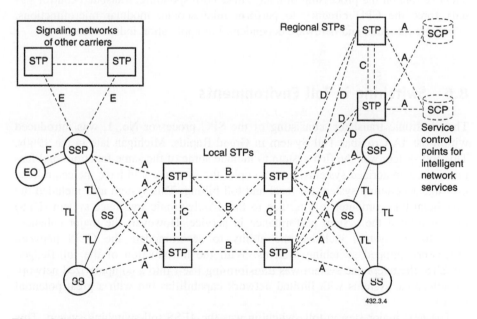

Figure 8.8 Typical interconnection of STPs in the CCS7 signaling network. The switches, which may hold other IN components, such as SSP, SLI, NID, and NRM, are also shown to indicate the voice/data paths in Bellcore's IN/2. The "A" lines are duplicated, and SSs may have SSP modules to detect and invoke IN services. The switches generally have numerous TLs to other switches. EO, end office; SCP, service control point; SSP, service-switching point; SS, switching system; STP, signal transfer point; TL, trunk lines.

transfer part (MTP) and different user parts. The MTP uses Q.702 at level 1 for the signaling data link, Q.703 at level 2 for the signaling link, and Q.704 for the signaling network functions and messages. The different user parts of SS7 at level 4 for the IN/1 environment are the signaling connection control part (SCCP), TCAP, and the operations and maintenance applications part (OMAP). It should be noted that other network forms and their appropriate parts are not implemented and are subject to changes and revisions as more experience with different public domain INs starts to occur. The signaling, engineering, and administration system (SEAS) provides the details and management of the functions and operations of the network signaling events. It operates via the STP and monitors the functions of the STP, SCP, and SSP, especially in IN/1 where the interaction and interconnection between the three signaling network components is clearly defined. One must realize that numerous SCPs, STPs, and SSPs do exist in most INs. The signaling network would still perform in the same form, using the same protocols in its communication but with extended addressing capabilities for the numerous components.

In computer systems, processing depends upon the interpretation of the operation code by the control circuits. From purely hardware considerations, at the control level, the translation of the operation code to the control signals plays a decisive role on the processing of data. These corresponding, translated control signals force the CPU circuitry to perform microscopic, modular microfunctions, which are intricate, and hardware dependent, but application independent.

8.6   Switching in Toll Environments

The electronic translator, consisting of the SPC processor No. 1, was introduced within the 4A Crossbar Toll System in Grand Rapids, Michigan late in the 1960s. This toll system was the first system to include some of the same functions and features of computerized systems. For example, the system could have the centralized message accounting system for local and toll billing. This system also included the peripheral bus computer to interface to the 4A/electronic translator system (ETS) that monitored the system performance in service. However, the major enhancement to the system included the ability to accommodate the CCIS between processor-equipped switching systems. With the introduction of the full-fledged 4A/ETS, the telephone system was transforming itself into a computerized network for telephone systems with limited network capabilities but with a great potential to grow.

The next major step in toll switching was the 4ESS toll-switching system. This machine is a logical (and managerial) extension of the No. 1 ESS switching system to reduce the fixed costs and the running expense and to provide flexibility with the changing socioeconomic climate of the early 1970s. The processing capabilities for toll, the more sophisticated toll network resource and channel allocation, and the pulse code modulation transmission and switching capabilities were also included in the 4ESS switch. The first 4ESS switch was capable of handling about half a million calls per hour with a trunk capacity of over 100,000 calls per hour. This switch provided a benchmark for the capacity and reliability of trunk-switching systems.

To a degree, the 4ESS switch initiated the impact of computerized control onto toll switching—what computers had initiated in the data processing field 29 years earlier. This trend in the communication industry funneled all the rewards to the digital processing and handling of telephonic information in the early stages. More recently, this same trend has evolved into networks that make any relevant information accessible to anyone authorized to receive it, at any time, and at any place with any degree of accuracy and resolution within the framework of security and the legality of exchange of information.

As a telecommunications switching facility, the 4ESS switch completes as many as 800,000 calls per hour as the call attempts to reach about 1,200,000 during peak calling periods as far back as early 1990s. More recently, similar strides have been made in retaining the compatibility between the 4ESS switch and the more modern communication systems and networks. Typically, the existing 4ESS switch is capable of interfacing with the SS7 via its common network interface and the ISDN implementation with CCITT (now ITU-T) Q.931 standards. The switching platform functions with a spatially separated time-multiplex switch capable of interconnecting numerous time-slot interchange units. The "B" (i.e., the DS0 at 64 kbps) channel integrity is retained in this switch. Total synchronization between the switching clock and the network clock is retained throughout the 4ESS switch. In its current design, the 4ESS switch can also interface with DS3 carrier systems initially and then with the SONET-based transmission facilities.

The introduction of the new processor (1B) to replace the original processor (1A) in the 4ESS switch has contributed to the increased call-handling capacity of the switch. The expanded volume that the switches handle is expected to increase at an approximate rate of 5% every year. The demand for the 800 number, cellular, fax, and video messaging is likely to remain high. Rather than replacing the switch with the newer 5ESS switch, a more economical and feasible alternative is to replace the processor. For this reason, the new processor is designed to function at a call-handling capacity 2.4 times greater than that of the original processor. The speed and memory access is more than doubled. The reliability is enhanced and operations and maintenance are streamlined. The overall switch (the 4ESS) capacity with the new processor is expected to be over one million calls an hour—a macro Pentium chip for a massive PC!

The introduction of the first single-module 5ESS switch in 1982 (in Seneca, IL), and then the introduction of the multi-module 5ESS switch in 1983 (in Sugar Grove, IL), started another major trend in Central Office capabilities. In essence, the integrated architecture and time division digital switching that is inherent in this machine provides for most of the distributed processing and multifunction capabilities for the expanding telecommunication market. This machine offers the following seven distinct features.

The more recent 5ESS is a single system that can serve all the applications: operator, local, toll, and international. It is generic and can interface with all carriers, with all media, and with all service providers. The versatility extends to providing IN, ISDN, SONET, ATM, Satellite, and specialized communication services. It provides for digital switching between numerous subscriber loop carrier systems and IC circuits (the T family or the E family), making the transition to ISDN easy and elegant. It also interfaces with the analog interexchange systems.

It has a modular approach in the hardware and software designs, which permits adding newer devices as technology evolves and which allows itself to interface with the older generation switching systems (e.g., the 4ESS switch or the older 5ESS systems).

Its hardware modularity permits gradual growth as the network and service demands increase. This permits a cost-effective deployment of Central Office resources.

Being mostly digital in devices and its control, it has a reliability comparable to, if not better than, most computer systems. Extra error correction stages and parallel functionality of the CPUs permit quick and dependable retract ability of any call-processing step(s).

The computer orientation of the switch design permits local and centralized maintenance by running diagnostics in any module, combined modules, extended subsystems, or global systems. The operations, engineering, and maintenance (OE&M) functions become much simpler.

The 5ESS operating system, being modular and encoded in a higher-level language (the C language), permits Central Office capabilities to be added easily. The system is portable and modular to be customized to the particular Central Office need. New digital services (such as ISDN) and new IN services within the SSPs can be accommodated by altering the flow control within the call-processing environment; such network services can include the detection of the trigger condition, database lookup in an NID or invoking an IP, or exercising an SLP.

Numerous other digital switches also exist. In Europe, for example, Siemens' EWSD® and Ericsson's AXE® systems perform comparable functions. Equivalent systems in Japan have also been built and function with similar precision and dependability.

The 5ESS-2000 switch (see Figure 8.5), in the American environment, contends with both the ISDN and the IN functionalities. In addition, this newer 5ESS platform permits enhanced processing capabilities, as they exist in the IN environments, and servicing capabilities with simpler operations, administration, maintenance, and provisioning (OAM&P). Servicing capabilities include handling as many as 200,000 lines, newer remote-switching modules with line capacities of 20,000 lines, wireless services, etc. The provisioning aspect is unique to most of the recently designed ESS platforms for the United States and Europe. The reliability of the 5ESS platform is better than that of most computer facilities and recorded (as of December 1994) to be at zero failure in the first 7 months of its installation in eight countries.

The newer wireless networks, SONET, independent packet networks (such as INTERNET, KNOWLEDGENET, or MEDINET (Ahamed, 2009)) are already tied into the public domain networks. The interfacing with the 5ESS-2000 permits it to perform as a totally software driven versatile switch. The switching module (SM-2000 5ESS) of this machine permits its interfacing with the fiber-optic nets using the synchronous digital hierarchy (SDH) (ITU, 1988), with OC-1 (in year 1994) and OC-12 (future) carrier capabilities. At the other extreme, the (mB + nD) servicing features of ISDN (proposed during 1990s) make provisioning of digital services quite easy and manageable with most of the new generation of ESS platforms (NGE Group).

8.6.1   From Switching to Intelligence

This section discusses the first 800 service, CCIS6, simplified message service interface (SMSI), billing validation and calling card services, international 800 services, CLASS™ services, software-defined network (SDN), and business/residence custom services (BRCS).

8.6.1.1   The First 800 (IN) Service

During late 1960s, the Bell System had extended the message accounting part of the administration function within the Central Offices. Unification and streamlining of certain types of incoming calls, such as sales, reservations, and centralized verifications, were established. Prior to this first 800 service in 1967, human intervention was used for collect calls, dedicated foreign exchange lines, and pre-authorized collect calls via operators. The automation of operations for offering newer services and automating services, such as enterprise services, by using the message accounting facilities, provided an incentive for making these services more attractive to businesses. Simplifying billing procedures and pre-authorizing acceptance of these calls formed the framework for initiating the 800 network and the continued growth of INs. The status of the network in 1965, 1968, and 1971 is shown in Figure 8.6.

8.6.1.2   The Role of CCIS6

In May 1976, the Bell System introduced the CCIS system (based upon the ITU's SS6) for the long distance part of its switched network. Trunk setup was first initiated between Madison, WI (4A ETS system: the 4A/ETS) and Chicago, IL (4ESS system). The multifrequency signaling system, which was used before this date, was going to be gradually replaced from this first CCS6 test in 1976. The architectural arrangements for the signal distribution and the signal transfer are shown in Figure 8.9. The numerous advantages of the potential of the CCIS system for IN functions were clearly established.

8.6.1.3 Simplified Message Service Interface

During early 1980s, an SMSI was introduced utilizing adjunct processors (for storage and retrieval of messages) and certain types of specialized Central Offices with built-in message storage systems. The capacity to provide memory and database access was made available on a limited basis within the network.

8.6.1.4 Billing Validation and Calling Card Services

This type of service was a precursor to the more sophisticated 800 services. The incoming call would be intercepted by an operator, who would query a distant and centralized database (an NCP) and complete the call if billing validation and/or calling cards were authorized. Figure 8.8 depicts the configuration of the network for billing validation and calling card services. This authorization was entered into the NCP from a database authorization system (DBAS, later enhanced as the SMS). In the automated version of the calling card service, the customer enters the calling card number, and then the personal identification number. The application

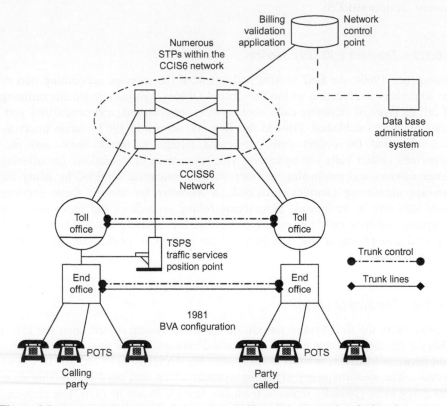

Figure 8.9 Databases for control of network switching. This illustration depicts the active use of database(s) at NCP to control the call progress and call completion through the network in 1981.

of billing validation is the first use of the CCS6 network for direct query transactions between the switching systems (operators or ESS) and the NCP. Figure 8.9 depicts the configuration of the network for NCP-based 800 services. This service was also introduced in 1981.

8.6.1.5 International 800 Service

In 1984, the international 800 service was introduced to permit calls in and out of the United States to be completed via an NCP, which did the final translation and interfacing between the United States and the selected foreign countries. As an independent development in 1984, the network was also able to support direct services dialing (DSD) and inward wide area telecommunication services (INWATS). Figure 8.10 depicts the configuration of the network for NCP-based advanced 800 service. The originating call-screening facilities permitted only selective call completion, and this is a key feature of the custom local area signaling (with special) services (CLASS). This feature was widely available as a composite group of network services until the individual RBOCs started to offer such services through the mid-1980s.

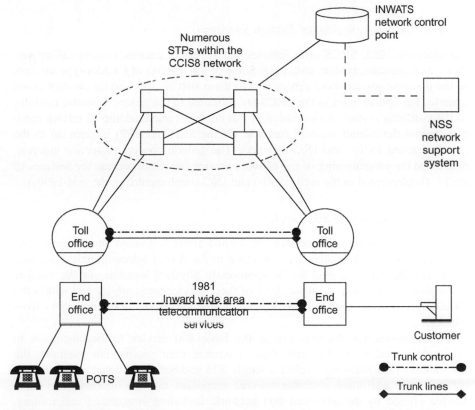

Figure 8.10 NCP-based wide area telecommunication services during early 1980s. POTS, plain old telephone service.

8.6.1.6   CLASS Services

In 1984, the CLASS was introduced on a trial basis in Harrisburg, PA. Automatic number identification (ANI) and CCIS6 signaling are essential for the early CLASS that consist of selective call rejection and auto recall/auto call back. The first switch-to-switch IN architecture was initiated, entailing the need for both interconnected Central Offices to retain all call-related information via CCIS6. In the same year, the direct services dialing capabilities (DSDC) was also introduced, thus permitting newer services (such as third party billing and call extension) to be added to the basic telephone service.

8.6.1.7   Software-Defined Network

The SDN service, introduced in 1985, is also a feature of INs. The SDN permits the circuit-switched network facilities to be quickly configured as PVNs with all the features of switched network operations, modernization, administration, and maintenance. This feature is domestic in the United States and was introduced at about the same time as DSD service.

8.6.1.8   Business/Residence Custom Services

Introduced in 1985, BRCS offer features that appear in centrex, custom calling services, and electronic tandem switching. Some of the features of CLASS-type services in the domestic service were generalized to these BRCS. This service concept is not generic. The options used in the BRCS are restricted to the generic software modules of the switching system. An extension of this concept (where additional service modules control the overall network function via the SCP and STP) is germane to the more advanced IN/1+ and IN/2 networks. The generic concept of service independence and the programming of the network service functions became the features of IN/1+ (implemented in the early 1990s) and IN/2 (implemented in the mid-1990s).

8.6.1.9   The Advanced 800 Service

For the national 800 number service, the United States is divided into six geographical service areas. The callers are connected to the AT&T telecommunications network and the call is routed to the appropriate physical location via the number translation and a lookup database. Five of these service areas are located within the 48 contiguous states and Hawaii. The sixth area serves the 800 subscribers from Alaska.

The advanced 800 features extend the basic 800 service to the customers to select their service offering and, thus, maximize their profits. For example, the 800 number customers may select a single 800 number for national and interstate callers. Eight additional customer-selected responses may be built into the exact service offered by the advanced 800 network, including customized call routing, routing control service, call attempt profile, call prompter, call allocator, command routing, time-of-day and day manager, and courtesy response.

Whereas the earlier 800 networks (discussed earlier) are INs in a limited sense of the definition of intelligence, the digital derived service network (the Bell operating company's 800 services) did not appear until 1988. These later 800 networks are specifically referred to as "IN/1" by the RBOCs. The stages in its development are depicted in Figure 8.11. In the scenario of IN evolution, IN/1 has an evolution of its own, and it can be traced through Figures 8.6−8.11. The architectures and generic building blocks of the RBOCs IN/1 are well defined and tailored to perform regional services and have features that are individualized to the local RBOC. These numerous 800 networks owned by the RBOCs are models of economic success for expanding the services of local businesses and generating telephone

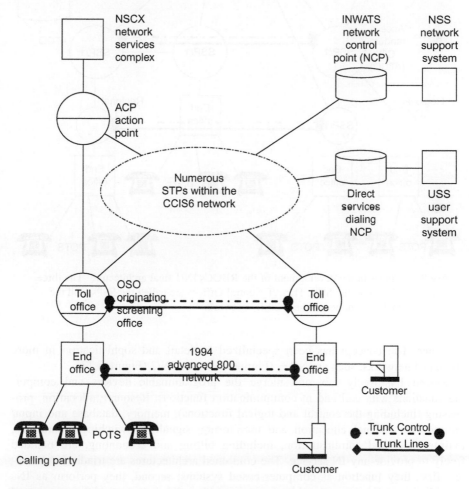

Figure 8.11 Architecture of an advanced 800 service network using direct service dialing capabilities.

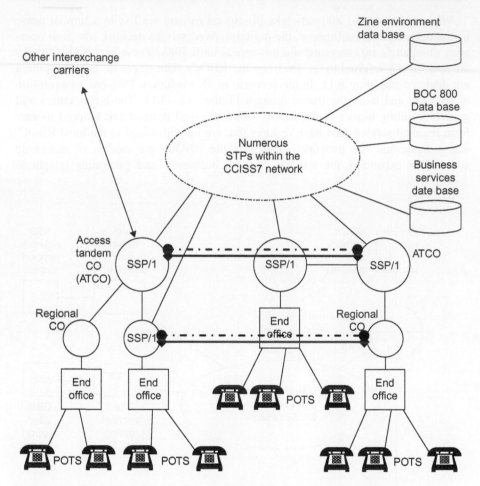

Figure 8.12 Stages in the development of the RBOCs IN/1 final architecture. The three databases reside within the SCP. The AT Central Offices are called the SSPs, and the interoffice signaling is done via the CCISS7 network.

revenues. The concept has been specialized in detail and sophistication in more advanced networks, such as IN/1+ (Figure 8.12) and IN/2 (Figure 8.13).

Recent INs freely mix and merge the programmable devices and computing functions with call and in communication functions. Resource allocation, processing (including the control and logical functions), memory, database and input/output with channel allocation and monitoring, signaling, switching, operations, maintenance, and administration, including billing and accounting, are blended freely to provide any IN service. The combined architectures are triadic in character: first, they function as computer-based systems; second, they perform as INs providing specific programmable services in a network language of their own; and third, they serve as sophisticated digitally controlled communication systems.

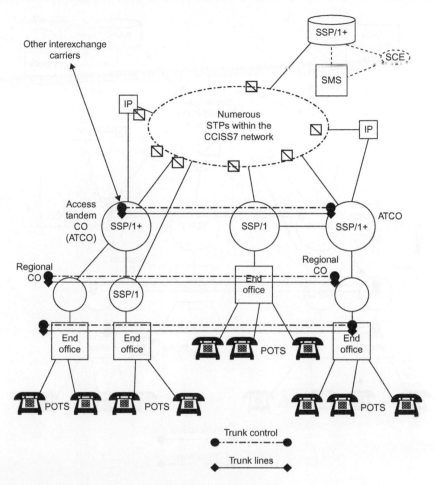

Figure 8.13 Architecture of the RBOCs IN/1+ . The SCP/1+ is a sophisticated database environment supported by SMS, and IP. The concept of service programming is introduced via the FCs of the SLI. AT Central Offices are enhanced and called the SSP/1+ . The interoffice signaling is done via the CCISS7 network.

The major steps toward the evolution of the INs during the last three decades are presented in Figure 8.14. There are no technical barriers to overcome for implementing the IN/2 and AIN-type of INs. For this reason, the implementation will progress through the 1990s. However, when the fiber backbone is sufficiently in place, it is expected that Service Net-2000 will incorporate SONET and ATM technologies to deliver IN services based upon frame relay and cell technologies. Typically, such services will be based upon processes now used in knowledge processing for medical, educational, and financial applications, and for video telephony and multimedia in entertainment. Service Net-2000 has an AIN/2 type of architecture.

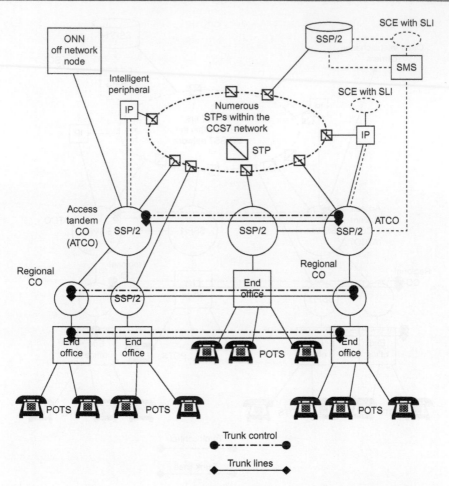

Figure 8.14 Typical architecture of the IN/2. This offers a wide variety of services to end users. The SCE has SLIs to be able to "write" SLPs for any new service to be introduced.

On the European scene, the ITU (formerly CCITT) had a dramatic effect in formalizing the INCM and defining its four layers during early 1990s. European, Canadian, and Japanese INs also evolved during this period. The impact of this standardization has been to make INs universal around the globe.

The INs provide extended control within the network and the vendor community, provide most of the flexible telecommunications functions (such as CLASS services), and provide a flexible format for services introduction (such as 900, 700, and 911 services) and their gradual implementation. By a collaboration of the ISDN and the INs, the true potential of high-speed, high quality, new services increases tremendously. Typically, E-mail, electronic directory, private network control (via the PVNs), and incoming call management (CLASS) can be independently carried out by these combined networks using one standard ISDN interface for all functions.

First, from the perspective of outsiders and user needs for the digital transport capabilities of the network, the rapidly evolving telecommunications networks, incorporating the circuit-switched, packet-switched, and message-switched networks, are shaping ISDN

Second, from the economic perspective, the tendency is to favor numerous evolving networks that are highly specialized and intelligent to serve segments of customers willing and able to pay for their specific needs (e.g., the 800 number and 700 number services).

Third, from the technological perspective, the force is the evolution of very high capacity, inexpensive optical fiber communication systems that enable long-haul data transport (via synchronous optical networks, SONET, and ATM). Such networks, though not intelligent, can influence the very architecture of INs and their use of SCPs, STPs, and the CCISS signaling backbone network, which is essential to the functioning of all INs. One option is the feasibility of evolving the current interoffice signaling network (now operating under the X.25 protocol in most countries) to a network based on ATM and having optical transport capability (if and when it becomes necessary).

The economic incentive of the service providers is already forcing many versions of the INs. For example, banks and financial institutions have their specialized networks. SWIFT™ (a financial networking system) network functions provide for the transport of most distributed banking and financial data. The needs of the housing industry and real-estate brokers will be quite different from those of the travel industry. Such diversification of needs is likely to bring newer and newer INs. If the IN concept can be implemented by PVNs, then ISDN and broadband capabilities will simply become the means of implementing the intelligent, personalized, and highly economic PVNs.

These new networks will deploy the advanced features of the new switching systems (AT&T's 5ESS switch, Siemens' EWSD, Northern Telecom's DMS-series switches, and so forth) and the five basic components (SSP, STP, SCP/NCP, IPs, and SCE) of AINs.

8.7   AT&T's Role in Evolution of INs

A universal and generalized interpretation of the network intelligence is implied by American Telephone and Telegraph Company. The INs proposed here have the capacity to introduce several physical and/or logical locations of intelligence in the network. The need, level, and location for the introduced intelligence are flexible and demand dependent. Newer technologies and services can thus be integrated in the network as they evolve. For example, the wireless and mobile radio networks can be integrated in the framework of national and international INs. In remote regions, very small aperture terminals (VSATs) interface to national networks, and their intelligence will also become desirable. Being more heavily geared toward global and national networks, the long-range survival of these networks depends upon being able to interface with many hundreds of "locally" INs. The capacity to accommodate the existing network infrastructure is one of the requirements of the newer INs.

8.7.1 The Switched Network and New Architectures

As far back as the late 1980s, the switched network, i.e., ISDN and SDN, with nodal services could be interconnected to different local access and transport area (LATA) networks, dedicated private networks, private switched networks, packet-switched networks, and international networks. Two key elements in the functioning of this integrated access architecture are the CCS network and the integrated access distributor (IAD). This 1987 configuration of the network is shown in Figure 8.15. The arrangement, though functional as a telecommunication and interconnect facility, does not qualify as an IN. However, the introduction of intelligence at the network nodes and at elements physically located away from network nodes is predicted to be offered by these global access providers, thus leading to universal and global INs.

The architectures proposed by the RBOCs are conducive to the evolution of the UISN concepts (see Section 8.3). These concepts parallel some of the IN/1, IN/1+, and IN/2 concepts but exceed their geographical range and localized access. Whereas the RBOC's initial goal is the effective operation within the regions and cooperative work with the surrounding regions, the longer distance-data transportation-services provided by the information carriers (AT&T, MCI, SPRINT, etc.) can also be enriched. The transport services that utilize a vast variety of media to communicate

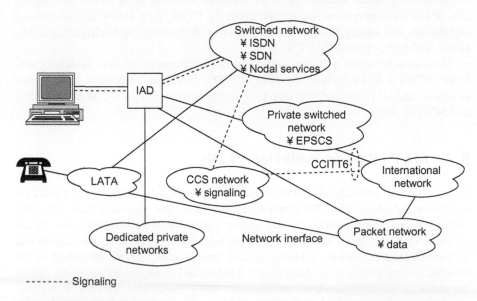

Figure 8.15 An earlier version of the communication network in the United States. CCS, common channel signaling; CCITT6, a provision of standards set by International Telegraph and Telephone Consultative Committee; EPSCS, enhanced private switched communications service; IAD, integrated access distributor; ISDN, integrated services digital network; LATA, local access and transport area; SDN, software-defined network.

information will be enhanced by UIS concepts at the national level and by the three major varieties of INs being implemented by the RBOCs.

The integration of digital services, as they are evolving with the ISDN, will interface with the national and regional INs via the more widely accepted CCIS/ (CCISS7 and via the ISDN Q.931 protocol). The inherent nature of the digital switches is driven by the stored program, which also facilitates the functional integration of all digital networks and INs. These digital-switching systems will house the service-switching systems for the newer network switches.

8.7.2   The Advanced 800 Services Network

The advanced 800 network was introduced in early 1980s as a precursor to the DDSN, the network-control-point-based billing validation application (BVA) services.

This network lacked the broad service-independence concept. However, this network had the makings of an IN/1 architecture with toll centers, rather than SSPs; CCIS6, rather than CCISS7; NCP, rather than an SCP; and a network support system, rather than an SMS. The long-distance services supported by this type of the network are evident from the INWATS database in the NCP as shown in Figure 8.10.

More recently, international efforts have been focused by the LECs in the United States, British Telecom in the United Kingdom, Societa Italian per l'Esercizo della Telecomunicazione (the postal administration, "SIP" in Italy), and Telefo'nica in Spain to build national IN platforms and offer services more uniquely suited to the particular national environment. Personal number service (or "Follow Me" service) is also being offered in other countries. The Advanced Services Platform of the A-I-Net, announced by AT&T, marks the beginning of the truly global networks where international mobility of customers and the data is a prime design consideration.

8.7.3   Universal Information Services Network

The UISN proposed in late 1980s was a precursor to AT&T's AIN. The proposed architecture shown in Figure 8.20 depicts the existing public-switched networks to facilitate Universal Information Services (UISs). UISN makes this existing network (Figure 8.16) intelligent and adaptive and provides an environment to blend and integrate numerous features existing in modern INs with distributed databases. This environment can blend any combination of services (voice, data, and video/image) with maximum convenience and economy. Network capabilities at the SSP nodes and carrier level are optimally used to meet the customer requirements. The architecture of this UISN is realized with the existing technology and components.

The services that these INs can provide include the existing 911 (Public Emergency) service, virtual private networks, and automatic calling card. These services correspond to the IN/1 functions. The more advanced INs (or the AIN Release 0 and AIN Release 1) from AT&T provide the 700 (personal number) service and the 900 (Televoting) service. These services can be performed in the public-switched networks and in private networks, and can be performed at a local and regional level, or at a national and international level. AT&T's AIN is depicted in Figure 8.17.

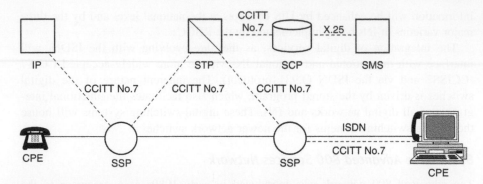

Figure 8.16 Simplified configuration of the AT&T UISN (ca. 1989).

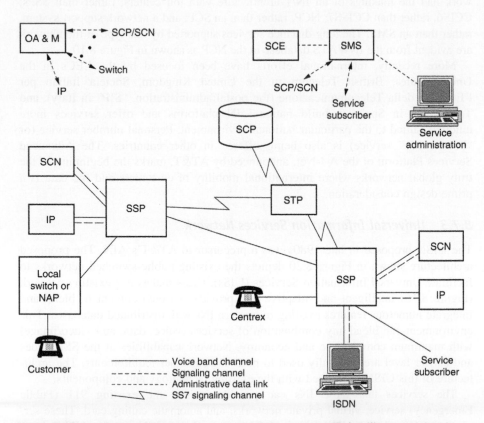

Figure 8.17 Architecture of the IN for using the AIN concepts. IP, intelligent peripheral; ISDN, integrated services digital network; NAP, network access point; OA&M, operations administration and maintenance; SCE, service creation environment; SCN, service circuit node; SCP, service control point; SMS, service management system; SSP, service-switching point; STP, signal transfer point.

The five major functional entities in the proposed UISN are the SSP, the STP, the SCP, the off-network node (ONN) or the IP, and finally the SMS. These components or entities perform much like any other special purpose and highly sophisticated computer systems. They are programmable at the operating system level through the special instruction level, and can perform intelligent functions in a localized geographical area for the RBOCs in the United States or on a national basis for major carriers and long-distance transport facilities of AT&T in the United States. In fact, any level of adaptation of an IN can be built for any amount of geographical coverage.

The SSP and SCE work together at the universal services nodes (USN) within the UIS network. The transport service of the UIS network will be monitored by the enriched service layer derived by the coordinated functions of SSP and SCE. Typically, the UISN may contain the STP, SCP, and SMSs to work in conjunction with any other IP or the ONNs as they exist within the framework of the INs proposed by Bellcore and discussed in Section 8.6.1.

8.7.4 Design Details of AT&T'S UISN

A certain amount of commonalty exists in the provisioning of basic switching functions common to all telecommunications networks. For example, the time-slot interchange concept is generic and has been deployed extensively in 4ESS™ and 5ESS® systems. It is the software modules and the inputs to such software modules that change the flavor of regionally intelligent functions versus the nationally or globally intelligent functions. In a sense, the same AT&T 4ESS and 5ESS, Siemens EWSD®, Nippon's Telephone and Telegraph DMS200, GTE's GTD 5EAX, NEC's NEAX61, or Stormberg Carlson's DCO core-hardware can perform as an RBOC tandem office switch or as a gateway office to another continent. To this extent, there is built-in programmability in most of the major switches around the world.

A similar argument exists for the STPs. Generically, the STPs used in networks are very high volume and very reliable, although not the fastest packet switches. These switches are placed in secure locations and are carefully deployed in matched pairs because their functions are crucial. They can deploy most of the applications interchangeably, since the STPs are stand-alone systems. In a broader sense, the functionality of the UISN components is akin to the functionality of components in Bellcore's INs.

8.7.4.1 SSPs in UISN

These SSPs have been integrated with the larger switching systems built by most of the major vendors, such as AT&T, Northern Telecom, Siemens, Alcatel, etc. The SSP of the advanced 800 network is built from the number 4ESS introduced by AT&T in 1976. The SSP of the DDSN deployed by British Telecom is derived from the 5ESS switch introduced by AT&T in 1982. This switch also incorporates the STP for the DDSN. This software module responds to the trigger condition existing within the network as the IN services become necessary. The call-handling information is obtained from the SCP via the service transfer point in the network at the USN. It is important to note that the manufacturers of the major switching systems provide the switching fabric for regional companies and for the gateway offices to national and international networks.

8.7.4.2 STP in UISN

The STP is a node within the CCIS network. In 1968, CCITT approved a common basis for signaling in response to the increased transatlantic telephone traffic. While still in the preliminary stages, the need for international signaling standards was evident. This early version, referred to as "System 6," went through a series of refinements, and the final specifications were approved in 1972. A digital version of the system was authorized in 1976. In the United States, the first CCIS6 link was installed between the 4ESS toll Central Office with 4A toll crossbar office in May 1976.

The earlier Bell System operated under the signaling provided by 10 geographically distinct regions. The STPs were duplicated in each region and provided communication between the various toll switches around the country. Three distinct link types were deployed: A-links for connecting toll offices with STPs, B-links for connecting STPs in different regions, and C-links to connect STPs in the same region with very specially selected, dedicated, and mated wire-pairs. This architecture of the CCIS6 network permitted interoffice and inter-region communication of call-connect and call-control information freely within the country. The CCS7 network is a much more elaborate manifestation of the CCIS6 that was deployed in the United States. CCS7, widely accepted throughout the world, permits international signaling around the globe for a vast variety of services, rather than the limited scope of network call-monitoring services that CCIS6 was initially designed to do.

The request for service is provided by standardized signals to appropriate service/information providers. These signals calling for such services/information have to reach the appropriate databases distributed within the network. The STP is a switch to forward the signals in real time and generate the response from the databases in the SCPs. The STP of the advanced 800 service is a stand-alone switch that functions in conjunction with the 4ESS.

8.7.4.3 SCP in UISN

This entity of the IN has two major components. First, the service logic module provides the capacity to interpret the type of service requested and the type of resources (such as databases) to be tapped. Second, the database(s) in the SCP contain updated information/resources to complete the request received by the SCP. These databases can be simple tables or a collection of extremely complex data structures, depending upon the type of service/information sought by the network or the user.

8.7.4.4 ONN or the IP in UISN

The type of services that an IN can provide can be highly specialized. All of these services may or may not be in the legal jurisdiction of the network owners to pro vide. To supplement the network services and enhance the attractiveness to the users, outside vendors may offer these services or support functions. The information/service can again be highly variable, ranging from language translation or voice recognition to delivering recorded messages, or digit collection based upon the multifrequency tones received at the ONN or IP. In the UISN, the ONN is a remotely located device or module and the IP is a network resident.

8.7.4.5 SMS in the UISN

Creating new network services and maintaining the associated databases calls for a considerable software effort. The SMS provides an authorized and efficient entry point for this work.

These five basic elements used in the UISN are the same as those in the RBOCs IN/1+ and IN/2. The flexibility offered by the elements make them serve as IN components in national environments, in the regional, or even in the private corporate network environments.

The architecture of the UISN is viewed in very broad terms with regard to the elements, and the individual functions and their management, as well as the cooperative functioning of the individual elements. A hierarchy with three levels has been suggested.

The five essential elements of the network reside at the lowest level. At the intermediate level, the collections of the local management of each of these elements exist, and of their individual functions. At the top level, the management of the cooperative roles of each of these elements constitutes a universal IN. This hierarchy for the management of the network (in its entirety) is classified as the universal network management architecture.

8.7.5 Two-Tier Services Architecture in UISN

There are two major service tiers in the provision of the UISs: the upper, enriched services tier, which is atop the second transport services tier. These two tiers facilitate digital access through the media between the universal network nodes. The enriched services of the UISN are partially realized by the universal operating system (UOS). The enriched services are capable of providing an adaptive admixture of the upper level functions of the OSI model. The UOS has access to the SSP and the service control environment, also operating in conjunction with the digital switch (5ESS or the 4ESS). The UOS also provides limited customer control of the network. These three modules, UOS, SSP, and SCE, together provide an enriched service environment for the UISN. These services may be activated at any of the nodes in the UISN. The transport services offered by the media are aimed to facilitate the realization of the lower-level open system interconnect model (see Section 3.4.1).

8.7.6 The Enriched Services Tier of the UISN

Newer services are supported by this enriched tier. Applications that need specialized implementation and service-switching functions are accessed at this level. The UOS, which is also a part of this tier, performs network management functions. Typical of these functions are customer control, cost-effectiveness, network problem and fault management self-healing diagnostics, and fault correction and service functions.

8.7.7 The Transport Tier of the UISN

Five levels are foreseen in the evolutionary model of the UISN: partitioning, multiplexing, dropping, adding, and cross connecting, all of which take place within this tier. Fiber-optic transmission media is seen to be an ideal environment to implement the transport tier. As ISDN starts to become more common, the transport tier can facilitate the ease of the basic channel functions listed. Basic rate, primary rate, and broadband ISDN are all expected to become substantial beneficiaries of the transport tier, controlling the mass capacity "digital pipes" in the national network environment. The subchannel facility becomes insidious to the functioning of this tier in the UISN. Looking to the future, the transmission media can become a well-controlled resource in the UISN environment by having a transport tier between the enriched services tier and the extremely large capacity national and international digital pipes of the near future.

8.7.8 Customer Interface for UISN

The customer access to the UISN is provided via standardized universal ports. The imminence of ISDN, broadband ISDN, and local high-speed (fiber and T1) networks requires a very generic interface with UISN. Standard data and signal paths are both necessary at these universal ports, ranging in data rates from 64 kbps to DS3 rates. The new technologies (fiberonics, multi-gigabit fiber transmission, switching, software, and ultra-large-scale integration) at the customer premises equipment and in the network can be gracefully integrated in the network by adhering to the interface requirements at the universal ports. With ATM gaining momentum through the 1990s, the universal ports of the AINs (rather than the slightly archaic UISN) will be able to interconnect with these networks.

In the final analysis, the emergence of network intelligence is neither a local nor a United States phenomenon. The services envisioned from INs will affect local street corner vendors and multinationals. For this reason, the platforms of INs can become vastly different. These implementations vary dramatically, even though the conceptual platform for designing and building these networks is essentially the same. This particular process has repeated itself in almost all aspects of technological growth. For example, the methodologies of the third- and fourth-generation computers are the same; yet there are many corporate entities building computers with their own private schemes.

8.8 The Role of Bellcore in Evolution of INs

In order to facilitate the orderly evolution of network intelligence in the public domain, Bell Communications Research (Bellcore), a research and development facility of the RBOCs, has proposed three distinct architectural variations (IN/1, IN/1+, and IN/2). Considerable collaboration in the phased introduction of these networks is essential to maintain uniformity and consistency of services throughout the nation. Vendors from all nations participate in supplying the network components, interfaces, and software modules. To maintain any resemblance of order, CCITT and ANSI publish stringent standards and well-defined protocol. Most companies follow these standards and implement networks, such as the CCS7 network and packet-switched networks. Based upon signaling and typical architecture, networks evolve, such as the 800 network, SDN, and others. These rudimentary networks meet all the basic interface and signaling requirements of the first version of the public domain IN, i.e., IN/1.

8.8.1 Intelligent Networks (IN/1, IN/1+, IN/2, IN/N)

Typical examples of these networks are Bellcore's IN/1 + and IN/2, which have been designed in considerable detail and are gradually being introduced. Similar architectures also exist for the long-distance networks. Several of these networks have been investigated by various long-distance carriers: AT&T (the Universal Information Services Network "UISN", AIN Platform 0, and AIN Platform 1), MCI (the Vnet™), and Sprint™ (the virtual private network or "VPN"). The UISN concepts are closely akin to the IN/1 and IN/1+ concepts. MCI's Vnet uses two data access points (or "DAPs," that are functionally similar to the STP) controlled by a network control system (or "NCS" having customer information management and a database administrator functionally similar to the SCP and SMS pair). Sprint's VPN also uses two STPs and numerous database control points (DCPs) managed by a DCP management system.

In the United States, major network standards, definitions, and functional devices with certain generic and interface requirements have been introduced. Three such networks, IN/1, IN/1+, and IN/2, are commonly accepted for phased introduction through the 1990s.

Numerous other networks are also associated with IN/1, for instance, the first generation of database queried networks. IN/1 is perhaps the first network to introduce other slightly different or slightly more intelligent versions of INs. This development has taken place in numerous countries and for various types of services in the United States. Under the architectural framework of IN/1, at least six other networks exist. These networks offer services widely known as GNSs, ABS, emergency response service (ERS), PVN, area wide centrex (AWC), and pay-per-view (PPV) services.

Though the type of databases and their access modality differ, the basic components and their configurations are essentially the same for these networks.

8.8.2   Design Details of Bellcore's IN/2

The architecture of a first-level IN, referred to as "IN/1" or the 800 network, is depicted in Figure 8.18. There are four basic components of IN/1, as it exists in the United States. These building blocks of IN/1 are SSPs/1, SCPs, SMSs, and STPs. Generally, there are numerous SSP/1 and numerous STPs within the Common Channel Signaling 7 (CCS7) network, even though there is only one SCP and SMS (duplicated for disaster recovery). This network barely meets the three requirements to be classified as an IN. Only the database(s) in SCP, CCS7, and

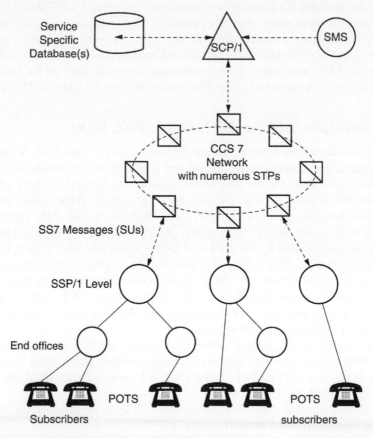

Figure 8.18 Simplified configuration of the Bellcore's first *IN/1* (ca. 1987). The subscriber-generated queries go up to the service-specific database(s), and the call-completion information is returned to the appropriate switching office. POTS, plain old telephone service; SCP, service control point; SMS, service management system; STP, signal transfer point; SU, signaling unit; SSP, service-switching point.

some service independence by having numerous databases in the SCP are incorporated. The more evolved IN/2 replaced the IN/1 in most of the networks.

8.8.2.1 Elements of IN/2

Five physical entities of IN/2 are the switching system (SS/2), SCP/2, IP, SMS/2, and vendor feature node (VFN) to accommodate the more advanced services and features of IN/2. VFNs are not necessary for all IN/2 configurations. These nodes may be added to train and/customize the network interfaces and software modules. Specialized services such as sales, presentations, communication, etc., for specific customers can thus be customized as special features of IN/2. Generally, VFNs are included in the SCEs.

The *four* rudimentary logical modules of the IN/2 are the: SSP/2 resident in the physical SS, SLI, which can reside in the SCP/2, IP, and/or SS, NID or NIDB, which can reside in the SCP/2, IP, and/or SS, service logic creation, also known as SCE under the jurisdiction of SMS/2.

These network elements and their associations are depicted in Figure 8.18. The interrelationships between the *five* physical entities and the *four* major logical modules are discussed further in this chapter. In Figures 8.19 and 8.20, a more complete

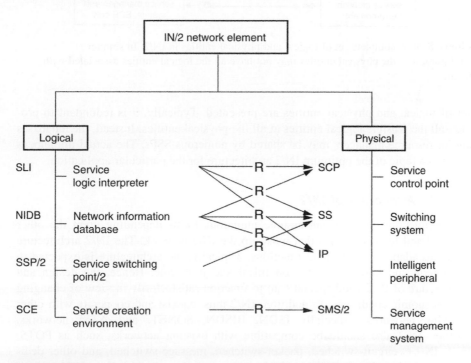

Figure 8.19 Typical physical and logical entities of IN/2. Additional units may be incorporated in IN/2 to enable the flexible service-provisioning feature of IN/2.
Note: R indicates where the logical module may reside.

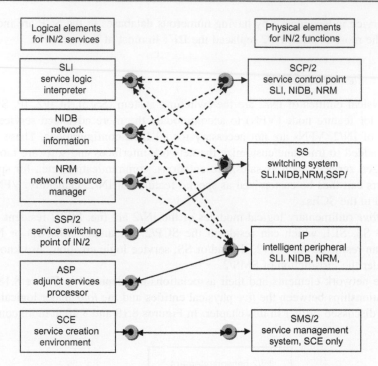

Figure 8.20 A complete set of logical and physical entities in IN/2. In simpler configurations, the physical entities may not have all the logical entities associated with them.

set of logical and physical entities are presented. Typically, it is redundant to provide all the feasible logical entities at all the physical entities. Instead, the databases and/or resource managers may be shared by numerous SSPs. The actual implementation is a topic of the optimum IN/2 architecture for the particular application.

8.8.2.2 Architecture of IN/2

The architecture of IN/2 can assume numerous forms depending upon the other physical and logical entities that make up the IN/2 network. The IN/2 architecture is just as adaptive as the IN/2 functions. Typically, the architecture is expected to be generic and universal, yet economical and justifiable. Hence, the design and architecture of IN/2 need special care to function satisfactorily in view of changing socioeconomic conditions. In addition, IN/2 must coexist and cooperate with other evolving networks, especially ISDN, BISDN, SONET, and ATM networks. Further, IN/2 also should be compatible with existing networks, such as POTS, IN/1, IN/1+, circuit-switched, packet-switched, message-switched, and other dedicated networks. Compatibility and interface are major considerations. This adaptability is proposed by a versatile software layer at most of the *five* IN/2 physical entities.

Figure 8.21 depicts the simpler IN/2 architecture that facilitates the transition from IN/1+. In this arrangement, fewer than five physical entities are deployed. The VFN is absent, but this configuration provides some VFN functionality via the IP interconnected to the SSP/2 and the STP, thus reaching the SCP/2. The SCE in this architecture (although considered independence of the SMS/2) provides the SMS/2 staff with SLPs to IPs, distributed throughout the IN/2. These SLPs become an integral part of the SLIs. The execution of the high-level code generated by the SLIs provides the IN/2 service. Customizing the service is as simple as altering the program structure of the individually written service programs that are presented to the SLIs for interpretation and execution of the network instructions.

Figure 8.22 depicts a more advanced version of IN/2 with independent VFN and for SSP/2 equipped for ISDN services. With this version of IN/2, the business community with ISDN capability can receive IN/2 and ISDN services via the same facilities. In this network, most of the IN/2 service can be introduced via the VFN, IP, or the universal customer interface (UCI) located under the jurisdiction of the SMS/2 to provide programming assistance for complex services.

In some cases (such as the No. 1A ESS, crossbar, and other systems), an adjunct service node (ASN) may also be included at the switch. In conjunction with the local-switching capability, the SSP functionality is added.

The customer line and its characteristics are maintained in the Central Office switch. In such cases, an additional module for memory management (memory administration system, MAS) becomes necessary. In most cases, this memory management is done remotely via the ASN. The MAS is also referred to as the remote MAS or simply RMAS.

This system (i.e., MAS) usually links the VFN, SS, SMS, and IP, thus providing the administration function for the IN/2 services. Each facility must be individually designed and interfaced, much like major computer systems being commissioned for computer networks.

Figure 8.23 depicts a still more elaborate IN/2 architecture where an adjunct service processor (ASP) and IP facilitate the introduction of new services in the network.

In this illustration, the switch contains the network resource manager (NRM), the service logic interpreter modules, and the NID, in addition to the SSP/2 modules in all switching systems. The NID and SSP/2 trigger detection module are also housed in the switch. In this configuration, the network can perform all the conventional and sophisticated IN functions.

The service provisioning in IN/2 is carried out by multiple network modules. The network services are realized by assembling modular and independently coded SLPs with appropriate interfaces. Standard signaling protocols are used between the various network elements. In the earlier network architectures, the introduction of new services are accomplished from a centralized point and introduced in one geographical area. In IN/2, these features are extended considerably. The features take advantage of the reusable network resources and their capabilities.

Since these networks function in real time, the management and allocation of network resources and capabilities become a greater challenge than resource

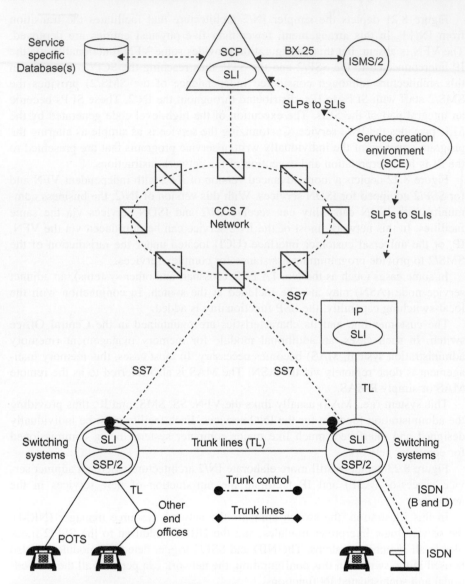

Figure 8.21 Typical architecture of IN/2. IN/2 offers flexible architecture and customized services. Additional elements may be incorporated if the newer services should be included. BX.25, a front-end processor for the SCP; CCS7, common channel signaling 7; IP, intelligent peripheral; ISMS/2, individual service management system/2; POTS, plain old telephone service; SCE, service creation environment; SCP, service control point; SLI, service logic interpreter; SLP, service logic program; SS7, signaling system 7; SSP/2, service-switching point/2; TL, trunk line. Trunk control may be accomplished directly or via the SS7 signaling network.

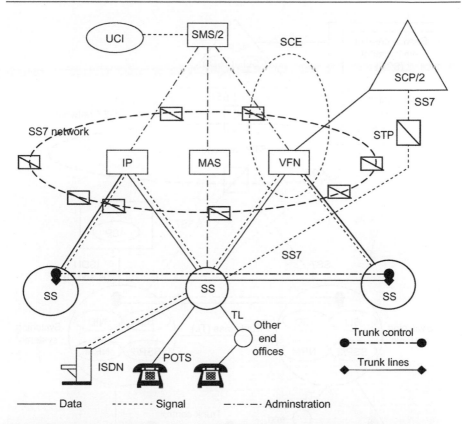

Figure 8.22 Typical IN/2 with a distinct VFN. This node is associated with a switch (SS) for new vendor-provided services. The MAS may or may not be necessary, depending upon the type of SS that is serving as the SSP/2. IP, intelligent peripheral; MAS, memory administration system; POTS, plain old telephone service; SS, switching system; SCE, service creation environment; SCP, service control point; SMS, service management system; STP, signal transfer point; TL, trunk line; UCI, universal customer interface; VFN, vendor feature node.

management in the conventional mainframe computer systems or the conventional telecommunication network systems. In IN/2, network services are offered to the network customers. These network service microfunctions are derived within the network environment from service application programs. The service application programs are written in a service-script format by assembling appropriate program modules and FCs that utilize reusable network resources and capabilities (Haas and Robrock, 1986). These reusable network resources and capabilities are truly service independent, and they exist by virtue of the network architecture, design, hardware, and supporting elements (such as LIDB*, NCPs*, SS7, network, and STP facilities). This is the marked difference between the service logic modules (housed in individual switching systems) for the specific network feature or service application in the earlier

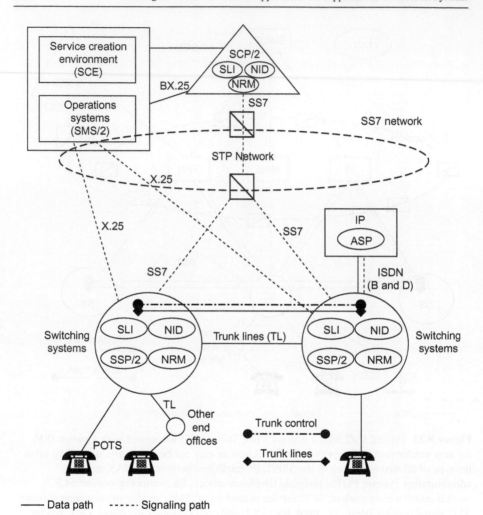

Figure 8.23 Complete architecture of IN/2. This architecture includes all the logical and physical entities. ASP, adjunct service processor; IP, intelligent peripheral; ISDN, integrated services digital network; NID, network information database; NRM, network resource manager; POTS, plain old telephone service; SCE, service creation environment; SCP/2, service control point/2; SLI, service logic interpreter; SMS/2, service management system/2; SS7, signaling system 7; SSP/2, service-switching point/2; STP, signal transfer point; TL, trunk lines; X.25, packet-switching protocol and links.

networks (especially the IN/1). In IN/2, the service logic controls numerous IN/2 modules and can communicate both the signaling and the data information.

The SCEs (shown in Figures 8.21 and 8.22) are another IN/2 feature. It is expected that the software architecture of the SLI in IN/2 will provide this environment to assemble and arrange the SLPs, together with the FCs of the network.

This will permit quick and efficient introduction of newer network service (such as opinion polling and stock market quotes) without reprogramming the service entities and the entire service-specific software (as is done in IN/1).

Three basic functions are essential in providing IN/2 service: service definition, service interpretation, and SLP execution.

First, the new service needs definition. This is done by the service logic programmer who, in turn, uses the SMS of IN/2. *Second*, the service interpretation function is done by the SLI. The input to this SLI is in the form of an SLP. The SLP defines the network actions specific to the service being introduced. *Third*, the new service provision includes the execution of the SLP. During this phase, the SSP/2 recognizes a request for the IN/2 service and dispatches a command to the SLI. The SLI then interprets the service logic and commands different network entities to provide the IN/2 service according to the SLP written for that specific service. In the service introduction phase, other aspects are also necessary, including the system design, service testing, network provisioning, and operations and billing.

8.8.2.3   IN/2 Architectural Elements and Capabilities

As many as *six* essential elements of IN/2 may exist in most architectures. Typically, these are named the SSP/2, SCP/2, STP, IP, SMS/2, and VFN specific to IN/2. Note that IPs are, in principle, independent entities with their own ASP, and the suffix "/2" is not used at this time. There are vast differences in the distribution of the sub-elements, and their functionality is expanded considerably. A more detailed discussion is given in the following sections.

8.8.2.4   Service-Switching Point/2

The SSP/2 resident at an ESS equipped with CCS7. The physical location of SSP/2 may be at an end office or a tandem office (a switching center for interoffice calls). Both are expected to be ESS with stored program control to facilitate the combined functionality of the switching system, the SSP/2, and the sub-elements of SSP/2. The trigger table in the SSP/2 recognizes the call-handling requirements for the IN/2 call. A trigger table is a set of unique network conditions and call requirements that force an SS to realize that an IN functionality is invoked. This initiates the IN/2 call-processing routines and sends queries to other routines seeking new processing information to complete the call or service of the particular caller or the called party. The SSP/2 may be a circuit-switched, channel-switched, or even packet-switched center. We foresee the SSP/2 being resident in most future ISDN switches.

In addition to the switching software, the host office also accommodates the SSP module (or the software), the SLI module, an NID, and an NRM module. These modules act in a coherent format to respond appropriately toward handling the IN/2 call with intelligent and adaptive response(s) or network functions. The three basic modules, the SLI, NID, and NRM, may be located at the SSP or at the SCP/2. Service performance, traffic consideration, and real-time response dictate the actual placement in the newer IN/2 environment. The customer interface is generally over the ISDN lines to the SSPs in IN/2. One or more VFNs may also be connected to the SSP/2 via the ISDN lines. These lines provide both the signaling path and the data path to and from the switch. Localized IN/2 service requests are attempted by scanning the information in the NID within the purview of the NRM. When the information in the NID is insufficient, the extraneous databases are queried.

8.8.2.5 SLI (Resident at SSP/2 and/or SCP/2 and/or IP)

The SLI forces the execution of the SLPs. These SLPs are a collection of FCs (see Section 8.3.5 and depicted in Figure 8.4), which use the network resources to accomplish specific sub-modular functions, for example, collect digits arriving from the customer, forward dialed number, and so forth. Generally confined to the IN/1+ and IN/2, the FCs constitute the real basis for service independence. The SLI also provides real-time response to network queries requesting call-handling instructions or IN/2 service provisioning.

Note: In a sense, the hierarchy of the network language (as it is evolving) is following the evolution of any higher-level languages in the computer environment. Typically, in the computer environment, the lowest level of an instruction is at the microinstruction level and corresponds to the FCs in the network environment. A microfunction is accomplished as a microinstruction is executed. These instructions are completely independent of the application program for which the microinstruction was written. In the hard-wired logic, the assembler instruction performs the lowest level sub-function. On the other hand, at the highest level, a specific applications program, or software package in the computer environment, corresponds to the SLP, which can be encoded in an SCE. The analogous assembler and compiler functions in the network environment are still very human-assisted by the SMS/2 staff and encoded by the service providers. Feature interaction, when interdependent modules are invoked for independent services, is a topic of serious concern in the IN/2 environment.

Such queries may arise from an SSP/2, an IP, or a VFN. The SLI may also respond to queries from other SLIs in the network. The execution of SLPs provides the answers to the queries. These SLPs may be written by network personnel or customers. The generic SLPs are encoded by network personnel (for accuracy and optimality), and the service-specific SLPs are written by the particular customer. Service logic and customer data may be embedded in such SLPs, which are administered from SMS/2. Most requests for the use of network capabilities are managed by the SLI. This breakdown of the coding responsibility is similar to the approach used in typical computer systems in which generic system utilities and mathematical libraries are written by system and compiler designers and the actual application-specific program is written by the programmer.

8.8.2.6 NID (Resident at SSP/2 and/or SCP/2 and/or IP)

The NID contains the customer access, network-connection information. It facilitates which type of calls can be routed and which services can be provided to each individual customer. This data is stored in the form of a networks capabilities map. The databases may be cross-queried by other modules dispersed in IN/2, via appropriate data lines on the X.25 packet networks linking different IN/2 elements, or even by ISDN lines between the network elements.

8.8.2.7 NRM (Resident at SSP/2 and/or SCP/2 and/or IP)

The node resource manager (NRM) of IN/2 locates and identifies the address of network resources required to continue call processing or provides the next increment of network service. The NRM may also provide the SLI with information required to establish a connection to an IN/2 module.

8.8.2.8 Service Control Point/2 (SCP/2)

The SCPs in IN/2 contain service-logic systems, databases, and SS7 interfaces. The SCP/2 has data communication with the SMS/2 and its associated operations system(s). The signaling information flows between STPs in IN/2. The databases (NIDs) in the SCP/2 may coexist with periodic updating (typically, a 15-min interval as in the 800 databases), or be entirely at SSP/2, or be located entirely at the SCP/2. Control logic and customer or network data are also stored at the SCP/2, which responds to the queries from SSP/2, IP, or VFN. The SCP/2 performs two functions: (1) service specific and (2) non-service related. The service-specific functions are handled by the SLI and NID discussed earlier. The non-service related functions include allocating network interfaces and protocols, and administrative and maintenance activities to offer high-quality service performance, such as low response times and high availability of system network services.

8.8.2.9 Evolution of the SLI

The SLI in IN/2 is not highly evolved. However, a *three-layer* SLI platform is envisioned. The *lowest* layer is termed the resource layer, and it retains control and communication with the network resources. Four such resources are the SS7 network, the disk holding the databases, the X.25 packet communication system for communication with other network elements, and the display terminal through which the network operators have access to the SCP operations. The *intermediate* layer of the SLI is termed the "server layer", and it holds the FC server, communications server, station server, and storage server. The *top* layer of the SLI is termed the application layer (not to be confused with the application layer of the OSI model). This layer holds the various SLPs, which will be used to introduce new services. Each service will have an independent SLP. Each SLP deploys a different sequence of FCs to suit the service.

8.8.2.10 Evolving SLPs

The SLPs in the SCPs compose the newer IN/2 services with FCs. The FCs uniquely tailored into the IN/2 architecture are modular call-processing routines that force the internal network resource to perform specific functions (such as playing an announcement, synthesizing voice, and collecting digits). These FCs provide the final basis on which service independence is achieved.

Defined as a physical or a virtual node within the IN, the SCP contains the active database of customer records. Three distinct types of databases (800 number, ABS, and PVN) can reside in the SCP. This database is actively queried from the SSPs within the network to seek and obtain service-completion information; hence, the optimal and effective management and utilization of this database is critical.

Certain sophistication in the hardware and software hierarchy is essential to make the SCP handle the high volume (several million calls per hour) and diversity in the information sought from the SCP, depending upon the types of services and subservices provided. In a sense, the design of the SCP should be considered a highly efficient parallel processor and data storage-retrieval computer system. The input and output processing need special attention. The SCP operating environment is relatively well defined, and its functional requirements are clearly delineated both by the architectures of IN/1 and by the CCSS7 requirements. Thus, the hardware design assures consistency with the operational environment (STP, SMS, and SSP), the type of processing accomplished (database functions, their updating, security, error-recovery, and duplication), and the interfaces with the other network components (SS7 network, other signaling networks, SMSs, security systems, and so forth).

8.8.3 Hardware Aspects

There are four major hardware components constituting an SCP, as depicted in Figure 8.24. First, an elaborate and highly dependable mass storage system (typically large-capacity disk drives and disk controllers) makes up the database storage. Second, a bank of parallel processors with their own dedicated memory blocks serves to access the bulk storage within the SCP, and communicates with the input/output devices in the database. Third, a series of front-end processors preprocess the queries received via the SS7 network, or any similar compatible network, with a well-specified protocol. Finally, a series of BX.25 front-end processors complete the major hardware components. These processors receive service management information from the SMS and provide the interface for maintenance, security, and operations of the SCP.

It is important to note that any computer hardware architecture with an optimally distributed bus structure can adequately perform the SCP functions. However, certain architectures are more suitable (such as parallel processor and multi-bus systems). In the interest of high dependability expected from the SCP, duplication of hardware and buses increases the confidence level in the functioning of these special-purpose computer systems. Typically, the downtime on the SCP is under 3 min a year (as of late 1980s), and the wait time in call completion demands both redundancy and speed from the SCP. With more advanced database machines and their software, the downtime is far less.

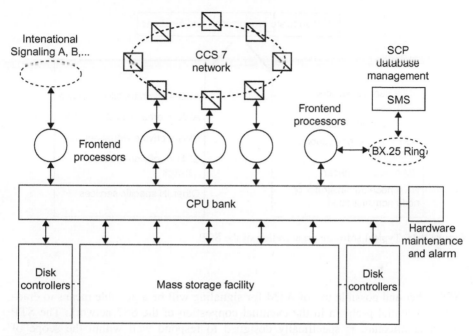

Figure 8.24 Possible hardware configurations for the SCP of INs. BX.25, a front-end processor (hardware); CCS7, common channel signaling 7; CPU, central processing unit; SCP, service control point; SMS, service management system.

8.8.4 Software Aspects

There are two groups of software structures in the SCP, as depicted in Figure 8.25. The first group deals with the functioning of the SCP as a coherent computational entity, which serves the hierarchical function of the SCP in the IN architecture. The second group deals with the applications that the IN (which hosts the SCP) is equipped to handle.

8.8.4.1 Signal Transfer Points

In IN/2, the function of the STPs is the same as that in the SS7 network. This fast packet switch provides the routing information and forwards SS7 messages through the network to the appropriate network elements. The exchange between SCP/2 and SSP/2 dominates most of the simple IN/1 and IN/1+ type of services. The number of messages will probably expand considerably with the newer 700, 900, and 911 services. At present, the capacity of the signaling network (SS7 backbone network) has not reached a crucial limit to cause excessive delays in the transfer of signals. The higher rates of signaling (9600 bps and 56 kbps) and redundancy of links are expected to provide enough buffering for the next few years. The role of

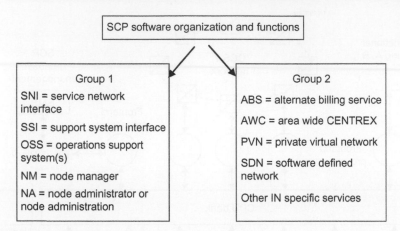

Figure 8.25 Typical software organization of the SCP.

ISDN fiber and possible use of ATM for signaling will be a possible means to eradicate a potential problem in the eventual congestion of the SS7 network. The STP switch architecture is specifically designed to respond well within the scope of VLSI technology for packet-switching systems.

8.8.4.2 Intelligent Peripheral

The functionality of the IPs in IN/2 can be quite extensive. Both network-based IPs and VFNs, which can be ONNs, are allowed in IN/2. If the ONNs do not have access to the SS7 network, then we see a provisional ISDN interface to be adequate for providing vendor services for IN/2. An IP-resident SLI may also be used if the services for the IP are extensive, and it can be customized to the needs of the particular IP. The basic concepts in the design of software engineering, within the context of computer systems, are equally applicable to the distribution of IN/2 software.

8.8.4.3 Operations Systems (SMS/2 and SCE)

There are two major elements in the provision of operations support for IN/2: the SMS/2 and the new SCE. The customer record administration, coordination, and control of the network databases are handled by SMS/2. The SCE provides the software environment to introduce customer-controlled capabilities, IN/2, and/or vendor services through the network facilities. Considerable coordination between the databases and the network facilities is essential for consistent customer services. Conditions leading to possible "deadlock" need special attention because the network resources may be actively contested in the IN/2 environment by vendor-provided services.

The creation of newer services within a fraction of the time generally required by the IN/1-type of network is the prime attraction of IN/2. The SCE offers the network users the hardware facilities and the software (the FCs) expertise to fabricate a new service. Typical of this service may be an opinion-polling service during an election or gathering the public response after a major event, such as an election or a catastrophe. Other examples of such services include SURF-LINE (a report of worldwide ocean surf conditions), Legal Services, FREIGHTLINER (on-the-road dispatch/delivery systems), and video shopping services. The SLPs necessary to generate the data for these new services can be encoded in the SCE and executed within a very short time in the real network. The public and business perspective of these new services within the realm of public domain networks still needs careful scrutiny.

8.8.4.4 Vendor Feature Nodes

The VFN is included especially in the network to allow outside service vendors to work in conjunction with IN/2 and provide services the network may not provide (due to regulatory or governmental constraints). Thus, some of the services that the network owners in the United States are specifically prohibited from offering to customers (such as stock market reviews, propaganda material, and telephone advertising) can be offered by outside service vendors.

Network access and the use of network resources must be provided for the outside vendors via two interfaces: (1) the service interface and (2) the capabilities interface. The service interface provides access to the network capabilities for a specific service the vendor is authorized to offer through the network. The service logic is resident in the SCP/2 or the SSP/2. The call forwarding may be carried out between the VFN and the network. The network–VFN interface is also monitored by the network. The capabilities interface is necessary because the VFN can achieve greater and greater sophistication. The objective of this interface is to permit the VFN to perform its functions without endangering the network or the database security. This interface is expected to ascertain that information is safely retained and routed without possible security leaks in the network.

8.9 Overview of Public Domain INS

The research at Bellcore has provided telecommunication scientists with an insight to implement elegant architectures and essential concepts in INs. The public demand for these new services envisioned by the IN/2 architects is at best slow, if not nonexistent. For this reason, the implementation of the networks to provide the true potential of IN/2 in the public domain has been delayed numerous times. However, the literature enriched by the research at Bellcore for IN/2 architectures is becoming a valuable resource for many private network designers. In particular, the implementation strategy by Bell Atlantic has been fruitful. The time spans between the research and the offering of services (such as CLASS, weather, emergency, and repair) have been quite short for Bell Atlantic. Numerous financial, medical, and educational networks stand to gain significantly by the documentation of the design of public domain networks. In Part 3, these architectures are extended to educational, medical, and personal computing networks.

8.9.1 Emergency Response Systems

Emergency response systems (ERS) have been evolving continuously over a time. In the early versions of ERS, operator intervention was necessary to identify the calling party and then inform the nearest emergency response unit. These functions were manual and required the verbal exchange of information, which placed a burden on the caller. Sometimes, even the lookup of the nearest response unit was manual, thus making the response slow and demanding on both the caller and the operator.

For these reasons, the more recent ERS units automatically identify the calling number (via the ANI), facility of the customer records, and the physical address of the calling party (via the automatic location identification (ALI) facility). In this way, these ERS units inform the nearest police unit, response unit, or public safety answering point (PSAP). The ERS databases in the SCP provide number translation (from 911 to the actual number), depending on the calling party number, time, day and date, and alternate response units if the original unit is busy or down. Generally, the public-switched telephone network handles such calls, even though private networks can also be built for businesses, homes, and corporations.

The ERS network implemented with more advanced networks may be programmed to perform numerous other individualized functions. A more recent version of ERS with access to the SCP database for ALI is shown in Figure 8.26. In this figure, some of the advanced CLASS features are embedded, such as ANI and ALI. Additional databases, such as directory assistance service, owned by individual operating companies may be invoked for the emergency response. Selective routing/default-routing algorithms and data, facilitated by the DBMS component of the SMS, may also be deployed based upon time, day, date, and the PSAP. These additional elements of data are enhanced with the TCAP or level of the CCS7 TCAP protocol data units. These same elements are sent via the CCS7 network to the participating SSPs. The VFN at the SSP plays a role in the ERS only if additional vendor services (such as ambulance, medical units, nursing care, and flood control) are included as a part of the ERS network.

8.9.2 Tsunami Early Warning System

There are many variables and uncertainties in the detection of a natural disaster such as tsunami or earthquakes. In some cases, there might be little or no information about the situation; in other cases, the available information may be vague or incomplete. In almost all these cases, the system has to operate under severe time constraints with little time to make a critical decision and warn about the catastrophe that is likely to occur. Complexity of the natural forces and events adds to the uncertainty of the entire process. The interaction between numerous independent players further jeopardizes the validity of human judgment or accuracy of machine

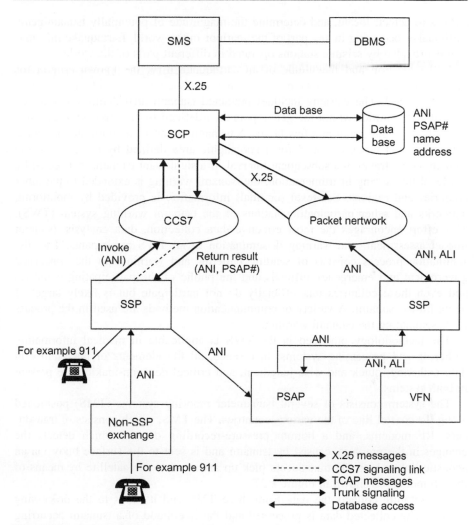

Figure 8.26 ERS implementation embedded in the IN/1 architecture. ANI, automatic number identification; ALI, automatic location identification; CCS7, common channel signaling 7; DBMS, database management system; PSAP, public safety answering point; SCP, service control point; SMS, service management system; SSP, service-switching point; VFN, vendor feature node.

processes. In the environment of uncertainty, complexity, and variability requires wise judgment, creativity, and initiative. The knowledge processing systems (KPS) should be able to handle such situations by falling back on artificial intelligence (AI), PR, and ES alike. The feedback from intelligent agents dispersed through the data gathering systems also plays a vital role.

The tsunami early warning system consists of two stages: the detection stage and the dissemination stage. As part of the detection process, the objective of the

KPS is to detect, locate, and determine the magnitude of potentially tsunamigenic earthquakes occurring in any part of the seafloor in the world. Earthquake information is provided by seismic stations operated in different parts of the world.

If the location and magnitude of an earthquake meet the known criteria for generation of a tsunami, a tsunami warning is issued to warn of an imminent tsunami hazard. The warning includes predicted tsunami arrival times at selected coastal communities within the geographic area defined by the maximum distance the tsunami could travel in a few hours. A tsunami watch with additional predicted tsunami arrival times is issued for a geographic area defined by the distance the tsunami could travel in a subsequent interval. If a significant tsunami is detected by sea-level monitoring instrumentation, the tsunami warning is extended to the other countries and regions. Sea-level (or tidal) information is provided by monitoring networks and other participating nations of the tsunami warning system (TWS). This effort encourages the most effective data collection, data analysis, tsunami impact assessment, and warning dissemination to all TWS participants. The dissemination process consists of sending bulletins and warnings to the concerned government and emergency officials and the public of the participating countries and even those countries that officially do not participate but is likely target of being hit by tsunami. A variety of communication methods are used in the process of disseminating the tsunami warning.

The methodology practiced in the TWS is applicable in medical information gathering and processing systems. In essence, all the elements of uncertainty in data gathering, quick and wise judgment, and critical decision-making are present in both systems.

The system consists of several tsunameter mooring systems (TMS) positioned along the coastal line of the various countries. The TMS, which consists of transducers, RF modems, and a bottom pressure-recording device, which detects the changes in the pressure, caused by tsunami and is sent to the surface buoy via an acoustic link, which the transducers pick up and send to the satellite by means of the RF modem as shown in Figure 8.27.

The satellite collects the data from these TMS and it sends to the processing centers. The collected data is processed and the likelihood of a tsunami occurring is determined. The path and the magnitude of the tsunami are also computed. The affected countries likely to be the targets of this disaster is determined and the necessary action is then taken and disseminated to these countries or regions within a country by way of tsunami alerts. In above two applications discussed, we clearly see a picture of chaotic environment filled with variables and unknowns.

A possible configuration of the medical and disaster KPS is presented and the applications arising from the implementation of such a system are discussed. The architectures and applications are extensive. Other complex problems can also be solved with improved accuracy. Numerous complex problems arising during routine situations that cannot ordinarily be solved by the existing computing infrastructure need the KPS leading to smart machines as presented in this section to make decisions which are time critical in nature.

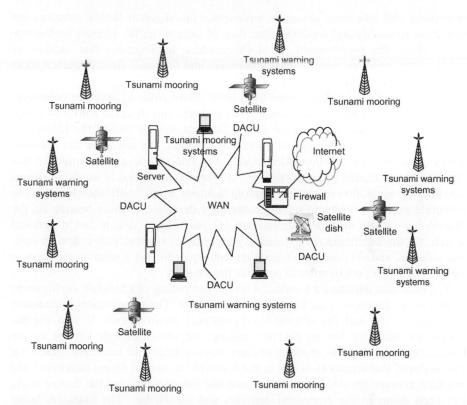

Figure 8.27 Deployment of network and processing intelligence for predicting tsunami and other natural disasters. DACU, data acquisition and control unit.

8.10 Conclusions

The Internet, broadband networks, and information highways provide ample amounts of raw data to seek and uncover relationships that are universal in nature. For medical applications, very large amounts of data are first filtered by high-speed computers and at the second level, the machines focus on information that carries medical knowledge and facts relevant to the medical classification of expertise. With an appropriate set of filter parameters, information, and knowledge are gathered in any given subject matter such as disease, treatment, and bone cancer. The complied information is then fine-tuned to search for cause—effect relationships based on models. Statistical correlation programs will unveil any fact that is unknown to the profession.

The proposed human—machine system supplements the inference that the immediate environment can offer in the raw digital format. The lower-level AI function(s) is programmed to sense and scan specific conditions within the environment. Knowledge generated from the machine's own knowledge banks of accumulated procedures and inferences about the topic under investigation further enhances the search for generality and wisdom in the flow of Internet traffic. Human intelligence firmly drives the programmed AI of the machine in directions that validate or repudiate an axiom of new medical knowledge and inference from a mathematical and scientific perspective.

The new medical machine stems from ideas drawn from AI systems, corporate-problem-solving strategies, decision support systems, and from the ability to assign a direction to search based on the Dewy Decimal System and/or the Library of Congress Classification of medical science. In addition, any inference that becomes a part of the derived axiom/relationship/concept retains a level of confidence that the machine evaluates and substantiates. A tree of knowledge is implicitly structured before any notion of medical wisdom is drawn at any confidence level. Three corporate executive problem-solving techniques that have a direct bearing on the functioning of the medical machine are (1) the limited search and directional search, (2) the satisficing (i.e., tentatively acceptable) solution rather than an optimal solution, and (3) constraint relaxation techniques to find a solution and then to tighten the constraints in order to optimize the solution.

We have also introduced a variation on the computing and network environment so that it can function as an intelligent human agent. The arrangement is inclusive of traditional AI and the scientific/computational environments. It also encompasses the realm of human decision-making and offers enough latitude to the human counterpart of the machine to carry out practically all humanoid functions. The realm of true creativity is still in the hands of the human driver who forces the machine to come close to doing to the data and information what the human being has been doing to the embedded concepts and knowledge. The machine, being adaptive and self-learning, becomes as effective as the computers that play (and win) most of the chess games against novices. The Internet features embedded in the addressing capability of the machine make it at least three times more powerful. The capacity of the WM to solve problems from a knowledge-based (not subject-based) perspective, with country and IP address-based access, provides sophisticated options for the medical community.

References

1. Abramson N, et al: *1969 Annual report the Aloha system*, Honolulu, Hawaii, 1970, University of Hawaii.
2. Schultz B: Tymnet's packet switched EMS leads debuts, Computerworld, March 24, 1980. See also Ahamed SV: *Design and engineering of intelligent communication systems*, Boston, MA, 1997, Kluwer Academic Publishers.
3. IBM, Manual: SNA Formats (GA-3136-20), United States. see www-01.ibm.com/support/docview.wss?uid=pub1ga27313620.
4. NYTimes: Text of Judge Greene's conclusion on A.&T.T. consent decree. www.nytimes.com, August 12, 1982.
5. Rayan KM, editor: *ATM and data networking*, Middletown, NJ, 1994, AT&T Technical Education Center.

6. Weber: Data base communication call processing method, U.S. Patent 4,191,860, 1980. Available from U.S. Patent Office. For a summary and implication of Weber.s Patent, see Ahamed SV: *The art of scientific innovation.* Upper Saddle River, NJ, 2004, Prentice Hall.

7. OPNET: Modeler, 2013 OPNET Technologies, Inc. OPNET is a registered trademark of OPNET Technologies, Inc. Bethesda, MD.

8. Sheffield Hallam University: An introduction to network modelling and network simulation using Comnet III, Howard Street, Sheffield, South Yorkshire S1 1WB, United Kingdom.

9. Ahamed SV, Lawrence VB: *Intelligent broadband multimedia networks*, ed 1, January 15, 1997, Kluwer Academic Publishers, 0792397479

10. Haas JM, Robrock RB: The Intelligent Network of the Future, IEEE Global Telecommunications Conference (December 1–4): 1311–1315, 1986. For AT&T perspective see Sable EG: Intelligent networks in United States, at the 1992 International Zurich Seminar on Digital Communications, Zurich, March 18, 1992. Also see Sable EG, Kettler HW: Intelligent network directions, *AT&T Tech J* vol. 70(Summer):2–10, 1997.

11. Wojcik RJ: Intelligent network platform in the U.S., *AT&T Tech J* 26–40, 1997. Summer

12. Ahamed SV, Lawrence VB: *Intelligent broadband multimedia networks*, Boston, MA, 1997, Kluwer Academic Publishers.

13. Ahamed SV: *Computational framework for knowledge: integrated behavior of machines*, Hoboken, NJ, 2009, Wiley.

14. Princeton University, 5ESS, www.princeton.edu/~achaney/tmve/wiki100k/docs/5ESS_switch.html.

15. ITU: Synchronous digital hierarchy bit rates, *Rec. G. 707*, 1988, Blue Book.Also see Chow Ming-Chwan: *Understanding SONET/SDH: standards and applications*, Holmdel, NJ, 1988, Andan Publishers.

16. NGE Group Siemens, *Next generation exchange PLUS*, nge.usa.siemens.com/docs/EWSDnextgen14fPLUS.

9 Intelligent Medical Networks and Machines

9.1 Introduction

The overt Web technology has brought about a profound revolution in the minds of all Internet users, researchers, and medical service providers (MSPs) alike. Information and knowledge that constitute the foundations of most human activities are being constantly altered, updated, and manipulated. Both affect the applications of most disciplines and the practice of most professions. Knowledge coupled with automation and seamless connectivity with standardized procedures makes any discipline and profession amenable to computer-aided practice and perhaps to automation. When the desirable feature of total integrity in practice of professions is overlooked, the use of information technologies becomes a pursuit of wealth and vanities.

Medical science and profession are exceptions because every patient is unique, and every doctor is an individual with a committed oath to deploy the profession to its best use. In the same vein, every patient is an individual committed to safeguarding health and welfare, just as every doctor is unique. An uneasy bilateral symmetry or a balance of power exists. The doctor being (perhaps) the more knowledgeable with endowed powers of prescription for drugs and services. Conversely, the patient having the capacity to choose the medical services' provider holds the grip of money (at least in the United States) payable.

In the same vein, this uneasily balanced relationship offers a vast amount of flexibility in the interpretation of medical knowledge and the treatment of patients. On the one hand, the practice of medicine is a science and every cure is a series of well-planned and sophisticated steps on the part of the medical staff. The procedures and subprocedures, medical objects (drugs, instruments, equipment, etc.) have a history of innovations and enhancements, and the medical knowledge is classified by the specialty and discipline, even though patients and their reactions are distinctly individualistic. The uncertainty in the chain of a scientific process leading to the cure brings in evaluation and discretion on the part of the medical staff. However uncertain the steps toward the cure may be, they are logical, inductive, and rational. Discretionary steps of the doctors are always liable to be queried by teams of specialists and medical boards, and unethical practice leaves them open to lawsuits.

On the other hand, the patients' role of being cooperative and willingly subservient during the treatment makes the position weak, especially during prolonged

Intelligent Networks: Recent Approaches and Applications in Medical Systems.
DOI: http://dx.doi.org/10.1016/B978-0-12-416630-1.00009-1

periods of treatment. In a sense, the Internet and Web knowledge bases (KBs) have diluted the power of doctors and their position in the exercise of the medical knowledge and information. In a complimentary sense, the distribution of information (via the Internet) and wealth (via the capitalistic society) has made the patients more selective from a larger and more sophisticated pool of MSPs. The delicate dyadic and symbiotic balance between patients and MSPs has shifted from country to country, place to place, and from decade to decade. The guidelines for reestablishing this delicate balance are now based on wisdom and ethics rather on power and monopoly.

Well-conceived and documented scientific procedures directed toward treating patients as unique human beings bring in a clear sequence of well-planned steps without too many discretionary choices for the individual doctors and medical staff members. In a sense, the entire global practice of medicine is well founded in science and its ensuing disciplines. Even though there is room for limited discretionary variation in the treatment of patients, the practice of healing patients needs firm scientific foundations.

This approach permits the machines to perform the standardized functions of being logical, inductive, and rational consistent with Web-enabled KBs and resources. It enables the doctors and medical staff to be rigorous in their interpretation, diagnosis, and their discretionary choices. The medical machines (MMs) in this part of the book have their foundations in the procedures within the medical profession as deeply rooted as computers have in the engineering profession.

From the hindsight of the processor technology of the last decade, the modern processors can indeed serve as medical processes. It is debt that computer scientists owe to the medical community to provide a methodology for programming the medical procedures and subprocedures that can be encoded as threads and elementary microprograms. Such microprogrammable steps aggregated, as a macroprocedure becomes a step in the global process of curing an ailment, treating a specific condition or even inventing a new cure for the patients. These medical microprograms reside in the caches of the new processors, and the operating systems of the medical computers guide the threads through the processes that the modern processors are built to execute.

It is evident from the processor development over the last decade that the integrated processors execute the numerous interdependently interwoven threads. This is feasible only because the numerous subfunctions in processes such as (graphics, visualization, MRI, surgery, etc.) were first established by specialists in the various disciplines and then presented to the computer scientists to unify these procedures as strings and threads for execution. Even though we present the architecture of medical processors as being the blueprints based on primitive VLSI techniques, the real purpose is to establish a neural pathway for human thought to bridge the gap between the prerequisite medical subprocedures and the programmable strings and threads in the modern processors.

Routine medical care and functions are especially amenable to computer and network processing. In this chapter, we indicate a methodology for processing the medical functions of any patient by the medical community using intelligent computer systems. It is our objective to present architectures to demonstrate that machines can enhance the productivity and efficiency of medical environments by confining the procedural steps, bookkeeping functions, and resource allocation to specially tailored computer systems. The human functions of pattern matching, judgment, and ultimate decision-making are also facilitated by a backbone of computers and networks organized to perform knowledge-based artificial intelligence (AI) functions. Similar existing and effective environments currently in use are the corporate management information systems/decision support systems (MIS/DSS), where decision-making tasks and analysis are performed routinely, and the stock market environments where vast numbers of routine transactions are handled quickly and inexpensively.

One situation where human intervention is constantly needed is in the maneuvering of an airplane or a spacecraft. In this case, the input conditions are so variable that trained human intelligence is likely to produce significantly improved results. In addition, the cost of failure is very high. The invocation of human insight and perception greatly influences the output and reduces the probability of fatal errors. In the case of an IP multimedia subsystem (IMS), we contend that the parameters lie halfway between these two extreme examples. With an exaggerated blend of man—machine teams, the environment may be adjusted sufficiently to generate an all-man-no-machine hospital, or an all-robot-no-man hospital. It is also our contention that the less expensive, electronic computer systems can take over some of the functions performed by the more expensive physician teams, thus generating more economical and more optimal medical environments in countries where physicians and their administrators are expensive.

Processor technology has undergone triple exponential growth in its features, availability, and applications during the last two to three decades. First, the switching speed has been enhanced to 3.3 ns. Second, the reduction in size has led up to 32 nm (1 nm is 10^{-9} of a meter or one ten-millionth of a centimeter) technology and its improved performance. Third, the cost has plummeted by at least by 6—9 orders of magnitudes implying that the processing power of a processor costing several thousands of dollars in the early 1980 time frame can be bought at a cost less than 0.01 cents in the early 2010 time frame.

The new strides in programming have eradicated the impression of a computer as being a faster calculator. The gating and switching (or simplest processing) of data are a millions of times faster than the conceiving that data in mind. Neural speeds along the pathways in the brain cannot compete with the switching speeds and clock rates in modern processors. However, at the higher end of the knowledge chain, conceptual, wisdom-based, and ethical functions, the mind can find the integrated effects of millions of such computations as easily as it can conceive an inspiration or create a scientific breakthrough. The functions of a human mind are barely comparable to those of quantum computers.

It is not our object to compare the power of mind with the power of machine. Each has a definite role to play. However, we propose to tame the gigantic computational powers encompassed in one-tenth penny gates or ten-dollar computers that will be built in the next generation to perform medical functions and handle medical codes. Human comprehension at the highest level is essential in writing the operating systems, and their multithreaded processing processes that become essential in the computer technology. The age-old practice is that if a horse is 10 times more powerful than a human is, the man learns to ride the horse.

In a conceptual framework, the ideology is still applicable by letting the computers perform routine, mundane, and artificially intelligent functions at incredible speeds, but retain the conceptual, wisdom, and ethical functions in the human activity to ride such machines. After all, wisest decisions are made after the most rigorous computations; and concepts, wisdom, and ethics reign supreme as the highest intellectual activity to deploy medical processors, MMs, and medical supercomputers to serve medical needs of nations and societies. Natural intelligence retains an aura of elegance, beauty, and excellence for decades, much longer than the milliseconds of precise computational decision-making. In the same vein, the contemplations of Aristotle, Buddha, and the philosophers retain a glimpse of eternity, unification of virtues, and generosity of actions, much longer than the transient humdrums of politicians, empire builders, and moneymakers.

9.2   Design Constructs of an MM

MMs hold the promise of the next generation intelligent medical assistants for the specialized medical community. These new machines cross the domain of knowledge and enter the realm of medicine. From a pragmatic perspective, the processing of information gives rise to knowledge and the processing of knowledge (in any subject of specialization) gives rise to the wisdom in practice and profession. Such wisdom endures longer than knowledge. Transitions and ripples in the knowledge domain are frequent and can become disjointed. There is a trace of embedded wisdom in the extraction of knowledge from information much as there is a trace of insidious human value and insight in the extraction of wisdom from knowledge. In the hierarchy of social progress, information, knowledge, and wisdom form the three distillates that lead to foundations of social norms, behavior and ethics. Historically, the role of philosophers, saints, and sages has paved the path of mature human societies and conversely, the role of plunderers, conceited and the selfish has robbed mature societies of their wisdom, knowledge, information and their affluence. History has a tendency to repeat. For this reason, when clusters of unbiased machines can moderate the human tendencies against greed and exploitation, then the art of medicine can be greatly beneficial for the society as a whole. The current trend of escalating fees for the expertise and services can also be moderated.

9.2.1   MMs Concepts

In Section 9.2, we explore the role of next generation computer systems that supplement the human vision and wisdom with hardware (HW) logic and programmed rationality. The outcome is expected to be that of a series of computed and premeditated steps in moving to provide medical services in the community and in the society. We also provide the design constructs for such machines to be built based on the platform of existing AI-based computer systems. More recently, computers and communications have merged gracefully to provide the Internet and its capacity to connect and communicate is an integral part of the design constructs for the MMs.

Nature has preceded humans by eons. The intricate schema of nature is indicative of the immense knowledge behind every microbiological and cellular process. Along the evolution of earth in the universe, cosmic forces have shaped the composure of the earth. Along the evolution of humans on the earth, intellectual forces have shaped the graceful and cooperative role of humans. Along the evolution of thought, social forces have shaped the achievements and inventions. A common mystic of universal order and deep methodology remains hidden through the innumerable parallelisms that span the origin of the universe and intricacy of the life and the ethics in the society.

Perception and comprehension are deeply ingrained in the thought processes. They become the corner stones for building a framework of knowledge, as we perceive it from the recent times. To avoid being trapped in a ring of reflective philosophy of the universe or the physiology of neurons in the brain, we can step onto the methodology of computation encompassing numbers, symbols, and the algebra of their manipulation in the processing units of machines and then extend such methodology to compiling and composing more complex medical processes.

Human mind is knowledge based and the simplistic computers are number and data based. The modern networks are address-code driven. They drive the data packets and cell through a cloud of interconnected switching systems. It becomes apparent that the logical approach to collapse the triangle between humans, machines, and networks is to make such machines and networks knowledge oriented and medically integrated. The evolutionary trend of the human mind is too well entrenched to make the human mind become number or bit oriented. Alternatively, we can make machine more human and benefit oriented. In this chapter, we propose a methodology for applying these evolutionary trends and truisms in developing MMs, medical networks, and mechanized medicine and Internet knowledge.

Integration and sophistication is a forte of modern machines, and broadband is the trend of almost all the recent communication networks. The synergy of both has made communication a dominant force in the society. An additional vantage point is the universality of the TCP/IP protocol making Internet the prime mover of data at fiber optic speeds. Data per se has very limited utility unless it is processed to a more appropriate format for human decision-making. A conversion gap exists between data that the Internet provides and the information that humans can assimilate. Data processing has been in vogue since 1950s and knowledge processing is (currently) application directed. The general graphics and video programs have limited use from a generic perspective. Even though information processing systems such as MIS and the medical information systems provide some relief in the daily decision-making activity, the true interface to the human intellect is lacking.

9.2.2 A Mathematical Basis for Processing Medical Knowledge

Processing of knowledge is based on the truism that any action (verb function) that is associated with any object (noun object) changes its status.[1] In the same vein, any medical process on a medical object changes its condition. If there is no artificial process (such as a treatment, surgery, and radiation), it can be a natural process (such as aging, digestion, and healing). Human actions and computational processes also cause change in the status and entropy of objects. Since there is no object that does not undergo change, there is some action or a set of actions inherently and inadvertently acting upon every object. An object without one or more verbs to act upon it is a nonentity, and a verb without corresponding one or more nouns to be acted upon is virtual. These truisms have been valid in the past and in present, and will continue to be valid in the future.

Objects in nature and their inevitable changes are the basis for the evolution of knowledge and thus the discipline of medicine. Changes occur over measurable and discernible parameters. The rate of change and innate forces (natural and artificial) in the environment bring about the change in the structure of objects; and around these objects, the structure of knowledge exists.

Indeed, it becomes the theme to construct the medical and computational framework. The validation of the normal usual equations relating the measurable parameters (such as, mass and momentum, force and movement, torque and rotation, energy and inertia, and so on) becomes necessary. As the real objects fill the physical space, hypotheses, concepts, and notions fill the intellectual space; humans, their needs, and their innovations fill the social space. Further, we contend that insight, logic, and reasoning fill the complex medical space. One of the objectives of the theory is to extend the domain of (statistical and probabilistic) computation coupled with the inference and directionality offered by AI techniques to extend the frontiers of art of medicine to a more stringent practice of medicine. Such a framework facilitates humans to derive notions leading onto concepts, axioms, and wisdom in the practice of medicine.

9.2.2.1 Elementary Medical Structures

Information/medical centric objects constitute the nuclei of knowledge/medicine. Other objects relate to such nuclei and bear dynamic hierarchical relations with them. A Web of relation between related objects constitutes an elementary knowledge structure. As shown in Figure 9.1, a body of knowledge may be symbolically represented by a collectivity of objects, their primary and secondary relationships, the attributes of objects, and their own relationships.

9.2.2.2 Elementary Knowledge/Medical Operations

A medical operation in an MM corresponds to a process in a computer. Typically, a microscopic operation in an MM convolves an element of the alphanumeric

---

[1] Human action regarding an object updates the individual memory(ies), and machine process updates the action taken about that object and its result (if any), unless it is a null operation.

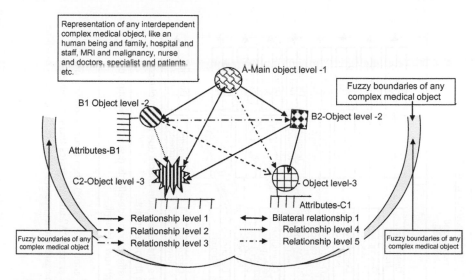

Representation of any interdependent complex medical object, like an human being and family, hospital and staff, MRI and malignancy, nurse and doctors, specialist and patients, etc.

A-Main object level -1

Fuzzy boundaries of any complex medical object

B1 Object level -2

B2-Object level -2

Attributes-B1

C2-Object level -3

Object level-3

Attributes-C1

→ Relationship level 1   ↔ Bilateral relationship 1
--→ Relationship level 2   ⋯→ Relationship level 4
-·-→ Relationship level 3   -·-→ Relationship level 5

Fuzzy boundaries of any complex medical object

Fuzzy boundaries of any complex medical object

Figure 9.1 Representation of the medical knowledge structure of a main object A, encompassing five lower-level surrounding objects. Strong, weak, casual, unilateral, and bilateral relationships are shown.

column constituting human comprehension with an element of the alphanumeric row of the "laws in the medical profession" in that particular Dewey decimal system (DDS) or Library of Congress (LoC) classification of medical knowledge. When such operations are sequenced as compiled and executable medical programs, then the machine will simulate humanist and medical domain functions and will offer optimized solutions to routine application programs dealing with individual, group, and/or medical objects or issues. The symbols in the rows and columns are alphanumeric entities that are partly descriptive and partly numeric. During the process of convolution, both the descriptor of the symbol and its numeric value undergo changes. The descriptor facilitates the change in the perceived (elements of the) law under the scrutiny of human comprehension. Elements of human comprehension are programmed as AI routines or as a series of medical programs, subprograms, or functions in machines.

The numeric value quantifies the extent of change incurred or that will be incurred. A cumulative index of a series of such changes (descriptive and numeric) is an estimate of the change of entropy of the old medical status of the objects. By relaxing proposed elements embedded in the laws are feasible and practical, the machine tracks every minute change that human beings may miss. The change between the entropies of the new medical objects from that of the old medical objects is the measure of the incremental change of the medical process thus invoked.

Figure 9.2 depicts the convolution process as the row—column process. Some of the descriptive/numeric entries could be 0/0 indicating the effects and side effects of a proposed step in the ith column entry on the jth row entry are zero both qualitatively and numerically.

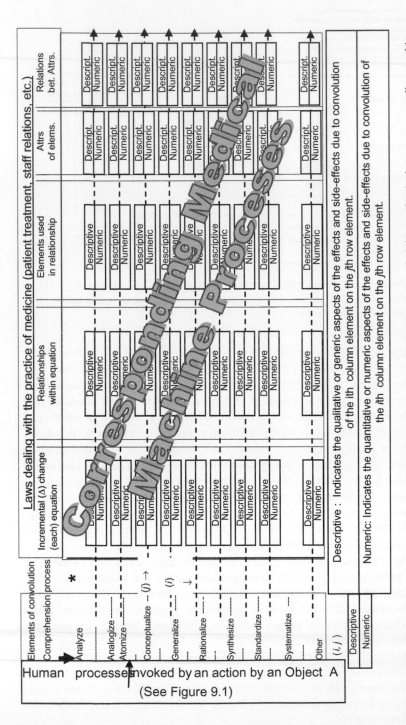

Figure 9.2 When a medical object "A" (Figure 9.1) accomplishes a medical function (e.g., administer a drug), then a corresponding machine action $KLP = \sum_1^n$ BKIs is invoked. The MM tracks these microscopic effects on all objects around "A" and integrates them to create a net effect of the action in a descriptive and a numerical format. Doctor's notes and laboratory measurements become a part of the human—machine subfunctions.

9.2.2.3   Procedural Steps in Medical Processing

To simplify the medical processing, any valid and executable process or a set of processes on any (complex collectivity of) medical noun object (MNO) is shown in Figure 9.3. In order to be accurate about the change in the status of objects, the machine tracks the noun object–verb function interaction in two ways. *First*, it tracks the noun object(s) that constitute the collectivity and *second*, it tracks the verb function(s) that operate as a group. In tracking the noun objects, the machine maintains a dynamic record of

a. objects in the collectivity(ies) (e.g., a medical status/structure that are inputs to a medical program),
b. attributes of each object,
c. relationships between the objects,
d. relationships between the attributes,
e. nature of the objects (unwilling, neutral, or cooperative),
f. linearity or nonlinearity of the response to each of the medical process (its magnitude, nature, and directionality).

   In tracking the verb functions, the machine also maintains a dynamic record of

i. medical processes in the group (e.g., the machine operations in the program),
ii. nature of each medical process (fixed, adaptive, or programmable),
iii. magnitude or intensity of each medical process,
iv. directionality (positive, neutral, or negative) of each of the processes.

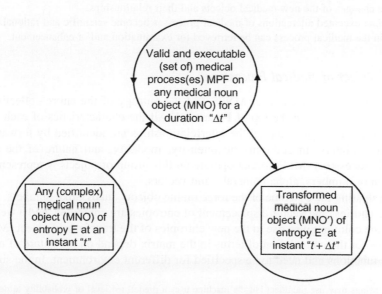

Figure 9.3 Change in entropy of a medical object MNO after a valid set of process(es) MPF resulting in a transformed (new) object MNO′.

9.2.3   Methodology for Medical Processing

At the next level of representation, if the medical process(es) can be symbolically represented as alphanumeric column and the noun objects are represented as an alphanumeric row, then the result would be a convolution matrix caused by a product-like effect. The rules for deriving the new noun object (i.e., the convolution matrix) are yet to be evolved. The representation of the interaction between the medical process(es), MPF(s) and MNO(s), is represented in Figure 9.3. There are seven underlying principles in order to process knowledge and are as follows:

1. Medical status is focused around dominant "noun objects," embedded in the overall status/entropy of numerous objects and such objects may have their own attributes.
2. Dominant noun objects bear "structural relationships" with respect to each other.
3. Medical processing can alter the composition of medical objects, their attributes, and their structural relationships, directly and/or indirectly via the attributes of the objects.
4. Machines like human beings can alter a "status of the cluster/group of medical objects" that constitutes a complex medical object (Figure 9.1) to suit the context and situation in which the medical process is accomplished.
5. The virtual boundary that encompasses the cluster/group of medical objects (a complex medical object) is governed by the relevance of the medical operation to the current context of the use of the objects, thus permitting machines and human beings to judiciously[2] terminate or extend the medical process(es) to manageable proportions.
6. Machine-executable medical operation codes (*mopcs*) are the accurate tools that are used to trim and readjust the status/entropy of the MNOs thus altering the status of an object. During the processing of medical function, transient objects may be created; convolved or deleted and new relationships may be evolved, convolved, or dissolved. The true test of the success of the (human or) machine medical process is its reflection of the "reality" of the changes of the new medical objects and their relationships.
7. Machine-executed altercations of medical processes become scientific and rational. Every step in the medical process can be retrieved for examination and/or enhancement.

9.2.4   Effect of Medical Processing

The entire status of a group of MNOs and the entropy of the entire collectivity is represented as a row in the top of Figure 9.4. All the characteristics of each of the noun objects are tagged and all the interrelationships are identified by forward and backward pointers. In addition, the intensity, modality, and nature of the set of medical process(es) (MPF(s)) that operate on this group of objects is represented as a column of numbers, alpha numerals, and vectors.

In evaluating the outcome of the force on the objects, matrix-like numbers, alphanumeric entities, and vector displacement of entropies are computed, and a weighted sum of the column gives rise to the new entropies of the transformed object (MNO'). The rules for the convolution of terms in the matrix depend on the nature of objects and the functions and need to be specified for different environment. In the simplest

---

[2] Human beings may use judgment but the machine uses a predefined level of probability to determine the relevance. Such probabilities are computed by the number of relevancies (in a similar context) derived from the past from the local and Internet knowledge bases.

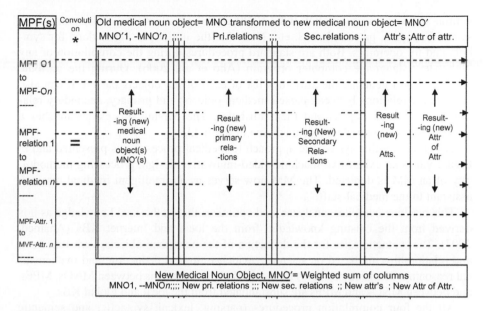

Figure 9.4 Change in status (entropy) of an old noun object MNO after a valid set of process(es) MPF(s) resulting in a transformed (new) object MNO'.

case when an electromotive force of V volts is connected to a resistor of R Ohms for "t" seconds, then the energy level within the resistor is enhanced by $(V^2/R) \cdot t$ watts. In a more complex case, when a group of "n" photons from an object enters the retina over a period of time t, then the entropy of the object in the eye of the beholder is altered dynamically. Neural-electric impulses are thus generated by the retina and transmitted via the optic nerve(s) over a period t. The sequence of such pulses conveys the change in the entropy (and the associated energy) for the object stored in the neural pathways in the brain. The perceived entropy (and the associated energy) of the object changes and conceived accordingly.

In every case, a physical and a scientific process occurs between MPFs and MNOs that can be computed with a good level of confidence. When the forces are social, cultural, and are even healing and medicinal, then an estimate of the intensity, modality, and nature becomes necessary and a confidence level of the outcome is feasible. Such methodologies have been deployed in AI-based programs (Bellazzi et al., 2007), Mycin (Shortcliffe, 1976), and NeoMycin (Kintsch et al., 1984) in medicine for diagnosing and treating common ailments.

9.2.5 Practical Use of MMs

Consider the possible use of an MM in its role of assisting a medical worker, an inventor in medical sciences, or a medical-mathematician. Such an MM can uncover the noun objects and verb functions in the existing medical banks of similar subjects under the DDS (OCLC, 2003) or LoC classification by parsing the scientific papers, patents, books, etc. Note that the initial parsing is done for symbols and for operators. Both are standard procedures during the compilation of any higher-level language computer program (Aho et al., 2006). During the attribute parsing, it will generate the attributes list of each of the objects parsed. It can also analyze the relations between parsed medical objects, and primary, secondary relationships between objects and their attributes. The parsing process establishes a structure of prior knowledge of medicine in the field.

In Figure 9.5, this systematic approach to medical processing is presented and in Figure 9.6 as an exhaustive machine-aided-innovative design, processing methodology of an MM is depicted. The MM now serves as an intelligent medical research assistant to the medical staff.

This machine compiles, analyzes, and optimizes the synthesized knowledge as it is derived from the existing knowledge from the local and Internet KBs (Ahamed, 2007). The syntactic rules for the deduction of the new noun objects, verb functions, and relationships are based on scientific evidence, logical deduction, and mathematical reasoning. The semantic rules for establishing the relations between MNOs, MPFs, and between MNOs and MPFs are substantiated from the local and global KBs.

All the four compilation procedures (parsing, lexical, syntactic, and semantic analysis; Aho et al., 2006) that have been well established in the complier theory of traditional computers are performed by the medical compiler software (SW) for the MM. The conventional compiler design concepts and their corresponding procedures become applicable in the compilation of medical programs.

In principle, the medical knowledge machine will execute medical programs as efficiently as a computer would execute any higher-level language programs in any

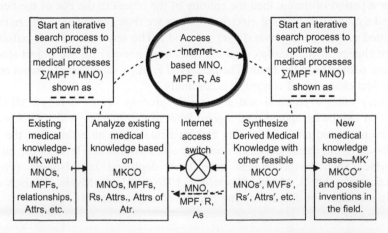

Figure 9.5 Parsing and analyzing the medical knowledge centric objects (MKCOs) in the existing KBs to generate synthesized MKCO that are optimized to suit the current socioeconomic settings. MNO, medical noun object; MPF, medical verb function; R, relationships between MNOs, MPFs, and MNOs and MPFs; Attr, attributes of MNOs and adjectives of MPFs.

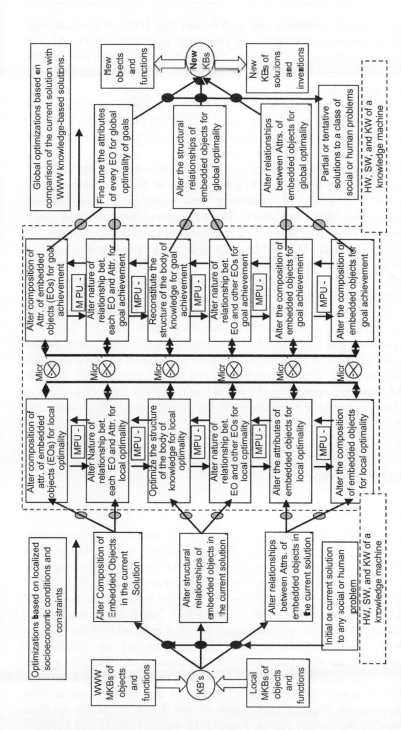

Figure 9.6 A computational framework for processing knowledge with KPUs that reconstitute objects, their functions, relationships to suit the solution to social and human problems. EO, embedded noun object; MPF, verb function; R, relationships between MNOs, MPFs, and MNOs and MPFs; Attr, attributes of MNOs and adjectives of MPFs.

computer system. It is our contention that well-constructed HW and medical-ware (MW) will perform the medical functions as efficiently as numeric, logic, AI, and object-oriented function as existing computer systems. In addition, the MM has the semihuman capacity to invent medical processes, objects, their attributes, etc., as it processes medical knowledge and information.

This innate ability to invent and innovate is built in MMs since it constantly checks the optimality of every noun object (MNO) and verb function (MPF) that it accesses and executes. The convolution between the two is examined thoroughly because of the network access to the Web KBs.

In this section, we present a computational platform for executing medical programs by deploying suitably designed MPUs and a series of medical compiler software modules. It is capable of generating new medical science—oriented knowledge from existing MPFs and MNOs. There is a possibility that these medical research assistants can invent based of WWW medical knowledge of current literature. The functioning of the MM can be made generic like the PCs that handle a large number of common programs for a large community of users or specific to specialized users in any discipline such as medicine, cardiovascular systems, cancer, radiation therapy, and so on. All the tools and techniques embedded in AI are transplanted in the science of medicine or any branch of medicine. The medical KBs are tailored accordingly to conform to the subject or profession.

Knowledge processing is based on object processing, and objects constitute the nodal points in the structure of knowledge. The links and relationships between the nodes offer different types of architectures that can be tailored to meet the user needs. Verb functions that operate on the nodes can transform existing inventions and literature into customized signatures for the next generation of computer systems.

9.3   Medical Processors

9.3.1   Simplest MPUs

MPU designs are firmly entrenched in the design of central processing units (CPUs), numerical processor units, digital signal processors, and knowledge processor unit (KPUs). In the section, we briefly review the architectures of the simplest CPU (von Neumann CPU) design to the more elaborate KPU design.

Simplest MPUs are brute-forced CPUs with elaborate firmware/medical-ware/ software (FW/MW/SW) modules that mimic the medical functions at a macrolevel. A simplest medical computer is a brute-forced business computer. From the perspective of 2030s, this approach appears like brute-forcing an Institute of Advanced Study (IAS) machine (late 1940s) to function as an IBM 370 system (late 1960s), or to force a manual switchboard (1920s) to function like a simplest electronic switching system (ESS) (1960s). The elegant and lasting solution is to modify the conventional Pentium architecture of the 1990s to handle medical objects and to modify the control units to respond the medical operational codes, if not design the MPU as a distinctly new entity built with the Intel 45 nm, 2007 technology.

9.3.2   Features of Medical Processors

MPUs have not yet specifically built for medical operation codes (*mopcs*). It is possible and viable that such processor chips will be tailored and geared to medical functions. A variety of such generic functions can be readily identified. One such medical operation code (*mopc*) is to instruct the MPU to compare bacteria strain i with all known bacteria (j, $j = 1$, n) from WWW bacteria banks and identify any settle change patterns. Certain amount of object processing and pattern recognition procedures will become essential to complete this task. For the computer scientists and VLSI designers, the modular tasks involved in executing this overall task have already been accomplished in other disciplines. The ordeal is to assemble an interdisciplinary team of scientists.

Other generic functions are the identification of ailments, patient complaints/cures, most effective treatments, and KPUs to bridge the various knowledge domains. Only a prolonged and consistent effort from the medical staff can lead to generic operation codes for MPUs that can be focal element of medical computer. For an initial step, the knowledge operation codes (*kopcs*) should suffice as medical operation codes (*mopcs*) discussed in this section. Medical processors and medical data banks work in tandem for executing numerous instructions, retrieving/storing, and processing pertinent medical information. Numerous medical processor HW units and modules (including conventional CPUs) coexist in the integrated system to track the confidence levels of the medical functions, individually and collectively.

Figure 9.7 depicts the schematic of an MPU derived from the designs of an object processor unit presented in Section 2.9 and the KPU presented in Figure 2.10. Patients and their attributes are treated in unison and as one synergy. Patient records are dynamic and reflect the most recent state of health and the attributes are updated with a history of changes. Procedures are configured from known procedures on similar patient but with slightly different attributes. The procedures are mapped against the attributes to ascertain the optimality and efficacy of treatments and procedures. The basic laws of medical sciences are not violated during administration of treatments and procedures. Administering n subprocedures on a patient with m (maximum) attributes generates an $n \times m$ matrix. The common, conflicting, and overlapping attributes are thus reconfigured to establish primary and secondary medical safety rules in the practice of medicine.

MPUs have not yet specifically built for medical operation codes (*mopcs*). However, it is possible and viable that such processor chips can be tailored and geared to medical functions. In fact, the current processor chips have tremendous amount of flexibility to be converted to MPUs. A variety of such generic functions can be readily identified.

One such medical operation code (*mopc*) is to instruct the MPU to compare bacteria strain i with all known bacteria (j, $j = 1$, n) from WWW bacteria banks and

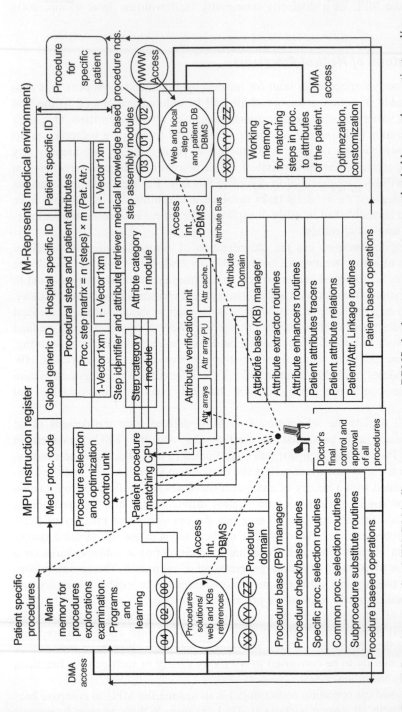

Figure 9.7 Architecture of an MPU. DMA, direct memory access; DBMS, database management system that holds procedure, patient, and/or attribute base(s), procedure management system(s), patient-specific characteristics, and medical resources of the hospital; KB, knowledge base(s). The medical procedure code is the *"mopc"* that forces the MPU to execute a micro- or nanomedical function.

identify any settle change patterns. Comparison of time-lapse images such as cat scans and X-rays yields inference about the progression or regression of infections, cancer, or any other ailments. Certain amount of object processing involving edge detection, pattern recognition algorithms may become essential to complete such tasks in the medical field. From the perspectives of computer scientists and VLSI designers, such modular tasks have already been accomplished in other disciplines (pattern recognition, signature and face identification, etc.). The ordeal is to assemble an interdisciplinary team of scientists.

Other generic functions are the identification of ailments, patient complaints/ cures, most effective treatments, and KPUs to bridge the various knowledge domains. Only a prolonged and consistent effort from the medical staff can lead to generic operation codes for MPUs that can be focal element of medical computer. For an initial step, the knowledge operation codes (*kopcs*) should suffice as medical operation codes (*mopcs*) discussed in this section. Medical processors and medical data banks work in tandem for executing a numerous instructions, retrieving/storing, and processing pertinent medical information. Numerous medical processor HW units and modules (including conventional CPUs) coexist in the integrated system to track the confidence levels of the medical functions, individually and collectively.

Modern medical computers constitute a special breed of cluster computers. Both have identifiable supersets of traditional computers for the routine functions. While it is viable to force a cluster computer to act as full-fledged medical computer, it is desirable to build medical computers on a distinctive track of its own medical operation codes (*mopcs*). The demand for such medical computers is likely to expand and grow like the specialized airborne computers for the aviation industry.

Patient databases, physician access points, patient access points, and service facilities are connected to the medical data banks and medical processor via several buses. In an alternative integrated medical computer system, numerous processors are included with their own memories and modules and are linked together to establish a processor net unit. Such systems are amenable to hospital-campus settings, where several buildings comprise the hospital, or where several hospitals are interlinked over local area networks.

9.4   Evolution of Medical KBs

The NIH funded research had been initiated by Internist-I as far back as 1988 at Stanford University. The ensuing GUIDON (i.e., an intelligent computer-aided instruction tool) and MYCIN do not provide the reason, structure, and the strategy in the diagnosis. Rationality for the expert system-based recommendations for recommended therapy is also missing.

Systematic accumulation of medical information into appropriate databases has been in vogue since 1970s by medical billing and insurance companies. In order to streamline the billing and payments, most financial activities related to medical profession have been handled by small systems. These systems now are multinational and global with the advent of backbone networks and then the transoceanic fiber nets that span most major nations in the world. Unfortunately, the activity was confounded to financial activities. However, since 1980s, the effort was shifted (only) slightly for sharing medical data and information. At the City University of New York, the initial steps for research directed toward sharing the medical knowledge was substantially accelerated by a numerous of doctoral candidates and their seminal contributions during the 1990–2007 time frame.

Elsewhere the contributions have been scattered and diversified. In a majority of cases, the activity has been commercial rather than academic and scholarly. The computational and network tools and techniques have been obscured by a blanket of profiteering from the sale of data to specialized medical teams and to desperate patients. As late as 2010, only a few nonprofit medical KBs have emerged. The authenticity and accuracy of the contents is by entry rather than by reason and scientific accountability.

9.5   Design Variations of the MPU

Traditional CPU architecture, shown in Figures 2.1 and 2.2 entailing a control unit, arithmetic unit, logic unit, control memory, interrelated with single- or multibus structures, is too rudimentary for medical applications. The MPU does not process data. It only generates a sequence of subprocedures for current or standard medical procedures consistent with the patient history, physician's expert system (Aikins et al., 1983; Kinney, 1987) capability/expertise and capability of the medical facilities available in that particular environment.

The typical operator–operand function of the MPU is neither traditional binary nor hexadecimal (Kinney, 1987) instead, it is based on knowledge of the patient (available in the patient database) and experience of the medical team in a general categorical sense and with reference to that particular patient. Both of these areas are dynamic and can vary significantly. For this reason, we propose that the expert and knowledge-systems based programs be used consistently with the capability of the medical facilities.

The microprograms (Detmer, 2001) in the MPU will function in *three* independent ways initially and subsequently in an interdependent fashion. *First*, any approved expert system database is referred for current concepts and breakthroughs. *Second*, the practice of the particular physician and the medical facility is referred to be consistent with the knowledge level of the physician and the capabilities of the medical facility. *Third*, the experience of this physician and earlier physicians with this particular patient is referred. All the necessary checks and verifications are made before administering any procedure to a patient in view of the patient history.

The output of this MPU is a series of instructions, which is based upon the opinion of the current experts, approved by a team of physicians (if necessary), and verified for processing and expectation by dual, independent processors. The output of the processor is a series of subprocedures that will be dispatched to the actual medical facilities after appropriate allocation of existing medical resources to the patient's subprocedures. Scheduling, resource sharing, time, and priority allocation will be done automatically depending upon the type or code of service being performed (emergency, standard, diagnostic, routine, etc.). This system is accountable for every step of its function, and no tampering of any sort is possible by encryption (Vacca, 2009) of subprocedure code and patient data. The decryption key and its code identification are available to the medical staff. Such measures of additional safety and streamlined handling of the procedures can make the overall service provisioning current, economic, and accountable at every subprocedure step.

9.5.1 Subprocedure Instructions

From preliminary considerations, we foresee numerous broadly definable instructions. *Three* such categories are knowledge-based inferential instructions, search instructions, and administrative or local housekeeping instructions.

In the *first category*, the medical structure of the cause—effect relation is queried, or the logical and predictable effect is being sought; or conversely, the preconditions for a given state are being investigated. It is important to note that certainty is never the strong point of this type of processing. Every step is subject to a confidence level. Thus, the chain of the subprocedures that make up a given medical procedure is based on such individual confidence levels. Fuzzy-set (Smith and Nguyen, 2007; Knuth, 1998) information processing is appropriate for the execution of this category of instructions.

In the *second category*, as the search (Ahamed, 1995) is being initiated, two groups emerge. The *first group* deals with search in the knowledge domain (professional, medical opinion, possible cures, diagnostics, etc.), and the *second group* deals with search in the data domain (files, patient information, databases, insurance company codes, service providers, drug vendors, etc.).

In the first group, the input is the incomplete input data to investigate which other branches of the knowledge tree are logically associated with the given inputs. Forward and backward pointers may be sought by this type of instruction, and similar symptomatic conditions may be queried. Associative and forward searches also may be initiated by this type of instruction. The first category and second set of instructions are not always orthogonal, and invoking the first set can invoke the second set and vice versa.

In the second group, the input is complete for the data processing units to offer a complete and definite response. An example of this type of search is the social security number of a patient or the latest visit to the hospital. Definite and precise answers are sought and secured from the IMS. By separating the searches into two groups, the instruction sets to the IMS can be separated as:

Searches dealing with the medical-knowledge domain.
(or)
Searches dealing with the data domain.

Thus, the HW, SW, MW, FW, and "people-ware" domains responsible for the execution of these two types of searches may be isolated and optimized.

In the *third category*, the administrative functions of the local medical facility may be activated. Typical of such instructions are scheduling of operating rooms, issuance of the hospital beds, allocation and consistency of physician teams, accounting and billing, updating of the patient databases, etc. This category of instruction is localized to the environment of the medical facilities, the personnel, the support staff, and the type of services it is expected to provide. We suggest that the input/output bus for this category of instruction be isolated from the input/output bus for the other two types of instruction to avoid any possible contamination of information to and from the established KBs. Standard techniques for the construction, maintenance, and use of such KBs in communication and intelligent networks are available (Haas and Robrock, 1986).

9.5.2 Speed and Capacity of the MPU

From the point of view of implementation, the speed of the MPU is not crucial, except when the physicians prefer a real-time look up of how the MPU would handle a certain situation. For this reason, we foresee two types of MPUs. The first type of MPU handles the batch type of job processing (Ahamed and Lawrence, 1998), and the second type handles the online processing. The architecture of the two systems differs.

9.5.2.1 Remote MPUs

These units are job-processing environments. Under normal conditions, any particular patient's ID may be submitted to the MPU with a desired procedure (or even a complaint or symptom) and the primary medical/vital data of the patient (e.g., temperature, blood pressure, and heart rate), as the paramedical teams dispatch this information to the physician. The nonreal-time response will be generated and mailed (dispatched electronically) to the doctor. Under the later conditions, the memory and database capability of the MPU to act in conjunction with the AI-based programs becomes the key element. Typically, in remote MPUs, the memory size and database capability can be compromised for speed. Dual, independent processing (as it is done in most ESS facilities; Alcatel-Lucent, 2013) can only double the cost of a high capacity, low-speed machine. Job priorities are assignable to the patient and procedures. Procedure sequences are forced in subsequent time slots, and time and resource sharing can thus be optimized. Almost all remote MPUs need to be network based since the medical KBs can also be remote, and one MPU can service many hundreds of remote input locations. The searches performed by remote MPUs can become more thorough and far-reaching in nonreal-time applications.

9.5.2.2 Hospital-Based MPUs

These units involve online processing. When real-time response is necessary for the MPU, the architecture can be readjusted for speed and response, rather than doing extensive searches for a large number of patients and subscribers. When certain procedures are necessary quickly, the cost of service provisioning and the economics of providing services from various hospitals, laboratories, diagnostic services, or even doctors may be sacrificed for urgency. However, under normal conditions, the patient can be provided with the most cost-effective strategy for the services to be performed. Specialized service providers who use all their resources optimally will be reinforced, and marginal service providers will be phased out.

Patients and their attributes are treated in unison and as one synergy. Patient records are dynamic and reflect the most recent state of health, and the attributes are updated with a history of changes. Procedures are configured from known procedures on similar patient but with slightly different attributes. The procedures are mapped against the attributes to ascertain the optimality and efficacy of treatments and procedures. The basic laws of medical sciences are not violated during administration of treatments and procedures. Administering n subprocedures on a patient with m (maximum) attributes generates an $n \times m$ matrix. The common, conflicting, and overlapping attributes are thus reconfigured to establish primary and secondary medical safety rules in the practice of medicine.

9.6 Microprogramming in Medical Field

Microprogramming was conceived as early as mid-1940s and brought in full use during 1970s. Numerous advantages such as flexibility and customization of the CPU follow. In a general sense, microprograms typically resident in "control memories" permit customized interpretation of the operation code or *opc* and operands used extensively in early assembly level programming of machines. The generic use of the computers could thus be increased if the same machines could be used for scientific and business computing by changing the microcoded ROM chips in the CPU. The corresponding operand(s) or *opr*(s) need to be placed (loaded) in the operand field of the binary instruction code. Even though this is a very attractive capability, the medical field appears too docile to embrace radical concepts in the practice of medicine.

However, the possibility of fragmentation of any medical procedures into finite number of subprocedures exists and the use of microprogrammed medical ROMs can be developed or burned in the PROMs. The process of curing of patients is an envisioned and well-anticipated series of well-planned and contemplated sequential and/or parallel steps. Adaptability in the admixing and administrating such finite subprocedures is a refined human skill of the medical staff but the sequencing of the necessary sub-subprocedures (or microprocedures) and the prerequisites and post-requisites for these microprocedures is well within the realm of machines. A successful partnership and boundary can thus be established. Standard sets of necessary microprocedure can be managed and delegated to machines while retaining the skilled contemplated judgmental choices in the realm of human activity.

9.6.1   Medical Procedures and Micro-MPU Programs

Human activity is a collection of smaller well-perceived series of steps. When the fragmentation of human activity is taken to an extreme, every activity has at least one verb function (equivalently, an operation code, *opc*) that acts upon at least one noun object (equivalently, one operand, *opr*). Single instruction single data (SISD) process methodology for computing is thus enabled. Many variations of human activity exist and correspond to single instruction multiple data (SIMD), multiple instruction single data (MISD), and multiple instruction multiple data (MIMD) process methodologies. Such instructions can be executed by CPUs that are derived by rearranging the von Neumann's CPU depicted in Figure 2.1.

Medical field is no exception and at the lowest level of any medical micro- or nanofunctionality must have at least one nanomedical function acting on at least one nanomedical object. Microprocedures become stylized collections of nanomedical functions acting on nanomedical objects. Subprocedures become macroassemblies of microprocedures, and major procedures become a macrocosm of finely well-perceived microprocedures. The bridge between curing a patient and the functions of the MPU can be visualized. The major hump exists at the judgmental level of the medical staff.

In the domain of knowledge processing, we have presented this concept by stressing that any microscopic knowledge function consists of a verb function (VF) that modifies at least one noun object (NO). The (interactive) process between VF and NO is represented as a convolution ($\circledast$). Thus, a basic knowledge instruction (BKI) becomes

$$BKI = VF \circledast NO$$

just as microscopic medical function could be represented as

$$BMI = MPF \circledast MNO,$$

where MMF represents a microscopic medical procedure and MNO represents a medical noun object.

In the computing field, a well-organized and well-programmed collection of assembly language instruction (ALI) represents an assembly level program or ALP; thus, we have,

$$ALP = \sum_{1}^{n} ALIs, \text{ or } \sum_{1}^{n} \{opcs \text{ corresponding } oprs\}$$

In the knowledge-processing field, we have

$$KLP = \sum_{1}^{nk} BKIs, \text{ or } \sum_{1}^{nk} \{VF \ast \text{corresponding NOs}\}$$

in addition, in the medical field we have

$$MLP = \sum_{1}^{nm} BMIs, \text{ or } \sum_{1}^{nm} \{MPF \circledast \text{corresponding MNOs}\}$$

In all of the symbolic representations, n denotes the number of steps of machine-executable instructions that constitute the program, ALP, knowledge program (KLP) or medical program (MLP). It is immaterial in the knowledge and medical fields whether the instructions are executed in the minds of humans or in the knowledge or medical processors. For the function the KLP or MLP accomplishes, these well-designed configurations of the $n \times k$ or $n \times m$ steps must be completed.

In Figure 9.8 for the traditional data processing systems, the basic steps involved in the flow of instructions (arithmetic logic instructions or ALIs, i.e., opc and $oprs$) within the arithmetic logic processors (ALPs), the corresponding operands data ($oprs$) in and out of a conventional CPU are presented. The steps in the modern processors are much more intricate and complex. These steps have changed and evolved dramatically over the decades even though the philosophy of execution cycle has prevailed. If an instruction cycle is not completed due to an internal or external interrupt or a machine dysfunction, a snapshot of all the registers, the caches, and status of requests is preserved until the interrupt request is serviced. CPU resumes the functions at a later instant from its previously saved condition.

The conventional computer environment had a very standardized procedure for the execution of programs. The fetch, decode, and execute cycle (FDE, in the simplest of instructions) has been conceptualized since the start of assembly language programming. This cycle has been enhanced many (many) times over as the HW and the architecture has evolved. Even during the intermediate era, the cycle became (single/multiple) instruction fetch (F1), separated it into opc part and opr part. Such instructions were classified as the type of opc, and number and nature of

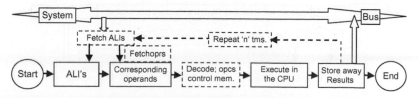

Figure 9.8 Flow chart of the simplest traditional data processing.

operands. In the microprogramming environments, these instructions resolved oper-
and (address(es)), fetched (F2) the operand(s) from memory/cache, or fetch microcode (μC) from the control memory. The decode part of the instruction (μD)
executes each microcoded instruction (μI) on the corresponding operand and stores
each (intermediate/final result) into data cache or main memory.

In the modern processors, the cycle become much (much) longer with the
multiplicity of subordinate processors, cache(s), multiplicity of bus arrangements,
nature of possible parallel/pipeline processing. Even though the (original FDE)
cycle may be deeper and nested, the processor and bus speeds have increased so
much faster that these present processors offer far greater flexibility and execute
much faster.

In the medical-knowledge domain, the legacy of the FDE cycle remains. The
complexity also becomes many layers deep and executed in numerous nested loops.
The resolution of the microsteps can be MW, HW, or micromedical program
(μmp) based. In a sense, the resolution attempted at all levels to make the medical
knowledge level assembly programming simpler and faster. It may take a long time
before we can expect another revolution in bringing home assembly level μmp
level programming in medical field processing. During the decade of 2010, the
medical industry appears to be too rudimentary to absorb all the sophistications of
the computer industry. However, coding microlevel assembly medical programs
appears attractive. The modern processors will serve this purpose well in forcing
this unprecedented VLSI technology one-step closer toward accomplishing human
thought-oriented and healing functions. The implementation of the computational
methodology in the knowledge domain is shown in Figure 9.9.

In an effort to hasten the instruction process cycle, all the steps feasible for
parallelism are processed simultaneously. Only the essential sequential and interdependent functions wait for one process to complete before the next one starts.
The maximum rate of processing coupled with the best utilization of every
resource is one of the chief goals of the operating system of almost all computing systems.

In the knowledge domain, if a KLP is represented as

$$ KLP = \sum_{1}^{n} BKIs, \text{ or } \sum_{1}^{n} \{VF \text{ corresponding NOs}\} $$

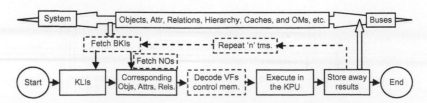

Figure 9.9 Flow chart of the simplest knowledge machine.

then the FDE cycle becomes considerably elaborate because the instruction fetched will have to be immediately decoded to determine type of instruction.[3] In the knowledge domain, even the simplest register to register (RR) instruction in traditional computing becomes at least a stack operation since an "object" is typically a compound tree-like structure with its own elements, i.e., branches, twigs, and leaves, and the BKI function may process one, multiple, and/all of the tree elements. Hence, the HW-based object processing needs enhanced processing capability. This capability may be interjected in the modern processors via the numerous embedded processors with their own dedicated caches, bus structures, and internalized switches. Hence, the concept of the FDE needs to be designed and validated for each BKI in its own processor environment. The programming becomes elaborate but manageable.

The methodology for grouping knowledge instructions as single instruction single object, as SISO, SIMO, MISO, and MIMO (Ahamed, 2009) is presented as the extrapolations of the SISD, SIMD, MISD and MIMD methodology in the tradition of conventional machines (Stone 1980). The mode of operation of the object-oriented computers differs accordingly. The design and architecture of the more elaborate object processors dealing with SIMO, MISO, and MIMO type of knowledge instructions becomes much more demanding and sophisticated but the architectural arrangements of these are also depicted in ref. Ahamed (2009).

9.6.2 Architecture of a Micro-MPU and Medical Code

Systems of specially designed chipsets from the traditional computer architectures have facilitated the solution of most scientific and business problems in society. Similar chipsets lodged in micro-MPU, itself lodged in a generic MM, will facilitate the solution of some of generic medical problems. Typically, seven such layers that exist in the computer[4] and communication[5] fields are projected in the medical field.[6] In a sense, the MW is expected to evolve in the similar fashion (see Figure 9.10 for a suggested medical code structure) as the software industry has evolved. Medical programs also have a hierarchical pattern ranging from

---

[3] The instructions are generally classified by the first few bits of the operation code. This is commonly done in most instruction decoders. Such typical procedures will become applicable in the knowledge and the medical processors.

[4] In the computer field, the seven levels consist of application code, higher level language code, the compiled code, assembly language code, loader and linked code, the machine specific (including the microcode) code, and the binary executable code. The HW of the machine executes this last code (one instruction at a time via the FDE cycle) to generate the result of the application program.

[5] In the communication field, the seven levels of instructions and header blocks correspond to the seven layers (application, presentation, sessions, transport, network, data-link, and physical) consist of the instruction standardized by the ITU and specifically defined by the OSI model.

[6] In the medical field, the seven proposed layers suggested are administrative commands, medical commands, hospital and support commands, staff commands, equipment and instrumentation commands, procedure commands, and subprocedure commands. In an initial format, the hierarchy of these commands is depicted in Figure 9.10.

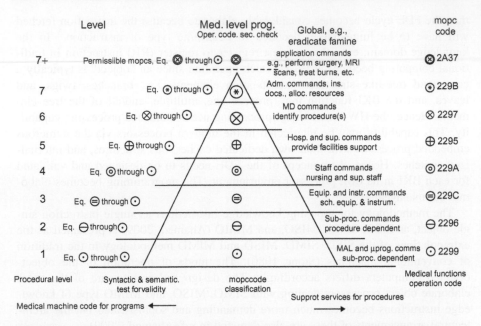

Figure 9.10 Search algorithms are matched depending on the level of the commands. By classifying these commands, the search time is minimized. Microprogramming at various levels can thus be tied into WWW search algorithm making medical computers as efficient as the RISC in the traditional computer environment.

higher-level (level-6) medical application programs (MAPs) with major (level-6) or macroprocedural commands (MPC), such as:

Abdominal Surgery (Patient X, Doctor D, Surgeon S, Hospital H)

The medical compiler will generate all the secondary commands from level-6 commands (Figure 9.10) and the micro-MPU commands of the most generic nature for the patient, doctor, surgeon, medical staff, hospital staff, resource allocation for each, anthologists, etc. Further, it will check with the human team(s) responsible for each major level 2 to level 7 procedures and issues commands to robotic units and instruction to the human participants. It will also provide a knowledge-base check to ascertain that the accuracy of the procedures, subprocedures, micro-, and nanoprocedures will be sound and medically valid and complaisant with all the human counterparts in the major medical procedure or subprocedure commanded at MPC level. Security and privacy will thus be guaranteed together with the accuracy and basis for each step will be cogent and coherent segment in the execution of the MPC. The MM will also "understand" the context of the problem in reference to the global medical knowledge of such problems in the WWW.

Further the MM resolves the steps necessary to solve any (initially simple, but finally more complex) problem at hand by (a) determining the medical procedures and/or actions necessary, (b) the medical objects (all objects) that will enable the solution of the problem, (c) the security and privacy issues, and (if necessary) the medical insurance and payment issues. Job scheduling and resource matching is well the realm of most management information and IT systems. In the traditional computing systems, priority resource management and monitoring of tasks are routinely performed by operating systems. Such functions will be performed by medical operating systems and will extend into the monitoring of the medical verb functions (mpf$_i$) convolving ($\circledast_j$) medical noun objects (mno$_k$) that are symbolized in Figure 9.11.

Threading of multiple (medical) tasks through medical supercomputers (see Section 10.8) becomes as logical and coordinated as the threading of multiple tasks through the processors of the 2010–2015 era (see Section 2.7). It appears that the time frame to conceive and build such medical middle-ware for the next generation MPUs is now during the decade of 2010. Such MPU chips will well serve the tiny doctor's offices, the midsized hospitals, community hospitals and networked medical regional medical centers, and finally, the national MSPs.

The array of personalized Internet services available to users via browsers is increasing. These Internet services attempt to satisfy the needs of the Internet users; however, they do not particularly meet the specialized needs of most of the members of any particular society or any specific groups of users. The conventional computer systems have attempted to provide services to computation and communication customers via more and more intelligent software layers atop very sophisticated special purpose CPUs. Typically, the types of functions are limited to a predefined set of computation and communication services. The user has very little ability to tailor these services to their specific needs and requirements. Meeting the increasing demand for personalized services has been difficult for several reasons.

$$\text{MNF} \circledast \text{MNO} \equiv \sum_{i=1}^{i=L} (\text{mpf}_i) \cdot \prod_{j=1}^{i=M} (\circledast_j) \cdot \sum_{l=1}^{l=N} (\text{mno}_k)$$

$$[\text{MPF} \equiv \sum_{i=1}^{i=L} (\text{mpf}_i)], \; [(\circledast_j) \equiv \prod_{j=1}^{j=M} (\circledast_j)], \text{ and}$$

$$\text{MPF} \equiv \sum_{l=1}^{l=N} (\text{mpf}_k)$$

Figure 9.11 Algebraic representation of an medical process ranging from a major medical program (such as "cure leukemia") to a micromedical operation ($\mu mopc$ such as sterilize surgical tools to prepare for an operation or "prescribe topical antibiotic cream"). It implies that any medical verb function (MPF) can be decomposed into a series of smaller (medical or related verb) functions, any medical process ($\circledast$) consists of a series of microprocesses, and the effect of the process on medical noun object (MNO) is the combined effect of the microprocesses on each of the elements (mno's) that constitute the main MNO.

One reason is that the traditional computer systems have too much generic capabilities and very little customization to solve individual problems quickly and optimally. Another reason is that standards take a long time to develop, approve, and implement computer systems to serve as generic knowledge/MMs. The solution proposed here fragments individual problems so finely that a well-designed micro-KPU/MPU chip will serve the wide range of knowledge/medical functions in the knowledge/medical domain as a well-designed CPU chip will serve in a computational domain.

9.6.3 Micromedical Instruction Execution

To initiate the solution, micro-MPU systematically decomposes any medical instruction level (MIL) μmedical *opc*odes ($\mu mopcs$ or *nano-mopcs*) into finer micro- or nanomedical instruction or a set of highly specialized reduced instruction set computers (RISC) micromedical commands (sterilize surgical instruments, preimmunize surgical patients, reserve operation theaters, book medical assistants—staff, reserve IC units and recovery rooms, tag patients and their allergies, etc.). When networked with hospital resources, resolution of conflicts for resources by the embedded-operating systems of any midsized computer facility is easily accomplished.

The micro-MPU chips find a generic "prototype" for the solution based on a collection of steps assembled from medical practices in most hospitals. Such steps are procedures in medical practice. Special hospital and staff features only modify the steps without changing the necessary procedural constraints. When monitored by authorized professionals, such modifications can indeed enhance the quality of care, treatment, or even the cure.

When only one MPF or mpf_i is "procedurized" with one MNO or mno_k, then a simple "procedurer" (Figure 9.11) will suffice[7] to bring about a (MPF, $\circledast$, and MNO) or (mpf_i, $\circledast_j$, and mno_k). Other architectural variations, such as one mpf, multiple mno's (equivalent of SIMD, or MISD, or MIMD) configuration, etc., can be derived based of the following architectures.

Medical processing is more complex than text, object, or knowledge processing, and the implication of each step of medical processing needs security, privacy, scientific, and/or economic justification. In addition, if a MAP calls for an optimization, then the utility of each of the steps of the MLAP needs to be evaluated and tallied against the resources required for that particular step or procedure.

In a wider sense, the utility/worth of every medical process (MPF, $\circledast$, and MNO) needs to be justified for its utility, efficacy, and its cost. Side effects of drugs,

---

[7] The term "procedurer" is designated as HW that enforces a medical verb function (mvf) on a medical noun object (mno). It is akin to simple VLSI device such as an adder or a multiplier. In the medical domain, at least one mvf and one mno is implied in every statement that modifies an mno. The implication is that an active mvf modifies an mno or alters its state. The action of the mvf varies dramatically depending on the medical procedure and the patient (or medical noun object) and becomes a procedure (however simple or complex) rather than a simple add, subtract, multiplier, divide, etc., or any logical, vector, matrix, etc., function. Hence, the symbol is chosen as a $\circledast$ and written between MPF and MNO or mpf and mno.

long-range implications of surgeries, drug rehab programs, etc. need consideration for any specific patient and the proposed procedure. Derived utilities are determined solely by the natures of (MPF, ⊛, and MNO) or by the natures of (mpf_i, $⊛_j$, and mno_k). In reality, however, a series of no_k's are involved since the process yields different utility for each no_k. Similarly, the utility is different for each possible variation of mpf_i, $⊛_j$, and mno_k. When these options are available, the utility of each combination is evaluated to find which combination or solution yields the best utility or results. Three different caches for mpf_i, $⊛_j$, and mno_k are necessary and shown in Figure 9.12. Other architectural variations (such as single mpf, multiple mno's, multiple mpf's, multiple mno's) of the micromedical processor will require multiplicity of stacks for MPFs, ⊛s, and MNOs.

The computation or the estimation of the expected utility of any $\mu mopc$ or micromedical function becomes necessary if the process involves optimization or the selection of the best utility that will result from one or more combinations of (mpf_i, $⊛_j$, and mno_k). A series of (mpf_i, $⊛_j$, and no_k) are stored in their respective caches and the process then selects the best combination of (mpf_i, $⊛_j$, and no_k). The resulting utilities are illustrated in Figure 9.13.

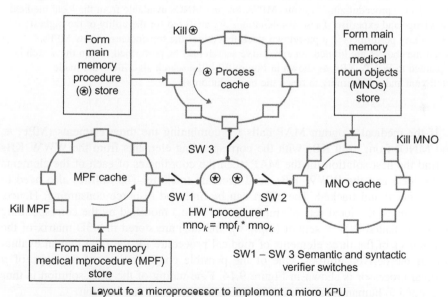

Layout fo a microprocessor to imploment a mioro KPU
for the convolution ($vf_i * no_K$) to generate a new noun object no_K

Figure 9.12 Location of a "procedurer" in a μMPU. The "procedurer" forces the completion of a micromedical procedure ($\mu mopc$) on one or a series of possible mno's. Typically, a series of mno_k's are involved since the process yields different utility for each $\mu mopc_i$ on mno_k. Similarly, the utility is different for each possible variation of mpf_i and for $⊛_j$. When these options are available, the utility of each combination is evaluated to find which combination or solution yields the best utility or results.

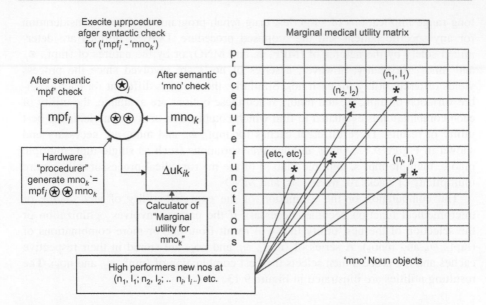

Figure 9.13 The plot identifies the combination of mpf$_i$, ⊛$_j$, and mno$_k$ yielded the highest utility from "procedurizing" various MPFs, ⊛s, and MNOs available from the local medical knowledge and expertise. These combinations are analyzed for the utility of the highest (procedure) performers in a pushdown stack that stores the top choices of new MPFs. When the choices are limited, an exhaustive search may be performed. When the search is expanded to WWW KBs, as shown in Figure 9.14, the search algorithms are made intelligent and self-learning to reach the best solution(s).

If the medical program MAP calls for combining the three elements (MPF, ⊛, and MNO) from local KBs with the corresponding elements from the WWW KBs to find the best solution for the MAP, then the coordinates of each of the elements in the local and the WWW KBs need accurate tracking. The utilities also need to be computed and tracked. The effort can be time and resource consuming. Hence, the tacking of the local sets of (mpf$_i$, ⊛$_j$, and mno$_k$) modified by the corresponding and documented WWW sets of (mpf$_i$, ⊛$_j$, and no$_k$) are stored in a 3D matrix of the coordinates of the three elements of medical procedure for the final human evaluation of the derived utilities. One of the possible configurations of this type of μ medical processor is shown in Figure 9.14. Fine-tuning of the final solution is thus postponed to human judgment in view of committee of joint decision.

One of the by-products of this type of micromanagement of the composition of medical knowledge is the enhanced creativity in the optimal combinations of the two sets of local and WWW (mpf$_i$, ⊛$_j$, and mno$_k$). New MPFs, ⊛s, and MNOs will be evolved to maximize the utility in one or more directions. When the criterion for selection is controlling violence, the machine yields the best social remedies against violence. When the criterion for selection is best molecular structures for drugs against flue, the machine yields possible sets of drug innovations only for flue, etc.

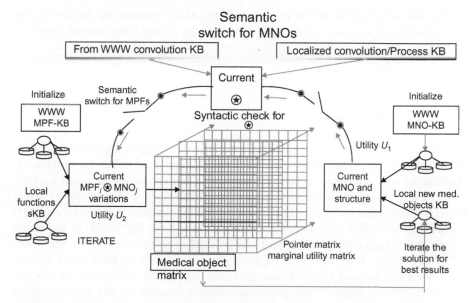

Figure 9.14 Medical "procedural" functions (MPFs) and MNOs are drawn from both local knowledge expertise and local KBs, and verified against the Internet KB to ascertain the "utilities" derived from the newly synthesized MPF and/or MNO. The marginal enhancement of utility is tallied against the marginal cost to make the most valid economic choice for the newly construed MPFs and MNO'. The derived MKCO is likely to be a flawless and perfected MKCO based on the constraints imposed on the choices of MPFs, ⊛s, and MNOs.

9.6.4 Mapping Medical and Internet Functions

When the entire medical care includes the verification of every microstep of every procedure, it becomes desirable to streamline the overall individual care that is delivered to the patients by ascertaining the validity, effectiveness, and justification of every microprocedural step, and check it out based on procedures published on the Internet. Even though the medical staff may provide the validity and connectivity of all the microsteps, the most recent and optimal steps may not be available to the staff. An MM deployed to streamline the patient care will delineate the steps and provide a reference for the doctors to expect the probability of estimate the success of the entire procedure. Such refinements do not currently exist in the present day medical care for the patients.

Such a methodology can be easily incorporated by matching the medical steps with the search for WWW medical KBs. If the functions (mpf_i, $⊛_j$, and mno_k) are synchronized with Internet searches on the WWW for the same, then the speed and efficiency are enhanced. A suggested encoding of the micromedical procedural steps is depicted in Figure 9.14.

The Internet complier for the execution of the MAPs matches the laws of syntax and semantics of the local (mpf_i, $\otimes_j$, and mno_k) with those of the Internet (mpf_i, $\otimes_j$, and mno_k) and any possibility of nonalignment of (mpf_i, with $\otimes_j$, and then with mno_k) is eliminated.

9.7 Conclusions

This chapter provides a conceptual framework for building an algebraic model for the practice of medicine. It provides a (semi) mathematical model for simulating, duplicating, and predicting effects, relationships, and consequences (with a confidence level) of any given medical procedure (MPF) upon a given medical object (MNO). Such steps are the basis of computer-aided analysis and design (CAAD) software in most technological establishments throughout the world. In the initial stages, the computational CAAD tool can be used as a fallback DSS for the medical professionals. With increased sophistication in the MW in the CAAD system, the system can be used to check and verify the procedural, subprocedural process, and microprocess steps of any proposed medical function in any given medical environment.

During the numerous steps in the machine generated "compilation" of a "MAP," the machine tailors the "medical verb functions" (MVFs) to the particular "MNOs. Any possible parsing, syntactical, semantic, loading, and linking misalignments are automatically detected and flagged, and "misprocesses" are eliminated.

The methodology for developing the CAAD computational tool (for medicine) is taken from the science of morphology and practiced in the art of systems programming in software design. When the art of medical programming is evolved, the probability of errors in the compiled machine-executable code will approach the probability of errors in computer and communication systems. The learning curve for the software environment has been approximately two decades and is comparable to the learning cure for the large-scale integration (LSI) industry during 1970s through 1990s. The medical CAAD is as unlikely to stop its evolution much as the VLSI industry is unable to reach its perfect status.

References

1. Bellazzi R, Abu-Hanna A, Hunter J, editors: *Artificial intelligence in medicine: 11th conference on artificial intelligence in medicine in Europe*, Amsterdam, The Netherlands, 2007, AIME.
2. Shortcliffe E: *MYCIN: computer-based medical consultations*, New York, NY, 1976, American Elsevier, See also Buchanan BG, Shortcliffe EH: *Rule-based expert system: the mycin experiment at stanford heuristic programming project*, Boston, MA, 1976, Addison Wesley.
3. Kintsch W: *About neomycin, methods and tactics in cognitive science*, Mahwah, NJ, 1984, Lawrence Erlbaum.

4. OCLC: *Dewey decimal classification and relative index*, ed. 22, Dublin, OH, 2003, OCLC, See also Comaroni JP: *Dewey decimal classification*, ed. 18, Albany, NY, 2003, Forest Press.

5. Ahamed SV: *Intelligent internet knowledge networks*, Hoboken, NJ, 2007, Wiley Interscience.

6. Aho AV, Lam MS, Sethi R, Ullman JD: *Compilers: principles, techniques, and tools*, ed. 2, Upper Saddle River, NJ, 2006, Prentice Hall.

7. Aikins JS, Kunz JC, Shortliffe EH, Fallat RJ: PUFF: an expert system for interpretation of pulmonary function data, *Comput Biomed Res* vol. 16(3):199–208, 2006. See also Medical Expert Systems Update. In *ADVANCE for Health Information Executives* (website). http://www.advanceforhie.com/accessed April 2013.

8. Kinney EL: Medical expert systems. Who needs them, *CHEST* vol. 91(1):3–4, 2006. doi: 10.1378/chest.91.1.3 See also Stuart NS: *Computer-aided decision analysis*, Westport, CT, 1987, Quorum Books, For decisions in medical diagnostics, see also Krol M, Reich DL: Development of a decision support system to assist anesthesiologists in operating room, *J Med Sys* vol. 24:141–146, 1987.

9. Detmer RC: *Introduction to 80 × 86 assembly level language and computer architecture*, 2001, Jones Bartlett Publishers, See also Rudd WG: *Assembly level programming and the IBM 360 and 370 computers*, Upper Saddle River, NJ, 2001, Prentice Hall.

10. Vacca JR: *Computer and information security handbook*, 2009, Morgan Kaufmann Series in Computer Security. See also Goldburt N: *Design considerations for financial institution intelligent networks*, Ph.D. Dissertation at the Graduate Center of the City University of New York, 2004, for Security in Communication Systems.

11. Smith JF III, Nguyen TH: *Autonomous and cooperative robotic behavior based on fuzzy logic and genetic programming*, The Netherlands, 2007, IOS Press.

12. Knuth DE: *The art of computer programming*, vol. vols 1–3, New York, NY, 1998, Addison Wesley, Professional.

13. Ahamed SV: Architecture for a computer system used for processing knowledge, US Patent Number 5,465,316, November 7, 1995. Aslo see, European Patent # 9437848.5: *Knowledge machine methods and apparatus*, European Patent Number 146248, US/ 05.11.93, Denmark, France, Great Britain, Italy. Issued date December 29, 1994.

14. Haas JM, Robrock RB: The intelligent network of the future. In *IEEE Global Telecommunications Conference*, December 1–4, 1986, pp 1311–1315.

15. Ahamed SV, Lawrence VB: *Intelligent broadband multimedia networks*, Boston, MA, 1998, Kluwer Academic Publishers.

16. Alcatel-Lucent, 2013, Alcatel-Lucent 5ESS® Switch (website). https://support.alcatel-lucent.com/portal/productContent.do?productId=5ESS. See also AT&T: *Telecommunications transmission engineering, vols 1–3*, Indianapolis, IN, 1985, AT&T.

17. Ahamed SV: *Computational framework for knowledge: integrated behavior of machines*, Hoboken, NJ, 2009, John Wiley & Sons.

18. Stone HS: *Introduction to computer architecture, computer science series*, New York, NY, 1980, Science Research Associates.

For high quality versions of the figures in this chapter, please visit the companion website for this book at http://booksite.elsevier.com/9780124166301/

10 Medical Machines

10.1 Introduction

This chapter explores the evolutionary path geared toward medical machines (MMs) and their processors. Such machines deal with medical objects (such as patients, medical staff, drugs, and biological entities) and medical actions (such as treatment, surgeries, therapy, and counseling). Together they blend into very major macroscopic (humanist achievements, accomplishments, procedures, etc.) deeds in medicine or very minor (subsidiary, supporting, inconsequential, etc.) steps or functions in medical practice.

The numerous steps of mechanization of the medical steps by numerous hardware units of machine hardware/firmware and/or of coordinated modules medicalware are streamlined in this chapter. The goal and the outcome are of prime importance. In the partitioning of such (medical) verb function on/by (medical) objects, computer science plays an unparalleled role. There are three such overlapping roles: *first*, the grouping (i.e., lexical analysis: classification of nouns and verbs); *second*, validating (i.e., syntactic analysis: validating the authenticity/legality of the desired verb on the appropriate noun), and *third*, contextual rendering (i.e., semantic analysis: validating the action of the verb on the noun in context to the medical goal that is to be achieved). The overall process is that of compilation a computer program. In this context, the medical compiler processes the request to the MM to accomplish a task or offer a series of steps to complete the task. The machine thus performs only valid task(s) for/by a valid operator(s) upon/for a valid noun object(s). Conversely, it also blocks illegal operation(s) associated with legal/illegal objects (syntactic check; verb → noun and noun ← verb) and prevents legal operations on illegal nouns (syntactic check; wrong verb → noun, verb → wrong noun, and wrong verb → wrong noun). Irrelevant operations to the overall task or out of context actions are flagged (semantic checks).

The science of medicine hinges on the knowledge. Knowledge like any other systematized information, inference, logic, and induction has its own rules for building new strings of knowledge or for concatenating old knowledge into new knowledge strings. The purpose of processing knowledge can be many fold, such as to evolve a series of steps toward a given goal (such as relieve a pain and perform a surgery), find the cause—effect relationship (such as cause and effect relation of a drug and the cause for inter-related ailments), and to find a cure. In

Intelligent Networks: Recent Approaches and Applications in Medical Systems.
DOI: http://dx.doi.org/10.1016/B978-0-12-416630-1.00010-8

handling such a routine, the MM stands to win as a computer can outperform a (an ordinary) human in game of chess or in arithmetic and logical functions.

In this chapter, we propose the seminal steps in interjecting the discipline of computer science onto the science of medicine. Simple machines for simple tasks are addressed first and then the architectures of more complex MMs are proposed. The trajectory is through the domain of knowledge and through the realm of knowledge machines. In developing the origin of MMs from the origin of computers, the MMs become "certain" about what (how many, what sequence, what scientific basis) needs to be done upon/to and from what object(s) before the task is even started by the MM. This scenario is identical to the scenario that a compiler compiles before the execution of a program. In an interpreter-driven machine, the procedure is limited to single statement at a time. Interpreter-driven MMs may be inappropriate except for the simplest medical functions (such as prepare an operating room for surgery and prescribe a pain reliever) and even at that, for a human being to inspect every step each time the machine proposes a step. However, these tiniest steps proposed by the machine may be superior to those selected by humans because of the artificially intelligent (AI) rules (such as pattern recognition of verbs and objects and permissible actions for existing noun objects) embedded in the interpreter.

MMs that can function as sophisticated computers are rare. Even though medical facilities for magnetic resonance imaging (MRI) and for radiology use sophisticated computer systems for graphics and imaging, the availability of general-purpose medical computers is nonexistent. Functional complexity, network connectivity, emergency care, and patient privacy add to the medical information processing at the processor level, network switching and worldwide implementation of the AI techniques add to the features of the MM and its networking.

The design of successful machine-network cluster for the hospital, medical community centers, or even a small nation medical service provisioning facility can be challenging, yet a controlled evolutionary process. Like the space science of 60s has been a careful blend of physics, computer sciences, astronomy, and rocket technology, the medical processing and communication science can be (or has to be) a customized blend of medical knowledge, human discretion with its own unique decision support system, computer science, and communication technologies. Such extraordinary blending of scientific knowledge and human judgment occurs in activities of wise politician, great artists, and excellent musicians and even in some (very well) polished corporate executives.

10.2   Requirements of MMs

MMs have all the functional and the architectural requirements of traditional computers, object, and knowledge machines. The five evolutionary stages of forcing an evolution from traditional computers to medical computers are shown in Figure 10.1–10.5.

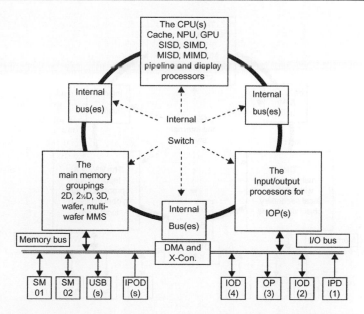

Figure 10.1 Functional components of a simplistic traditional computer, 2D, 2½ D, 3D, etc. Typical memory structures of 1980–1990s. Bus usually refers to the bus structure(s). CPU, central processor unit; DMA, direct memory access; GPU, graphics processor unit; NPU, numerical processor unit; IOD, input/output devices; IOP, input/output processor unit; SISD, SIMD, MIMD, and MIMD typical CPU design configurations. X-Con, cross-connect switches.

10.2.1 The CPU(s)-Based Computers

For most modern computer systems, the five architectural components (CPU, memories, bus structures, I/O subsystems, and switch) are shown in Figure 10.1. Additional processors, devices, and/or memory/device access may be added to enhance the main task of data processing in the computers.

10.2.2 The OPU(s)-Based Object Computers

For the object computers shown in Figure 10.2, a hardware object processor unit (OPU) is added together with CPU(s), I/O processor(s), graphical processors, etc. The OPU handles the objects, their attributes, and the attributes of attributes (if any). The object-oriented command to the OPU forces it to execute an object-oriented instruction in its entirety. Similar command to an array processor forces the APU (not shown) of a computer to perform an entire array or a matrix function. The hardware of the OPU generally needs considerable enhancement. Numerous classifications of the OPUs to handle single or multiple objects are discussed in Section 2.9 and ref. OCLC (2003).

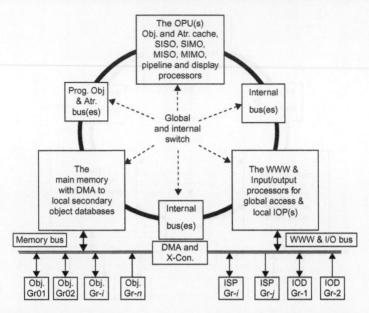

Figure 10.2 Functional components of an Internet-based object computer. DMA, direct memory access; GPU, graphics processor unit; NPU, numerical processor unit; IOD, input/output devices; IOP, input/output processor unit; object bus(es) become quite elaborate; OPU, object processor unit including numerous CPUs, SISO, SIMO, MIMO, and MIMO typical OPU design configurations. X-Con, cross-connect switches. WWW, web connect facilities.

In progressing toward architecture and design of MMs, the platform for enhancement is the object machine with an OPU and the four additional components (the memory, the bus structure, the switch, and input/output devices) of typical computers. In processing objects as computers process data and logical entities, the role of the CPU becomes essential since objects do have numerical and logical attributes. In a sense, numerous CPUs become necessary to handle complex objects. In addition, the bus structure also become more elaborate since the processing of objects involves changes in the attributes of the objects. The registers, their stacks, and the logical operations of the registers call for specialized architecture and interconnectivity.

10.2.3 The KPU(s)-Based Knowledge Machines

For the knowledge computers depicted in Figure 10.3, a hardware knowledge processor unit (KPU) is added together with one or more OPU(s), CPU(s), I/O processor(s), graphical processors, etc. It becomes evident that the architecture of knowledge computer cannot be derived by adding lower-level components. An entirely new systems configuration/organization may become necessary.

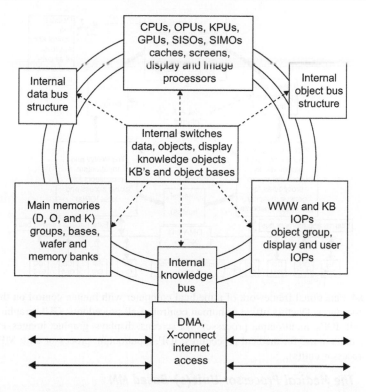

Figure 10.3 Functional components of a knowledge machine with Internet access. D,O, and K, data, object, and knowledge; GPU, graphics processor unit; IOPs, input/output processors, IOD, input/output devices; IOP, input/output processor unit; KB, knowledge bases; KPU, knowledge processor unit(s); OPU, object processor unit including numerous CPUs.

Knowledge processing involves handling and manipulation of knowledge centric objects (KCOs) and the hierarchy of subobjects to which the KCOs are related and connected.

The OPU handles the objects, their attributes, and the attributes of attributes (if any). The object-oriented command to the OPU forces it to execute an object-oriented instruction in its entirety. Similar command to an array processor forces the APU (not shown) of a computer to perform an entire array or a matrix function. The hardware of the OPU generally needs considerable enhancement to serve as an integral part of a knowledge machine.

Internet and external knowledge base (KB) access is provided with I/O systems or high-speed switches that provide a short-quick linkage of the knowledge bus with the system switches. Once again the design and the architecture of the interfaces need considerable enhancement to be able to transfer entire KCOs, the other linked-in objects, the attributes, the attributes of the attributes, depending on the complexity of the knowledge object.

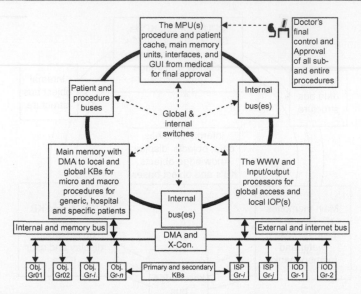

Figure 10.4 Functional framework of a medical computer with human control on the medical procedures. Doctors office or human control of all procedures; GUI, graphics user interface unit; IOPs, input/output processors for screens, displays, graphic, images, etc. IOD, all devices units in use for medical procedures; IOP, input/output processor unit; MPU, medical processor unit(s).

10.2.4   The Medical Processor Unit(s)-Based MM

The conceptual framework of the MM, shown in Figure 10.4, needs one or more human interfaces, to ensure that all the features (error checking, privacy, administrative approvals, scheduling, staff availability, etc.) are addressed and executed.

Examples where such multiple controlled software and application programs are executed in flight simulation and spacecraft landing missions. Synchronized data processing (such as those in call processing and switching systems of electronic switching systems) and multifaceted I/O devices are essential. Generally, the architecture of an intermediate-sized computer facility provides a good blue print for front end systems of MMs.

In Figure 10.4, only the control by the medical staff is shown, but the interfaces for administrative, operations/resources-control staff may also be added with memory overwrite protection and firewalls between the various sectors of a medical center or a hospital facility. The software to accomplish these routine safety and precautionary measures are abundant for computer software developers.

10.2.5   Structure of a Medical Processor Unit(s)-Based MM

In Figure 10.5, the bus structure for an MM is presented. The number of bits for communicating the medical computer elements or bus width may be considerably greater than those in the recent graphics or gaming processors.

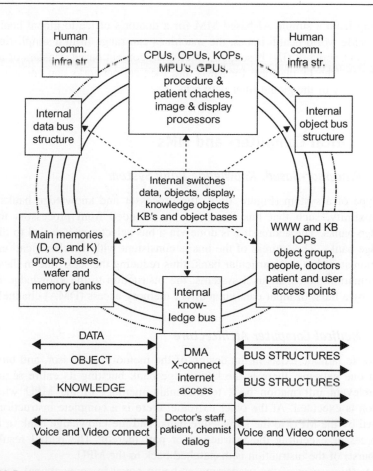

Figure 10.5 Functional components of a medical computer with internal control and communication within the medical community of a hospital of MSP in a community. Such facilities generally exist but their design is not standardized, even though there are numerous applications in almost all health facilities around the world.

Bit channel addressing or separating busses for various functions (graphics, imaging, administrative, etc.) are both feasible options. The details of architecture of components and busses need considerable care to ascertain the quality of the medical service that an MM can provide. An interaction with the medical teams becomes necessary, in case the medical processor unit (MPU) may generate inconsistent output. A conceptual arrangement of the MM with multimedia interaction facility is shown in Figure 10.5 by separating out the human communication bus within the MM.

Debugging of the MPUs and MMs could become more complex than the debugging of the IBM 360/370 CPUs (1960–70s) and defense surveillance machines. Much as customized computer systems are tailored to the application, MMs can assume numerous customized profiles.

Ranging from a simple AI-based MM for a doctor's office to global health systems to tackle world health issues, the machines can range from a simplistic PC to the intelligent network (IN) based, AI, intelligent content based, clusters of analytical machines. The IT platform for MMs and medical networks can encompass the optical capacity of the global fiber networks.

10.3   Medical Computers and MMs

10.3.1   Processor-Based, Knowledge Bank System

In this type of a system (Figure 10.6), the processor and knowledge banks are in close proximity, such that bus lines can be extended from processors to these knowledge banks. The addressing is done via a bus-selector switch tied to different knowledge banks. The address of the bus is consistent with the classification of the information stored in that particular bank, thus reducing the seek time in these massive information stores. In such systems, the instruction to the knowledge bank is followed by a burst of input data via a direct memory access (DMA) channel.

10.3.2   Medical Computer Architecture

Considerable latitude exists in the design of the memory, processor, and bus structures. At one extreme, there is the knowledge bank bursting its entire segment of all the relevant information back to the main memory of the MPU where the instruction is executed. At the other extreme, there is a complete instruction being dispatched by the MPU to the knowledge bank, and the knowledge bank in its own local processor executing the instruction or part thereof. The partial result (in a shorter burst) of the instruction is dispatched back to the MPU.

We see this aspect of the processing as being novel in conventional computing environments where part of the execution of the instruction takes place in the memory. Some of the sophisticated database software packages can perform these functions for the IMS. The compromises in the cost and performance are evident from the two hardware configurations.

Thus, every subprocedure is executed, and the net result of the procedure is conveyed to the user (or the user program). The output is generated from subprocedures, procedures, runs, and the entire usage of the IMS in an orderly and systematic fashion. Debugging of the IMS functions becomes as easy as reading the registers and core dump of the MPU or the registers and the core dump of the local processing units of the knowledge banks.

If the MPU is considered as a single entity, it is logical to isolate the input and the output bus of the medical processor. System dependability is greatly enhanced. Since IMS is generally network based, it would be desirable to separate the input and output ports on all the MPUs in the network to reduce any risk of malfunction concerning the logical processing of inputs and coordination of corresponding outputs.

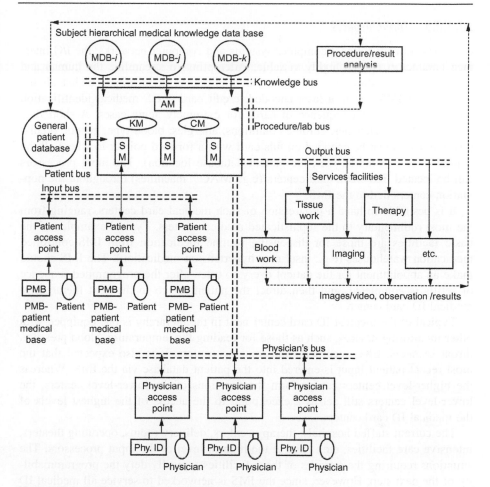

Figure 10.6 Architecture of a hospital-based MPU with six buses. The buses monitor the flow of information in a large medical complex. The contact between the patients and the physicians may be in real time or via the processor unit or remote access. MDB, medical database; AM, administrative module; KM, knowledge module; CM, communications module; SM, switching module.

If the argument for the separation of the input and the output ports is taken further, we can design the I/O architecture of any MPU. Inputs from numerous medical ID card centers will follow the input path to the most logically accessible MPU via the type of medical service request. If certain MPUs can handle specialized services (depending upon the contents of its own knowledge banks), then the logical address of the MPU is determined by the network by mapping the service request for the patient with the service capability the MPU is specially capable of handling. The type of hierarchical addressing reduces the complexity of the lookup tables for the particular MPU and the service provider for any service request for any patient.

10.3.2.1   Input Aspects

Compared to conventional computer systems and computer networks, the I/O interface parameters can be highly variable. Attempting to streamline the human and verbal communication appears futile. For this reason, it is proposed that all the input to the IMS be via a laser-encoded, credit card-sized, medical identification for routine cases or a sequence of cards for extremely acute cases. A short data structure of vital statistics, chronic conditions, allergies, blood type, genetic predisposition, etc., must be encoded on this card with a forward pointer to where all the patient history is stored (i.e., the patient database location). The input processors can be located like credit card centers (e.g., MAC® machines) throughout the population centers tied to the IMS.

It is desirable to have a progression of such medical card centers, ranging from the most rudimentary to the sophisticated medical centers. Typical examples of the basic facilities are those for dispensing routine medication from IMS-controlled medication warehouses (e.g., insulin or hypertension medication). The IMS should make an appointment for the patient every so often after the programmed sequence of refills is completed, and then direct the patient to go to the next hierarchical medical ID card center.

Typical of the medical ID card center next in the hierarchy is one equipped with other monitoring devices, such as those for reading the temperature, blood pressure, throat scanners, EKG recorders, and imaging centers. It is also expected that the most recent patient input is entered into the patient database via the IMS. Whereas the higher-level centers can perform the functions of the lower-level centers, the lower-level centers still act as a checkpoint to the access of the highest levels of the medical ID card centers.

The current staffed hospitals, therapy centers, delivery rooms, operating theaters, intensive care facilities, etc., exist at the highest level of the input processors. The situations requiring the services of these facilities typically defy the programmability of the next step. However, since the IMS is networked to service all medical ID card centers, access and referral throughout card centers on the network is automatic.

10.3.2.2   Output Aspects

The output from the IMS can also have significant variations. Ranging from no action to immediate hospitalization or surgery, the IMS reaches all medical service facilities, such as drug dispensing machines, physical therapy centers, blood banks, nursing homes, and the higher levels of the medical card centers discussed earlier.

One of the possible ways of handling the outputs of the IMS is via specialized nodes created on the network. Similar to the knowledge processing where nodes are addressed by the subject matter they hold, the output nodes are addressed by the type of service that is scheduled through them. For example, if the architecture is equipped via a node for physical therapy, all requests for this service would go through this node. The geographical dispersion of the patient and service centers is managed by mapping the zip codes of the patient and of the service provider. One example where such service is already provided is by matching the real estate agent with clients moving into a new area.

Patient databases, physician access points, patient access points, and service facilities are connected to the medical data banks and medical processor via several buses. In an alternative integrated medical computer system, numerous processors are included with their own memories and modules and are linked together to establish a processor net unit. Such systems are amenable to hospital campus settings, where several buildings comprise the hospital or where several hospitals are interlinked over local area networks (LANs).

The medical computer architecture must focus on specific experience and knowledge. Typical data processing functions are not involved. This section discusses the MPU, instruction sets, and speed and capacity.

10.3.2.3   Processor Speed, Confidence Level, and Patient Load

One of the more time-consuming tasks of the processor is the search through numerous KBs to achieve a high confidence level in the inference it draws about the next logical step or the next inferential step. One can defeat the IMS by insisting upon a 100% confidence level with insufficient input data and with exhaustive KBs, or conversely, with sufficient input data and with inadequate KBs. To be realistic about the results that the medical systems can generate, a compromise in what is being queried is essential. Being a programmed system, it can provide only inferential results with varying degrees of confidence. Exhaustive searches take a longer response time, as do the peak-hour, high-patient load queries. Here, the processor speed provides a compromise. Expensive high-speed systems can yield high-confidence inferences at the busiest hospital hours and vice versa. Smaller medical facilities will thus need a lower-power processor. Job scheduling algorithms in the operating system (as they are used in traditional computer systems) will prove useful in generating an acceptable response time from the more sophisticated medical systems.

Other tasks, such as patient scheduling, shared resource allocation, sequence of subprocedures, and minimum hospital stay requirements, are relatively trivial for the sophisticated medical systems. At this seminal stage, we do not foresee these secondary functions as causing significant reduction in the throughput.

In the network-based medical systems, the results of the procedure are conveyed to the user (or the user program) by a series of packet transactions. Such transactions between a single hospital-based medical system and the multiple knowledge banks are systematically processed, and the output is accumulated from subprocedures, procedures, and runs. The entire usage of the network-based system is as orderly and systematic as job processing in distributed computer environments. Debugging of this type of function becomes easy by studying the packet contents of any given procedure.

10.4   Knowledge-Based Medical Facilities

The specialization of the MPUs, coupled with that of the service providers, thus provides the logical addressing of these nodes in the IMS. It is expected that if the IMS architecture is designed based upon the separation of specialty, and the separation of the input and output ports of the individual MPUs, then the flow of information can be significantly streamlined, thus reducing the probability of any possible errors in processing the medical information for any particular patient.

Medical computers constitute a special breed of cluster computers. Both have identifiable supersets of traditional computers for the routine functions. While it is viable to force a cluster computer to act as full-fledged medical computer, it is desirable to build medical computers on a distinctive track of its own medical operation codes (*mopcs*). The demand for such medical computers is likely to expand and grow like the specialized air-borne computers for the aviation industry.

Figure 10.7 depicts the four basic modules of the KPS and one of the ways of interconnecting the components. In this arrangement, the switching module (SM) is located between the communication module (CM) and the KBs. If the various KBs

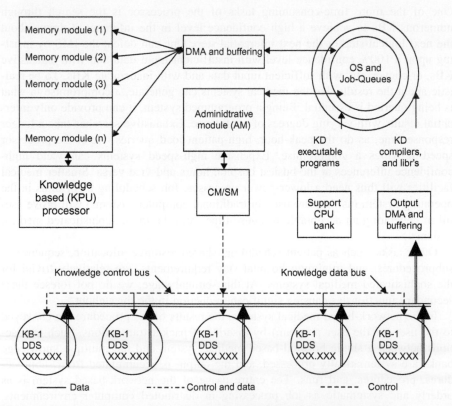

Figure 10.7 Architecture of a local hospital-based MKPS with a single processor. CM, communication module; SM, switching module; KB, knowledge base.

are arranged in some well-defined hierarchical format (such as the Dewey Decimal System (DDS) (OCLC, 2003) or the Library of Congress classification [9.1]), then a network configuration (star, bus, ring, dropped bus, etc.) can be used to retain the access methodology in and out of vast databases. Under these conditions, one BISDN (broadband integrated services digital network; United States Government, Library of Congress Classification) links or one access point may be provided between the SM and the KBs.

With its resident operating system, the administrative module (AM) dynamically allocates resources, monitors performance, and prevents deadlocks. The operating and accounting functions of the KPS are confined to the AM. The engineering and maintenance functions are also performed by the AM, such as updating of the KBs, altering the structure and hierarchy of the stored information in the KBs, and modifying the compiling and interpreting processes of the CM for its many tasks. The knowledge rings (KRs) depicted in Figure 10.8 are organized according to the disciplines based on the DDS or the Library of Congress (LoC) classification.[1]

The AM is also responsible for the execution of each subprocess in the problem solution or query handling by the KPS. In a sense, it becomes the hardware host for the KPS "operating system." We foresee that the AM is a parallel processor system, assuming that the KPS is going to be shared between a large numbers of user tasks. Since any processor (in the AM) can access any information in the KB, the SM will switch between the processors of the AM and the read/write capability of the KBs. The quantity of information and its directionality may now be identified. In the great majority of cases, the KBs share large chunks of information with the memory modules of the AM.

After performing the knowledge functions (e.g., pattern recognition, matching, forward/backward pointing, and inference drawing), the contents of the memory may be discarded. Whereas the interrogation may be only one instruction long, the returned information can be a large block. Thus, the modality of communication between the AM and the KBs can be made asymmetrical, and for this reason serial query ports and DMA for burst back are a feasible implementation. The SMs may also be segregated for the low/high rates of data/knowledge communication.

10.5 Communication of Medical Information

In traditional electronic switching systems, the SM is located between the nodes from one geographical area to the next. In the medical knowledge-processing systems (MKPS), the SM accesses the various processors (and memory modules) in the AM and the extensive fragments of knowledge in the KBs. In essence, the SM

---

[1] To be consistent with the memory addresses in 2½D, 3D, and multiple wafer memories, the numbering of the "knowledge rings" can also be binary. The need for external address translation is eliminated and the linkers/loaders can generate the executable code for any given machine. To some extent the scalability of the knowledge bases may be sacrificed because of the limited binary addresses available. This is truly a matter of detailed design of the entire knowledge processing system.

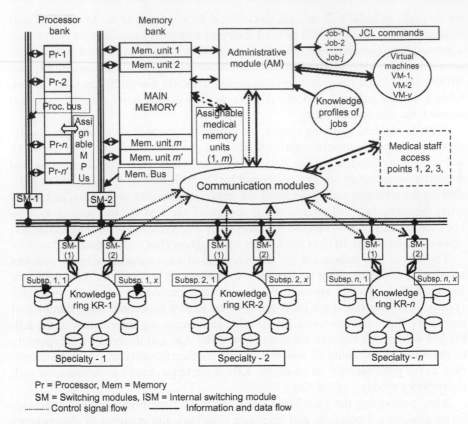

Figure 10.8 Typical architecture of a local MKPS with multiple processors, independent communication module, and switching modules. The "medical knowledge rings," i.e., KRs are partitioned by the subject matter and or the specialty of the services provided; however, any numbering or addressing system is appropriate. SM, switching module; MKPS, medical knowledge processing systems or machines. Secondary cache memories (not shown) can also be used to "fetch" object groups from the KBs during processing.

in MKPS is identified by the specialty of the contents. When these areas of specialty are identified, the packet switching paths are routed via the physical address decoding done by packet switching facilities of backbone networks.

The addressing in the MKPS is done by the classification of knowledge and its hierarchy. Typically, the addressing is done via the area codes and exchange numbers or the Internet Protocol (IP) addresses in the Internet environment. The address translation and seek time are dramatically reduced by the addressing of the subject material, on which the knowledge function is being performed by its decimal code. The same code thus provides the exact address of that specific piece of knowledge in the medical knowledge bases (MKBs).

The bus capacity and memory allocation algorithms affect the performance. Since the amount of information necessary to perform knowledge functions can be vastly different depending on the topic and the type of operation, fixed memory allocation algorithms are soon likely to become constrictive. However, if the operating system has sufficient flexibility (such as dynamic memory allocation), the active memory size is made sufficient to handle complex KPS functions (such as, pattern recognition, cross-compare, find analogies, find supplementary knowledge, and scan other sciences). Then the SM provides access between all the AM processors and the file segments in the KBs in real time, and an architecture for intelligent knowledge processing may be generated.

The difficulties that we foresee in this methodology occur when all the users need or access the same information, for example, a class of students handling the solution to a given problem during the laboratory hour. Queue management techniques still lead to long response times. Another instance of such a situation arises if all the users are using memory-intensive subprocesses at the same time. Even though we have listed such functions as "bottlenecks," they are also encountered in all computer systems. Smart network operating systems handle contingencies of this nature by allocating more resources when bottlenecks start to appear or by dynamically circumventing the congested node(s).

10.6   Network Configurations Based on INs

In this section, we propose two architectural arrangements to build localized and independent intelligent medical networks. These networks constantly monitor the specific needs of the patients and resources of the locality with the involvement of medical service providers (MSPs). The MSPs would serve the medical and informational needs of their client patients. A large number of these MSPs would serve a community or a region. Each MSP i will retain a portfolio of each of the client patient j and perform a daily check on the changes of status in the local or global information or service as it pertains to the medical history of the particular client patient and makes the patient aware of any detail as it may affect the course of action. If the patient goes through the MSP, then the incremental change is updated in the patient database. In addition, the system performs the routine medical functions as a hospital staff would perform but retains the information over the life of the individual in and out of every ailment and its treatment. The details of the databases and their distribution or their aggregation are presented in the two architectural arrangements.

Large groups of independent hospital networks may be integrated (and programmed) to coexist independently within one larger wide area, medical network as independent INs sharing the network infrastructure. The functionality can also be forced to perform as a group of localized medical network (Krol, 1996) for the particular hospital rather than one massive medical network for a region or a country. The role of the numerous MSP will thus be confined to the local area services and information access rather than that of a few global MSPs. The main advantage of having a large number of smaller and localized MSP is that the cost and complexity of a localized MSP are much lower than a large MSP. The new competition at the localized MSP services thus available will reduce the medical expenses and the overall customer costs. Local MSPs and businesses can offer the medical information and services such as discounted prescription drugs, hospital and nursing services, and physical therapy. Such an increase in the supply side of medical information will facilitate the medical field to become more competitive and bring down the medical costs in the end.

10.6.1   Feasible Network Configurations

Although some of these services can be accessed by the smart Internet users, such services have not been tailored to the medical profession. The specialized services that the physicians and hospitals provide and the associated patient costs are still not available to most patients. Over the next decade or so, it is envisioned that the specific medical information may be supplied by medical KBs rather than by doctors and their staff who have an embedded profit motive. In a sense, the initial information gathering and the search for appropriate low-level medical treatment are facilitated by MSPs, medical KBs, and intelligent medical knowledge processing that tailors the medical services and the hospital facilities to the patients. The current approach is to place the patient at the lowest level of service provisioning rather than placing the patient as the paying customer. In a majority of the cases, the patients are forced to accept the medical services and the hospital facilities at an unknown quality of service and an unclear billing system. It is also foreseen that the specific information for an individual patient can be retrieved by smart medical databases based on the patient-specific conditions.

10.6.2   Merits of Traditional IN and MSP-Based IN

In the enhancement of the basic IN architecture of the 1980s to suit the TINA architectures (CCITT Recommendations M.3010), the network designers have brought a sense of interoperability within the framework of all the INs within the globe. Whereas it is commendable and desirable to have this ideology already build in every network, there at least four penalties. The standards need a long time to evolve, the standard interfaces and software modules to perform the functional components (service specific feature of the TINA Network) or functional components (FCs) may not be readily available, and more importantly, the backbone network should be ready to host and execute the network programming language for each of FC's for each of the medical subscribers. A possible configuration of the hospital-based integrated medical computer systems for processing medical and patient information using specialized functional modules (FC) is presented in ref. Ahamed (1998). However, the setbacks in the full implementation of such a network environment cause a delay in bringing the intelligent medical Internet services to the patients and users.

At the same time, the market place is dynamic and volatile. The business drivers are anxious to get the network services now and take a risk if the price is small enough. In a sense, the proposed network architecture shifts the responsibility back to the MSP to use their own customized package that will accomplish their specific goals. These goals are specific for the MSP and the community of the patients and users whom the MSP is willing to serve. Such goals can offer a menu, as the Internet does, but from their own database and via the telephone all fixed and wireless network. Thus, the blend of services is discretionary, the waiting time is short, and the patient and user control on the content is made local and immediate. This is a stark contrast to the philosophy of other IN service providers and owners who wish to offer generic and universal services to all customers.

From the architectures of the advanced INs (AIN) discussed in ref. Ahamed and Lawrence (1998), the adjunct service provider (ASP) and the IP-based switching systems provide similar capabilities for their telecommunications clients. However, the programs within the ASP and IP are mentored, monitored, and maintained by the network owners. In the MSP-based Internet, it is proposed that the user/patient-specific functions be programmed and fine tuned on the local computers owned by the MSP subscribers who will offer a blend legitimate medical functions (such as dispensing of drugs, physiotherapy, nursing care, paramedical services, and radiation therapy) with authorization from the community of medical professionals and hospitals. Whereas it may take a long time for all the telecommunication-based AIN standards to be written and standardized, debugged, and made available to the clients, the MSP-based network environment provides the patients and users what any current network technologies have to offer now. These network and medical functions are blended harmoniously under the supervision of the MSP within the framework of the risk that the MSP is willing to take with the local community of patients and users.

10.6.3   The Proposed MSP Network Configuration

The proposed MSP-based architecture would permit the doctors and hospitals to have an open information policy brought about by competition on the supply side. It also facilitates a trend for numerous specialized MSPs to participate in the regional, national, or global medical economy. This step is akin to the distribution of localized medical information (from the supply perspective) from local medical data banks rather than sharing very large data banks via global or Internet access. In the ensuing knowledge society, these MSPs will be akin to local banks functioning in cooperation with the Regional banks, National banks, and the Federal Reserve System. Many such MSPs can serve a large number of patients who do not need the very high speed nor the high intricacy that the high technology global Internet is capable of providing excellent services to *all* its users. Smaller databases, localized customers, and larger local area traffic will permit the smaller MSPs to customize and target their services to a specific clientele and the user community.

Under program control, the localized medical knowledge networks (MKNs) that interconnect the MSPs may also be forced to work interdependently, exchanging the current information as it becomes available to perform a variety of functions hitherto possible only by human beings. The individual patient and user databases are based on the patient (SS) numbers and assigned logical address within the host network. Each logical MKN functions as personal intelligent networks (PINs) developed in ref. Miller et al. (1982). It is dedicated to that particular patient only for the illness or for the life. These MKNs provide all the MIN (medical IN) and PCN (personal communication network) services and operate under a patient-driven programmable code. The patient has the privilege and freedom to "instruct" the host network to perform all the legitimate and ethically acceptable backbone medical and communication network functions. These functions may be as simple as the banking services (such as account balance, online payments, and credit card activity) currently offered by the local banks or as complex as the services that TINA network is capable of performing a set of highly sophisticated hierarchical and cascaded intelligent telecommunication functions.

Figure 10.9 depicts one of the possible regional medical network architectures that permits the regulation, the authentication, and monitoring the medical services by a government or a nonprofit entity. The network management system, Medical Services Management System (MSMS), monitors and tracks the activity to prevent abuse of the medical services in a region, a state, or a nation. Many other possible uses of such a network infrastructure (such as childcare, nursing home, and emergency care) are also possible.

10.6.4   Relative Merits of MSP-Based Network Compared to the Internet

In designing web-based programs, the range and extent of network services become apparent. In a sense, the IN functions of the circuit switch networks can be duplicated by the HTML programs for the Internet. Whereas these services are mostly information based, applications-specific client services are usually confined to be stereotyped and minimal. Most of the application programs are based in distant servers and are communicated via the Internet by packet switches. This can cause substantial delays between screens and during the downloading the programs and data. In addition, when the network programs are uploaded, they reside in the local or a distant server and program execution occurs based on the capabilities of the server. As the volume of data to be exchanged becomes large, the response time also starts to increase to the extent that any multimedia traffic becomes too distant awaiting the broadband networks to be implemented. Typically, the bottleneck is in the local fixed line or the wireless loop. This can be enhanced by the integrated services digital network (ISDN) line or the ADSL capability now available in some metropolitan areas.

On the other hand, using local high-capacity servers and a local high-speed LAN may alleviate the problem. For large-scale users, this methodology uses the TCP/IP protocol, high-speed LANs (typically campus networks, educational or medical networks, etc.), and much localized high-capacity servers to serve their

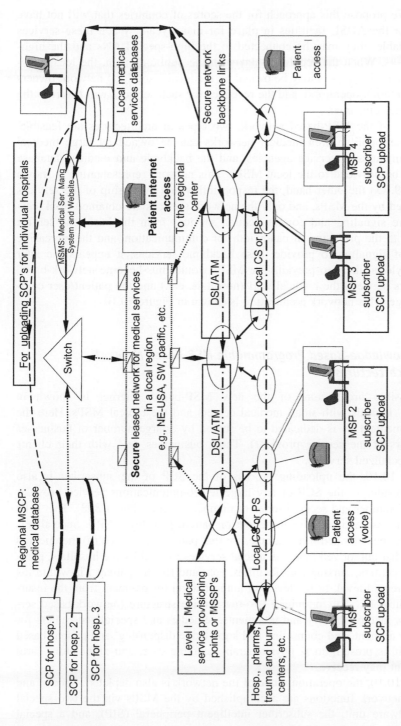

Figure 10.9 Representation of numerous medical networks being hosted in one larger medical WAN. Each Micro Medical Net is uploaded by the individual MSP subscriber who can program the network to function as an IN/1, IN/1 +, IN/2 or any version of the advanced version of an IN or the AIN. MSP subscribers may also interject their own customized programs to be executed during the operation to provide specialized services to suit the client needs.

customers. We propose this approach for the scores of countries that will not have their ISDN or the ADSL facilities in place for many years. When these services become available, they may be connected to the high-speed LANs and the high-capacity servers. When the problem is taken in the public domain, the local high-speed LANs and the servers may be owned by the local-fixed loop network owners (rather than Internet operators), and the revenues for such services will revert to the local telephone companies.

In the case of the MSP-based network, two types of architectures are feasible. The larger metropolitan area medical networks can be owned by large medical insurance companies or service agencies, and the backbone and medical database services will be provided to the local MSPs. This network representation is shown in Figure 10.9. On the other hand, the responsibility and ownership of the services can be retained by the MSPs, and only the network services are obtained from leasing the secure signaling and communication services from the backbone service providers. With the profusion of bandwidth for communication, and the increasing complexity of signaling to provide these backbone services, it appears the later ownership style is likely to prevail. The MSPs would thus become network-based intermediators between the medical staff (hospitals, etc.) and the patient/user community at large. This network architecture is shown in Figure 10.10.

10.6.5 Knowledge-Based Programmable MSP-Based Network Architectures

Another possible architecture of the new MSP-based Internet is shown in Figure 10.10. It deals with small medical centers and the typical MSPs. Here the SCP of this medical IN is dedicated to be shared by a large number of businesses (the customers of the service provider). These businesses deal with their clients who need specialized services.

In Figure 10.10, the uploading process of the SCP of the subscriber is also depicted. It resides in the SCP of any large telecommunications service provider (under a new number and *s*ecured series of numbers such as 899 or 898). This is an integrated database activated for the client or patient j of any MSP i. Special services may thus be activated, for example, for that patient j provided (a) the client is within his or her authorized range of special services offered by the hospitals, pharmacies, burn centers, nursing care facilities, etc., and (b) the patient j is within his or her own prepaid level, or the levels of authorization for payment from the insurance companies, etc. This permits a two-tier service structure (network-based services, such as medical history and treatments, remedies and specialized centers for the particular ailment, and counseling and knowledge dispensing, and patient-based services, such as prescriptions, physiotherapy, nursing care, and ambulatory care) that the patient may receive.

In Figure 10.10, the operation mode of the network is also depicted. Special and permissible network functions are accomplished by the MSPs via the two special units: a hardware unit, the subscriber intelligent peripheral (SIP), and a special

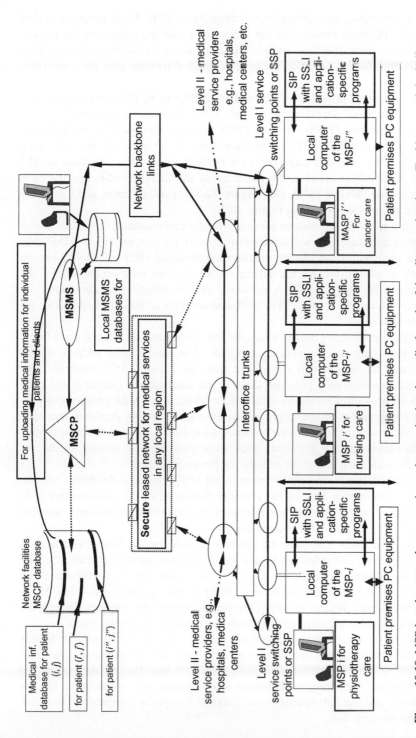

Figure 10.10 MSP-based system always remains active monitoring the medical needs of the clients and patients. To this extent, it is similar to hospital environment. SIP and SSLI are two special software packages supplied by the MSP for their clients and patients.

software unit, the subscriber service logic interpreter (SSLI). These units are scaled down (into the PC size) versions of the IP and SLI that are present in the typical service switching point (SSP) of an IN. These units are necessary for the modern IN (typically the IN/2) to provide the special MSP functions akin the subscriber services.

These two functions provided by SIP and SSLI (Figure 10.10) also can be traced back to the functional architecture of the TINA network documented in ref. Ahamed and Lawrence (1998). In this TINA network proposed by International Telecommunications Union (ITU), the functions of IP and of the SDP (see Figure 12-3b in ref. Ahamed and Lawrence (1998)) parallel the functions of SLI shown in Figure 10.10. Likewise, the functions of the CCF, the SSF, and the SCF at the service node (SN) of TINA (see Figure 12-3b in ref. Ahamed and Lawrence (1998)) parallel the SSLI shown in Figure 10.10.

Largely, if a telecommunications service provider can condense the SN of TINA to a PC-based hardware and software environments for the individual MSP subscriber, then the specialized service creation environment (SCE of TINA) can be handed back to the MSPs. All the advanced IN features now acclaimed by the next-generation INs, like the TINA network, can be offered in rudimentary IN environment with the basic SCP, STP, SSP, and an SMS as the building blocks for the MSP-based network.

When any patient/client j makes a call for the specialized services to the MSP i, it activates the client-specific service program. The track sector address of the executable code for the client is dispatched from the network SCP database. This facilitates that an executable program code in the databases of patient client j, be executed in view of most recent medical information, at the MSP premises to provide the best service for patient client j. The enhanced network database furnishes a program address in the subscriber database and redirects the call to the appropriate secondary-level service provider, such as a pharmacy, a nursing center, or counseling for additional treatment or help for the patient/client.

In Figure 10.10, the ownership of the regional MSCP medical databases and the MSMS can be negotiated. One of the possible variations of the architectures is to permit Internet access to the databases to keep the hospitals and patients updated about the specific changes in these databases.

The blending of MSP and network services is done by the MSCP and MSMS programs customized and uploaded by the MSPs for their patients and clients. The segment of the KB that is tagged as (i, j) is invoked and serves exactly according to the contents of the KB uploaded by the MSP i for the client/patient j. The MSP-based network is thus capable of taking the patient request for services through the Internet access or service authorizations from the medical staff or hospitals.

In Figure 10.10, the local subscriber database for the SCP is depicted. In this configuration, the subscriber retains his or her own specific database. The SCP now contains all the information to handle customer specific and the authorized network functions. The program database also contains the information for the SSLI functions, and the SIP functions are handled by special hardware to network signaling and network data.

The architectures presented in this chapter offer a series of added benefits to the medical community. First, by incorporating the role of the MSPs between the hospitals, medical/diagnostic centers, and the client/patients, the client/patients are provided with *all* the information and details of the medical condition germane to that particular client/patient. The human interface is practically eliminated unless it is called for by the patient/client. At the supply side, the MSP has all the most recent medical information available to them. Their databases include all the codes and coverage and the list of options for treatments. Second, when the client/patient is ready for treatment/hospitalization, the MSPs act as mediators between the secondary-level MSPs (Figure 10.10) and their clients/patients. Third, the MSP services provided are based on the procedures of electronic transactions on networks. For this reason, the service and turnaround are quick; they are also efficient and cheap thus facilitating the reduced cost for operating the health industry. Fourth, very large medical network KBs owned by the hospitals and universities can now be fragmented as the thousands of small server environments (in any localized area) necessary for smaller specialized MSP in the local area. Fifth, numerous sophisticated medical IN services can be readily offered by executing special SIP and SSLI programs within the MSP premises computers (Figure 10.10). Sixth, prepaid and authorized medical services can be dispensed immediately. Each of the MSPs can tailor and tune the medical service provided and include a personal touch to the attention of the client/patients.

The MSP-based network environment effectively taps into the Internet and the wireless telephone networks. Both these networks are growing at an enormous rate with an increasing coverage and popularity. The proposed medical networks bring the impact of the new digital technology, knowledge society, and network revolution to the medical community. The MSP-based network quickly and profoundly closes the gap between the medical community and the high mobile clients and patients within a growing segment of the social population.

10.7   Alternate Architectures

10.7.1   Human Factors

At the high-end MKPS, there is ample flexibility. Human participation in the processing can be adjusted to suit the expectations of the medical community. On the one hand, we have a situation of all-human and no-machine system going back to the 1800s, and on the other hand, we have a system of all-machine and no-human medical system where Spock replaces the Jim on a spacecraft. The robot in Spock is replaced by a humanist MM. In the social setting of the twenty-first century, the MKPS driven and controlled by medical experts appear to be a likely compromise.

This type of a system is depicted in Figure 10.11, where the human expertise starts to augment the machine-generated solutions more and more at the higher levels (see Levels 6 and 7 in Figure 10.11). Conversely, the machine performs the ISP and MSP functions much like the switching systems in communications

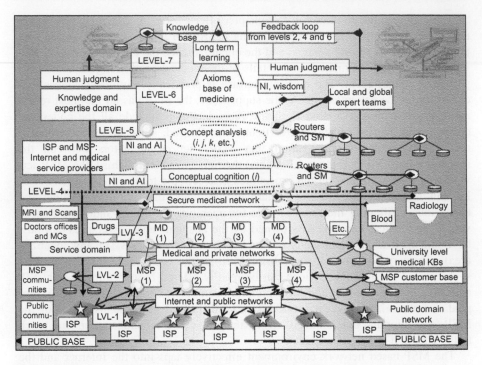

Figure 10.11 Seven-level intelligent medical environment. This arrangement provides the public medical needs via the WWW entry (Level 7) into the hospitals. The routine physician—patient transactions are handled at the lower three levels (5—7). The facilities at the higher levels (1—4) provide venues for the physicians and hospital staff to consult with local medical communities and interact with subject matter specialists around the globe. Limited access to the public provides patients to check the medications, procedures, and expert opinions. Network security is essential.

technology (see Levels 1 and 2 in Figure 10.11). The system is adaptive and self-correcting because of the natural intelligence (NI) and expertise of the medical professionals at the intermediate level.

10.7.2 Computation and Communication Factors

The balance between the extent of computer storage, processing, and the KBs storage is negotiable in MKPS shown in Figure 10.5 from computers and communications perspective. A slightly more sophisticated embodiment of the system, shown in Figure 10.5, is also shown in Figure 10.11. The admixture of public and private networks at the Levels 1 and 2 is selected to be optimal from a current technological perspective in the developed countries. Conversely, when the MSP network is not evolved, the Internet and public networks can be designed to function well at both Levels 1 and 2.

At the higher Levels 6 and 7, the nature and style of the medical environment play a dominant role in the blending of AI programmed in the machines and of the NI and expertise that constitute the axioms of medical wisdom resident in that particular medical community. Both extremes are feasible though not desirable. All wisdom and no machines become as undesirable as all machines and no wisdom. In a sense, the constitution of the medical boards of health and medicine is an indication of the evolution of the MMs in any community or of a migration (or lack of it) in a hospital complex.

All storage and no processing lead to massive transfers of data from the KBs to the memory modules of the AM whose processor performs all the knowledge-oriented functions. Because this capacity is evidently enough, no storage in KBs eliminates the need for them and SMs. However, as a compromise, with some processing in the KBs, rudimentary knowledge functions may be attempted and only relevant information may be forwarded to the AM, thus reducing the channel access time and wait time. The INs have solved this problem partially by having some processing in the SCP. The problems of achieving such a balance are far more delicate in the MKPS, and detailed study is desirable.

The resolution and accuracy of the knowledge profile is also a subject of optimal design of the MKPS. On the one hand, with perfect granularity in the knowledge profile, the compile time of the problem is longer, but users get the exact response from the KBs. On the other hand, incomplete or imperfect representation of the KBs in the profile will prevent legitimate use of the MKBs or cause execution time errors from the MKBs. However, we view these issues as secondary but relevant to the design consideration of the particular MKPS.

Most hospitals and medical centers have private networks. Intelligent knowledge processing and research capabilities are generally not automatically provided except in research and teaching institutions. Rudimentary searches based on string matching are feasible by the extended capabilities of the operating systems. Customized requirements from hospital and community-based networks need the network operating system compatibility with the special purpose software for special purposes.

10.8   Medical Applications of Supercomputers

Specific computers are feasible for specific tasks if the initial development costs, VLSI die costs, and production costs can be justified or fall under the development of other products. However, from a business and investment perspective, these costs need to be recovered in a short enough duration before the competitive firms begin to start to claim the market share. From a historical perspective, the chip manufacturers have been predicting the demand and their market share accurately enough to be profitable. The success of the earlier chips for PCs, and then the more sophisticated Pentium chips for laptops, the duo series for scientific and business applications are good examples of the strategy to mass produces of low-cost, more-flexible chips rather than high-priced, very-specialized chips. Further, the low-priced chips can be used in parallel operation (e.g., array processors, SIMD and MIMD machines, duos, quads, etc., for the potent laptops and desktop machines) or configuration (e.g., massive VLSI memories).

Specially designed VLSI chips for medical applications are limited by their demand. The chip manufactures have not commercialized medical chips to be inexpensive and to be profitable. Being specific to the medical applications, the demand is limited. On the other hand, the vendors of medical equipment generally assemble chips from other applications to accomplish specified medical functions. Supercomputers become partially attractive because these machines are oriented toward numerical and scientific computing and related applications. The capacity is measured by their petaFLOPs (floating-point operations per second) rather than their peta-MOPS (medical operations per second) capability.

Image processing, pattern recognition, and expert systems (ES) applications are common in the computing for medical and scientific applications. For this reason, application in MRI and cancer detection are most amenable to the use of supercomputers. Computer graphics is extremely common in almost all medical systems from retina scans to neural conduction, microsurgery to transplants.

10.8.1 Medical Supercomputers

In extrapolating this strategy for supercomputers, it can be taken to extremes. In reality, as many as trillion plus (1.6 trillion) lesser-expensive chips arranged in pipeline/parallel operation or configuration for supercomputers has been proposed. This appears as the logical business choice. IBM's new supercomputer (Sequoia of the 2011−2012 of period) uses as many as 1.6 trillion processors and 1.6 petabytes of memory. It deploys IBM's Blue Gene technology (reaching a speed of 500 teraflops, i.e., 500 trillion flops) and offers an estimated 20 petaflops (i.e., 20,000 trillion flops) of computing power. The power efficiency is also high offering 3050 calculations per every watt of power. The infrastructure deploys advanced fiber optic switching for internodal data transfers. Examples of the deployment of such supercomputers are for astronomy, human genome, and energy research. Being built at the DoE's Lawrence Livermore Laboratory, Sequoia is expected to be operational in 2012. It uses variations of the Linux operating system.

The top level of these supercomputers is usually built with a cluster of MIMD multiprocessors. Each processor of the MIMD is SIMD based. Each multiprocessor controls series of multiple coprocessors, thus achieving the extremely high flops. Six orders of computing power become feasible by this three-level hierarchical design of the supercomputers. These supercomputers can vary radically with respect to the number of multiprocessors per cluster, the number of processors per multiprocessor, the number of simultaneous instructions per SIMD processor, and the type and number of coprocessors. Based on the specialized (yet simple) MIMD and SISD configurations, the supercomputer speeds can reach the many tens of petaflops processing power. These clusters are interconnected by high-speed very well-connected data highways within the supercomputer. Each cluster generally runs under its own operating system. The core clusters share the tasks in a balanced fashion thus giving rise to symmetric multiprocessing environment. They share the memory with non-uniform memory access and each of the cores may be from one to many thousands of multicore processors. The coprocessors can themselves be the new breed of general-purpose graphics processor units that are very powerful in their own right with their customized FPUs, ALUs, and integer processors and coprocessors. The computing power is thus pushed from a few million flops (10^6) to several tens of petaflops (10^{15}). Interconnection, bus switching, operating systems, and multithreading of task are the toughest but not insurmountable issues in the design of the modern supercomputers. Currently, social sciences and medical problem solving are not on the list of the application of either of the two supercomputers, and Sequoia being built by IBM.

The use of supercomputers in medical applications is limited, partly because the VLSI and software designers have not visualized the medical application as being profitable to them. This scenario was prevalent in the automobile industry about two or three decades back, but over time, almost all aspects of automobile industry are computer, communications, and graphics oriented. The dependability, precision, and the speed that sophisticated digital systems can bring into the medical field are yet to be harnessed.

Full-fledged medical computer systems need architectural, firmware, and software enhancements. In this chapter, we have eluded to the changes that will be desirable and necessary. The design of the MPU can also become radically different from the design of ultra large-scale integrated circuits.

10.8.2 Design of a Medical Computer

Figure 10.12 depicts an initial design of medical computer. Human intervention in the computational aspects is minimized in this configuration to permit the machine to deploy its AI programs exhaustively before offering its analysis and conclusions to any medical problem. Such problems are loaded by the users as ill-defined or partially defined problems.

The compilers, loaders, and linkers systematically breakdown the problem posed by the users into segments of what is known, what is uncertain, and what is unknown by the analysis of the medical noun objects (MNOs), medical verb functions (MVFs), and their convolution ($\circledast$). The primary entities (i.e., the dominant MNOs), their crucial functions (i.e., the principal transactions or interactions MVFs), and the resulting effects of these crucial actions (i.e., the dominant convolutions $\circledast$s) are classified and compiled at the initial stages of medical computation. The segments of problem that are identifiable and documented in the KBs around the world (see the left and right links to Internet KBs in Figure 10.11) are assigned high confidence in the

$$(MPF \circledast MNO)\text{s} \quad \text{or} \quad (mpf_i \circledast_j mno_k)\text{s}$$

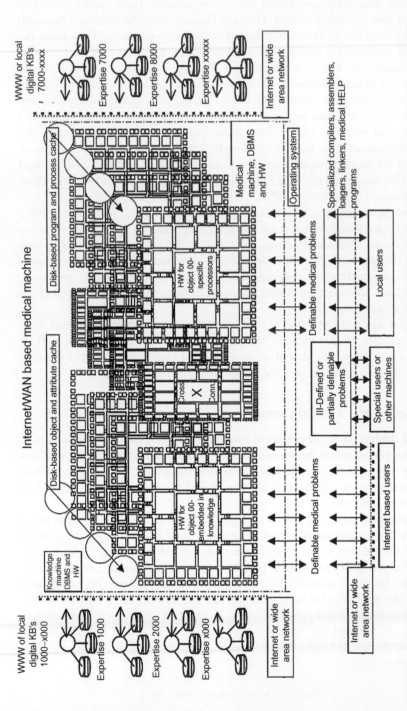

Figure 10.12 Architecture of a MM and MKPS/machine with multiple wafer level MPUs and KPUs. Modern CPUs and IOPs of *circa* 2010 can handle the intricate functions expected from the MM and provide connectivity to the WWW medical knowledge bases, backbone networks, and WANs.

segment(s) of the final solution. Conversely, the remaining MNOs, MVFs, and $\otimes$ s are assigned lower confidence levels. Their functions, i.e.,

$$(MPF \circledast MNO)s \quad \text{or} \quad (mpf_i \ \circledast_j \ mno_k)s,$$

become less confident, suspicious, or error prone. This forces the AI segments of the machine to research the nature of (MPF, $\otimes$, MNOs or mpf_i, $\otimes_j$, mno_k) more extensively and offer a solution and a confidence limit associated with these unknown medical parameters. The machine is thus forced into offering an uncertain result. Such scenarios are common on medical ES problems such as Internist-I (Miller et al., 1982) or NeoMycin (Shortcliffe, 1976).

10.9 Other Medical Systems

Specialty centers for ailments and medical conditions need access to networks that are already linked into worldwide KBs. The advent of network switching technology access is generally easy to achieve. The address translation technology, based on INs (Ahamed and Lawrence, 1998; Ahamed and Lawrence, 1997) first developed by AT&T and other similar communication corporations has been in use since 1980s. Multiple database lookups offer selections based on specialty, region, research institution, etc., is as a Google search followed by intelligent connectivity matrix to the most logical search destination. Intelligent Google searches have still to follow even though text-based searches are abundant.

Intelligent medical searches are proposed (Mollah, 2005; Waraporon, 2006) by various researchers at the City University of New York during the last decade. The intelligence is enforced by detecting the tree-graph between the various search (noun) objects and/or (verb) function posed in the query and isolating the KCO and its location that encompasses the entire tree rather than the text strings in the query. Such detection procedures can be and should be programmed in the intelligent Internet switches proposed in ref. Ahamed (2006). Intelligent international telephone switching based on the string of dialed numbers has been in service since late 1990s. The privacy and security aspects essential in medical networks are already implemented in global financial networks (Goldburt, 2004). Well-integrated global intelligent medical networks have been long time in becoming a reality. The inertia appears to be social rather than technical and a deliberate resistance to making medical processing more scientific and technological.

10.10 Intelligent Medical Environments

Medical networks can range from small hospital networks to multinational global specialty-based networks for special conditions and rare diseases. In the current environment, the search engines provide access to information but lack the human consultative platform for interactive sessions between experts. The financial and economic aspects of the transactions are not handled by the plain old search engines. The inclusion of the MSPs (Figures 10.9–10.11) who maintain extensive information ranging from the patient ailments to the medical insurance coverage and medicines will complete the treatment program for each of their customers much like the credit card companies can track the financial activities of their clients.

General patient databases, physician access point units, patient access point units, and service facilities are connected to the medical data banks and medical processor via several buses. In an alternative integrated medical computer system, numerous processors are included with their own memories and modules and are linked together to establish a processor net unit. This system can be used in a campus environment, where several buildings comprise the hospital or where several hospitals are interlinked over LANs. Two such configurations are shown in Figures 10.10 and 10.11. The nature of components and their capacities are matched to the variety of services provided, and sizes of the links and routers are matched to the expected client base that is served by the medical facilities.

Large groups of independent hospital networks may be integrated (and programmed) to coexist within one larger medical network as independent INs sharing the network infrastructure. The functionality can also be forced to perform as a group of localized medical networks (Ahamed and Lawrence, 1997) for the particular hospital rather than a single massive medical network for a region or a country. The role of the numerous MSPs will thus be confined to local area services and information access rather than to a few global MSPs. The main advantage of having a large number of smaller and localized MSPs is that the cost and complexity of a localized MSP are much lower than a large MSP. The new competition at the localized MSP services will reduce the medical expenses and overall customer costs.

More of the local MSPs and businesses can offer the medical information and services such as discounted prescription drugs, hospital and nursing services, or physical therapy. Such an increase in the supply side of medical information will facilitate the medical field to become more competitive and thus contain medical costs substantially over time.

10.11 Conclusions

We have presented numerous versions of the medical systems and two versions of IN-based medical networks. The classification of subject matter and the design of modular software oriented to the performance of medical subprocedures become essential. Coordinating these medical subprocedures with the expertise of the medical staff and the use, and availability, of medical facilities in the hospital or the medical center becomes the crucial step in deploying the IMS in practice.

The separation of the input and output processing at the nodes of the MPUs in the network is desirable to streamline the multitude of input—output transactions at any medical system node. The hierarchical separation, based upon the specialization of the medical processors, makes network addressing of these nodes flexible and straightforward. Additional nodes may be added or removed from the IMS. The hierarchical separation, based upon the services provided by the service providers, also makes the network addressing of these vendors flexible, straightforward, and programmable. Such vendors may be added or deleted from the numerous medical systems to offer the most optimal and economical service.

We consider this approach feasible in light of the recent developments in database storage and access technology. This approach supports the hierarchical organization of medical information, its real-time access and associative searches, AI techniques (for knowledge processing, such as forward/backward linking, inductive and predictive logic, pattern recognition, and expert system consultation capability), and specialized operating systems (for resource management, allocation, conflict and deadlock resolution, accounting, billing and record keeping). With the cooperative role played by the interdisciplinary team of systems designers, medical system can be as useful to the health industry as airplanes are to the transportation industry or as computers are to the scientific community.

References

1. OCLC: *Dewey decimal classification and relative index*, ed 22, Dublin, OH, 2003, OCLC, See also Comaroni JP: *Dewey decimal classification*, ed 18, Albany, NY, 1976, Forest Press.
2. United States Government, Library of Congress Classification. http://catalog.loc.gov. Accessed June 2003.
3. Krol M: Intelligent medical network, Doctoral Dissertation, 1996, City University of New York.
4. CCITT Recommendations M.3010: Principles for a Telecommunication Management Network (TMN) TINA Architecture; M.3200. TMN Management Service; M.3400. TMN Management Functions; M.3020. TMN Interface Specification Methodology; M.3180 Catalogue Network Information Model; M.3300. TMN Management Capabilities.
5. Ahamed SV: Hospital-based integrated medical computer systems for processing medical and patient information using specialized functional modules, 1998. US Patent No. US6,272,481 B1 issued on August 7, 2001. Assignee Lucent Technologies, Holmdel, NJ.
6. Ahamed SV, Lawrence VB: *Intelligent broadband multimedia networks*, Boston, MA, 1998, Kluwer Academic Publishers, ISBN 0792307479.
7. Miller RA, Pople JE Jr., Myers JD: INRRNIST-I, an experimental computer-based diagnostic consultant for general internal medicine, *New Engl J Med* 307:468—476, 1982.
8. Shortcliffe E: *MYCIN: Computer-based medical consultations*, New York, 1976, American Elsevier. See also, Buchanan BG, Shortcliffe EH: *Rule-based expert system: the mycin experiment at stanford heuristic programming project*, Boston, MA, 1984, Addison Wesley, and see also, Kintsch W, et al: *About neomycin, methods and tactics in cognitive science*, Mahwah, NJ, 1984, Lawrence Erlbaum.

9. Ahamed SV, Lawrence VB: Personal computer-based intelligent networks, 1998, US Patent 5,715,371 issued on February 3, 1998, Assignee Lucent Technologies, Holmdel, NJ.

10. Ahamed SV, Lawrence VB: *Intelligent broadband multimedia networks*, Boston, MA, 1997, Kluwer Academic Publishers. See also, Ahamed SV, Lawrence VB: *Intelligent networks: architecture and implications*, Encyclopedia of physical science and technology, 2, 1992, Academic Press, 229–261.

11. Mollah, N: *Design and simulation of international intelligent medical networks*, PhD Dissertation, 2005, Doctoral Center, City University of New York.

12. Waraporon N: *Intelligent medical databases for global access*, PhD Dissertation, 2006, Graduate Center of the City University of New York.

13. Ahamed SV: *Intelligent internet knowledge networks: processing of concepts and wisdom*, 2006, Wiley-Interscience.

14. Goldburt N: *Design considerations for financial institution intelligent networks*, PhD Dissertation, 2004, Graduate Center of the City University of New York.

For high quality versions of the figures in this chapter, please visit the companion website for this book at http://booksite.elsevier.com/9780124166301/

11 MPUs for Medical Networks

11.1 Introduction

This chapter introduces analogical and deductive methodologies for the design medical processor units (MPUs). From the study of evolution of numerous earlier processors, we derive the basis for the architecture of MPUs. These specialized processors perform unique medical functions encoded as medical operational codes (*mopcs*). From a pragmatic perspective, MPUs function very close to central processor units (CPU). Both processors have unique operation codes (*opcs*) that command the hardware to perform a distinct chain of subprocesses upon operands and generate a specific result unique to the opcode and the operand(s). In medical environments, MPU decodes the *mopcs*, executes a series of medical subprocesses, and sends out secondary commands to the medical machine or its peripherals. Whereas operands in a typical computer system are numerical and logical entities, the operands in medical machine are objects such as such as patients, blood samples, tissues, operating rooms, medical staff, medical bills, and patient payments. We follow the functional overlap between the two processes and evolve the design of medical computer systems and networks.

11.2 History and Background of MPUs

The infusion of scientific methodology in the practice of medicine and art of surgery has been slow but is steadily gaining momentum. Tools and technology are much more prevalent now in diagnosing ailments and curing of chronic conditions than ever before. The scientific discoveries and innovations have given the modern doctors a firm rationale over the mere blending of skill and experience of the less scientific approaches of medical practitioners of the 1980s and 1990s. Science is as much a part of modern medicine as aerospace technology was a part of the aircraft industry during the 1980s. Yet the infusion of science and technology from the National Aeronautics and Space Agency (NASA) has substantially transformed the design and manufacture of aircraft and the future of the spacecraft industry.

In the medical field, the first wave of infusion of science and technology has resulted in superb tools. Streamlined procedures and scientific methodologies in

Intelligent Networks: Recent Approaches and Applications in Medical Systems.
DOI: http://dx.doi.org/10.1016/B978-0-12-416630-1.00011-X

the diagnosis of disease and disorder and the subsequent cure of patients are the norms of medical activity. At the current snapshot of time, the infusion has dissipated, and the process is now waning into diffusion. In perspective, the second wave of infusion that is still to follow is from the major contributions in processing of information and knowledge. It is slowly but surely replacing processing of numbers and data structures in the computer field. Machines are taking over human functions at an unprecedented rate. Learning from human reactions and bylaws of rational behavior, humanist machines can outperform any unskilled labor force. In these new machines, local reasoning is infused with global wisdom, and the immediate outcome is truly beautiful as much as it is socially valuable.

In this chapter, we take the bold step of blending the steps in processing of knowledge and information with the effectiveness and dispersion of global medicinal/surgical practices. The outcome should be a blend of efficiency and accuracy of digital techniques in computers and networks with the strides of scientific discoveries and innovations in the field of modern medicine. Further, in this chapter, the basis of modern medicine is assumed to be in some documented form of computer and network accessible (textual, graphical, accounting, observational, statistical, etc.) files. Opinions and experience of the professionals are summarized as derived expert system knowledge bases and/or computer-driven artificial intelligence (AI) generated files that can be used as reference nodes in the deduction and derivation of new hypothesis, conclusion, or inference. Information and knowledge processing techniques merge and process the current local conditions and constraints with those observed in the past and documented in the medical knowledge bases around the globe. Two major effects become evident.

First, the medical machines provide sound and documented sets of recommended procedural steps to solve the local problem dealing with diagnosis and/or cure. The confidence in each of the derived inference is numerically displayed for the local team of specialists to verify and modify (if necessary), thus forcing the practitioners to keep abreast of global knowledge. The machine processes approach the methodologies now in vague for forensic studies and for crackdown of the breach of computer security.

Second, the medical machine tracks the difference between its prediction based on prior historical facts in the knowledge bases and the observed (or preferred) outcome or treatment. The AI-based learning algorithms validate the cause−effect relationship in the current/local problem and log the findings for more human (humanist) consideration.

Both actions of the medical machine make its functions complimentary and subservient to the surveillance of human judgment. Major modification to the medical and procedural knowledge bases is completed only under the consensus and validation of global medical experts. Such practices are frequently undertaken in most national and international knowledge bases in any given discipline (such as economics, finance, banking, economics, or any expertise) only if there is agreement and consensus among the experts in that particular discipline.

11.3 Medical Knowledge Bases

The contributions to systematic accumulation of knowledge pertaining to medical sciences have been scattered and diversified. In a majority of cases, the activity has been commercial rather than academic and scholarly. The computational and network tools and techniques have been obscured by the influence of profiteering from the sale of data to specialized medical teams and desperate patients. As early as 2010, only a few nonprofit medical knowledge bases have emerged. The authenticity and accuracy of the contents are by entry rather than by reason and scientific accountability.

Three key components to deploy medical knowledge processing techniques in existing global networks are identified as follows:

1. the Internet accessible knowledge bases that hold, share, and validate the current medical knowledge and procedures in every well-defined area of expertise and information;
2. optimal and efficient MPUs to analyze and resolve local medical issues and distribute the procedural commands to the medical computers, their peripherals, networks, and knowledge bases;
3. accessible and efficient broadband backbone and global networks.

Unified, integrated, and streamlined, these three components constitute the next generation medical networks that can be programmed and tailored to individual, community, and regional of national needs of developing countries.

In the United States, the National Institute of Health (NIH) funded research at Stanford University[1] has yielded noteworthy contributions such as Internist-I (Miller et al., 1982). The ensuing GUIDON (an intelligent computer-aided instruction tool) (Clancey et al., 1979) and MYCIN (Shortcliffe, 1976) lack the knowledge about the structure and the strategy in the diagnosis and the rationality for the expert system based recommendations for procedures and/or therapy. Initially, they were used for consolidating the recommendations for bacteremia and meningitis. MYCIN has a nonpsychological, expert system, probability driven knowledge base primarily used for referencing rather than for analysis, derivation, and enhancement of medical knowledge. The heuristic approach has serious limitation for the creative deployment of medical knowledge for the particular ailment of a particular patient. Patients are unique and highly individualistic; only medical knowledge is generic and the role of the medical machine is to compliment the generic knowledge with unique circumstance and individuality of the patient. Conversely, the medical machine actively deploys the scientific reasoning and methodology to suit the unique needs of patient. The medical team monitors the reason and logic that

---

[1] The long list of contributions from NIH funded Stanford University's scientists is remarkable. In particular, Internist, MYCIN, MYCIN-II, and NeoMycin have transformed the methodologies for merging heuristic programming into the practice of medicine.

the medical machine is currently using to fine-tune the outcome to be flawless and meets the desired goal within a present level of confidence. Surely, it may not circumvent the inevitable, but it will leave search exhaustively (in the worldwide medical knowledge domain) for every possible option. At the least, the machine will strive to delay or even bypass the inevitable for long span of time. This is the last resort for the incurable diseases in patients.

Initial medical procedural codes, their associated details, ensuing methodology, and their databases were initiated at the City University of New York by Krol (1996). Integrated medical network (IMN) configurations and their architectures have been studied by numerous other researchers such as Mollah (2005) and Kazmi (2002). A novel encoding of the procedural codes in ATM cell was proposed by Leung (2005). Waraporon (2006) introduced graphing of symptoms and deduction ailments and their treatments in the medical field in his dissertation and the following publications Ahamed and Lawrence (1998) and Waraporn and Ahamed (2006).

The concept of multidimensional Hamming codes was introduced in 2007 (Ahamed, 2007, 2009) to the medical field in order to identify the nearest set of documented symptoms of diagnosed ailments to those of the patients. Being programmable, these steps facilitate quick, efficient, and quantifiable results in the diagnosis and then the treatment of the patient condition by matching the personal history and data of the patient with those of successfully treated patients. Medical knowledge bases are an integral part of the studies by Mollah (2005) and Waraporon (2006).

In order to integrate the AI techniques in the Web environment, Ahamed (2007, 2009) has extended this methodology over the last few years. Rahman (2010) have also documented the most recent finding. Numerous configurations that utilize the intelligent Internet architectures and the national medical expert teams are presented in Section 11.5. These intelligent medical systems environments, based on Internet access, constantly scan the activities in hospitals and medical centers in order to filter out the routine activity and select the unusual circumstances to add to the medical knowledge bases around the country or the world.

In a recent IBM patent Basson has indicated the crucial use of sensing techniques to develop a (mobile network based) vehicle control system when the driver suffers from potentially debilitating conditions. A database including such conditions and symptoms is accessed. The findings are processed by a traditional CPU with network access to central control point. The system attempts to rescue the situation and the medical emergencies for the drive. In an earlier paper, Park highlights the concept of an "intelligent" garment worn by human beings that monitors the Georgia Tech Wearable Motherboard (GTWM) to monitor the vital signs in an unobtrusive manner. The sensing of EKGs, temperature, voice recorders, and so on permits the wearer to transmit data and information to external devices. Doukas (2006) have proposed advanced telemedicine services to the context-aware networks.

11.4 Processor Designs

11.4.1 Platform of Current Processors

MPU designs are firmly entrenched in the design of processors. CPUs,[2] numerical processor units (NPUs), digital signal processors (DSPs), and knowledge processor units (KPUs) are indeed the forerunners of MPUs. In the section, we briefly review the architectures of the simplest graphical processor unit (based on the vintage von Neumann CPU) design to the more elaborate KPU design.

CPUs have been the generic hardware for numeric, arithmetic, and logic functions since the von Neumann machine (Hayes, 1988) in 1945. The architecture of the IAS (Institute of Advanced Study) machine (Neumann, 1945) was the first blue print of many more machines that were built for a decade or so after the basis of the IAS machine was well received by the computer manufacturers. The earlier CPU architectures are briefly presented in Chapter 2 and described in detail in Ahamed (2007).

11.4.2 Display/Graphics Processor Units

The earlier display processor units (DPUs) for cathode ray tube (CRT) technology are obsolete. Cursor input in the CRTs has been long outdated. The software was primitive and the display functions and colors needed considerable enhancements. The flat panel technology and the availability of very fine granularity and color options have rendered new venues for machines to carry the visual impact deep in the minds and thoughts of scientists and researchers alike. The impact in every scientific and social direction of progress is monumental.

During their introduction, the graphics processor units (GPUs) served as the intermediate processors between the CPU and the graphic devices. The GPUs were initially built to relieve the CPU from the display functions and continue with the application-based processing. Earlier designs (e.g., Intel 82786 graphics coprocessor) adapted a separate configuration, but the later CPU architectures absorbed the basic GPU configurations within the larger VLSI chips that were offering larger capacity, dependability, and yield. Typical configuration of a CPU from the 1980s that could also be deployed as a GPU is shown in Figure 11.1. The GPUs for movie industry are far more specialized and sophisticated.

The internal bus structure within the GPU is based on the word length and the instruction set of the graphics/display processor unit. Typically, the older (1980s and early 1990s era) graphics processors and accelerators (the Intel 80860, i860, 1989) delivered 13 MFLOPS or approximately half a million vector transformations for graphics applications. The architecture deployed 10 bus structures, integer and floating-point adders and multipliers, 2 cache memories, and numerous

---

[2] In the modern days, the number of processors has increased dramatically. It is possible to build a processor for almost any function or task, ranging from arithmetic functions to automatic robotic responses. In this section, we present the trail of only a few pertinent processors that form a basis for the evolution of the MPUs.

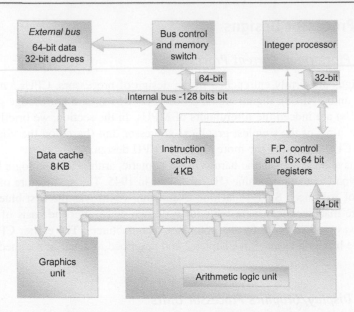

Figure 11.1 A typical CPU configuration that could be used as a GPU unit from the late 1980 era.

switches and multiplexer units. The algorithms for computer graphics functions are highly optimized to deliver the most desirable processor power consistent with desired level of visual impact to the viewers based on the application requirements.

Recent graphics processors are as powerful as the CPUs. In fact, the VLSI technology is the same and some GPUs outperform traditional CPUs for specific applications. Movie making has initiated a whole new era of graphical computer systems. Processors for graphical inputs and outputs have specialized requirements. Lapse-time and real-time processing are both prevalent. In real-time applications, the GPUs keep pace with the application-based computations. When the entire systems are designed for special applications (such as distance learning, remote surgery, MRI, stock market, and games), the response time of the two (application oriented and graphics oriented) subsystems needs consideration. The communication capacity is influenced on channel capacity, and the three (computation, graphics, and communication) basic design parameters influence the accuracy, clarity, and quality of the output displays, movies, and pictures.

Graphical user interfaces (GUIs) provide the user inputs to application programs that generate the resulting displays. Graphical devices are main output devices for computer to communicate with the users. In certain applications such as computer games and movie making, the perception time of the users and viewer becomes crucial. When the computer systems are dedicated to movie making, the graphics processing systems can become as elaborate and intricate as mainframe computers. The balance between the processing power and graphics display capability becomes an option for most of the designers of standard desktop and laptop computers. In the customized systems, the processing powers are based on the choice of the CPU, GPU processor chips and the opcodes that drive them.

For intensive graphics application, independent graphics processors are deployed. Most modern computing systems have integrated GPUs built in the overall architecture. GPU computing has become a specialty in its own right. It is seen as a viable alternative to the traditional microprocessor-based computing in high-performance computing environments. When used in conjunction with selected CPUs, an order of magnitude gain in performance can be expected in game physics and in computational biophysics applications. The parallel architecture of the GPU is generally used to accelerate the computational performance. These GPUs handle a broad range of process-intensive complex problems with a visual insight into the nature of changes that occur as the computation progresses.

11.4.3 Object Processor Units

The architectural framework of typical object processor units (OPUs) is consistent with the typical representation of CPUs. Design of the object operation code (*Oopc*) plays an important role in the design of OPU and object-oriented machine. In an elementary sense, this role is comparable to role of the 8-bit *opc* in the design of IAS machine during the 1944−1945 periods. For this (IAS) machine, the *opc* length was 8 bits in the 20-bit instructions, and the memory of 4096 word, 40-bit memory corresponds to the address space of 12 binary bits. The design experience of the game processors and the modern graphical processor units will serve as a platform for the design of the OPUs and hardware-based object machines.

The intermediate generations of machines (such as IBM 7094, 360-series) provide a rich array of guidelines to derive the instruction sets for the OPUs. If a set of object registers or an object cache can be envisioned in the OPU, then the instructions corresponding to register instructions (R-series), register-storage (RS-series), storage (SS), immediate operand (I-series), and I/O series instructions for OPU can also be designed. The instruction set will need an expansion to suit the application. It is logical to foresee the need of control object memories to replace the control memories of the microprogrammable computers.

The instruction set of the OPU is derived from the most frequent object functions such as (i) single-object instructions, (ii) multiobject instructions, (iii) object to object memory instructions, (iv) internal object−external object instructions, and (v) object relationship instructions. The separation of logical, numeric, seminumeric, alphanumeric, and convolutions functions between objects will also be necessary. Hardware, firmware, or brute-force software (compiler power) can accomplish these functions. The need for the next-generation object and knowledge machines (discussed in Section 11.5) should provide an economic incentive to develop these architectural improvements beyond the basic OPU configuration shown in Figure 11.2.

The designs of OPU can be as diversified as the designs of a CPU. The CPUs, I/O device interfaces, different memory units, and direct memory access hardware units for high-speed data exchange between main memory units and large secondary memories. Over the decades, numerous CPU architectures (single bus,

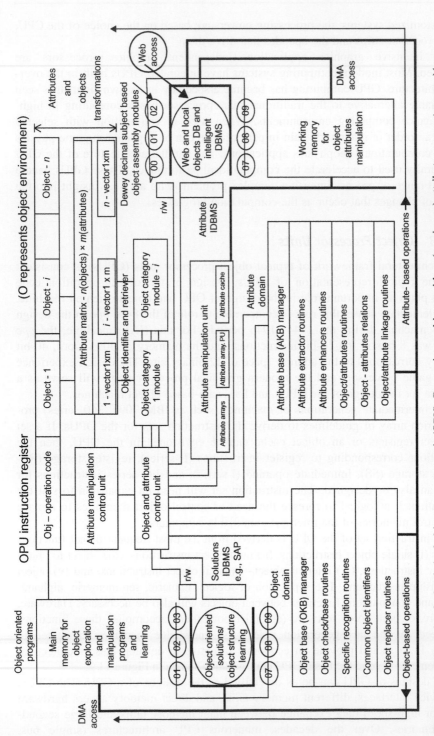

Figure 11.2 Schematic of a hardwired object processor unit (OPU). Processing n objects with m (maximum) attributes generates an $n \times m$ matrix. The common, interactive, and overlapping attributes are thus reconfigured to establish primary and secondary relationships between objects. DMA, direct memory access; IDBMS, Intelligent, data, object, and attribute base(s) management system(s); KB, knowledge base(s). Many variations can be derived.

multibus, hardwired, micro- and nanoprogrammed, multicontrol memory-based systems) have come and gone.

Some of microprogrammable and RISC architecture still exist. Efficient and optimal performance from the CPUs also needs combined SISD, SIMD, MISD, and MIMD, (Stone 1980) and/or pipeline architectures. Combined CPU designs can use different clusters of architecture for their subfunctions. Some formats (e.g., array processors, matrix manipulators) are in active use. Two concepts that have survived many generations of CPUs are (i) the algebra of functions (i.e., opcodes) that is well delineated, accepted, and documented and (ii) the operands that undergo dynamic changes as the opcode is executed in the CPU(s).

An architectural consonance exists between CPUs and OPUs. In pursuing the similarities, the five variations (SISD, SIMD, MISD, MIMD, and/or pipeline) design established for CPUs can be mapped into five corresponding designs; single process single object (SPSO), single process multiple objects (SPMO), multiple process single object (MPSO), multiple process multiple objects (MPMO), and/or fractional process pipeline, respectively (Ahamed, 2003).

11.5   Knowledge Processor Units

Knowledge is derived from objects, their nature, attributes, and their interactions. Thus, the processing capability of knowledge entails processing objects, their attributes, and object interactions. Numerous designs of KPUs become evident and in fact, they can be derived from the varieties of CPUs initially and then the GPUs that can function as OPUs, and the finally the GPUs that can also serve as CPUs. The creativity of the individual KPU designer lies in matching the HW architecture to the application needs. KPU chips, being more expensive and process intensive than CPUs, are unlikely to become as numerous as CPUs that can be personalized to any whim and fancy of the chip manufacturers. The function of the KPUs depends on the capacity of the HW to manipulate or juggle (global and local) objects, based on their own syntax and environmental constraints in the semantics of the user objective.

The CPU's functionality depends on the capacity to execute stylized *opcs* on arithmetic and logical operands (in highly specialized formats and date structures). The configuration of a simple KPU (Ahamed, 1995) operating of object operands is shown in Figure 11.3. Other variations based on SIMD, MISD, and MIMD[3] and

---

[3] A brief explanation of acronyms for this section is presented. CPU, central processor unit; KPU, knowledge processor unit; ALU, arithmetic logic unit; NPU, numeric processor unit; SISD, single instruction single data; SIMD, single instruction multiple data; MISD, multiple instruction single data; MIMD, multiple instruction multiple data; OPU, object processor unit; SKI-SO, single knowledge instruction-single object; SKI-MO, single knowledge instruction-multiple object; MKI-SO, multiple knowledge instruction-single object; MKI-MO, multiple knowledge instruction-multiple object; SO processor, single object processor; MO processors, multiple object processors; SOI-SO, single object instruction-single object; SOI-MO, single object instruction-multiple objects; MOI-SO, multiple object instruction-single object; MOI-MO, multiple object instruction-multiple object; SKI-SOI-SO, single knowledge instruction-single object instruction-single object; MKI-MOI-MO, multiple knowledge instruction-multiple object instruction-multiple objects.

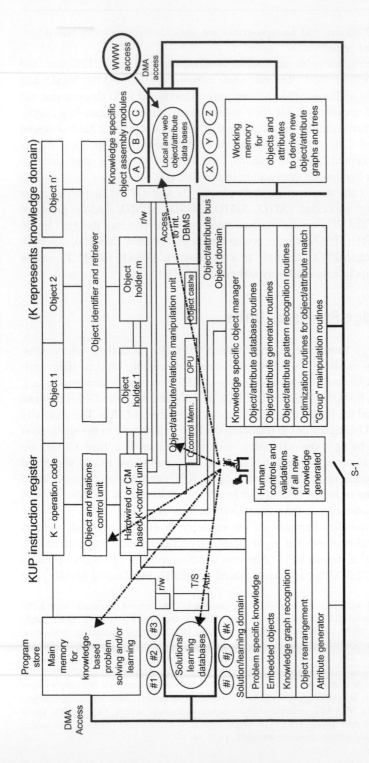

Figure 11.3 Switch S-1, open for execution mode for knowledge domain problem solving; closed for learning mode. The learning programs "process," the existing solutions and are able to extract objects, groups, relationships, opcodes, group operators, modules, strategies, and optimization methodologies from existing solutions and store them in object and corresponding databases. The architecture permits the KPU to catalog a new object in relation to existing objects and generate/modify existing pointers to and from new objects.

pipeline architectures of the CPU have been built, and such variations can be transfused in the OPU designs. Object processors that lie in between CPUs and KPUs bring in another degree of freedom because KPUs can deploy OPUs, much like CPUs can deploy ALUs and NPUs. Sequential, pipeline, and parallel execution of operations on objects in KPUs gives rise to at least eight possibilities: SKI-SO processors, SKI-MO processors, MKI-SO processors, and MKI-MO processors. Now, if SO and MO processors have SOI-SO, SOI-MO, and MOI-SO processors (pipeline structure), and MOI-MO (pipeline and/or multiprocessor structure) processors have variation embedded within themselves, then at least eight design variations become evident. The SKI-SOI-SO is the simplest to build while the MKI-MOI-MO is the most cumbersome to build. From the first estimate, the HW for the simplest KPUs should be an order of magnitude more complex than the IBM 360 CPUs (even though these CPUs deployed the microcode technology).

Knowledge processing is based on rudimentary yet pragmatic knowledge theory (Ahamed, 1995). Stated simply, human knowledge is clustered around objects and object groups. Such objects can be represented by data and information structures. Data has numerous representations, and information has several forms of graphs and relationships that bring order and coherence to the collection of objects. Such a superstructure of data (at the leaf level), objects (at the twig level), and the object clusters (at the branch level) constitute a tree of knowledge. Specific graphs, moreover, relationships that bind information into a cogent and coherent body of knowledge, bring (precedent, antecedent, and descendant) nodal hierarchy in a visual sense that corresponds to reality.

KPUs should be able to prune, build and shape, reshape, and optimally reconfigure knowledge trees, much as CPUs are able to perform the arithmetic (and logic) functions on numbers and symbols and derive new numbers (and logical entities) from old numbers (and logical symbols).

In the design considerations of the CPU, the more elaborate AU functions are known to be decomposable into basic integer and floating-point numeric (add, divide, etc.) operations. Similarly, complex logical operations can be reconstituted as modular (AND, OR, EXOR, etc.) functions. In this vein, we propose that all the most frequently used knowledge functions are feasible for the KPU to perform the basic, elementary, and modular functions on objects.

Knowledge-bearing objects can be arbitrarily complex. Numerous lower level objects can constitute a more elaborate object entity. Similar to bacterial colonies, knowledge superstructures have dynamic life cycles. The order and methodology in the construction and destruction of such knowledge superstructures lead to "laws of knowledge physics" in the knowledge domain under the DDS classification 530–539.

Traditional laws of Boolean algebra and binary arithmetic do not offer sufficient tools for the calculus of the dynamic bodies of knowledge undergoing social and technological forces in society. A brand new science of knowledge would be appropriate for medical/knowledge machines to perform in the human domain and computers to perform in the numerical domain. Object and knowledge machines would pave the way. If the new laws for the flow, dynamics, velocity, and acceleration of knowledge and knowledge centric objects (KCOs) can be based on a set of orderly, systematic, and realistic knowledge operation codes (*kopcs*), then these laws can be written as machine executable routines that operate on the KCOs. This approach is a bold digression from the approach in classical sciences where the new concepts enter the sciences as symbolic and mathematical equations. In the modern society, information erupts as multimedia WWW streams, rather than as a graceful expansion of coherent and cogent concepts embedded in knowledge. Time for extensive human contemplations is a rare luxury to reset the origin of knowledge. Much as we needed digital data scanning systems for DSPs in the past, we need a machine-based common sense, sensing systems to separate junk level information (Ahamed, 2007) from knowledge bearing information. Knowledge filtering (Ahamed, 1995) accomplishes this initial, robust, sensible, and necessary task.

The current scenario of science and innovation has given rise to the deployment of technology before it gets obsolete. To accommodate this acceleration of knowledge, we propose that we have a standard set of basic and modular *kopcs* (Ahamed, 2009). The complex knowledge operations that encompass the newest concepts are then assembled from the basic set of internationally accepted standard of *kopcs* (Ahamed, 1995). The proposed representation for the dynamics of knowledge paves the way between concepts that create new knowledge and the technology that uses such knowledge. The international telecommunication union (ITU) effort has standardized efficient protocols for the seven-layer OSI model for communication of data, and then again as the TCP/IP.

11.6   Design of Medical Processors

11.6.1   Medical Processor Units

MPUs are not yet specifically built for *mopcs*. It is possible and viable that such processor chips will be tailored and geared to medical functions. A variety of such generic functions can be readily identified. One such *mopc* is to instruct the MPU to compare bacteria strain (i) with all known bacteria ($j, j = 1, n$) from WWW bacteria banks and to identify any settle change patterns. Certain amount of object processing and pattern recognition procedures will become essential to complete this task. For computer scientists and VLSI designers, the modular tasks involved in executing this overall task have already been accomplished in other disciplines (such as face/fingerprint recognition in criminology or cell shape recognition in medicine). The ordeal is to assemble an interdisciplinary team of scientists.

Other generic functions are the identification of ailments, patient complaints/ cures, most effective treatments, and knowledge processing units to bridge the various knowledge domains. Only a prolonged and consistent effort from the medical staff can lead to generic *opcs* for MPUs that can be focal element of medical computer. For an initial step, the *kopcs* should suffice as *mopcs* discussed in this section. Medical processors and medical data banks work coherently (Ahamed 2001) in tandem for executing a numerous instructions, retrieving/storing, and processing pertinent medical information. Numerous medical processor hardware units and modules, (including conventional CPUs) coexist in the integrated system to track the confidence levels of the medical functions, individually and collectively. Figure 11.4 depicts the schematic of a MPU derived from the OPU shown in Figure 11.2. Some of the features for automated learning procedure from the KPU shown in Figure 11.3 are included for the medical systems to activate AI procedures and to suggest improvised procedures to the medical teams. A typical wide area based medical network with advanced learning features and retrieval capability is shown in Figure 11.5.

Patients and their attributes are treated in unison and as one synergy. Patient records are dynamic and reflect the most recent state of health, and the attributes are updated with a history of changes. Procedures are configured from known procedures on similar patients but with slightly different attributes. The procedures are mapped against the attributes to ascertain the optimality and efficacy of treatments and procedures. The basic laws of medical sciences are not violated during administration of treatments and procedures. Administering n subprocedures on a patient with m (maximum) attributes generates an $n \times m$ matrix.

The common, conflicting, and overlapping attributes are thus reconfigured to establish primary and secondary medical safety rules (diabetes and sugar control, alcohol and drugs precaution, etc.) in the realm of medical practice even by a machine. Rules that are more complex are deducible based on medical database (MDB) information for any specific condition/patient.

11.6.2 Medical Computer and Typical Network

Medical computers constitute a special breed of cluster computers. Both have identifiable supersets of traditional computers for the routine functions. While it is viable to force a cluster computer to act as a full-fledge medical computer, it is desirable to build medical computers on a distinctive track of its own *mopcs*.

The demand for such medical computers is likely to expand and grow like the specialized air borne computers for the aviation industry. Patient databases, physician access points, patient access points, and service facilities are connected to the medical data banks and medical processor via several buses. In an alternative integrated medical computer system, numerous processors are included with their own memories and modules and are linked together to establish a processor net unit. Such systems are amenable to hospital campus settings, where several buildings comprise the hospital, or where several hospitals are interlinked over local area networks.

11.6.3 Intelligent Medical Computers

In the intelligent and integrated medical facilities, numerous MPUs and knowledge banks are linked via a high-speed backbone network as depicted in Figure 11.5. Isolated packets of information arrive at the knowledge banks from numerous medical centers and hospitals. Optimal protocol design and packet structure for medical functions need to be evolved for this type of medical environment, even though the existing TCP/IP will suffice. The addressing of the distant knowledge banks is

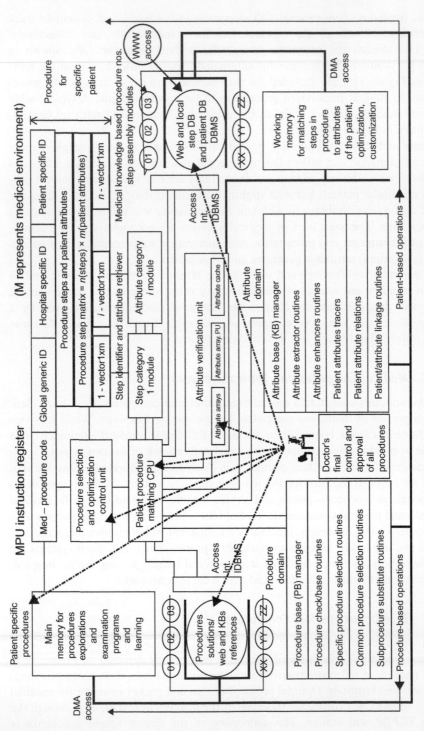

Figure 11.4 Architecture of a medical processor unit (MPU). DMA, direct memory access; DBMS, data, procedure, patient and/or attribute base (s) management system(s); KB, knowledge base(s).

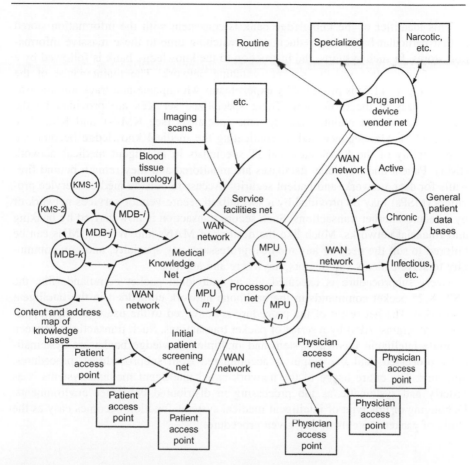

Figure 11.5 Architecture of a WAN based intelligent medical network. A cluster of MPUs shares the overall task of running the medical facilities of any regional area. Existing hospitals and medical centers are networked to use their facilities optimally and economically. The resource allocation for the most expensive facilities is done by the operating system driving the processor net. Knowledge processing is also done by the processor net, thus sharing its own resources. KMS, knowledge machine(s); MDB, medical database; MPU, medical processor unit; WAN, wide area network that facilitates resource sharing from numerous participating centers and hospitals.

done via a subject matter identifier allocated to the distant knowledge banks. Content and address map of the entire network are housed in specialized medical service "control point" that facilitates[4] the high-speed backbone network to quickly access the information for real-time or emergency conditions.

---

[4] Some of these concepts dealing with service control point (SCP), service management system (SMS), and network partitioning are borrowed from typical designs of various intelligent networks (United States, French, Japanese, Swiss, etc.) and now in use by (almost) all communication and mobile networks around the world.

This identifier of the knowledge bank is consistent with the information stored in that particular bank, thus reducing the switching time to these massive information stores. In such systems, the instruction to the knowledge bank is followed by a burst of input data via the packet switching network. The maintenance of the MDBs (Figure 11.5) is provided by expert teams who update and track any innovations/changes in the profession. These specialized services are provided by the team of knowledge maintenance systems specialists (see KMS-1 and KMS-2 in Figure 11.5). Maintenance and authenticating the medical knowledge become the responsibility of the KMS staff and IT specialists in intelligent medical network (IMS). Patient and physician databases are monitored and they remain behind firewalls for data, network, and patient security. Access to outside medical service providers (MSPs) may be provided by a specialized secure vendor services network or by a secure Internet transactions. Such secure transaction is now carried by banking and financial networks. Much like the designs of MANs and WANs, IMNs can be tailored to suit the need of any medical profession, any specialty, and any community to serve patients and doctors, anywhere and anytime.

Every subprocedure is executed via an individual packet command (like the SS7, X.25 packet commands in the backbone network embedded in the intelligent networks). The net result of the procedure is conveyed to the users (or their application programs, APs) by a series of packet transactions. Such transactions between a single intelligent medical system and multiple knowledge banks are systematically processed, and the output is accumulated from subprocedures, procedures, and runs. The entire usage of the network-based intelligent medical systems is as orderly and systematic as job processing in distributed computer environments. Debugging of this type of intelligent medical systems function becomes easy as the study of packet contents of any given procedure.

11.7 Conclusions

We evolve and present the architecture of an MPU in this chapter. The platform for MPU design is based on the designs of classical GPU, the OPU and the KPU. Such specialized processors are being pursued by moviemakers, games/graphics chip designers, and designers of intelligent educational, instructional, and knowledge-based systems. Each of these specialized application environments calls for optimality of architectural design and chip layout. In the OPU, KPU, and MPU architectures presented here, numerous functions specific to the application are all built in the processor architecture. However, it is also possible to fragment the most frequently used and complex functions into modular arrays of simpler functions and then recombine them at a systems level.

We also provide a basis for building a medical machine and IMNs by combining the architectures of the MPU with the object memory modules, the switch, and the bus configuration(s) for object flow and operational code control signals. The IMN components and architectures can be highly customized to the functional and geographical distributions of medical facilities in a campus, region, nation, or the globe. In this chapter, we have delineated the issues and offered generic methodologies to address and resolve the issues specific to the medical environments.

The innovations and achievements in network design during the last two decades have made the dreams of communication designers a reality now. Looking back, we propose a migration to IMNs by replacing the architecture of electronic switching systems (AT&Ts and ESS, which also process data and information) with medical machines and by replacing the functions of massively parallel processed 32-bit communication processor (3B2) with medical processors. The blending of medical, AI, and communication processes is always the purgative of the next generation IMN designers.

References

1. Miller RA, Pople JE Jr., Myers JD: Internist-I, an experimental computer-based diagnostic consultant for general internal medicine, *New Engl J Med* 307:468–476, 1980.
2. Clancey WJ, Shortliffe EH, Buchanan BG: Intelligent computer-aided instruction for medical diagnosis. *Proceedings of the third annual symposium on computer applications in medical care*, IEEE, pp. 175–183, 1979. See also Clancey WJ: Tutoring rules for guiding a case method dialogue, *Int J Man-Mach Stud* 11:25–49, 1980.
3. Shortcliffe E: *Computer-based medical consultations*, New York, NY, 1976, Elsevier, See also, Buchanan BG, Shortcliffe EH: *Rule-based expert system: the MYCIN experiment at Stanford Heuristic Programming project*, Boston, MA, 1984, Addison-esley, and Kintsch W: *About neomycin, methods and tactics in cognitive science*, Mahwah, NJ, 1976, Lawrence Erlbaum.
4. Krol M: Intelligent medical network, PhD Dissertation, City University of New York, 1996.Krol M, Reich DL: Development of a decision support system to assist anesthesiologists in operating room, *J Med Sys* 24:141–146, 2000.
5. Mollah N: Design and simulation of international intelligent medical networks, PhD Dissertation, Doctoral Center, City University of New York, 2005.
6. Kazmi TH: Simulation and design studies of knowledge processing in intelligent knowledge processing networks, Ph.D., Dissertation, Doctoral Center, City University of New York, 2002.
7. Leung L: Design and simulation of international intelligent medical networks, Ph.D., Dissertation, Doctoral Center, City University of New York, 2005.
8. Waraporon N: Intelligent medical databases for global access, PhD Dissertation, Graduate Center of the City University of New York, 2006.
9. Ahamed SV, Lawrence VB: *Intelligent broadband multimedia networks*, Boston, MA, 1998, Kluwer Academic Publishers, also in Springer Verlag 2008.
10. Waraporn N, Ahamed SV: Intelligent medical search engine by knowledge machine. Proceedings of the 3rd international conference on information technology: new generations, IEEE Computer Society, Los Alamitos, CA, 2006. Waraporon, N: Results of real time simulation of medical knowledge technology (MKT) system for medical diagnosis on distributed knowledge nodes. Las Vegas ITNG, 265–270, 2007.
11. Ahamed SV: *Intelligent internet knowledge networks: processing of wisdom and concepts*, Hoboken, NJ, 2007, John Wiley & Sons.

12. Ahamed SV: *Intelligent computational framework for knowledge: integrated behavior of machines*, Hoboken, NJ, 2009, John Wiley & Sons.
13. Rahman S, Ahamed S: Intelligent network applications for medical systems, recent trends in wireless and mobile networks. Second international conference, WiMo 2010, Ankara, Turkey, June 26–28, 2010. Proceedings, DOI 10.1007/978-3-642-14171-3_36, ISBN 978-3-642-14170-6 (Print) 978-3-642.
14. Basson SH, Fairweather PG, Kanevsky D: Medical applications in telematics. US Patent No. 7266430, Sep. 4, 2007, Assignee International Business Machines, Armonk, NY.
15. Park S: The wearable motherboard: a flexible information infrastructure or sensate liner for medical applications, in Westwood JD, Editor, editor: Medicine meets reality VII (studies in health technology and informatics), IOS Press. See also other books in *Medicine meets reality*, series edited by Westwood JD, Editor, Fairfax, Virginia, 2011, IOS Press.
16. Doukas D: Advanced telemedicine services through context-aware networks. Paper presented at 6th international networking conference (INC2006), July 11–14, 2006, Plymouth, England.
17. Hayes JP: *Computer architecture and organization*, ed 2, New York, NY, 1988, McGraw Hill.
18. von Neumann, J: First draft of a report on the EDVAC. Contract No. W-670-ORD 4926, Between the United States Army Ordnance Department and the University of Pennsylvania, Moore School of Electrical Engineering, June 30, 1945. Burks AW, Goldstine HH, von Neumann J: U.S. Army Report Ordnance Department, 1946. Estrin G: *The electronic computer at the Institute of Advanced Studies, mathematical tables and other aids to computation*, Princeton, NJ, 1953, IAS, pp. 108–114.
19. Stone HS: *Introduction to computer architecture (computer science series)*, New York, NY, 1980, Science Research; Associates.
20. Ahamed SV: The architecture of a wisdom machine, *Int J Smart Eng Sys Des* 5 (4):537–549, 1980.
21. Ahamed SV: Architecture for a computer system used for processing knowledge. US Patent No. 5,465,316, November 7, 1995. European Patent No. 9437848.5, Knowledge machine methods and apparatus, European Patent No. 146248, US/05.11.93, Denmark, France, Great Britain, Italy. Issue date 29/12/94.
22. Ahamed SV: Hospital-based integrated medical computer systems for processing medical and patient information using specialized functional modules. US Patent No. 6,272,481 B1 issued on August 7, 2001.

For high quality versions of the figures in this chapter, please visit the companion website for this book at http://booksite.elsevier.com/9780124166301/

12 Procedure-Based Medical Machines

12.1 Introduction

In this chapter, we present the architectural configurations of the Internet-based medical procedure-based medical machines that scan the knowledge bases around the world to suit the medical needs of patients and the specification of the doctors. These machines and facilities initially search and analyze the established global (and standardized) medical procedures. The medical staff, doctors, and the administration, in consultations, determine the exact nature of the procedure, subprocedures, and their customization to suit the local conditions of the hospitals, availability of the equipment, and expertise of the staff.

There are four major implications listed as follows. *First*, the machines match the global Internet resources to the patient needs and generate a preliminary evaluation. In addition, it identifies the possible knowledge and physical addresses. *Second*, the machines serve to modify, enhance, and customize the detailed step-by-step operations in any given local medical center, hospital, and medical team; their features, limitations, and strengths and validate all the subprocedures. *Third*, the machines serve the medical community to validate and propose possible alternative approaches to solve the patient needs; and *finally*, they perform an economic analysis of the steps and their justification from a medical and patient perspective. At the discretion of the users, the extent and depth of search can be tailored to suit the preferences of the local medical community.

Error proofing is accomplished at every step in the procedures and subprocedures. Critical procedures are identified as the critical paths in the flow graph of the medical treatment. As much as financial transactions are secure in Internet banking and as much as critical stages are safeguarded in VLSI, the medical machines validate and authenticate every step in patient care. Much of the burden is shifted from humans to humanist machines thus streamlining the treatment of patients like the (almost) flawless assembly line processes of airplanes. The human relations and personal care are shifted back to the human beings where they really belong. As much as humans are being displaced by robots in routine duties and functions, highly trained doctors can be relieved from performing routine, repetitive, and cumbersome administrative, housekeeping functions by intelligent medical machines.

Cost justification needs a detailed economic and financial study. As humans tend to live longer, and their needs demand customized solutions, the need for such

Intelligent Networks: Recent Approaches and Applications in Medical Systems.
DOI: http://dx.doi.org/10.1016/B978-0-12-416630-1.00012-1

humanist machines becomes urgent. In an economic sense, the marginal gain in the utility derived by the investment for such machines may not be justifiable in cases where both highly trained doctors and the supporting staffs are cheap and abundant. However, as the medical costs (i.e., doctor's fees and hospital costs) escalate every major investment needs a justification based on its own rate of return on investment. The lesson from Japanese stagnation during 1980s and 1990s is glaring: as the interest rates fall and the investors get fearful. Only the initiative from the government sector (i.e., the variable, G from Keynesian economics) can pave the way out of the capital freeze. Social rewards in the new information age should also regulate the older Keynesian equations, rather than the dollars and cents. Dollars and cents are the basis of decisions proposed by intelligent humanist machines.

Intelligent medical machines are not robots, nor smart social computers. Instead, these machines have a distinct flavor of scientific and social computing with all the flavors and variations of artificial intelligence (AI) embedded in the medical processes. This pinnacle of science has been the privilege of the doctor—patient relation. From the recent historical perspective, the machine-based medical diagnosis and consultation was deemed unnecessary by the medical profession during the evolution of 1980s (especially MYCIN (Clancey et al., 1979; Clancey, 1979; Shortcliffe, 1976), and NeoMycin (Kintsch et al., 1984), and medical expert systems (Buchanan and Shortcliffe, 1984). However, the recent strides in technology, (especially processor-based, network-, and AI-based technologies) make the medical machines a means for designing integrated hubs of the medical ware (MW), computer system software (SW), and specialized hardware and networks (HW). Network- and processor-based technologies are reviewed in Chapters 2 and 3. In this chapter, we suggest the ways and scientific venues for the interoperability and for the integration of WM, SW, and HW into medical machines, facilities, and backbone medical networks.

Medical and procedural steps have a distinctive humanist flavor and interactive process control by doctors, administration, and staff. In a sense, the role of the staff becomes comparable to the role of security staff and systems in airports and financial institutions. The authenticity and functioning of machine invoked medical processes secured by multiple processing of the functions by interlayered hardware and to this extent the dependability is as reliable as the network and telephone systems connectivity. The human element is generally needed to oversee and intuitively verify the highest levels medical functions. The details are checked by dual layers of software and hardware and made as secure as the financial transactions of banks or of the credit card companies.

12.2 Customized MW Layer

Care in ICUs, operating, and emergency rooms are perhaps at the highest level. The level of care can vary depending on the status and condition. Accordingly, MW also needs numerous hierarchical levels depending on the patient condition, physician's preference, and dependent on the stage of treatment, much like semantic analysis that follows syntactic analysis that follows lexical analysis in traditional steps in compilation of computer programs. Human beings the most adept readily grasp the sequence of steps but these steps need to be carefully programmed in MW. Such sequences of steps need the consultation and approval of the medical professionals. These steps have been successfully implemented in emergency room situations and ambulatory services. Customization of MW is the joint responsibility of the medical and computer professionals. Such joint collaborations have been successfully implemented in the remote surgeries and remote intelligent educational systems. In a sense, these steps in medical machines have precedence in other joint area of computer sciences.

The methodological steps in morphology (Aronoff and Fudeman, 2010) are well established in scientific literature. These very powerful and generic steps can be extended for the development of MW for procedures. When the major functional blocks in medicine or medical procedures are reconstructed as project flow diagrams[1] (as they are done in operations research or OR), then the simpler lines between the nodes become the subprocesses and the nodes become the state of the objects before and the end of such processes. For example, patients, physicians, staff, operating and emergency rooms, the MRI, and radiation machines make up the object group; the diagnosis, treatment, procedures, surgery, medications, transplants, implants make up the function group; and the syntactic and semantic relations between each of the functions and nouns form the convolution group between corresponding elements of the functions and the object groups.

The nature and extent of this morphological disintegration process has finite depth limited by VLSI and network technology and by human comprehension. It is necessary to keep the process (es) cogent and coherent, since any disorder in the functional steps, minor objects, and the convolution links can become chaotic and uncontrolled. This morphological process has been exploited at a processor level in the micro-medical processor unit presented in Chapter 9.

At the finest granular level of process and object disintegration, the microscopic processes are seen as verb functions (VFs), objects as noun objects (NOs), and convolutions as syntactic and feasible operations. At the macroprogramming level, these VFs constitute macrocommands; the NOs constitute macrooperands, and the convolution protocol would already be completed by the programmer or application level programs (ALPs). At the next level, these "vf's" and "no's" become the operation codes (opc's) and operands (opr's) and get executed in medical processor.

Intelligent medical processors collect all feasible medical opc's or mopc's, and medical operands opr's or mopr's and verify the effectiveness and utility derived by each of micro and macro levels of the execution of the medical processors. Human beings can achieve this level of morphological breakdown and detailed match between mopc's and mopr's; however, the effort would be far too tedious

---

[1] OR-flow charts and flow diagrams consist of nodes and process links. Nodes are generally stable states of the subobjects as they undergo subprocesses. Hence, if processes and objects that participate in any major procedure are decomposed into minor steps and minor objects, then the science of morphology becomes application in most practical situations.

and prolonged. This effort may be downgraded to systematic machine instructions and MW for medical machines.

12.3 The Medical Component

This component has four[2] major blocks: diagnosis, identification of problem, treatment, and prognosis. In Figure 12.1, these typical human functions can be handed over to the machines block by block. Expert medical systems already perform some functions at a superficial level since the 1980s. What has been missing is the exploitation of software, switching, and Internet technologies. The advantage is monumental. For instance, the pattern recognition (PR) methodologies offer a much higher level of confidence in identifying the ailments. Intelligent deductive and inductive reasoning based on current level of medical knowledge make the inference far more accurate, the Internet knowledge-base scanning makes prevents the medical team(s) from reaching hasty/erroneous conclusions at any one of the conclusion of one of the four blocks, etc.

In Waraporon and Ahamed (2006), the concept of medical Hamming distance between ailments has been introduced. This concept is based on the notion of the every identifiable ailment is unique depending on the precision of the tests and combination the test results. When there is doubt, more tests are (ordered or) designed to separate the overlapping possibilities. In a sense, the process is based on probability and the confidence level is thus achieved. The medical machines track such confidence levels based on Internet and local medical knowledge banks. The patient thus stands a very good chance that the treatment is most accurately matched to symptoms and test results. This generic concept performs very dependably in error control in communication systems and stands a good chance it will perform dependably (or much better) in medical systems and hospital care. The results provided by medical machines are backed by the (mathematically derivable) confidence level(s) so achieved. Double and triple error corrections are feasible by a larger number of independent/interdependent tests.

12.4 The Machine Component of Medical Machines

This part of the processing is based on the established concepts of designing and fabricating computers. Typical processor, memory, bus, and switching technologies are coupled with human interface devices to deal with input and output requirements in the Internet-based medical environment. Over the last two or three decades, the fivefold impact of these five (processor, memory, bus, switching, and input/output) technologies has been phenomenal if not monumental.

---

[2] Any number of blocks can be added and tied into corresponding subroutines in the MW. After the steps in the humanist effort are identified accurately, the macrocommands within the subroutines are equally accurately transferred, translated, transliterated, and encoded as macros. That is the ultimate goal in forcing medical machines to perform as accurately as a physician, a medical team, a medical center or facility would perform.

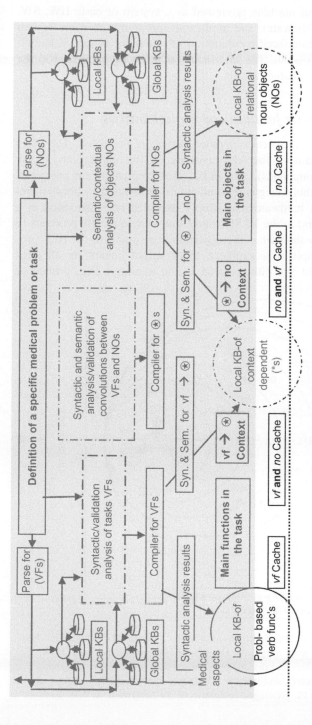

Figure 12.1 A composite MW–SW–HW configuration of the medical machine with medical expertise (procedure and patient matching) and MW at the top and the software (MW + traditional SW) and HW at the bottom. The initial medical language instructions from the medical staff undergo the typical higher level language instruction procedures by the compiler of the language. These steps are designated as lexical analysis, syntactic analysis, and semantic analysis. These three steps ensure that the user is not violating any rules for the choice of objects and symbols that will be processed in the machine. In the compiler for medical procedures and processing similar, verification that is more stringent and validation are necessary The design of a medical compiler becomes more elaborate and detailed to verify that both the language rules and medical rules are strictly adhered.

In a nutshell, if the medical machine is viewed as a system of basic HW, SW, MW (not to be taken as middleware), and application programs, then the system can be configured as a well-interfaced combination of computer system, a knowledge system, and a medical system. The interfacing is to be accomplished in the HW and SW domains and in the time domain.

12.4.1   Traditional Computer for Data and Logical Entities

In Figure 12.2, an overview of typical computer system is presented. The users enter the computational domain via the ALPs (simply via the applications) or the high-level language (HLL commands). The initial user commands are compiled, assembled, encoded (in assembly language), and finally converted to binary level executable instruction to the hardware that simply executes one instruction at a time (in each of the processors) in the VLSI circuits and systematically proceeds to generate the results sought by the user in the application programs or the HLL programs. If the programs, compilers, assemblers, loaders, and linkers are all error free, the results are generated and either stored in the memory, disk, printed or

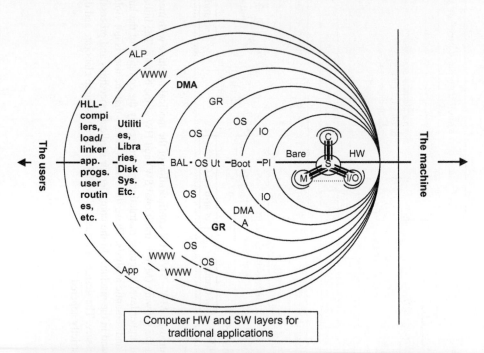

Figure 12.2 Overview of a typical binary database computer system. ALP, application level programs; BAL, basic assembly level programs; Boot, boot systems instructions; DMA, direct memory access; GR, graphics and display programs; HLL, higher level programs including utilities, compilers, loaders, and linkers; HW, basic hardware; IO, input/output systems; OS, operating systems; PI, privileged instructions; SW, software; WWW, Internet access and control.

displayed via the output routines. The operating system ensures the correct functionalities of the HW and SW modules for the machine to serve as a spectrum of users and solve problems that are appropriately programmed.

12.4.2 The Object Computer for Information and Knowledge

The binary system digital machines are CPU oriented and the intermediate SW layers convert the user commands to binary level operations as bit, nibble, byte, word, word-groups, arrays, and matrices dimensioned and partitioned in the declaration statements in the higher level programs.

The object computer (OC) is a new breed of machines in its own right. It has essentially the same five HW components (OPUs, object memories, object bus structures, object switches, and object oriented I/O systems) as the traditional computers but functions at an object level rather than at a data level. The OPU works with objects and the operation on such objects as efficiently and as gracefully as the CPU works with numbers and logical entities based on $opc's$ and $opr's$. The HW and SW layers of an OC are depicted in Figure 12.3. These intermediate SW layers shield the application level programmers and users from the details of the CPU functions.

Whereas the CPU level functions occur at binary level and at nanosecond speeds (see Chapter 2), the object level functions in the human mind occur at knowledge-bearing object(s) level and at a much slower pace. When the two operation methodologies are brought closer and closer, the possibilities of conceiving functions at object level emerges and the architecture of a HW-based object processor unit (OPU) appears as feasible at VLSI level. The speed of the machines can become slow while executing object level functions.

12.4.3 The Medical Computer for Medical Environments

In extending the evolution of OCs from traditional computers, the medical computers deal with medical operations and functions upon medical objects and medical centric units (MCOs). In the same vein, the evolution of OPUs from central processor units (CPUs) leads to the evolution of the medical processor units (MPUs). However, the MPUs retain a degree of human (physicians and staff) control that is atop of the MPUs that command the OPUs and CPUs to perform the dependent functions. In addition, since the MCOs can assume life objects, special care and procedures are associated with such medical operands ($mopr's$).

From a computer systems perspective, specially written interface SW and HW subsystems deals with data structure, objects such as arrays, images, radioactive materials, and nuclear plants. These objects can be quite rudimentary or complex. Example of a complex objects are human beings, patients, medical centers, hospitals, and even nations. When objects become complex and cumbersome, the capacity of the SW systems to deal with such objects also diminishes. Specialized SW packages provide additional flexibility. In this vein, the MW is a setoff SW package to deal with medical environments.

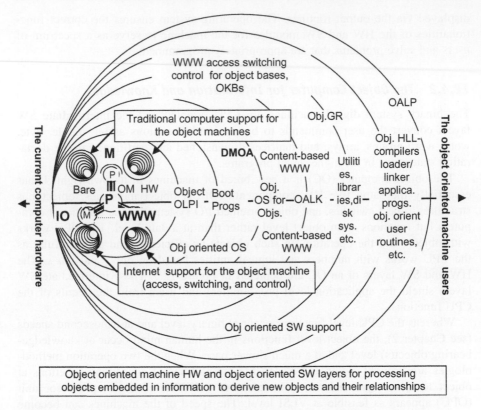

Figure 12.3 Overview of a typical object-based computer system. Note: P is object processor unit, M is memory for objects, I/O is input/output systems for the object machine. OLAP, object level applications programs (major/minor object functions can be processed); OALK, basic assembly level programs for object oriented instructions; Boot, boot systems instructions; DMOA, direct memory object access; Obj.GR, object graphics and display programs; HLLK, higher level programs including utilities, compilers, loaders, and linkers for object functions; HW, basic object functions/hardware; IO, object-based input/output systems; OOS, operating systems for object functions; OPLI, object-based privileged instructions; OSW, traditional and object-based software; Ut., utilities; WWW, access and control of object bases; OKBs, other supporting/associated objects.

In a sense, the use of specialized SW by the users shifts the creative potential of problem solving to the designers of the SW packages. The SW designers are focused toward solving routine problems rather than exploring novel solutions. To some extent designer packages in the computer-aided design (CAD) environments offer design choices rather than creative solutions.

Medical machine MW and its HW bring the creativity closer to the medical community because the functions in the MPUs become evident to the users. The extra layers of SW to convert complex medical objects to binary data structures are thus eliminated. A typical configuration of the medical machine hardware and the surrounding MW software layers is shown in Figure 10.12.

12.4.4   The Medical Computer System

In Figure 11.4, a feasible arrangement of the processor architecture is shown. The focus of processing is centered on one or more A-register(s) executing one or more instruction(s) in sequential (SISD) mode, or in multiple/parallel (MISD, MIMD, and SIMD) modes. The other components such as registers (IR (instruction register(s), DR (data; object register(s)), data and object cache(s), data and object stack(s), their local buses, and localized register and bus switch(es) are suitably arranged.

Figure 12.4 presents an architectural overview of a medical machine that uses a knowledge machine for its subordinate (medical) knowledge-based functions. The architecture is general enough to use it for an educational or a corporate management information system (MIS). The bus interconnectivity and the security issues are addressed. Switches that interconnect the four major buses configurations offer the security and firewall protection against information leakage, browsers, and spammers.

Figure 12.5 depicts a possible configuration of the middle layers of a medical computer system. At the hardware level, the three basic constituents of a typical computer system (processor, memory modules, input/output processors and devices, and switch) are shown as MP, M, I/O, and S. The application layer MALP, consists of medical application programs (MAPs) and major/minor medical functions can be processed at this level. The basic assembly level programs for medical instructions are shown at the BALM layer. The traditional layers for booting the medical computer (boot systems instructions), direct memory medical objects access (DMMA) for medical objects and functions depicts the disk/Internet access capability are also shown. Object oriented graphics and display programs, the higher level language medical (HLLM) programs including utilities, compilers, loaders, and linkers for object/knowledge functions also are depicted in the middle layers of the medical computer. HW basic object functions/hardware, MIO medical objects-based input/output systems, MMOS operating systems for medical and object functions, MLPI, knowledge/object-based privileged instructions, KSW traditional and knowledge/object-based software, and WWW Internet access and control components are also necessary for the functioning of the entire medical machine.

Figure 12.5 also depicts a configuration of a composite MW−SW−HW arrangement of the medical machine and the role of the medical compiler (to check the syntactic and semantic rules of the medical practice).

The medical expertise (procedure and patient matching) and MW (the compiler part) are shown at the top (Figure 12.6). The software (i.e., MW and the traditional SW) and HW is shown at the bottom with the "A" register(s) of the medical machines. In this particular setup, only the local (hospital or medical center and patient) databases are searched. An extended version of the complier is also feasible where the syntactic and semantic rules are checked on a global basis accessing the Internet and shown in Figure 12.8.

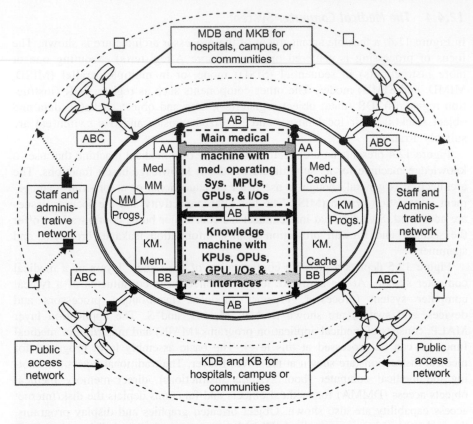

● Secure – limited access switching point for medical/knowledge data
■ Secure – limited access switching point for administrative and staff data
□ Open public domain information

Figure 12.4 Overview of a typical medical computer system that encompasses the functions of the medical machine that also uses medical knowledge and knowledge objects via local KB or Internet-based KB. The network ABC is protected by a secure firewall to the external Internet traffic. The internal security is preserved via the four bus arrangements and the switching points shown in the figure. Note: AA, internal—secure broadband optical bus for medical machine; BB, internal—secure broadband optical bus for knowledge machine; AB, shared—secure broadband medical knowledge machines communication; ABC, secure medical or knowledge objects bus for knowledge machine.

12.5   Comparison of the Software Arrangements

A comparison of the software arrangements for the traditional computer systems and the next generation knowledge ware of a typical knowledge machine or KM are shown in Figure 12.7. The knowledge level functions encompass the object level functions and significantly enhance the hierarchical structure of SW for the KM.

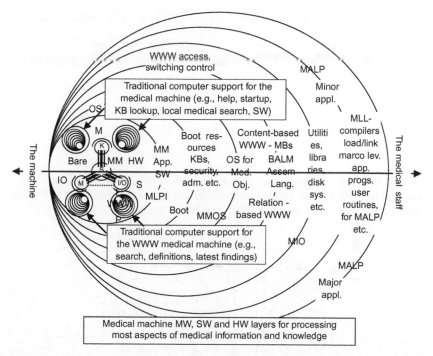

Figure 12.5 Overview of a typical medical computer system that encompasses the functions of traditional computers, OCs, and the medical functions of the medical staff of any medical facility. Note: MP is medical object processor unit, M is memory for medical objects, I/O is input/output systems for the medical machine. MALP, medical applications level programs (major/minor medical functions can be processed); BALM, basic assembly level programs for medical instructions; Boot, boot systems instructions; DMMA, direct memory medical-objects access for medical functions; Obj.GR, object graphics and display programs; HLLM, higher level language medical programs including utilities, compilers, loaders, and linkers for object/knowledge functions; HW, basic object functions/hardware; MIO, medical objects-based input/output systems; MMOS, operating systems for knowledge and object functions; MLPI, knowledge/object-based privileged instructions; KSW, traditional and knowledge/object-based software; WWW, Internet access and control.

The medical level functions encompass both the knowledge level and the object level functions and become at least two orders of magnitude more complex than the SW for traditional computers. In evaluating the hierarchical nature of the SW for medical machines, the suggested hierarchy of medical language instruction sets (Figure 9.8) and the complex structure of the MPU (Figure 11.4), both need to be examined. With the recent sophistication in the SW industry, the task is as feasible as organizing the FORTRAN V compiler and SW in 1960s or the design, debugging, and final implementation of the operating system for the 360/370 in the same era.

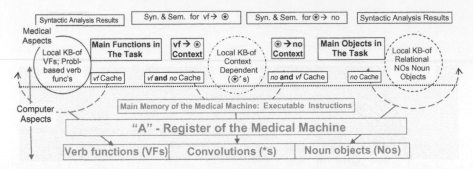

Figure 12.6 Detailed configuration of a composite MW−SW−HW arrangement of the medical machine with medical expertise (procedure and patient matching) and MW at the top and the software (MW + traditional SW) and HW at the bottom.

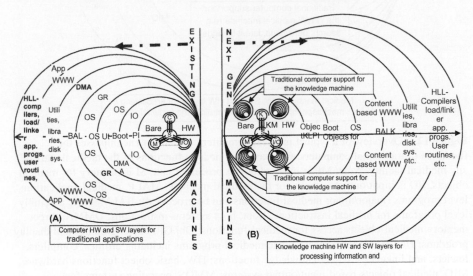

Figure 12.7 A comparison of the SW arrangements for the traditional computer systems and the next generation knowledge ware of a typical knowledge machine or KM. A similar comparison between the SW is of knowledge machines and medical machines.

12.5.1 Human Interactions with Medical Machines

The human skill for interacting with a modern medical machine gets sophisticated as the machine executes a large number of interwoven functions. In some cases, the functions may be made sequential and the single-threaded medical programs (e.g., billing, diagnosis, and analysis of patient history) are executed. When interdependencies exist (e.g., ICU care, patient monitoring during surgery, and emergency room treatment), the machine needs to function in real time and when the medical parameters are likely to be interdependent, then the medical machine has to track each parameter independently and interdependently. Trained medical staff executes such functions routinely. The infusion of such training onto a medical machine needs sophisticated SW and MW skills.

The degree of sophistication of the human being to monitor the medical machines functions can increase faster than the complexity of the medical function is executing. However, human beings have been extremely adept and complex machine functions have been managed efficiently in the past. For example, ships were navigated before GPS evolved; airplanes were flown before drones were designed; pilots flew planes before computer-based autopilot systems were conceived. In the later stages, the machine functions can perform significantly better than those of an average human being can. Embedded AI of the expert systems becomes better than the mediocre adaptation of a typical college graduate. In the medical machine, all aspects of AI (PR, expert systems, heuristics, estimation, computer graphics, use of intelligent agents, etc.) appear to be necessary for the machines to compete with medical staff and to perform better. However, speed, accuracy, logic, and accountability are the features of machines.

Figure 12.8 depicts the programmed stages in the functions of the compiler of a medical machine. When any task medical task (MPF $\otimes$ MNO) is to be accomplished, the application level command is analyzed by the compiler and checked for the origin and level of the source (and thus its security), for syntactic rules, semantic rules, in the structure of the command. Two variations of checks for syntactic rules, semantic rules, become necessary. *First*, the syntax of (MPF$\rightarrow\otimes$) and the semantics of (MPF$\rightarrow\otimes$) in context of in the overall framework of the MAP are both checked. *Second*, the syntax of ($\otimes\rightarrow$MNO), the semantics of ($\otimes\rightarrow$MNO), in context of in the overall framework of the MAP is checked.

The two implications of syntactic check are as follows: (a) Can the medical function MPF be convolved in the fashion commanded to the machine? (b) Can the convolution $\otimes$ be operated on the medial noun object MNO? Analogous to implications of semantic checks are also verified and ascertained. Only valid and legal operations from legitimate sources will pass the compiler check.

The SW configurations presented in Figures 12.6 and 12.8 are similar. However, access to the global knowledge bases in Figure 12.8 permits the machine to verify that the local instructions or commands to the medical machine in any hospital or medical center are consistent with their global usage. The local medical functions MFPs and local medical objects MNOs will have a medical correspondence with those used in the global medical community, thus removing any abuse or misuse of functions and objects.

12.5.2   *Typical Deployment of Medical Networks*

Medical services and expertise are directed toward a purpose of great importance and value exceeding those of financial or corporate services. Security networks have a high priority but the size and services are limited to fewer users. In essence, the requirements and demands on medical networks are stringent and extensive

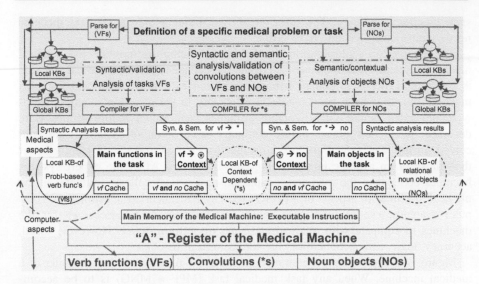

Figure 12.8 A composite MW−SW−HW configuration of the medical machine with medical expertise (procedure and patient matching) and MW at the top and the software (MW + traditional SW) and HW at the bottom.

requiring medical networks to have more elaborate and extensive interfaces than most other networks. Generally, the medical setting and environments dictate the customization of these networks. Patient security and quality of service are usually prioritized. It is generally not feasible to have a blue print for all medical networks or machines.

In most cases, the limited practice of individual medical practitioners can be characterized as a local area network (LAN) with a patient database facility, a server, Internet connection(s), and numerous computers or laptops. Billing and scheduling software can be readily purchased. In essence, such networks and the SW are only a little larger than the private user LANs.

As medical practice and patient load grows, the capacity of individual components is enhanced. The network capacity rarely needs new wiring or major ductwork. Higher network capacity can be gained by newer interfacing with the existing copper, coaxial, or fiber-optic backbone facility. Installing a wireless router and server with wireless link(s) is also a feasible for medical centers, small hospitals, and specialized care units. Small town hospitals, medical practices, educational institutions, businesses, etc. can also grow in a cost effective and elegant fashion.

Figure 12.9 depicts a medical platform that can be customized to most medical establishments. The two networks for data and administration services do not need to be physically distinct; dedicated addressing, logical, and channels isolation (enforced by allocated router ports in the network) permits both networks to be embedded in the same physical or wireless media. Flexible network operating systems permit great variations in the exact architecture of the network.

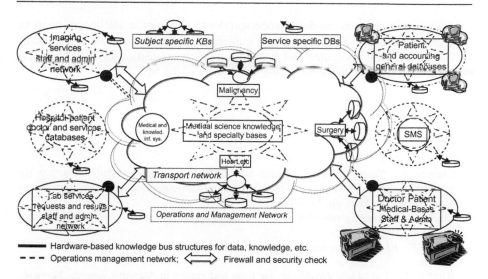

▬▬▬▬ Hardware-based knowledge bus structures for data, knowledge, etc.
− − − Operations management network; ⟨⟨⟩⟩ Firewall and security check

Figure 12.9 Human interactions and machine functions with the medical machine. Knowledge bases are invoked during the patients and the treatment of patients and implementation of medical procedures. KMS and SMS are knowledge and service management services, respectively. Service specific databases are invoked during billing and service, scheduling, service requests, etc.

12.6 Conclusions

The monumental strides in the computer and network technologies have not broken ground in the medical field. The medical technologies seem to lag behind in deploying the configurations and enjoying the rewards of information and Internet age. The tendency of the medical profession was been evident in the 1970s when the profession posed reluctance to incorporate even the medical billing systems databases for patient billing. In the decade of 2010, intelligent computer systems and (AI) SW is only showing a small dent in the practice of medicine and even than in a few specialized fields.

Intelligent networks and intelligent Internet techniques appear to have a long struggle before they can be assimilated in the main stream of medical practice. Fears of technology, errors possible due to untested MW, and the ensuing lawsuits seem to be one of the causes. In the telecommunication industry, a similar situation was corrected by enforcing two processor banks and switching systems (as in the 4ESS and 5ESS) offer identical results in real time. In the medical profession, the deployment of a medical machine as an AI-based medical assistant is a feasible approach to debugging these new medical machines.

From the perspective of computer science, the issues appear complex but not insurmountable. Sustained efforts by the computer-based medical technologists (in academia) are likely to create a breakthrough in tunneling through the computer field into the medical field. Both fields are now mature in their own right.

A process map in the medical processor(s) and a step-wise intellectual map in the expert's mind will close the gap and train the machine. A core map in the memory of the medical computer and a snapshot of the transition of MNOs in the expert's mind will tackle the programming aspects of the MW.

References

1. Clancey WJ, Shortliffe EH, Buchanan BG: Intelligent computer-aided instruction for medical diagnosis. *Proceedings of the third annual symposium on computer applications in medical care*, IEEE, pp. 175–183, 1979.
2. Clancey WJ: Tutoring rules for guiding a case method dialogue, *Int J Man-Mach Stud* 11:25–49, 1979.
3. Shortcliffe E: *MYCIN:* computer-based medical consultations, New York, NY, 1976, Elsevier.
4. Kintsch W, et al: *About NeoMycin,* methods and tactics in cognitive science, Mahwah, NJ, 1984, Lawrence Erlbaum.
5. Buchanan BG, Shortcliffe EH: *Rule-based expert system: the mycin experiment at Stanford Heuristic Programming project*, Boston, MA, 1984, Addison Wesley.
6. Aronoff M, Fudeman K: What is morphology (fundamentals of linguistics) 312 p. ed 2, 2006, Wiley-Blackwell. See also, Schwartz Jeffrey H: *Skeleton keys: an introduction to human skeletal morphology, development, and analysis*, Oxford, England, 2006, Oxford University Press.
7. Waraporon N, Ahamed SV: *Intelligent medical search engine by knowledge machine*, *Proceedings of the 3rd international conference on information technology: new generations*, Los Alamitos, CA, 2006, IEEE Computer Society. See also, Waraporon N: *Intelligent medical databases for global access*, PhD Dissertation, Graduate Center of the City University of New York, 2006.

For high quality versions of the figures in this chapter, please visit the companion website for this book at http://booksite.elsevier.com/9780124166301/

List of Abbreviations

⊙

⊙	convolution markers
μD	microdecode function
μmp	micromedical process instruction

1
| 1A | processor special communication processor for call-processing applications in electronic switching systems |

2
2B + D	ISDN basic rate
2B1Q code	two binary to one quarternary code
2D	trellis coding, two dimensional ($x + iy$) code algorithm for data communication
2G	2G + coding standards by ITU cordless telephone (CT) usage

3
| 3G | third generation wireless technologies for CT applications |
| 3GPP | third-generation partnership project |

4
48	octets payload in the ATM cell
4A	crossbar toll system
4A/(ETS)	electronic translator system
4ESS, 5ESS, 5ESS-2000 switch	Alcatel-Lucent switching system
5 octets	ATM header block

5
51.840 Mb/s	SONET-1 rate
53 octets	ATM cell size
5ESS	A generic electronic switch for handling a wide variety of telephone switching services

8
800, 900, 700	numbers reserved for special services
802.x	ITU standards for packet switched networks
899 or 898	numbers and numbers for specialized services to the customers

9

900	services reversed charges special services network services
911	public emergency service
9-row/13-row SONET	frame configuration debates and deliberations

A

AAL	ATM adaptation layer
ABS	alternate billing service
ADCCP	advanced data communications control procedure
ADM	adaptive delta modulation
ADMs	add-drop multiplexers for the new and older generation networks
ADPCM	adaptive delta pulse code modulation
ADSL	asymmetric digital subscriber line
ADSL/HDSL	asymmetric digital subscriber line/high-speed digital subscriber line
ADSL+	specialized version of ADSL
AI	artificial intelligence
AIKN	advanced intelligent knowledge network
AIN	advanced intelligent network
AKSP	adjunct knowledge processor for knowledge functions in knowledge environment
ALI	automatic location identification
ALKP	application level knowledge program
ALUs	arithmetic logic units in the CPU environment of a computer
AM	administrative module; also used for amplitude modulation
AM, CM, and SM	administrative communications and switching modules in an ESS facility
AMPS	advanced mobile phone service
AND, OR, EXOR	logical functions
ANI	automatic number identification
ANSI	American National Standards Institute
AP	adjunct processor
APC	adaptive predictive code
APs	applications programs
AS	access stratum (RRC and UP)
ASN	adjunct service node
ASP	adjunct service processor
ASP	adjunct service point or adjunct service processor
AT&T	American Telephone and Telegraph Company, no longer in existence
Atlantis-2	one of the many Atlantic crossings for voice and data communication
ATM	asynchronous transfer mode for cell relay systems
Attr.	attribute or attributes of NOs
AUs	Arithmetic units embedded in the ALU and CPU environments
AW	artificial wisdom
A-WAB	wisdom axiom base for the type A human being (philosopher)
AWC	area wide centrex

B

B	bearer channel of the ISDN
BAL	basic assembly language
BALK	basic assembly language knowledge instructions
BALM	basic assembly-level medical instructions
BB	broadband
BC	bearer control
BCC	Bell client companies
BCR	Bell Communications Research
Bellcore	Bell Communications Research
BISDN	broadband ISDN
BRCS	business/residence custom services
BRISDN	basic rate integrated services digital network (ISDN)
BS	base station
BX.25	special interoffice x.25 protocol
BX.25	version of X.25 protocol/network developed by Bell system

C

CACC	customer access and call control
CAD	computer-aided design
CANTAT-3	one of the numerous transatlantic cables for data/voice services
CAT	MRI Scans of tissue for cancerous malignancies
CATV	cable television
CCF	INCM component of the Intelligent Network Conceptual Model in the TINA network
CCIS 6 or 7	common channel interoffice signaling 6 or 7 in communication systems
CCIS	common channel interoffice signaling
CCISS	common channel interoffice signaling system
CCITT	consultative committee of ITT, now ITU-T
CCS	common channel signaling
CCS7	common channel signaling #7, especially developed in view of the increasing number of intelligent network services and the earlier ISDN services.
CCSN	common channel signaling network
CDMA	code division multiple access
CEPT	central European post and telegraph
CLASS	special group of IN/2 services provided by second generation INs
CM	communication module in networks
CM	control memory in CPUs
CMA	centralized message accounting
CMAC	customer mobile access control
CN	campus networks
CO	central offices
COMNET	an event-based computer simulation program to evaluate network performance
CPDFM	continuous phase discrete frequency
CPM	critical path method

CPU	central processor unit
CSA	carrier serving area
CSPDN	circuit switched public data network
CT2	cordless telephone second generation
CT3	enhanced CT-2 telephone services toward the third generation

D

D	channel banks CO equipment for multiplexing and demultiplexing the DS0 and DS1 signals through the circuit switched networks
DACS	digital access cross connect systems
DB	database
dB	decibell
DBAS	database administration system
DBM	database management
DBMS	database management system
DCS	digital cross connect systems in the SONET environment
DDS	Dewey Decimal System
DDS	digital data services (in context to digital transmission systems)
DDSN	Digital Derived Services Network
DECT	digital European cordless telecommunication
DMA	direct memory access
DMS	Nippon's Telephone and Telegraph
DNS	Domain Name System
DPSK	differential PSK
DPU	display processor
DPUs/GPUs	display/graphics processor units
DS	D-system digital hierarchy in Americas
DS0	digital signal 0 is 64 kb/s channel at the lowest level of digital hierarchy
DS1	digital signal 1 is 1.544 Mb/s signal with 24 DS0 channels + signaling bits, also known as T1 signal
DS1, DS1C, DS2, DS3	American digital hierarchy
DS1C	digital signal 1C is at 3.152 Mb/s
DS2	digital signal 2 is at 6.312 Mb/s also known as T2 signal
DS3	digital signal 3 is at 44.736 Mb/s
DSD	direct services dialing
DSDC	direct services dialing capabilities
DSL	digital subscriber line
DSS	decision support system
DWDM	dense WDM

E

E system	European digital hierarchy for data transmission
E1	CEPT digital hierarchy signals at 2.048 Mb/s
E2, E3	CEPT digital hierarchy signals
EC	echo cancellation
EO	end office

EPC	evolved packet core
ePDG	evolved packet data gateway
ERMES	European radio messaging
ERS	emergency response service
ES	expert systems
ESS	electronic switching systems
ETSI	European Telecommunications Standards Institute
E-UTRAN	evolved UTRAN
EWSD	a series of ESS facilities built by Siemens

F

FCC	Federal Communications Commission
FCs	functional components of the intelligent network conceptual model
FDE	fetch, decode, execute cycle of any CPU
FDM	frequency division multiplex
FEPs	front end processors of the SCP facility
FH-DPSK	frequency hopped differential phase-shift keying modulation
FLAG	one of the numerous transoceanic fiber-optic networks
FM	frequency modulation in signal transmission systems
FM	functional modules in TINA model for intelligent networks
FO	fiber optic
FORTRAN	one of scientific programming languages
FPLMTS	future public land mobile telecommunications
FRS	Federal Reserve System
FSK	frequency shift keying
FTTC	fiber to the curb distribution data/voice/video networks
FTTH	fiber to the home distribution data/voice/video networks

G

Gb/s	gigabits per second optical rates in FO networks
GERAN	GSM/EDGE radio access network, facilitates the smooth evolution of GSM and its real-time services
GMSK	Gaussian minimum shift keying
GNS	green number services
GPGPU	general purpose GPU
GPRS	global packet radio services
GPU	graphical processor unit
GSM	global system for mobile communication
GTFM	Gaussian timed frequency modulation
GUI	graphical user interface
GUMTS	generic universal mobile telephone systems
HD	Hamming distance
HDLC	high-level data link control
HDSL	high-speed digital subscriber line
HDTV	high definition TV
HLL	higher level language
HLR	home location register
HSS	home subscriber server

IAS	Institute of Advanced Study known for von Neumann's SPC machine
IC	integrated circuits
IC	interexchange carriers
IETS	interim European technical standard
IKN	intelligent knowledge network
IKPS or I-KPS	intelligent, Internet-based, or IN-based knowledge processing system
IKW	intelligent knowledgeware
IM	intermodulation
IMF	International Monetary Fund
IMN	intelligent medical network
IMS	intelligent medical systems
IMTS	improved mobile telephone service
IN	intelligent network
IN/1	first-generation intelligent network
IN/1 +	enhanced version of the IN/1
IN/2	second-generation IN
INCM	intelligent network conceptual model
INOs	intelligent noun objects
INTERN	an AI program for medical diagnostics
INWATS	inward wide area telecommunication services
I/O processors	input/output Processors
IP	intelligent peripheral or Internet protocol
IPTV	Internet protocol TV
ISDN	integrated services digital network
ISN	information storage node
ISO	International Standards Organization
ISP	Internet service provider
IT	information technology
ITU	International Telecommunications Union

J

JCL	job control language
JDC	Japanese digital cellular

K

KAP	knowledge action process
kb/s	kilobits per second
KBMS	knowledge base management system
KBs	knowledge bases
KCO	knowledge centric objects
KCP	knowledge control point
KCPU	a hardware unit to accomplish knowledge functions and CPU functions
KD	knowledge domain
KIP	knowledge intelligent peripheral
KIR	knowledge instruction register

KLP	knowledge logic programs
KM	knowledge machine
KMM	knowledge management module
KMs and WMs	knowledge machines and wisdom machines
KMS	knowledge management systems
KN	knowledge network compilation of knowledge programs
kopc	knowledge operation code
kopcode	operation code within BAL knowledge instructions
KP	knowledge processing
KPE	knowledge processing environment
KPS	knowledge processing systems
KPU	knowledge processing unit
KSCP	knowledge services control point
KSS	knowledge sharing system
KTP	knowledge transfer point

L

LA	lexical analysis
LAN	local area network
LATA	local access and transport area
LECs	local exchange carriers
LED	light-emitting diode
LoC	Library of Congress
LPC	linear predictive coding
LT	line termination
LTE	long-term evolution for NGMN

M

MAC	medium access control
MAN	metropolitan area networks
MAP	medical application programs
MAS	memory administration system
Mb/s	megabits per second
MCN	mobile control node
MCOs	medical centric objects
MCPN	mobile customer premises network
MDB	medical database
ME	mobile equipment and hand phones
MIMD	multiple instruction multiple data CPU architecture
MIMO	multiple instruction multiple object KPU architecture
MIN	medical intelligent network
MIS/DSS	management information system/decision support system
MISD	multiple instruction single data CPU architecture
MISO	multiple instruction single object KPU architecture
MKCO	medical knowledge centric object
MKCP	medical knowledge control point
MKI-MO	multiple knowledge instruction multiple object KPU architecture
MKI-SO	multiple knowledge instruction single object KPU architecture

MKNs	medical knowledge networks
MKTP	medical knowledge transfer point
MLAP	medical language assembly program
MME	mobility management entity
MMOS	operating systems for medical and object functions
MNMS	medical network management systems
mno	medical noun object
MNO$'$	newly synthesized medical noun object
mno$_k$	medical noun object k
mopc	medical operation code
moprs	medical operands
MP	medical processors
MPC	medical program code
MPF(s)	major medical program functions
MPF⊛MNO	major medical function convolved on a major medical noun object
mpf$_i$ ⊛$_j$ mno$_k$	minor medical function convolved on a minor medical noun object
mpf$_i$, ⊛$_j$, and no$_k$	multiple minor medical convolutions
mpf$_i$	minor medical program functions
MPU	medical processor unit
MRI	magnetic resonance imaging
MSI	medium scale integration
MSMS	medical services management system
MSPs	medical service providers
MTP	message transfer part
MTS	mobile telephone service
MTSO	mobile telephone switching office
MUA	mobile user agent
MVFs	major medical verb functions
MW	medical ware
MYCIN	an artificially intelligent SW system for medical diagnostics

N

$n \times m$	$m \times n$ matrix operations or convolutions
NA	node administration
NADC	North American Digital Cellular
NAS	nonaccess stratum
NCOM	network communication unit
NCP	network control point
NGMN	next generation mobile network
NIDB	network information database
NIH	National Institute of Health
NKSP	network knowledge service provider
NNI	network-to-network interface
NO	noun object
NOs and VFs	noun objects and verb functions
NPU	stands for numerical processor unit. In the CPU environment, the NPU performs accurately within the precision of the ALUs. In the KPU environment, the NPU works with imprecise rules for manipulating the attributes of objects.

NPU	numerical processor unit in the CPU or KPU environment
NRM	network resource manager
NT-1 and NT-2	network terminations 1 and 2 for ISDN services
OA&M	operations, administration, and maintenance
OAM&P	operations, administration, maintenance, and provisioning
OC	optical carrier designation
OC-12, OC-48, OC-192	optical carrier data rates
OC-*n*	optical carrier systems in the SONET environment
OMAP	operations and maintenance applications part
ONN	off-network node
OOL	object-oriented language
OOP	object-oriented programs
OP	object processors
opc	operation code
OPNET	discrete event networks simulation package
opr	operand
OPU	object processor unit
OR	operations research; also OR logical function
OSI	open systems interconnect
OSS	operation support system
P	
PBXs	private branch exchanges
PC	paging control
PCM	pulse code modulation
PCP	processor control point
PCRF	policy and charging rules function
PCS	personal and wireless communication system
PCU	program control unit
PDCP	packet data control protocol
PDN	packet data network
PDNGW	packet data network gateway
PE	paging entity
PIN	personal intelligent network
PLCP	physical layer convergence protocol
PLMN	public land mobile network
PMPC	patient medical process cycle
PMR	private mobile radio in the United Kingdom
PON	passive optical network
POTS	plain old telephone service
PPNs and EPNs	processor port network and expansion port network
PPV	pay per view
PR	pattern recognition
PROCEDURER	A HW unit that executes microprocedures (vf) on micromedical (mno) or knowledge objects (no)
PS	packet switched
PSK	phase-shift keying

PSPDN	packet switched public data network
PSTN	public switched telephone network
PUCI	protection against unsolicited communication in IMS
PVN	private virtual network

Q

QAM	quadrature amplitude modulation
QoK	quality of knowledge
QoS	quality of service
QPSK	quadrature phase-shift keying

R

RACE	research and development for advanced communication in Europe
RAN	radio access network
RAT	radio access tandem
RBOC	regional Bell operating company
RDTs	remote data terminals
RF	radio frequency
RLC	radio link control
ROM	read only memory
RRC	radio resource control
S, T, U, and V	ISDN standardized interfaces
SAE	system architecture evolution
SAFE	spanning the globe, a global network
SAN	storage area networks
SAP	one of a series of intelligent MIS and EIS programming systems
SAT-3/WASC	one of the newer fiber-optic transoceanic network
SAT-3/WASC/SAFE	also one of the newer FO transoceanic network but following different routing or protocol
SCCP	signaling connection control point
SCE	service creation environment
SCP	service control point
SDLC	synchronous data link control
SDN	software defined network
SDSL	symmetric DSL
SDTV	standard TV
SEA-ME-WE 2,	segments of the fiber-optic transoceanic network
SEA-ME-WE 3,	spanning the globe fiber-optic transoceanic network
SEAS	signaling, engineering, and administration system
SGSN	support node
SGW	serving gateway
SIMD	single instruction single data CPU architecture
SIMO	single instruction multiple data CPU architecture
SIP	service intelligent peripheral
SLCS	subscriber-loop carrier system
SLI	service logic interpreter
SLP	service logic programs
SM	'S' interface for the mobile roamer

SM	switching module
SMDS	switched multimegabit digital service
SMS	service management system (in conventional INs)
SMSI	simplified message service interface
SNI	service network interface
SNMP	simple network management protocol
SNR	signal-to-noise ratio
SONET	synchronous optical network
SONET/SDH, SONET/SONET	digital hierarchy
SPC	service control point (in conventional INs)
SPSO	single process single object KPU architecture
SS	switching system
SS7	signaling system 7
SSB	single sideband
SSB-F/A	single sideband frequency/amplitude
SSI	small scale integration
SSKO	single simple knowledge object
SSLI	special services logical interface
SSP	service switching point
SST	spread spectrum transmission
STM-i, STM-i	designation, with i $(=n/3)$ for the STS-n designation
STP	service transfer point (in conventional INs)
STS	synchronous transport signal
STS-n	synchronous transport signal at level n

T

T1,	Signal at DS1 rate of 1.544 Mb/s
TAT-8, TAT-9	global optical networks
TCP/IP	transmission control protocol, connection-oriented transport protocol of the Internet architecture; reliable byte stream delivery service. Internet protocol (IP) that provides a connectionless best effort delivery service across the Internet
TCPAP	transactions capabilities applications part
TDMA	time division multiple access
TE	terminal equipment
TEm	terminal equipment microwave
TINA	European advanced intelligent network also known as TMN + IN (telecommunication management network + intelligent network)
TMM	transaction management machine
TPC-5	transpacific cables

U

U	T and S interfaces for ISDN
UCI	universal customer interface
UE	user equipment
UIS	universal information services
UISN	universal information services network

UMTS	universal mobile telecommunication system
UNIX	a powerful operating system developed by Bell system to operate ESS type of telecommunication nodes and network functions. It is generic enough to operate most computing environments
UNMA	universal network management architecture
UOS	universal operating system
UP	user plane
UPT	universal personal telecommunication
USIM	universal subscriber ID module
USIN	universal services intelligent network proposed by AT&T during the late 1980s, but never finally implemented
USN	universal services nodes
UTRAN	UMTS terrestrial radio access network

V

VCs	virtual circuits through the network environments
VDSL	variable rate DSL, one of the numerous versions of the digital subscriber lines
VF	verb function
VFN	vendor feature node
VHDSL	very high-speed DSL
VLSI	very large scale integration for IC chips
VoIP	voice over Internet protocol
VSAT	very small aperture terminals
VSELP	vector sum excited linear prediction
VT	virtual terminal

W

WAN	wide area network
WARC	World Administrative Radio Conference
WC	wire center of a typical switching node where the subscriber line terminate at the central office
WDM	wave-length division multiplex for FO transmission
WWW	World Wide Web

X

X.21	one of the earlier packet data protocols
X.25	ITU recommendation that specifies the interface between users data equipment (DTE) and the packet-switching data circuit terminating equipment (DCE)

Z

Z_0	characteristic impedance of transmission media

Printed and bound by CPI Group (UK) Ltd, Croydon, CR0 4YY

03/10/2024

01040418-0005